# Music, Sound and Space

*Music, Sound and Space* is the first collection to integrate research from musicology and sound studies on music and sound as they mediate everyday life. Music and sound exert an inescapable influence on the contemporary world, from the ubiquity of MP3 players to the controversial use of sound as an instrument of torture. In this book, leading scholars explore the spatialisation of music and sound, their capacity to engender modes of publicness and privacy, their constitution of subjectivity, and the politics of sound and space. Chapters discuss music and sound in relation to distinctive genres, technologies and settings, including sound installation art, popular music recordings, offices and hospitals, and music therapy. With international examples, from the Islamic soundscape of the Kenyan coast, to religious music in Europe, to First Nation musical sociability in Canada, this book offers a new global perspective on how music and sound and their spatialising capacities transform the nature of public and private experience.

GEORGINA BORN is Professor of Music and Anthropology at the University of Oxford. Formerly Professor of Sociology, Anthropology and Music at the University of Cambridge, she is currently directing the international research programme 'Music, Digitisation, Mediation: Towards Interdisciplinary Music Studies', funded by the European Research Council. Her publications include *Rationalizing Culture: IRCAM, Boulez, and the Institutionalization of the Musical Avant-Garde* (1995), *Western Music and Its Others: Difference, Representation, and Appropriation in Music* (edited with D. Hesmondhalgh 2000), *Uncertain Vision: Birt, Dyke and the Reinvention of the BBC* (2005) and the forthcoming *Interdisciplinarity: Reconfigurations of the Social and Natural Sciences* (edited with A. Barry).

# Music, Sound and Space

## Transformations of Public and Private Experience

*Edited by* GEORGINA BORN

CAMBRIDGE
UNIVERSITY PRESS

# CAMBRIDGE
## UNIVERSITY PRESS

University Printing House, Cambridge CB2 8BS, United Kingdom

Cambridge University Press is part of the University of Cambridge.

It furthers the University's mission by disseminating knowledge in the pursuit of
education, learning and research at the highest international levels of excellence.

www.cambridge.org
Information on this title: www.cambridge.org/9781107504127

© Cambridge University Press 2013

First published 2013
First paperback edition 2015

*A catalogue record for this publication is available from the British Library*

*Library of Congress Cataloguing in Publication data*
Music, sound and space : transformations of public and private experience /
edited by Georgina Born.
    p.   cm.
Includes bibliographical references and index.
ISBN 978-0-521-76424-7 (hardback)
1. Music–Social aspects.   2. Sound–Social aspects.   I. Born, Georgina.
ML3916.M879 2013
781.2′3–dc23
2012027131

ISBN 978-0-521-76424-7 Hardback
ISBN 978-1-107-50412-7 Paperback

# Contents

# Figures

# Tables

# Music examples

# Contributors

PHILIP V. BOHLMAN, FBA, is the Mary Werkman Distinguished Service Professor of the Humanities and of Music at the University of Chicago, Honorary Professor at the Hochschule für Musik, Theater und Medien, Hannover and Artistic Director of the New Budapest Orpheum Society. His publications include *World Music: A Very Short Introduction* (2002), *The Music of European Nationalism: Cultural Identity and Modern History* (2004), *Jewish Music and Modernity* (2008) and *Focus: Music, Nationalism, and the Making of the New Europe* (2010).

GEORGINA BORN is Professor of Music and Anthropology at the University of Oxford. She is the author of *Rationalizing Culture: IRCAM, Boulez, and the Institutionalization of the Musical Avant-Garde* (1995) and *Uncertain Vision: Birt, Dyke and the Reinvention of the BBC* (2005), and co-editor of *Western Music and Its Others* (with David Hesmondhalgh 2000) and *Interdisciplinarity: Reconfigurations of the Social and Natural Sciences* (with Andrew Barry forthcoming). She directs the research programme 'Music, Digitisation, Mediation: Towards Interdisciplinary Music Studies', funded by the European Research Council.

ERIC F. CLARKE, FBA, is Heather Professor of Music at the University of Oxford. He is the author of *Ways of Listening: An Ecological Approach to the Perception of Musical Meaning* (2005) and co-author of *Music and Mind in Everyday Life* (with Nicola Dibben and Stephanie Pitts 2010). He is co-editor of *Empirical Musicology: Aims, Methods, Prospects* (with Nicholas Cook 2004) and *Music and Consciousness: Philosophical, Psychological and Cultural Perspectives* (with David Clarke 2011).

NICHOLAS COOK is 1684 Professor of Music at the University of Cambridge and former Director of the AHRC Research Centre for the History and Analysis of Recorded Music (CHARM). His books include *Music: A Very Short Introduction* (1998), which has appeared in fourteen languages, and *The Schenker Project: Culture, Race, and Music Theory in Fin-de-siècle Vienna* (2007), which won the Society for Music Theory's 2010 Wallace Berry Award. He is a Fellow of the British Academy and of Academia Europaea.

SUZANNE G. CUSICK is Professor of Music at New York University. Her writings appear in such journals as *Early Music, Musical Quarterly, Perspectives of New Music* and *Journal of the Society for American Music. Francesca Caccini at the Medici Court: Music and the Circulation of Power* (2009) received the 2010 book prize of the Society for the Study of Early Modern Women. Her current work addresses the use of noise and music for interrogation in the 'war on terror', work for which she received in 2007 the Philip Brett Award of the LGBTQ Study Group of the American Musicological Society.

TIA DENORA is Professor of Sociology of Music at the University of Exeter. Her books are *Beethoven and the Construction of Genius* (1995), *Music in Everyday Life* (2000), *After Adorno: Rethinking Music Sociology* (2003) and *Music in Action: Selected Essays in Sonic Ecology* (2011). She recently completed a longitudinal research project on music and mental health and, with Dr Gary Ansdell, is preparing a three volume 'Triptych' on this work. With Gary Ansdell, she co-edits the Ashgate Series on Music & Change.

NICOLA DIBBEN is Senior Lecturer in Music at the University of Sheffield and joint co-ordinating editor of *Popular Music* (Cambridge University Press). Her research addresses music, mind and culture, with a focus on the science and psychology of music and on popular music studies. She has published over forty journal articles and book chapters, is the author of *Björk* (2009) and co-author of *Music and Mind in Everyday Life* (2010). She also collaborated with Björk on the artist's multimedia app album *Biophilia* (2011).

BYRON DUECK is Lecturer in Music at the Open University. His research has encompassed indigenous music and dance in Canada, popular music in Cameroon and jazz performance in the UK; it is crossed by several themes including musical public cultures and the social implications of rhythm and metre. He is co-editor of *Migrating Music* (with Jason Toynbee 2011) and *Experience and Meaning in Music Performance* (with Martin Clayton and Laura Leante, forthcoming); and a monograph, *Musical Intimacies and Indigenous Imaginaries*, is forthcoming.

ANDREW J. EISENBERG is Postdoctoral Research Associate in the Faculty of Music at the University of Oxford, where he is working on an ethnography of the Kenyan music industry as part of the European Research Council-funded 'Music, Digitisation, Mediation' research programme directed by Georgina Born. He holds concurrently a three-year Junior Research Fellowship at St Catherine's College, University of Oxford. He has an article on youth music on the Kenyan coast forthcoming in the journal *Africa*.

SUMANTH GOPINATH is Assistant Professor of Music Theory at the University of Minnesota. He is currently working on two book projects, one on the global ringtone industry and another on the politics of race in the music of Steve Reich. He has also edited, with Jason Stanyek, the forthcoming *Oxford Handbook of Mobile Music Studies*. His other research interests include post-Second World War (American) art and popular musics, cultural theory (especially Marxism), intersections of politics and music (or culture generally), and the globalisation of cultural production.

ANNELI B. HAAKE is a researcher and music psychology consultant on music-listening. Her doctoral research into music in workplaces has been presented at international conferences and published in the journal *Musicae Scientiae* (2011). She has been awarded the ESCOM/ICMPC Young Researcher Award (YRA) and is also a reviewer for the *Psychology of Music*.

RICHARD MIDDLETON, FBA, is Emeritus Professor of Music at Newcastle University. He is the author of *Pop Music and the Blues* (1972), *Studying Popular Music* (1990), *Voicing the Popular* (2006) and *Musical Belongings: Selected Essays* (2009), editor of *Reading Pop: Approaches to Textual Analysis in Popular Music* (2000) and co-editor (with Martin Clayton and Trevor Herbert) of *The Cultural Study of Music: A Critical Introduction* (2003; revised edition 2012). He was a Founding Editor of the Cambridge University Press journal, *Popular Music*.

GASCIA OUZOUNIAN is Lecturer in the School of Creative Arts at Queen's University Belfast. She is a musicologist, composer and violinist, and has performed in North America and Europe with such ensembles as the Silk Road Ensemble, Sinfonia Toronto and Theatre of Eternal Music Strings Ensemble. Her research focuses on experimental music and sound art, with particular interests in site-specific sound, sound installation art and intermedia composition. Her writings are published in *Journal of the Society for American Music, Journal of Visual Culture, Computer Music Journal* and *Organised Sound*.

TOM RICE is Lecturer in Social Anthropology at the University of Exeter. He held an ESRC Postdoctoral Research Fellowship at the University of Cambridge, during which time he co-organised the 2008 conference 'Music, Sound, and the Reconfiguration of Public and Private Space' from which this volume derives. His publications on 'auditory anthropology' appear in the *Journal of the Royal Anthropological Institute*, *Journal of Material Culture*, *The Senses and Society* and *The Sound Studies Handbook*. His book *Hearing the Hospital: Sound, Listening, Knowledge and Experience* is forthcoming. His future research addresses the nature of prison soundscapes.

JASON STANYEK is University Lecturer in Ethnomusicology at the University of Oxford, where he is also Fellow and Tutor in Music at St John's College. He is the author of numerous articles and of a forthcoming book on music and dance in the Brazilian diaspora. He co-edited *The Oxford Handbook of Mobile Music Studies* (with Sumanth Gopinath) and *Brazil's Northern Wave: Fifty Years of Bossa Nova in the United States* (with Frederick Moehn), both forthcoming.

JONATHAN STERNE teaches in the Department of Art History and Communication Studies at McGill University. His research focuses on sound and music, media technologies and the politics of culture. He is author of *The Audible Past: Cultural Origins of Sound Reproduction* (2003), *MP3: The Meaning of a Format* (2012) and numerous articles in such journals as *Social Text*, *New Media and Society*, *Ethnomusicology* and *Media, Culture and Society*. He is the editor of *The Sound Studies Reader* (2012). Visit his website at http://sterneworks.org.

# Acknowledgements

This book began life as an interdisciplinary conference organised by myself and Tom Rice at the aptly named CRASSH (Centre for Research in the Arts, Social Sciences and Humanities), Cambridge University. Those involved found it an exceptionally stimulating event because it succeeded in bringing into dialogue fields – sound studies, sound art, ethnomusicology, musicology, popular music studies and the anthropology, geography, psychology and sociology of music – that toil adjacently but rarely talk. This was a particularly fertile period at CRASSH, then under the creative leadership of Mary Jacobus, whose openness to experimental directions between the arts and social sciences was quite inspirational. At this time I was also privileged to be a Fellow of Girton College, Cambridge, the Fellowship of which includes a spirited and progressive group of musicians and geographers, and where music, space and the social are lively intellectual and creative concerns. My greatest debt is to Tom Rice, in terms of the co-organisation of the conference and the early stages of work on this book. Tom's knowledge of sound studies greatly exceeds my own, and I was fortunate, through our collegial relationship, to be infected by the sound bug. Unfortunately, due to other demands, Tom's editorial involvement in the collection was cut short. He goes from strength to strength as one of the most significant and talented younger scholars in the anthropology of sound. My other serious debt is to my contributors for their enthusiasm and willingness to be enrolled in this project, for providing a feast of research and ideas to grapple with, and for their generous patience as progress towards publication was slower than expected.

My work on the book has benefited greatly since late 2010 from my research for a programme funded by the European Research Council: 'Music, Digitisation, Mediation: Towards Interdisciplinary Music Studies'. This research has brought me into intensive dialogue with a range of practitioners in the UK, Canada and Austria engaged in distinctive ways in the artful exploration of the mutuality of music, sound and space. My thinking also gained from co-editing a volume with Andrew Barry, *Interdisciplinarity: Reconfigurations of the Social and Natural Sciences*, based on earlier research funded by the UK Economic and Social Research Council, which stoked my awareness not only of the challenges but also the powers thrown up by inventive interdisciplinarity. In a way the volume on interdisciplinarity is a silent twin to this one, even though there are no explicit references in that book to music and sound. (For those interested, however, a series of proposals concerning music, stimulated by our wider research on interdisciplinarity, can be found in my article: 'For a relational musicology: Music and interdisciplinarity, beyond the practice turn', *Journal of the Royal Musical Association*, 135(2), 2010.)

I am grateful to Kyle Devine, Clare Oxenbury and Jean-Luc Jucker for assistance in the preparation of the manuscript. Warm thanks are due to my editors at Cambridge University Press, Vicki Cooper, Fleur Jones and Rebecca Taylor, who made the whole process as supportive as it could be. Final thanks go to my family, Clara, Theo and Andrew, for their love, good humour and resilience in the face of my devotion to the study and the sound system.

# 1 | Introduction – music, sound and space: transformations of public and private experience

GEORGINA BORN

## Topological music, sonic-spatial practices

When new instruments will allow me to write music as I conceive it, the movement of sound-masses, of shifting planes, will be clearly perceived in my work, taking the place of linear counterpoint. When these sound masses collide, the phenomena of penetration or repulsion will seem to occur. Certain transmutations taking place on certain planes will seem to be projected onto other planes, moving at different speeds and at different angles ... We have actually three dimensions in music: horizontal, vertical, and dynamic swelling or decreasing. I shall add a fourth, sound projection ... [the sense] of a journey into space. Today, with the technical means that exist and are easily adaptable, the differentiation of the various masses and different planes as well as these beams of sound could be made discernible to the listener by means of certain acoustical arrangements ... [permitting] the delimitation of what I call 'zones of intensities'. These zones would be differentiated by various timbres or colours and different loudnesses. [They] would appear ... in different perspectives for our perception ... [They] would be felt as isolated, and the hitherto unobtainable non-blending ... would become possible. (Varèse 2004 (1936): 17–18)

Over the past few weeks the Old Schools Combination Room has been buzzing with workshops, talks, film showings and a steady stream of visitors and participants. Today, it was properly pumping. Responding to the refusal of University management to engage in any sort of discussion with the occupation of the Old Schools, protesters staged a noise protest in the afternoon, blasting music towards the Vice Chancellor's ... office out of the windows of the Senior Combination Room ... We launched the noise protest – which involved amplifiers blasting music, an electric guitar, drums, pots, pans and chants over megaphones – in response to the

I am grateful to the following colleagues for their perceptive and valuable comments on this Introduction: Robert Adlington, Lionel Bently, David Borgo, Don Brenneis, Andrew Eisenberg, Martin Kretschmer, Katharine Norman, Gascia Ouzounian, Deniz Peters, George Revill, Tom Rice, Jonathan Sterne, Patrick Valiquet and Simon Waters, as well as anonymous reviewers. Many of their suggestions were enormously helpful. None of them, however, are responsible for the final cut.

University's refusal to engage in discussion ... and a group of students took drums to the main entrance of the Old Schools to be heard there ... If the University is more willing to implement a forcible and violent eviction than to speak to the students it claims to speak for, we must hold them to account for their choice ... We have collectively agreed upon and implemented a safer spaces policy, as a framework for addressing these concerns within our space.[1]

The two opening quotations between them lay out the terrain of this book. The juxtaposition of these vivid tableaux is intended to highlight the mutual relations between music, sound and space, as well as the generative potential of bridge-building between, on the one hand, the study of music and sound and, on the other, the study of spatial and social processes. In the first quotation, the French–American composer Edgard Varèse – who described his music as 'organised sound' and himself as 'a worker in rhythms, frequencies, and intensities' – inaugurated a discourse on twentieth- and twenty-first century music that has since grown exponentially in both influence and extent. The copious topological, spatial and mobile metaphors coined by Varèse to imagine and describe the sonic material of his musical works – shifting planes, colliding masses, projection, transmutation, repulsion, speeds, angles and zones – not only prefigure the later interest in spatialisation in electronic and electroacoustic music and what has come to be called sound art, but they point in the direction of the themes of this volume, echoing some of the core conceptual terms that it summons up. The second quotation comes from a website statement issued by students who occupied a central building in Cambridge University for several weeks in late 2010 in protest against major cuts to British university funding by the government. In reaction to the cuts, a campaign to defend public universities gathered pace in a number of cities: the 'defend education' movement.[2] What is striking in the statement is the prominent role given to music- and noise-making in the actions intended to elicit a public dialogue with the authorities, particularly collective acts of noisily mobilising in and occupying public space, as well as the insistence on creating independent 'safer spaces' to foster self-organisation and participatory political dialogue. Issues of sound and space therefore had a focal place in the movement's political imagination.

The subject matter of the present collection congeals at the intersection of a series of related terms: music, sound, space, and how these phenomena

---

[1]  Statement by students occupying the Senior Combination Room, Cambridge University, in protest at the threatened cuts to university funding, 1 December 2010, www.defendeducation. co.uk/old-schools-occupation/safer-spaces-agreement (last accessed 18 August 2012).

[2]  For the Cambridge branch of 'defend education', see www.defendeducation.co.uk/ (last accessed 18 August 2012).

have been employed to create, mark or transform the nature of public and private experience. While music and sound have long been employed to cultivate realms of both public and private experience,[3] these capacities accelerated with the burgeoning of sound media from the late nineteenth century. The early telephone, for example, was 'startling and pleasurable in its capacity to transmit bodily and intimate physical sounds, suggesting a fluid interchange of separated spaces, in which the interior of the body is transmitted … to the inner ear of the listener' (Connor 1997: 206); indeed 'a long series of literary phantasms … rewrite eroticism itself under the conditions of gramophony and telephony' (Kittler 1999: 56). In parallel, the gramophone and its precursors made it possible in the first decades of the twentieth century for music-listening to be relocated from the music hall, jazz club or concert hall to the home or brothel, while radio broadcasts enabled music to accompany not only domestic life but factory labour and political meetings (Korczynski and Jones 2006). Already apparent is a dual movement that is characteristic of this history: both interiorising, in the domestic provenance of early sound media and the inter-corporeal, prosthetic uses of telephony, and exteriorising, in those media oriented more to engendering collective forms of life and work.

At the base of this collection is the conviction that 'perhaps the most important distinguishing feature of auditory experience … [is] its capacity to … reconfigure space'. With the development of modern sound media, according to Steven Connor, 'the rationalized "Cartesian grid" of the visualist imagination … gave way to a more fluid, mobile and voluminous conception of space … Where auditory experience is dominant, we might say, singular, perspectival gives way to plural, permeated space. The self defined in terms of hearing rather than sight is a self imaged not as a point, but as a membrane … a channel through which voices, noises and musics travel' (all Connor 1997: 206). As the chapters that follow demonstrate, however, the auditory self is also an embodied self that responds and re-sounds: in the words of Jean-Luc Nancy, sound is 'tendentially methexic (that is, having to do with participation, sharing, or contagion)'; it 'spreads in space, where it resounds while still resounding "in me"' (Nancy 2007: 10, 7). But the contributors to this volume go further, proposing that the auditory self, as listener, musician, sound artist or sonic *flâneur*, can be positioned equally as a boundary point that impedes or stops the flow of music

---

[3] Corbin (1998), for example, a historian of sound and the senses, charts how church bells produced communal experiences of sonically mediated public space long before modern sound media, sonic publics that were traversed by hierarchical social relations while also engendering collective ritual, memory and passion.

and sound, as well as being potentially initiatory in relation to sound and music – as much agentive and mediating as mediated.

The first section of this Introduction aims to identify key conceptual themes running through the book, while suggesting how these themes link to existing discussions and move them in generative new directions. In this light, the second section gives an overview of the individual chapters, bringing out their singular contributions to the volume. The book, which has its origins in an interdisciplinary conference held at the Centre for Research in the Arts, Social Sciences and Humanities at Cambridge University, brings together scholars of music, sound, mediation and modernity.[4] It does so in order to address a series of changes in the contemporary experience of music and sound – changes that, as the chapters make clear, are associated with but not limited to their evolving forms of technological mediation. In this combination of preoccupations, the volume explores new ground. But it is also framed by a web of disciplinary and interdisciplinary areas of enquiry. Recent years have seen a veritable avalanche of scholarship devoted to the interconnections between sound and space, in some cases making links also to music and audio technologies. This is evident in the emergence and evolution of the overlapping interdisciplinary fields of film sound studies (Altman 1992a, 1992b; Chion 1994; Lastra 2000), sound-scape and sound studies (Schafer 1994 (1977); Connor 2000b; Kruth and Stobart 2000; Sterne 2003; Hilmes 2005) and auditory or aural culture studies (Bull and Back 2003; Drobnick 2004), as well as in the growing attention paid to these matters in history (Attali 1985; Chanan 1995; Corbin 1998; B. R. Smith 1999; M. M. Smith 2001, 2004; Thompson 2002), anthropology and ethnomusicology (Feld 1982, 1996; Born 1995, 2005; Lysloff and Gay 2003; Erlmann 2004; Feld and Brenneis 2004; Fox 2004; Hirschkind 2006; Samuels *et al.* 2010), sociology (Bull 2000, 2007; DeNora 2000; Back 2007) and geography (S. J. Smith 1997; Leyshon, Matless and Revill 1998; Revill 2000; Connell and Gibson 2003; Wood, Duffy and Smith 2007). To these can be added developments in two further, sociologically influenced inter-disciplinary fields: science and technology studies (Pinch and Bijsterveld 2004; Bijsterveld 2008) and popular music studies (Whiteley, Bennett and Hawkins 2005; Krims 2007). Manifestly, sound, space, music and techno-logical mediation are high on the scholarly agenda.

---

[4] The conference, held in April 2008, is archived at www.crassh.cam.ac.uk/events/70/ (last accessed 18 August 2012). I am greatly indebted to those speakers, musicians and artists who gave presentations but have not contributed to this volume: Michael Bull, Ruth Davis, John Levack Drever, Brandon LaBelle, James Lastra, Martin Stokes and David Toop, as well as the respondents, Steven Connor, Ben Etherington, George Revill and Ben Walton.

However, such a profusion of research poses its own challenges; as one commentator observes, 'these various venues of academic work on sound phenomena so rarely speak to or take heed of each other' (Hilmes 2005: 252). A core aim of this collection is, then, to create productive cross-currents between fields that have hitherto developed without much mutual reference. A first way in which the volume experiments is by placing chapters that address questions of music and space, from the perspective of the music disciplines, into dialogue with others that examine sound and space. A founding observation of the collection is that musicology and the burgeoning literatures on sound and auditory cultures have proceeded largely in isolation from each other. On the one hand, research in sound studies has had little to say about music's inhabitation of and entanglement with the encompassing acoustic environment. This is despite the fact that the work of R. Murray Schafer and other seminal writings in this area have registered music's interconnections with the wider soundworld (Schafer 1994 (1977), Chapter 7; Bull and Back 2003, Part V). It is also despite the fact that from the outset soundscape research provided the stimulus for compositional activities, as in the music of Barry Truax, Hildegard Westerkamp and others. On the other hand, musicology and music analysis have continued to focus in recent decades primarily on those score-based lineages of twentieth-century Western art music that conceive of musical materials primarily in the terms of orthodox music notation. They have been slow as yet to respond to those parallel waves of post-1950s developments – experimental music, electronic, electroacoustic and computer music, interactive, site-specific and installation-based sound art, as well as electronic popular musics – in which musical thought and practice are irreducible to a score, where the ontological distinction between music and sound is disturbed,[5] and which foreground the creative possibilities – whether in recorded media, live performance or installations – of the mutable boundaries between music, sound and space.[6] The dominant academic music disciplines therefore continue to uphold the nineteenth-century formulation of musicology 'as a kind of musical philology' (Cook 2008: 58), making it difficult to address not only music as performance and event, but also

---

[5] See Nattiez 1990: Chapter 2 on the heterogeneous and relational semantic content of, and the shifting classificatory distinctions between, concepts of music and sound as well as sound and noise with reference to both historical and cross-cultural research.

[6] For an attempt to classify and define the various movements composing this broad historical field of developments, and a commentary on musicology's relative neglect of them, see Landy 2007: 1–19.

those many genres of twentieth- and twenty-first-century music that have embraced new materials, new performance practices and new media.

As if in response to this impasse in the academic music disciplines, one of the most cogent implications of the growing attention to sound across the humanities and social sciences has been methodological and epistemological. In part this amounts to a 'critique of "visualism"' (Erlmann 2004: 1; cf. Connor 1997): a concerted attempt to wrest the bases of human knowledge away from the long-standing hegemony of visual, text-based and representational models. For Veit Erlmann, a key figure in forging close relations between sound studies and the anthropology of the senses and of sound, a methodology attuned to 'hearing cultures' partakes in a larger project of 'sensuous scholarship': '"Hearing culture" suggests that it is possible to conceptualize new ways of knowing a culture and of gaining a deepened understanding of how the members of a society know each other' (Erlmann 2004: 3). Steven Feld (1996: 94–5) traces the twin origins of this approach, showing how from the outset conceptual links were drawn between sound and space. He finds them in the work of music philosopher Victor Zuckerkandl (1956) and anthropologist Edmund Carpenter (1960), both of whom propounded the idea of 'auditory space'. Zuckerkandl's writings, for instance, which drew on Bergson, William James and Heidegger, detailed how 'space is audibly fused with time in the progression and motion of tones', stressing 'the interpenetration of auditory space and time' (Feld 1996: 95). While Zuckerkandl's influence was felt among a generation of anthropologists of music, ritual and symbolism, Carpenter's was evident in the founding in 1970 of Schafer's World Soundscape Project, which, integrating art and science, was the first research programme to focus on the nature of the sonic environment and resulted in the coining of soundscape studies and the concept of acoustic ecology. As Feld (1996: 95) explains, 'Schafer's group began recording, observing, and acoustically analysing the sonic experience of space and place … and developed an analytical vocabulary, a notation system, and a comparative framework for the study of acoustic space and its human interpretation and feedback.'

While acknowledging the significance of the Schaferian lineage, Feld criticises its tendency to reify 'a visual-auditory great divide' (1996: 96).[7]

---

[7] See Ingold 2000b for another insightful commentary, with reference to James Gibson and Merleau-Ponty, on the tendency to draw an opposition between vision and hearing in the work of such writers as McLuhan, Ong and Carpenter, and to equate vision with objectification or 'speculation' in the work of Jay and others. Ingold stresses instead the complementarity between visual, auditory and other sensory modalities, arguing from ethnographic evidence that in certain cultures vision as well as hearing amounts to a mode of participation or 'being' that is elicited by particular environments. He makes the ironic point that the critics of visualism

Rather than dichotomising vision and hearing, anthropology today – in the work of Feld, Erlmann, David Howes (Howes 1991) and others – advocates the embedding of interdisciplinary research on sound and hearing in wider cultural and historical analyses of the interplay between the senses: the study of 'sensory ratios' (Feld 1996: 96). Feld himself is a pivotal figure in both sound studies and the anthropology of the senses; he exemplifies a particularly generative direction, one that takes its orientation from another key turn in sound studies: to phenomenology, via Merleau-Ponty and later writers. Feld's work is exceptional in addressing both music and sound and their interrelations as part of a broader framework of enquiry, which, in a classic paper from 1996, he identifies as a combination of 'social phenomenology and [a] hermeneutics of senses of place' (Feld 1996: 91).[8] In this way he points to a second innovative dimension of this book, which responds to a common feature of the various (inter)disciplinary initiatives: the relative *under*development of analytical approaches to the *social* dimensions of the interweaving of music, sound and space. Each of the chapters in this volume addresses the social mediation of music, sound and space, whether from the perspective of their capacity to engender modes of publicness and privacy, their constitution of forms of subjectivity and personhood, their affective resonance, or their embedding in capitalist dynamics of commodification and reification. A core aim of this Introduction is to show how, taken as a whole, the contributions augur a new kind of social phenomenology of music and sound, and one that expands considerably upon previous conceptions.

---

invariably have their source 'in the very Cartesian epistemology that they seek to dethrone. What they offer, then, is … a critique of modernity dressed up as a critique of the hegemony of vision' (Ingold 2000b: 287).

[8] It is beyond the scope of this Introduction to address the important questions posed in anthropology about the relations between space and place (Feld and Basso 1996), and by ethnomusicology about the significance for music of place and locality (e.g. Stokes 1994; Solomon 2005a, 2005b; Wolf 2009), although certain chapters do address these issues (see Chapter 2 by Ouzounian, Chapter 8 by Eisenberg and Chapter 11 by Dueck). Suffice it to note Edward Casey's cogent critique, by way of a sensuous phenomenology, of any conception of place in which it is subsumed by what are thought to be primary, universalised categories of space and time, such that 'generality, albeit empty, belongs to space; [while] particularity, albeit mythic, belongs to place' (Casey 1996: 15). With reference to the philosopher A. N. Whitehead, Casey argues against 'the tendency to posit a plane of abstract perfection and purity [i.e. space or time] onto which complexities and dirty details come crowding [i.e. place]' (Casey 1996: 45). Rather, 'space and time are themselves coordinated and co-specified in the common matrix provided by place' (Casey 1996: 36). Casey's remarks are highly salient to the alternative accounts of space as well as the sonic–social phenomenology elaborated in what follows. My thanks to Don Brenneis for suggesting that I mention these issues, and in particular for referring me to Casey.

Feld (1996: 97) stresses the embodied and spatialised nature and the affective entailments of sound perception:

Sound, hearing and voice mark a special bodily nexus for sensation and emotion … By bringing a durative, motional world of time and space simultaneously to front and back, top and bottom, and left and right, an alignment suffuses the entire fixed or moving body. This is why hearing and voicing link the felt sensations of sound and balance to those of physical and emotional presence.

With reference to his seminal ethnography of the Kaluli people of the rainforests of Papua New Guinea (Feld 1982), Feld introduces the concept of acoustemology (acoustic epistemology). With it he points to 'acoustic knowing as a centrepiece of Kaluli experience; how sounding and the sensual, bodily, experiencing of sound is a special kind of knowing, or put differently, how sonic sensibility is basic to experiential truth in the Bosavi forests' (Feld 1994). 'Acoustic knowing', then, is an experiential knowledge based on the intimate relations between sound, space and place. Acoustemology invokes the way that 'space indexes the distribution of sounds, and time indexes the motion of sounds. Yet acoustic time is always spatialized … And acoustic space is likewise temporalized' (Feld 1996: 97–8). This orientation is amplified by Feld's ethnography, in which Kaluli socialities more fully enter the frame, and in which he shows how Kaluli musical experience cannot be understood without reference to their wider ontology and ecology. For Kaluli, music is embedded in and constitutive of not only their environmental ecology and collective experience of space and time, but their social relations and rituals, emotions and labour. Feld charts in both ordinary and ceremonial music-making a series of ambiguities and fluidities concerning the boundary between collective emotion and the aesthetic and symbolic valencies of musical performance, as well as between improvisation and composition, music-making and everyday work and play, and individual and collective experience. Musical expressions therefore weave through and form an indissociable part of Kaluli socialities.

Several fruitful insights can be derived from Feld's work. First, he indicates the significance of a sonic-social phenomenology, one that is generalisable as both epistemology and method. Second, he shows convincingly that at the core of our embodied experience of sound and music lies the interrelation between, and mutual modulation of, space and time. Third, Feld portrays these modes of experience – sound, music, their spatialities and temporalities – as immanently affective and as generative of subjective impression, expression and transformation. And fourth, his insistence on the mutuality of these modes of experience, and of the sounded imbrication of bodies and environment, gestures also in the direction of a theory of mediation of sound and music:[9] of their complex and multiple, sensory and affective, material and social forms.

## Space in/and music

If sound studies and the anthropology of sound have drawn illuminating links between sound and space, how have the music disciplines understood the relations between music and space? While 'space' has often been used in ambiguous and metaphorical ways in relation to music, it is possible to distinguish three broad ways of conceptualising space in/and music in these literatures: three distinct lineages of practising and cognising musical spatiality.

A dominant, formalist approach to musical spatiality, allied to score-based, visual and graphic representations and analyses of music, limits itself to a concern with the internal operations of musical sound conceived primarily in the terms of what is called 'pitch space'. To illustrate from recent work: Edward Campbell, in his study of the music and philosophy of Pierre Boulez, writes that 'the concept of musical space, in the sense of pitch space, is a fundamental one for many writers' (Campbell 2010: 220) and cites approvingly the metaphorical reading of musical space in Zuckerkandl (1956) and Roger Scruton (1997) in this regard. Campbell explains that 'From a spatial perspective, tonal music can be thought of as tracing paths through pitch space by means of the system of keys and their

---

[9] It is important to clarify the term mediation in relation to music and sound. In earlier writings I pointed to the importance of understanding music as 'inherently "mediational" – liable to mediation' (Born 1991: 158), in the sense that music is always (but variably) experienced through a constellation of aural, notational, visual, performative, corporeal, social, discursive and technological forms – forms that mediate the music (or sound). Such an approach makes it possible to 'move beyond ... impoverished and essentialist notions of how music conveys meaning by developing an analysis of the multiple, specific forms in which it is experienced', allowing us to grasp 'the multitextuality of music-as-culture, and the need to analyse its particular forms – aural, visual, technological, social, discursive – as an ensemble' (Born 1991: 159). This conception (which I developed independently) in some ways converges with the general definition of mediation given by Bruno Latour (2005), which he draws through a contrast: 'An *intermediary*, in my vocabulary, is what transports meaning or force without transformation ... *Mediators*, on the other hand ... transform, translate, distort, and modify the meaning or the elements they are supposed to carry' (Latour 2005: 39, emphasis in original). Mediation, then, transforms both elements in the relation posited by it: thus, in writing of music's social mediation I refer to how music is transformed by its social manifestations or embodiments, as well as to how the social is produced and transformed by music. On these issues see later sections of this Introduction as well as note 81 on the concept of 'musical capitalism'.

modulation to distinct but related regions', and he continues by way of the Second Viennese School's alternative, dodecaphonic manipulation of pitch space in the form of the twelve-tone series and its transpositions, as well as Schoenberg's idea of the 'unity of musical space' (Campbell 2010: 220). Campbell is persuaded to engage in the analysis of pitch space because of its central place in Boulez's musical poetics. He charts its changing status in Boulez's writings, particularly the efflorescence of spatial concepts in his Darmstadt lectures in which Boulez identified "'the conception and realisation of a *relativity* of the various musical spaces in use" as an urgent objective' (Campbell 2010: 220, citing Boulez 1971: 83) and distinguished two main pitch-space states, 'smooth' and 'striated', as the basis for an expanding taxonomy including such sub-species as curved, regular and irregular striated pitch spaces (Campbell 2010: 221–5).[10] A similar spatial ontology is palpable in dialogues between composers, for example in commentaries by Boulez and Alexander Goehr on what they perceive to be problems with Messiaen's compositional style. As Arnold Whittall describes, they charge Messiaen with having 'no idea of musical levels: all was surface' (Goehr 1998) and with accomplishing the mere juxtaposition as opposed to development of musical ideas, a failing linked to his lack of interest in constructing 'organic wholes' in the tradition of Germanic organicism (Whittall 2007: 244–5).

It is intriguing that since the 1970s analogous spatial metaphors have been a feature of psychoacoustical research. Here space is no longer conceived intramusically, but as a property of the interface between sonic or musical object and perceiving subject. This stance is manifest both in theories of auditory perception that focus on the way that sonic sensory data are grouped and segregated by individual listeners into what are called 'auditory streams' (McAdams and Bregman 1979; Bregman 1994 (1990); Bregman *et al.* 2000),[11] and in theories concerned with the analysis of perception of musical timbre in terms of 'timbre space' (Wessel 1979). The latter paradigm is symptomatic of the close interconnections that arose between research on psychoacoustics, music synthesis techniques and new aesthetic possibilities in computer music (Born 1995). In the words of David Wessel (1978):

[10] Boulez's distinction between smooth and striated space was given wider philosophical and political resonance by Deleuze and Guattari (1987: Chapter 14), which has in turn stimulated further spatial orientations in social theory, e.g. Osborne and Rose 2004: 211.
[11] On the intuitive deployment by composers of Bregman's psychoacoustical principles, see Harley 1998.

In our research on musical timbre ... [s]ubjective judgments of perceptual contrast between sounds provide the basic input data to multidimensional scaling programs that produce geometric representations ... [and] a good statistical relationship is sought between the distances in the space and the contrast judgments between the corresponding tones. The spatial representation is given a psychoacoustical interpretation by relating its dimensions to the acoustical properties of the tones.

In sum, a Euclidean and statistical model of timbral space is derived from subjective perceptions in order, in part, to drive sound synthesis controls; we might say that the normative and technical enfold and order the subjective and perspectival.

Despite the prominence of such spatial thinking in twentieth- and twenty-first-century music and music analysis, it has not been uncontroversial. The philosopher Vladimir Jankélévitch (2003: 91–3), to cite an outspoken critic, rejects spatial metaphors:

In effect, the general characteristics attributed to 'music' often exist only for the eye, by means of the conjuring trick of graphic analogy. The simple particularity of writing ... will suffice for us to characterize the melodic 'arch'; and a melody that is outside all space, as a succession of sounds and pure duration, is subjected to the contagion of graphic signs ... Music is not calligraphy projected into space, but a lived experience analogous to life.

Katherine Bergeron, in turn, interrogates the musical canon and the learning of scales as disciplinary musico-spatial formations. Scale-playing presupposes a particular discipline: 'playing "in tune". This also implies an ordering of the body, a disciplining of the ear'; while the canon amounts to 'an ideal of order made material, physical, visible. In the scale ... such order is also audible, materialized as a finite set of intervals, perfectly tuned by mathematical calculation, by the ratio – the numerical representation ... [of] "reason"' (Bergeron 1992: 2). For Bergeron, the canon and the scale combine musical and social regulation; each advocates 'a collection of discrete values produced out of a system that orders, segments, divides' (Bergeron 1992).

A second conception of space in/and music is evident in diverse practices and discourses of 'spatialisation' associated with multichannel techniques of studio recording and manipulation and loudspeaker projection as they developed in both popular musics and electronic, electroacoustic and computer art musics from the 1950s onwards. In these traditions, the localisation of sound in physical and perceptual space, as well as the creation of senses of virtual space and of sonic-spatial movement and evolution both between and within sound objects (Chowning 1977), are harnessed to aesthetic ends either as part of the desired musical effect or as a primary element in the compositional imagination. Like 'pitch space' formalism, this second discourse of space prominent in electroacoustic and computer music invokes notions of spatial and musical autonomy. But in the absence of score-based methods of analysis for these mainly non-notated musics, it has necessitated the invention of quite different frames of reference. These can be gleaned from reflections by electroacoustic composers who have also become theorists. Trevor Wishart, for instance, poses the notion of aural 'landscape' against the compositional philosophy espoused by Pierre Schaeffer and the Groupe de Recherches Musicales, which centred on the idea of 'acousmatic' music: music based on the 'abstraction of the recorded "sound-object" from any dependent relationship to its origins' (Wishart 1986: 43). With 'landscape' Wishart aims to valorise the aesthetic salience of modes of sonic experience 'related to our recognition of the source of the sounds' (1986: 42). Comparing the approaches to 'landscape' adopted by the composers Luc Ferrari and Bernard Parmegiani, Wishart notes that 'changes in aural perspective on an object' obtained by certain recording techniques 'produce quite different acoustic results and when they are jux-taposed in the aural landscape our sense of aural perspective is transformed' (1986: 42). He distinguishes various types of 'acoustic space', such as the illu-sion of two-dimensional space, movement of sound-objects through virtual space, and 'convolution' – imposition of 'the acoustic characteristics of any pre-analysed sound environment upon a given sound object' (1986: 45).

An alternative perspective on spatialisation comes from the composer–theorist Denis Smalley, who claims unequivocally that 'acousmatic music is the only sonic medium that concentrates on space and spatial experience as aesthetically central' (Smalley 2007: 35). Smalley's writings travel from an early focus on 'spectro-morphology' – 'an approach to sound materi-als and musical structures which concentrates on the spectrum of available pitches and their shaping in time' (Smalley 1986: 61) – to a recent concern with 'space-form and the acousmatic image' (Smalley 2007). The later art-icle attempts nothing less than a phenomenology of the potential spatial forms afforded by acousmatic music. Several features are notable, not only in themselves, but for what they reveal about the strengths and limitations of distinctive styles of phenomenology of sound and listening. Smalley's 'space-form' mode of analysis, while acknowledging the co-evolution in music of space and time, offers emphatically 'an approach to musical form, and its analysis, which privileges space as the primary articulator. Time acts in the service of space' (2007: 56). On the basis of a nuanced auto-ethnographic description of an evening soundscape in a village in southern France, Smalley derives a remarkable taxonomy of analytical terms for the perception of spatial sound: zoned, proximate, behavioural, perspectival, distal, utterance, agential, vectorial, panoramic, ouverture/enclosure, approach/recession, diagonal forces and so on. Distilling his initial analysis, Smalley arrives at a 'holistic view. This holistic space comprised an array of zoned spaces'. With reference to a group of prominent sound sources, he observes: 'I could regard the frog-river-crow zone as a *nested* [sonic] *space* (spaces within a space)' (2007: 37, emphasis in original).[12] He proceeds to identify a sonic vector, 'the space traversed by the trajectory of a [moving] sound' (2007: note 8) caused in this instance by passing cars, which 'delineates the peripheral border of the whole', as well as shifting figure–ground spatial relations between fixed (a river, cicadas) and emergent-passing (bird song) sound sources. Smalley's analysis, which moves from the acoustic ecology to its implications for composition, is a tour de force. We will have reason to return to the idea of zoned and nested sonic spaces.

In addition, however, through its detailed investigation of the relational nature of spatialised sounds, and of the propensity of sounds to create a sense of spatial boundaries via shifting and nested sonic horizons, Smalley's analysis compares favourably with that of the philosopher Don Ihde (Ihde 1976), often considered the standard work in the phenomenology of listening and sound. Ihde himself acknowledges the relational nature of perception and of phenomenological knowledge. He establishes a series of principles: that human auditory focus is omnidirectional, while sound is generally experienced as located and as directional; that sound perception proceeds through a variable focus on one or other sound, through backgrounding and foregrounding; that sound perception is characterised by its continuity, by the 'ebb and flow of noise' and movement of sound; and that sound can be perceived spatially in the guise of hearing sonic shapes, surfaces and interiors. Yet despite these findings, Ihde does not develop a conceptual inventory as rich as Smalley's to account for the multiplicity of sonic forms, trajectories and interrelations composing the sonic environment. And in discussing sound's capacity to create boundaries or horizons, Ihde insists that, perceptually, such boundaries can only be temporal, not spatial: 'Although I may be "immersed" in this "sphere" of sound, I cannot find its boundaries spatially. The spatial signification of a horizon is obscure' (1976: 102). If sound has a boundary, Ihde contends, 'in the case of the auditory field that horizon appears most strikingly as *temporal*' (1976:

---

[12] Smalley's notions of perceived sonic zones and nested sonic spaces bear comparison with Simon Emmerson's concept of nested 'soundfield frames' (Emmerson 1998).

103). Later, indicating the confines of Ihde's a-historical, a-social phenomenology of sound, we will see that this is problematic: that music and sound can articulate spatial and socio-spatial as well as temporal boundaries.

Returning to Smalley, it is notable that his analytical taxonomy acknowledges the spatiality both of sound's technological mediation and of its social mediation in performance. Yet these elements of his conceptual scheme are barely developed. Smalley's phenomenology certainly extends that of Ihde, but given its minimal account of social and technological mediation, it offers ultimately an expanded, if rigorous and elegant, sonic formalism. Moreover, while Smalley's initial analysis is garnered reflexively from auto-ethnography and is perspectival, derived from embodied listening, subjective experience and location, the essay is oriented to discerning normative principles. Overall, his scheme therefore exhibits a tension between the perspectival and a certain objectivism. This interpretation gains support from Patrick Valiquet (2011), who highlights the presumption of structural autonomy that tends to prevail in discourses of spatialisation in electroacoustic and computer music. As Valiquet shows, such claims to autonomy are accompanied by the occlusion of how, through 'discursive, social, and technical work … composers and theorists were able to rationalise their appropriation of the technical apparatus of multichannel stereophony from the telecommunications and entertainment industries while simultaneously constructing an aesthetic of spatialisation which delegitimised commercial music and sound design' (Valiquet 2011: 41).

A commitment to spatialisation continues to characterise electroacoustic and computer music and related research today, and takes diverse forms. As attested by recent computer music symposia, sessions on 'spatial sound' combine technical, psychoacoustical, philosophical and aesthetic concerns.[13] Despite this breadth and the current interest in virtual spatialities, musically oriented virtual worlds and the 'strange ontologies' that they might entail – for example, 'worlds that present alternative models of being-in-time' (Wakefield and Smith 2011: 14) – what is striking about ongoing work in this second lineage is its resiliently Euclidean orientation. If 'strange ontologies' are envisaged, it is generally by engineering sensibilities bound still to the orthodoxies of 'computer–human interaction'.

A third distinctive set of understandings of space in/and music departs radically from the two previous lineages described, subsuming a heterogeneous range of aesthetic and ideological orientations. If they exhibit any unity, it is by virtue of a determinedly post-formalist stance that responds to

---

[13]  See, for example, the papers collected in Adkins and Isaacs 2011.

the two formalisms outlined, in the process exploding their conceptions of space.[14] This third lineage is associated today with soundscape composition and sound art, as well as live and experimental electronic and computer music.[15] It is perhaps particularly identified with sound art, by which I refer to such practices as sound installation, site-specific and public sound works, practices that operate at the borders of an array of conceptual, performance, intermedia and digital art practices (Kahn 1999; LaBelle 2006; Salter 2010). This broad interdisciplinary field includes performance events, installations and works that involve electronic and computer mediation, and others that do not, or only minimally so. The genealogy of sound art is often traced back to Varèse's notion of organised sound, through the post-war tradition of Cageian and post-Cageian experimental music delineated by Michael Nyman (Nyman 1974),[16] including the work of such figures as Christian Wolff, LaMonte Young, Alvin Lucier and Max Neuhaus, as well as the Fluxus movement, happenings, installation and minimalist art (LaBelle 2006; Landy 2007; Demers 2010). For sound artist and writer Brandon LaBelle, Cage's experimental practices set 'the stage for a heightened consideration of listening and the "place" of sound', positioning music 'in relation to a broader set of questions to do with social experience and everyday life' (LaBelle 2006: xii–xiii). He adds to the genealogy Group Ongaku, an avant-garde Japanese improvising collective of the early 1960s who – manifesting a 'radically physical relationship to the material world' (2006: 37) – met at different locations to improvise using found objects and instruments, radios and tape recorders. Through Group Ongaku, LaBelle expands the forefathers of sound art to encompass movements and figures committed to a sonic–spatial politics of the urban condition and the everyday, from anthropological surrealism to Situationism, Henri Lefebvre to Michel de Certeau (2006: Chapter 3). Indeed, practices in this lineage strain against

---

[14] But for attempts to forge potential links or a transition between the second and third lineages, see Myatt 1998 and, in particular, Truax 1998.

[15] The definition of these music and sound art movements, as implied above (note 6), remains fluid and contentious, and writers take different views on the substance and meaning of, and the relationship between, sound art, soundscape composition and live electronic music (see, for example, Demers 2010 and, for a critique of the term 'sound art', Kahn n.d.).

[16] The term 'experimental' in relation to music is also contentious. Demers criticises Nyman's (1974) historical analysis, preferring a structural use of 'experimental' to refer to 'anything that has departed significantly from norms of the time' (Demers 2010: 7). However, such a structural understanding is itself weakened by lack of historical specificity and lack of attention to musicians' self-understanding. Piekut 2011, in contrast, follows these self-understandings (adapting a methodology from Bruno Latour), arguing that the term 'experimental' is performative and that the network of discourses, practices and institutions that it engendered should be understood as historical achievements (Piekut 2011: 5–8).

the very category of art: for Guy Debord, Situationism's 'experimental attitude' (Wark 2009: 9) informed a poetics of space that necessitated 'collective
experiences of space and time that have their own singular coherence but
[must not] ossify into mere art artifacts' (quoted in Wark 2009: 25).[17]

Space in this third lineage therefore moves out beyond the musical or
sound object to encompass 'exterior' spatialities: the spatialities configured
by the physical, technological and/or social dimensions of the performance event or sound work. While it is plain that none of these dimensions
are limited to musics of the last century, let alone to sound art, live electronic or computer music, recent decades have witnessed an escalating and
self-conscious creative engagement with them on the part of artists and
theorists. Within this broadly post-formalist camp it is helpful to make
three further distinctions in regard to the orchestration of space, which are
not mutually exclusive and indeed may overlap: between, first, those events
and works that focus experimentally on the performance space or situation; second, those events and works that encompass the wider sounding
environment or acoustic ecology ('natural', built, architectural or human),
as well as those attentive to a specific site or place; and third, those events
and works that by means of digital technologies such as the internet, virtual
environments, massive multiplayer game networks, mobile telephony, loca-
tive media, GPS or ubiquitous computing technologies configure several
simultaneous and shifting locations or virtual spatialities.[18]

In contrast to the previous lineages, space in this broad area of practice is
conceptualised, therefore, not in terms of the internal operations of musical
form, nor in terms of the perception of evolving musical or sound objects,
but as multiple and constellatory. Creative practices in this lineage attend to
a spectrum between the space of musical or sonic performance or practice,

---

[17]  I am grateful to Robert Adlington for drawing my attention to the conflict over the question of
art between Debord and Walter Olmo, one of very few composers involved in the Situationist
International. Debord criticised Olmo's attempted contribution to the SI via his idea of 'musical
experimentation' because he was still working with 'a 19th-century conception of the composer
presenting his personal works', an attitude that Debord abhorred and contrasted with how
the 'acoustic portion of a Situationist event' should '[be] *unitary* in its means and in its ends'
(Debord 2009: 83). On the core SI tactic of 'unitary urbanism' as a type of collective creativity,
see Wark 2009: 12–16.

[18]  See Salter 2010: Chapter 8 (especially pp. 338–48) on art and sound works centred on
interactive installations, environments and performances that combine a number of these
digital media to effect the exploration of public space or to mobilise vastly distributed human
collectivities. See also Borgo forthcoming on the distributed musical performance potentials of
cyberspace; and Rebelo 2003 on the several orders of space potentially animated by interactive
digital environments, in which the musical work yields a 'configuration of interactions' such
that the user becomes a 'performer of space'.

on the one hand, and the space of everyday, 'found', designed or techno-logically enhanced sonic environment or site, on the other. By virtue of an engagement with acoustic environment or soundscape, any a-priori dis-tinction between sound and music tends to be effaced, just as the bounded, ritualised scenario of the concert hall is troubled or replaced by the migra-tion of focal musical and sonic experiences into quotidian life or the social or virtual world. Being inventive in relation to space, site and movement has become integral to the creative imagination. Moreover in sound art, as in electroacoustic music, practice and theory appear closely conjoined, as is evident in LaBelle's articulation of the conceptual grounding of sound art: 'Sound is intrinsically … relational', and at the core of sound art is an 'acti-vation of the existing relation between sound and space … Sound and space converse by multiplying and expanding the point of attention, or the source of a sound: the materiality of a given room shapes the contours of sound, moulding it according to reflection and absorption, reverberation and diffraction' (LaBelle 2006: ix, xi). At the same time, 'sound makes a given space appear beyond any total viewpoint: in echoing throughout the room, my clapping describes the space from a multiplicity of perspectives and locations, for the room is here, between my palms, and there, along the trajectory of sound … What we hear in this clapping is more than a single sound and its source, but rather a spatial event' (2006: x). Sound art, LaBelle contends, effects a transition from the concert setting 'toward environments, from a single object of attention … toward a multiplicity of viewpoints, from the body toward others, [thus emulating] the very relational, spatial and temporal nature of sound itself' (2006: xii). It should be obvious how significant is the challenge issued by sound art to the prior lineages of space in/and music described. Because of sound's perspectival and relational nature – in the sense that it is always experienced from particular subjective and embodied, physical and social locations – and thus sound's multipli-city, its capacity to overflow measurement and containment, in sound art it is knowingly employed to produce modes of sonic–spatial experience that transcend Euclidean forms.

It might be thought that a precursor to these practices can be found in the 'musicalization of space' (Sterken 2001: 268) envisaged by Iannis Xenakis in works such as the *Polytopes*, a series of large-scale multimedia and archi-tectural installations created between the late 1960s and early 1970s. In them, light and sound were projected while changing over time, producing multiple, dispersed and overlapping sound spaces, with the intention that listeners would perceive 'the music in a different way according to his or her location … The acoustical space is no longer homogeneous, but divides itself into different spatial areas' (Oswalt 1991). In this way the 'abstract and multi-layered *Polytopes* try to open the audience's mind to diversity and simultaneity' (Sterken 2001: 271). In subsequent works Xenakis also pursued temporal differentiation, such that '[t]ime is no longer absolute. Several time divisions and different tempi exist side by side' (Oswalt 1991). The aim was to elicit active participation by the audience, who have themselves 'to effect the operation of synthesising the poly-temporality of the proposed spectacle' (Sterken 2001: 271). Yet despite the apparent anticipation of sound art's relational universe in these works, they remain resolutely if ambiguously formalist, crafting audience participation and the staging of multiplicity through expanded compositional controls. Rather than affirming audience participation, such works pose acutely the need to assess its nature and extent, as well as the limits of the transformation of the socialities engendered by the work.[19]

It is by contrast with the formalism of the *Polytopes* that a last element in the third, post-formalist lineage can now be discerned. For it is here that we encounter explicit, if uneven, attempts to engage with the social dimensions of musical and sonic practices. This is evident in social, political and ethical preoccupations woven through the works and writings of a number of sound artists, live electronic and computer musicians, commonly with reference to ideas of participation, interactivity, collaboration or community. They take a range of forms. Perhaps most prominently, in a tradition seen to originate in Cage's *4' 33"*, the focus is on performing and listening bodies as they enact forms of spatiality, on reconfiguring the musical division of labour through experiments in composer–performer–audience relations. Because this 'exterior' spatiality – the performance 'context' – encompasses aspects of the sociality of performance, it is often taken to be equivalent to an engagement with social or political dimensions of the musical work or event per se – an assumption that will later be questioned. Other artist–theorists are concerned with the distributed interactions and virtual spatialities engendered in network or telematic performances (Renaud and Rebelo 2006; Rohrhuber 2007). Julian Rohrhuber, for example, portrays network music as comprising 'a broad range from collaborative composition environments to sound installations and improvised music ensembles' (Rohrhuber 2007: 140). He charts the transition from an objectivist

---

[19] Art theorist Claire Bishop makes an analogous point in her critique of the paradigm of relational aesthetics (Bourriaud 2002): '[E]very art work – even the most "open- ended" – determines in advance the depth of participation that the viewer may have with it ... The tasks facing us today are to analyze how contemporary art addresses the viewer and to assess the quality of the audience relations it produces' (Bishop 2004: 78).

'information aesthetics' model in the 1950s through the 'interactive, conversational' network paradigm of the 1960s and 1970s in the work of groups like the League of Automatic Composers and The Hub. Rohrhuber argues that these groups advocated the 'active participation of the algorithm' and 'opened up the social relations among the musicians' (2007: 148), redefining interactions between artists and audiences and raising questions of 'power-structure, rules, authorship and group-formation' (2007: 155). Yet other writers consider the ethics of the use of naturalistic recordings in soundscape works. For John Drever, the creative appropriation of such recorded sounds by extraction from their original environment risks a 'psychic usurpation' or plundering that can be mitigated only by cultivating sonic responsibility and reciprocities (Drever 1999: 28).[20]

At this point it is productive to bring out the implications of the relational understanding of music, sound and space immanent in this third lineage. They centre on three kinds of irreducible multiplicity at work in musical and sonic experience. All three depart from Euclidean and Cartesian understandings of space in/and music, all are interwoven and all may be operationalised in different ways in musical or sound art practices. The first is the multiplicity of any human subject's experience of music and sound as s/he inhabits a particular physical or virtual space, performance venue or site: music and sound as mediated by subjectivity and corporeity, as well as by a given location and by (potential) movement through it. The second is the social multiplicity given by the existence in the same performance space, site or event of many (diverse, often previously unrelated) human subjects, whose gathering, however, constitutes a novel set of social relations, and whose experiences of music and sound are variant – mediated, as before, by subjectivities, corporeities, locations and movements. The third foregrounds temporal mediation: it is the multiplicity effected in any musical or sound performance or work by the continually evolving sonic–spatial–temporal constellation composed of the mutual modulation – the relative ebb and flow, beginning and ending – of component sound events in a given, durative acoustic environment. Taking account of all the elements in these multiplicities – music and sound, space and time, subjectivity and sociality – all are immanent in the experience of music and sound, and all are continually involved in the mediation of the other terms. Abstractly, the six elements can be conceived as composing a dynamic matrix in which

---

[20] Drever's concerns take on a post-humanist cast in Jason Stanyek and Benjamin Piekut's reflections on the ethics of human–non-human sonic assemblages, where they question the 'human exceptionalism' invariably present in discussions of the ethics of recording; see Stanyek and Piekut 2010: 34.

each term potentially mediates all the others, together forming a constellation of multidirectional, virtual transformations.[21] But this tidy image pins down what is more aptly portrayed as a decentred, mobile and unruly flux of mediations. Nonetheless, in phenomenological terms we have arrived via the third lineage at a position close to Feld's, detailed earlier; and the common aspiration of the heterogeneous musical and sonic practices gathered under this lineage is that, in principle, all of these elements and their mutual mediations *can* be the locus of experiment and invention.

In sum, in all three lineages of cognising spatiality in music and sound addressed in the previous pages, space is regarded as an element of the creative imagination and as an artefact of musical or artistic practice: space is both *produced* and *transformed*. But only in the third lineage is the ineluctably *social* nature of these processes to the fore; space is conceived as multiple and constellatory, as mediated and mediating. In their reflections on social, ethical and political matters in an array of musical and sonic practices, artists in this broad camp animate in diverse ways and to different degrees sound's multiple mediations, pointing beyond the formalisms of the pitch space and electroacoustic lineages. The attempt is made to think music, sound, space and the social together.

## Theorising space

How do these ways of conceptualising space in/and music, as well as the perspectives outlined previously from sound studies, the anthropology of sound and the senses, compare with thinking on space elsewhere, particularly in geographical and social theory?

The theorisation of space in contemporary geography is remarkably consonant with the ideas presented so far. In the most general terms, for geographers today space is the focus of an epistemological revolution involving a rejection of Kantian conceptions of space as an 'absolute category' in favour of the tracing of a series of 'species of space' (Crang and Thrift 2000: 24). For Nigel Thrift, it is necessary to 'abandon the idea of any pre-existing space in which things are embedded for an idea of space as undergoing continual construction … through the agency of things encountering each other in more or less organized circulations. This is a relational view of space in which, rather than space being viewed as a container within which the

---

[21] By 'virtual', I point to the emergent properties of this matrix of mediations, as synergistic pluripotentialities – a term that I borrow and adapt from William Connolly (2011: 38).

world proceeds, space is seen as a co-product of those proceedings' (Thrift 2009: 96). Space is here conceived as plural, as the outcome of social and material practices, and as indivisible from time; indeed, space and time should be understood as 'combined in *becoming*' (Crang and Thrift 2000: 3, emphasis added). It follows that rather than think of space as static, unitary and unconnected to time, it should be interpreted as inherently mobile and in motion (Thrift 2006). A variant of this stance is articulated by Doreen Massey, for whom space is 'the product of interrelations', the realm in which 'distinct trajectories co-exist … Without space, no multiplicity; without multiplicity, no space' (all Massey 2005: 9). 'What is needed', Massey contends, 'is to uproot "space" from that constellation of concepts in which it has so unquestioningly … been embedded (stasis; closure; representation) and to settle it among another set of ideas (heterogeneity; relationality; coevalness)' (2005: 13).

Other directions in spatial thinking connect more precisely with the ideas already outlined. One such direction is evident in the philosophical geography of Michel Serres who, in contrast to a 'metric theory' of space-time, proposes a topological account of 'spacing and timing' focused on 'relation-propositions'. Topology is regarded here as the 'science of proximities and ongoing or interrupted transformations' (Bingham and Thrift 2000: 290), and the aim of such a topological enquiry is '[h]ere and there, locally, [to] identify fractures and discontinuities, elsewhere, on the contrary, relations and bridges' (Serres 1977: 200, quoted in Bingham and Thrift 2000: 291). The topological undertaking is concerned with articulating processes that lie 'outside of measurement but within relations' – 'the closed (*within*), the open (*out of*), intervals (*between*), orientation and directionality (*toward, in front of, behind*), proximity and adherence (*near, on, against, following, touching*), immersion (*among*)' (all Serres 1994: 71, quoted in Bingham and Thrift 2000: 290) and so on. It is striking how Serres's topological lexicon echoes Smalley's inventory of sonic–spatial relations as well as Varèse's evocative opening to this Introduction. A different link is provided by the current geographical turn to non-representational theory (Thrift 2008). This stance is evident in Derek McCormack's writings on dance, which reverberate with similar challenges in the analysis of music. Of particular salience is his intention to supersede representational models by cultivating corporeal and affective understandings of spatial experience. McCormack (2008: 1828) remarks on the 'contagious and visceral' affectivity occasioned by dance, which is 'poorly understood if framed by theories of representation'. Noting the 'relation between rhythm and the spaces of which moving bodies are generative' (2008: 1828), and with reference to

Lefebvre's notion of rhythmanalysis (Lefebvre 2004), McCormack adopts a concept of rhythm in order to think through the coexistent yet disjunct, 'lively and chaotic' (2008: 1829) flows and fluxes that compose the spatial experience not only of dance, but of urban and everyday life.[22]

An alternative, direct link between geography, music and sound is found in the work of geographers who write specifically on music. This sub-field ranges from a concern to probe 'the production of spaces of classical music [as well as] the variegated spaces of contemporary pop culture ... [while questioning] the socially constructed boundary between these spheres' (Leyshon, Matless and Revill 1998: 5) to attempts to create 'musical methodologies' informed by ideas of music-making as an 'emotional process that builds identities, [creating] spaces of community and belonging' (Wood, Duffy and Smith 2007: 885). Scholarship in this area has learned from the tendency to reduce the study of musical spatialities to 'practices associated with music rather than music's sonic qualities' (Revill 2000: 597). In reaction, consideration is given to the properties of musical sound as they inform 'the moral geographies of landscape, nation, and citizen' (2000: 597), registering how aesthetic codes mediate this relationship and, for example in the case of nationalist musics, how 'cultural geographies of exclusion and inclusion are performed in sound' (2000: 598). The geography of music recognises both that music and sound can be enrolled as means of social regulation and control – through the production of subjectivities, the enactment of power, the organisation of spatial boundaries and the affirmation of identities – and that they may also be used to contest and evade such regulation (S. J. Smith 1997; Revill 2000). Particularly significant for this volume is the attention paid to the way that music and sound can create, mark or reconstruct social and spatial boundaries. Susan Smith, for example, argues that music, like art, 'is a medium through which boundaries are established and transgressed, and in which difference is marked out and challenged' (S. J. Smith 1997: 502). Taking 'three cuts across history', she examines the role of aural and musical cultures in the socio-spatialities of Renaissance Italy, Edwardian England and post-civil rights black America. On the latter, with reference to jazz and rap, she contends that music both embodies and illuminates the struggle over access to public space, community resources and the interpretation and valorisation of black expressive cultures. In this way her work converges with ethnomusicological and other scholarship

---

[22] For an application of rhythmanalysis to sonic experience through the notion of 'sonic warfare', entailing the extension of an 'ontology of vibrational force into the ... context of viral capitalism', see Goodman 2009: xix.

concerned with music's capacities to articulate, reinforce or reshape the boundaries of social identity formations (Stokes 1994; Born 2000; Born and Hesmondhalgh 2000). The geography of music therefore shows how music and sound mediate wider socio-spatial relations. It is perhaps less attuned to the ways in which music and sound can engender socialities and spatialities that are irreducible to, if crossed by, those prior relations – to music and sound as *initiatory* of socio-spatial relations.

Just such a perspective is offered by a last direction in geographical theory relevant to this book: the work of Henri Lefebvre, in a compelling contemporary reading by Stuart Elden (2004). It is Lefebvre's *The Production of Space* (1991 (1974)) that is taken to have inaugurated the theoretical shift away from Kantian categorical conceptions of space and time to a focus on space as a 'historical production', where '[p]roduction ... deriving from Marx, Hegel, and Nietzsche's notion of creation ... [is] grasped as both a material and a mental process' (Elden 2004: 184). Of particular interest for this volume is the combined influence on Lefebvre's oeuvre of both Marx and Heidegger, the legacy of which is his emphasis on the multiple, concrete and abstract modalities of socially produced space, and in particular his conceptual triad of space as perceived, conceived and lived: *l'espace perçu, conçu, vécu*. Spatial practices, in this scheme, result in a constellation of physical, conceptual and lived spaces. Heidegger's influence is tangible in the focus on lived experience and the use of the active verbs 'to inhabit' and 'to dwell' in relation to space (2004: 190); while Elden (2004: 193) brings out Lefebvre's Marxist orientation when he affirms that 'Just as the social is historically shaped, so too is it spatially shaped. Equally the spatial is historically and socially configured.' For Lefebvre, Elden argues in what amounts to an abridged version of the six-term matrix of mutual mediations proposed earlier in this Introduction (pp. 19–20), 'The three elements of the social, spatial and temporal shape and are shaped by each other ... [S]pace is not merely "the passive locus [*lieu*] of social relations"' (Elden 2004: 193, citing Lefebvre 1991 (1974): 11). Lefebvre's singular contribution is therefore to propose an approach that is not only phenomenological but also critical, attuned to the social, and concerned with the spatialised operations of power. His example has been taken as the stimulus for analyses of 'struggles over the organisation and meaning of space' and the 'production of "counter-spaces" of resistance', as well as 'juxtapositions within social space and its nested spaces within spaces in which very different rules apply' (all Shields 2006: 149).

If geographical theories of space resonate well with the themes of this book, it is also striking that in terms of phenomenological acuity they are

matched, if not surpassed, by the adventurous conceptual turns advocated
by certain writers on electroacoustic music and sound art. This raises the
provocative thought that music and sound – in their capacity to catalyse and
augment the relational propensities of lived space, in this way generating
complex and motile topological forms – elicit especially subtle reflections
on spatial processes. Music and sound, we might say, are particularly fertile
conduits for spatial experience in that they have the capacity both to compound and to orchestrate in novel and affective ways the spatial affordances
of social life writ large. It is to this set of possibilities that we now turn.

## For a critical phenomenology of musical/sonic publicness and privacy

While the perspectives outlined in the previous two sections are productive
in opening out the conceptualisation of music, sound and space, in order
to address the material presented in this book a further conceptual move
is necessary – one that is largely missing from those bodies of literature.
It is the need for systematic consideration of the ways in which the social
and technological mediation of music and sound enter into and animate
their spatialities. If music's technological mediation has received growing
attention in recent decades in ethnomusicology, popular music and media
studies,[23] its social mediation, as I mentioned before, has been relatively
neglected.[24] It is not, however, these general processes that form the core
of this collection but a pronounced and spatialised facet of them: the capacity of music and sound, through their social and technological mediation,
both to produce or initiate and to reconfigure public and private experience. Reference to the categories 'public' and 'private' sparks long-standing
critical debates over their regulative, normative and gendered overtones
associated in particular with their status as the bedrock of certain traditions
of liberal thought (Pateman 1983; Strathern 1988; Coombe 1998; Landes
1998).[25] When sundered from those usages, however, the concepts continue to have salience as ways of capturing key dynamics at different scales

[23] For an overview, see Born 2009a.
[24] With the notable exception of writers in the anthropology and sociology of music: see, for
important contributions, DeNora 2000, 2003 and Hennion 1993, 2003.
[25] See Weintraub 1997 for a standard interpretation of the categories of the public and private,
which, it is suggested, invoke two 'fundamental, and analytically quite distinct' criteria: degrees
of visibility, and degrees of collectivity or the relative priority of private or public interests
(Weintraub 1997: 4–5).

and across a range of temporalities of social life (Gal 2002; Warner 2002; Hayden 2010).

For the purposes of this book, the terms public and private are generative in several ways. To begin with, when interpreted adjectivally – in the active sense of the public-ising (or public-making)[26] and privatising propensities of music and sound – they register processes that are at once social, material and spatial. Moreover, abandoning any merely dualistic conception of the terms makes it possible to highlight the relational nature of their articulation, their mutual constitution and multiplicity. Productive here is Susan Gal's semiotic analysis of the public/private distinction in which she portrays the categories as not only encultured and relational, but fractal-like and recursive, such that they are capable of generating 'multiple nestings' (Gal 2002: 81). Note the echo of Smalley's account of nesting as a relational dynamic in spatialised sound (p. 13); and in some of the chapters that follow we trace how, in part through the profusion of experiential forms engendered by the consumer audio industries of late capitalism, music and sound can effect both a zoning and a recursive nesting of publicness and privacy. Without succumbing to static, dualistic accounts of the public and private, it is nonetheless important for this book to retain an analytical sense of the terms as potentially antithetical. Only in this way is it possible to grasp how the privatisation of music and sound can indeed entail the erosion or occlusion of certain public modes of experience. Where Gal takes the categories public and private to be primarily conceptual and linguistic, however, when examining their constitution by music and sound the evidence from this volume is that it is necessary to expand the analytical frame to encompass their material and social, corporeal and affective qualities: to move, in short, from a semiotics to a critical phenomenology of the lived, embodied and institutionalised forms of music and sound.

In calling for a critical phenomenology of the musical or sonic orchestration of public and private experience, in all its socio-spatial dimensions, the present collection joins with a spate of efforts in anthropology, cultural, media and sound studies to recast phenomenology in fully historical (Sterne 2003; B. R. Smith 2004), cultural (Csordas 1997; Connor 1999, 2000a) and social (Feld 1996; Porcello 1998; Born 2011, 2012) terms. In Jonathan Sterne's resonant words, 'There is no "mere" or innocent description of

---

[26] Michael Warner draws attention to the processes, and paradoxes, of public-making in relation to literary–textual publics. As he notes, 'when people address publics, they engage in struggles … over the conditions that bring them together as a public. The making of publics is the metapragmatic work newly taken up by every text in every reading. What kind of public is this? How is it being addressed?' (Warner 2002: 12).

interior auditory experience. The attempt to describe sound or the act of hearing in itself – as if the sonic dimension of human life inhabited a space prior to or outside history – strives for a false transcendence. Even phenomenologies can change' (Sterne 2003: 19; cf. B. R. Smith 2004: 41). While for Steven Connor, what is at stake is a cultural 'enlargement of phenomenology' such that it encompasses the 'affective, somatic dimensions of cultural experience', as well as the 'conditions of temporality, corporeality' and collectivity (Connor 1999: 23, 18, 21). In turn, the social phenomenology demanded by the chapters that follow departs from the models provided by Alfred Schutz (1971 (1964)) and Pierre Bourdieu (1990: 130)[27] in that it necessarily encompasses not a singular 'social', but the multiple valences of social mediation immanent in music and sound including hierarchical and antagonistic dimensions of human sociality (Born 2012). As we shall see, while a culturally and historically enriched phenomenology is necessary, it is not sufficient to account for the diverse types of socio-spatial mediation of music and sound described in this book. For what is required, as the chapters show, is an analytics that – following Lefebvre – combines such a phenomenology with a critical analysis of their social and institutional forms.

Central to this volume are questions to which this conceptual scheme responds: how is it that music and sound, catalysed by their social and technological mediation, engender such a profusion of modes of publicness and privacy? Sometimes constructing strongly bounded zones of experience, sometimes also recursive and nested assemblages – a range of forms of private-within-public, virtual public-within-private, public-within-public, private-within-public-within-private and so on? How is it that, contra Ihde, music and sound can produce not only temporal but spatial horizons and boundaries – boundaries the physical, aesthetic and moral obduracy of which are attested to as much by the leakage of sound across them as by its containment within them?[28] Recall the extent to which present-day audio media are used to effect a series of radical transformations of musical and auditory experience: the mobile phone affording a genre of private-in-public communication; the iPod and headphones engendering

---

[27] See Throop and Murphy 2002 for a critical comparison of the social phenomenologies of Bourdieu and Schutz.

[28] See the chapters by Rice and Bohlman. Stanyek and Piekut (2010: 22) coin the twin terms 'perforation' and 'leakage effects' for the 'paradoxical co-process of connection and disconnection' inherent in sound recording from the outset: Edison's recording studio of 1888. The spatial segmentation of the studio, they argue, has always been accompanied by 'perforated' means of channelling sound from one zone of sonic isolation to another, as well as by leakage of sound beyond the channels, so eliciting attempts to control the leakage.

mobile, individuated listening enclaves nested within the wider acoustic and social environment; soldiers using personal audio media and headphones inside tanks in battle to construct a sense of intimate, affective space and identity that occludes the ambient sounds of violent warfare; and the virtual musical publics afforded by internet-based distributed music-sharing and music-making encountered within the privacy of participants' domestic settings and offline lifeworlds. The proliferation of audio media therefore results in a situation in which acoustic environments are increasingly multiple, recursive and topologically malleable. This in turn depends on the potential of music and sound media both to demarcate and reinforce social and psychological boundaries through the creation of sonic autonomy and segregation, and to overcome such boundaries through sound's omnidirectional, mobile and enveloping materiality, as well as through the mediated weaving of translocal sonic connections.[29]

That the questions posed above pertain not only to the technologically mediated music cultures of the twentieth and twenty-first centuries but also to other cultures and earlier eras is evidenced by anthropological and historical scholarship. Bourdieu's classic analysis, for example, of the socio-spatiality of the Kabyle house (Bourdieu 1979), in which he anatomised the gendered classification and spatial segregation of male and female habitation and movement, is also inter alia an analysis of attempted sonic segregation – whatever subversive leakages may have occurred. Focused on the social discipline manifest in unyielding physical and symbolic boundaries, the study implicitly attests also to the gendered zoning of sound in this environment. Indeed Bourdieu's account culminates in what amounts to a fractal analysis – in terms of 'the endlessly repeated application of the same principle of division' – of the gendered classification of space as it is equated in this 'mythico-ritual system' with a series of spatialised oppositions between public and private life (Bourdieu 1979: 142–3).

Cultural–historical research offers similar insights. By examining 'sonoric landscapes' represented in seventeenth-century European painting, Richard Leppert shows how they convey a 'concern for ordering the world sonically' (Leppert 1998: 294) through depictions of the hierarchical social organisation of music, sound and speech, and in particular by figuring an evolving 'tension between the public and private in music' (1998: 291). In the foreground of a painting from 1607, for example, serfs labour in the garden of a chateau, while in the background a musical performance with an 'amatory

---

[29] For an analysis of these tendencies in relation to 'sonic Afro-modernity', see Weheliye 2005: Chapter 4.

function' evokes contemplation by a group of nobility, 'an etiquette that turns music from an inherently participatory activity into a passive one in which the listener maintains physical stasis by exerting the cultural force of will against the body's desire' (1998: 300). In this image, ironically, 'the political capital of privacy, [and] the sonoric-visual signs of that privacy, music making and lovemaking together, have to be made visually public' (1998: 303). Leppert argues that the contemplative listening of the aristocracy and other elements of the public–private tension materialised in these images prefigure the later 'troubled fetishization of privacy that serves as a defining characteristic of the bourgeoisie in the 19th century' (1998: 314). Yet they are also different: here, '[c]ontemplative listening is not philosophically removed from the world, as later aesthetic theory would have it; it is instead the sign of one's control and domination of the world … As such, it *is* an exercise of power' (1998: 302, emphasis in original), wherein the capacity to command music into existence, to create an enclave of passive consumption and to be subjectified by it have become focal.

Research on later centuries continues to highlight the evolving, relational construction of the socio-spatialities of musical publicness and privacy. James Johnson in his account of opera and concert hall listening in late eighteenth- and early nineteenth-century Paris identifies the emergence in the 1770s and 1780s both of 'individuals *qua* individuals [who] formed and announced their own musical judgements' and of 'a corresponding sense of unity through sentiment, [giving] birth to the notion of a single musical public' (Johnson 1995: 92). Musical experience 'turned listeners simultaneously inward and toward other like-minded spectators' (1995: 94), while the musical public, composed of a small elite, 'effectively challenged traditional absolutist patterns of judgment' (1995: 93). The first decades of the nineteenth century, he argues, saw in turn the rise of bourgeois individualism and its manifestation in 'intensely subjective' modes of musical experience in which 'interior communion met … romantic spirituality' (1995: 277). Absorbed listening and attention to music's abstract meaning were accompanied by a policing of manners and 'anonymous and rule-bound' (1995: 233) allegiance to notions of decency and respectability, as well as a belief in the harmonious social unity thought to be reflected in such experiences. In his wider analysis of the same period, Richard Sennett traces a series of urban social and architectural transformations that wrought an obsession with privacy. In concert life the changes were evident in the development of silent, self-disciplined, contemplative and interiorised spectatorship allied to the cultivation of personal feeling – a bourgeois 'act of purification' that amounted to 'a defense against the experience of social relations' (Sennett

2002 (1977): 214, 213). 'Silence made it possible to be both visible to others and isolated from them' (2002 (1977): 217). For Sennett, escalating processes of individuation and privatisation in urban life, as in music, effected an erosion of social interaction; by the end of the nineteenth century 'the whole rationale of public culture had cracked apart' (2002 (1977): 218).

What these works reveal is the extent to which the production of privacy and publicness by music and sound, manifest in the individuation and aggregation of experience, was fuelled by social and cultural processes and transformations that long predate the modern audio technologies that would later compound these tendencies. But the mediation is emphatically *two-way*: just as distinctive social hierarchies are ensounded – embodied in music and sound – so music and sound produce their own irreducible socialities and spatialities, which, however, are traversed by wider social relations.

If these studies attest to large-scale transformations in the nature of musical privacy and publicness – changes that are at once aesthetic and subjective, social and spatial – then other writers augment this scheme with reference to the catalysis provided by changing technologies. In his innovative study *The Audible Past*, Jonathan Sterne (2003) traces the evolving, inter-medial materiality of recorded music and sound through relations both of imitation or borrowing and of differentiation from adjacent media, and the resulting semiotic and phenomenological affordances.[30] By uncovering how these shifts are entangled in social, cultural and economic dynamics, Sterne makes good the neglect of technological mediation while avoiding the errors of technological determinism.[31] He outlines the technical and industrial correlates of the processes analysed by Sennett in the emergence in the late nineteenth and early twentieth centuries both of the technical capacity to isolate and localise sound and of 'audile technique', a type of listening associated

---

[30] James Lastra offers an alternative framework for analysing the evolving materiality of audio media in relation to contiguous media as well as broader social, cultural and economic conditions: 'a four-term dialectic' of 'device, discourse, practice, and institution' (Lastra 2000: 13).

[31] Technological determinism is the critical term applied to reductive models of history that portray changes in technology as the prime movers in, and as determining, wider historical transformations; the standard critique is MacKenzie and Wajcman 1999. Alternative approaches trace the industrial, scientific, political, social and cultural conditions that foster technological change, noting its contingency and path-dependence and how it is catalysed by forces – existing and emerging markets, the interests of the state, social relations and cultural developments – that synergistically condition the technologies that ensue. Sterne's is a particularly compelling example of such a history focused on an account of the processes by which, after periods of experimentation and instability, technologies emerge as fully-fledged media when they finally become stabilised (Sterne 2003).

initially with medical use of the stethoscope and with sound telegraphy (Sterne 2003: Chapter 3). This technicised listening, he argues, entailed the extension of hearing and its separation from the other senses, as well as the individuation of the listener in a novel kind of personal acoustic space. As a result, '[b]y the 1920s, the possibilities for collective listening to sound reproduction technologies presumed a prior individuation and segmentation of acoustic space', the 'sonic equivalent of private property' (2003: 159, 161). Audio technologies therefore heralded the 'collectivised isolation of listeners' (2003: 166), promoting music's burgeoning commodification.

Technological mediation features also in Jody Berland's seminal account of the contribution of radio in constituting the plural spatialities of Canadian cultural life. Her work makes three valuable contributions. First, she augments our understanding of the public-making capacities of music and sound by highlighting the role of twentieth-century cultural technologies such as radio in the creation and sustenance of 'stranger' publics: publics that exist 'by virtue of being addressed' (Warner 2002: 67). These are publics engendered solely by participation in mediated discourses or other circulating forms of cultural material. It is a participation that demands attention but which is otherwise quite minimal and does not 'saturate identity' (Warner 2002: 71), so that individuals may belong to multiple publics and counterpublics. Berland's second contribution is to insist that processes of subject formation are as central to the constitution of the technologically mediated stranger publics of the twentieth and twenty-first centuries as they were to the historical developments reviewed earlier. It is through emotional identification that listeners are both subjectified and constituted as a public or publics by audio media: 'musical sounds, radio practices, social institutions, and listeners collaborate in "placing" listeners in their affective and topographic worlds' (Berland 1998: 138). Her third contribution is to observe how the interplay between public and private in audio media has to be traced recursively both within and across scales, not only in the spatialities of individual listening practices but, importantly, in the spatialities constructed by radio's industrial forms. Thus, on the imbrication of spatialities in quotidian listening: 'CDs, boomboxes, and car radios enable music to mediate personal and public space ... connecting us to something outside the actuality of physical space. And just as cultural technologies like radio mediate between the production of music and the production of us as audiences, so [radio's spatiality] mediates between us and the diverse spaces we inhabit' (Berland 1998: 131). Berland shows, moreover, how the competing institutional bases of Canadian radio proffer distinctive forms of subjectivity, spatiality and imagined community, a provision evidencing twin dialectics of private and public: transnational commercial music radio industry as opposed to national public broadcasting, on the one hand; local or community radio as opposed to national radio, on the other.

A final example of the relational constitution of public and private, in the context of the legal conditions of late capitalism, takes us to the heart of the digital music economy in the guise of BitTorrent: a filesharing protocol designed in 2001 to enable the transfer of large files, which has been used to circulate software, computer games and video as well as music. BitTorrent attracted notoriety through its association with the Swedish website, The Pirate Bay, where it was deployed to facilitate downloading and file-sharing practices involving systematic copyright infringement. BitTorrent invokes not only the public-isation–privatisation dialectic, but the mutual articulation between copyright law and inter-medial materiality. The BitTorrent software architecture draws on wider developments in distributed computing; its circulatory architecture has the effect that any single music file being sought by a file sharer is itself 'socialised' or collectivised into a cloud of fragments of the file, dispersed across the personal computers of thousands of anonymous users – the so-called 'swarm'. The Pirate Bay, as an 'index service', supplied 'tracker' files that provided users of the service with the coordinates of ongoing, independent BitTorrent swarms, thereby enabling users to reassemble the fragments and experience the files musically. Through the combined individuation and socialisation of digital files wrought by the BitTorrent architecture, and the 'balanced reciprocity' (Sahlins 1974) that this necessitates, The Pirate Bay encouraged copyright law to be circumvented; in effect, there was no one-to-one relation between a supplier, a downloader and a complete musical track. And indeed, in a legal case brought in 2009 against The Pirate Bay, the criminal convictions related to 'assisting' the making available of copyright-protected content rather than distributing the material. Months later, The Pirate Bay decentralised further by replacing their centralised tracker files with 'distributed hash tables' (Anderson 2009), reshaping the protocol and its instrumentally engineered virtual public into a fully rhizomic system. The intention of these manoeuvres was, then, to enable music to circulate freely among dispersed individuals while socialising risk and evading music's corporate–legal privatisation.

## Social mediation, multiaccentuality and the ontological politics of space

Earlier we encountered a dynamic matrix of six mutually mediating terms – music and sound, space and time, subjectivity and sociality – all of which are immanent in, and may be creatively reimagined by, musical and sonic assemblages (pp. 19–20). But to develop an analysis of the public-making and privatising capacities of music and sound it is necessary at this point to zoom in closer on the sixth term: the social mediation of music and sound. For, rather than a singular sociality, music engenders four planes of social mediation. In the first plane, music produces the intimate microsocialities of musical performance, music ensemble and sound installation site: the social and corporeal interactions and intersubjectivities set in motion among performers and audience or other participants. In the second plane, music animates imagined communities (Anderson 1991 (1983)), aggregating its listeners into virtual collectivities or publics based on musical and other identifications. In the third plane, music is traversed by and refracts wider social formations: the hierarchical and stratified social relations associated with differences of class and age, race and gender, ethnicity and religion. In the fourth plane, music is mediated by a range of institutional forms that enable its production, reproduction and transformation, including market and non-market exchange, elite, religious and state patronage, and late capitalism's multipolar cultural economy.[32] All four planes of social mediation enter in dynamic ways into musical and sonic assemblages. The four are irreducible to each other and each has a certain autonomy; yet they are articulated in contingent ways through relations of synergy, affordance, conditioning or causality.[33]

Two key points follow. First, such an analytics of social mediation makes it possible to distinguish between the different degrees and kinds of co-present and virtual sociality, as well as of individuation and aggregation, privatisation and public-isation, afforded by today's ramifying musico- or sonic–social–technological assemblages – from BitTorrent-enabled file-sharing, to iPod-listening, to live laptop ensemble, to internet-based distributed music-making. The framework amounts to an anti-metaphysical, non-essentialising, empirical analytics of the diverse and changing forms of the social mediation of music and sound; and it permits us to discern such differences without succumbing to a tragic metaphysics of musical

[32]  The topological metaphor of the plane is intended to capture both the autonomy of and the mutual interferences between the four dimensions of social mediation described. The metaphor clearly has limitations, failing as it does to convey the fleshy, embodied and human qualities of these distinctive socialities.

[33]  On the analytics of four planes of social mediation, see Born 2011, 2012, and on the concept of a musical assemblage, Born 2005, 2012. The idea of a musical assemblage addresses the way that music's mediations take a number of forms – social, corporeal, discursive, visual, technological and so on – which cohere into constellations that endure and take particular historical shapes.

co-presence and its loss, or a dualism that valorises the aurally authentic over what is deemed to be artificial or secondary.[34]

Thus, in addition to a phenomenology that incorporates culture, history and materiality, we require one attuned to the social: a sonic–social phenomenology that attends to the ways in which musical or sonic assemblages are traversed by the four planes of social mediation and their complex and non-linear interconnections. This in turn allows us to uncover a universe not of consensual social relations, but of sometimes agonistic and dissensual relations – pointing to music and sound as the terrain on which not only aesthetic differences but also social, cultural, religious and political differences, inequalities and oppressions may be played out. Here we might recall Leppert's feudal socio-musical hierarchies, or Johnson's bourgeois imaginary of harmonious social unity, both associated with the creation of privatised subjectivities and bounded enclaves of elite musical experience. We might refer to how, in the massified public consumption of BBC radio by women workers in British factories during the Second World War, broadcast music was used to impose industrial discipline and motivate workers engaged in repetitive manual labour. While singing by workers was generally prohibited, spontaneous singing would sometimes erupt on the shop floor: a resistant appropriation of 'Music While You Work' fuelled by class- and gender-based antagonisms (Korczynski *et al.* 2005; Korczynski and Jones 2006). We might consider children's use of audio media to create 'private' environments within 'private', domestic space, evading the 'universal' music played by middle-class mothers in the 'public' areas of the home by sequestering themselves in the acoustic of the iPod or the zoned privacy of the bedroom – dynamics redolent of generational struggles and incommensurable musical tastes.[35] Or, finally, we might invoke the conflictual Cairo soundscape created as legions of competing mosque loudspeakers and cassette recorders blast out the calls to prayer of Islamic groups, a threatening 'cacophony' that is perceived by secular Cairenes and adherents

---

[34] See Sterne's (2003: 20–2) critique of the metaphysical privileging of co-presence in sound studies; and Auslander's deconstruction of ontologies of live performance that associate it with notions of presence, immediacy or 'community', posited as 'other' to mass mediatisation and 'the economy of repetition' (Auslander 1999: 44 and Chapter 2). Instead, he argues persuasively, 'the historical relationship of liveness and mediatisation must be seen as a relation of dependence and imbrication' (Auslander 1999: 56).

[35] This interpretation is based on unpublished research in the mid 2000s by an American IT corporation on how the use of audio and other media in middle-class American homes – and particularly the main 'public' family room, the 'great room' – were crossed by conflictual family dynamics of generation and gender.

of other religions 'as the violent imposition of religious discourse onto the nonreligious space of public life' (Hirschkind 2006: 125–6).

In other words, the analytics of social mediation proposed here recognise the multiplicity and multiaccentuality of the spatialities of musical and sonic performance and co-presence (the first plane) as they are traversed by wider social differences (the third plane). This takes us a considerable way in theorising the social multiplicity of musical and sonic space identified earlier (p. 19), beyond ideas of the self-presence of space or of its universal or unifying qualities. The concept of multiaccentuality draws on an analogy with Vološinov's theory of the embedded nature of the linguistic sign in, and its generative transformation by, social relations. As Vološinov explains, social multiaccentuality refers to the way that '[e]xistence reflected in [the] sign is not merely reflected but *refracted*. How ...? By an intersecting of differently oriented social interests within one and the same sign community' (Vološinov 1986 (1973): 23, emphasis in original). By moving (again) from a semiotics to a phenomenology, the idea of the social multiaccentuality of the sign can be taken to sonic–spatial experience and its agonistic and antagonistic, dynamic and experimental potentials. Several later chapters point to a politics of space played out in musico–social or sonic–social interactions that are mediated by entrenched social divisions of ethnicity, religion, nationality, ideology or expertise. What is extraordinary is how such divisions can produce both extreme sonic violence[36] and, on the contrary, attempts through music to assuage the damaging consequences of social division and disadvantage.[37] More common is the playing out in sonic–social interactions, involving more or less explicit conflict, of disjunctive and competing, encultured and embodied experiences of sounding space. As certain chapters attest, such disjunctures can engender an ontological politics over the nature of and the boundaries between public and private space, as well as over the stewardship of, and the right to dwell in and travel through, such spaces.[38]

The second key point arising from the analytics of social mediation detailed in this section is that all four planes can be the locus of significant transformations. Indeed, it is the subtle potentialities engendered by both the autonomy of and the mutual interference between the four planes of social mediation that may be generative of experimentation and emergence in musical and sonic assemblages. This can take the form of

[36] See the chapter by Cusick.

[37] See the chapters by Cook, Dueck and DeNora.

[38] My thanks to Andrew Eisenberg for this application of the concept of multiaccentuality, which he develops in Chapter 8. Similar issues are portrayed in the chapters by Rice and Bohlman.

experimentation with the microsocialities of performance, practice or site, with the assembling of novel musical publics, with the crystallisation via musical affect of innovative social identity coalitions, or with the nature of music's institutional forms. Thus, whether the amatory music of feudal nobles, with its experiment in privatised and hierarchised performance socialities (Leppert 1998); or Canadian music radio's iterative performance in domestic spaces – against a default global–American audio imaginary – of a national imaginary through a 'project involving distinct activities and values with respect to location, publics, scale and community' (Berland 1998: 130); or the fostering through the performance socialities of music therapy of a space of asylum that supports clients' psychological and social integration;[39] or the inventive amplification of voices from the aboriginal community in their confrontation with the state in the sound installations of Anishnabe Canadian artist Rebecca Belmore:[40] what we confront is an array of experiments that turn on intervening in and juxtaposing in novel ways the distinctive planes of social mediation of music and sound.

## On musical and sonic publics

Music's public-making capacities are also elucidated by the analytics of four planes of social mediation. Of the four, it is the first two – the micro-socialities of performance, ensemble or site, and musically imagined community – that most obviously entail the production of lived space, *l'éspace vécu*: through the spatiality of performance and sonic co-presence, and through the space of circulation and of affective contagion (Brennan 2004; cf. Goodman 2009).[41] These spatialities are produced by two types of musical public-making, as a number of chapters show: by the co-present publics assembled by performance or site, and by the virtual or stranger alliances and collectivities generated by the mediated circulation of music and sound. At issue is the capacity of music to engender emotional identification in its listeners, an identification that is at the same time musical, cultural and social. A musical public is, in this sense, an aggregation of the affected, of those participating in or attending to a musical or sonic event (DeNora 2003: 45–56; Born 2009b: 88). As the anthropologist Karin

---

[39] See the chapter by DeNora.

[40] See the chapter by Ouzounian.

[41] Of course, the third and fourth planes are also immanently spatial and demand their own musical geography, contributions to which have been made by the scholarship in geography alluded to earlier by Andrew Leyshon, David Matless, George Revill, Susan Smith and others.

Barber puts it, writing of the public for the African musical genre *kiba*, we should consider 'not so much how *kiba* [performances] address audiences as how audiences constitute themselves around *kiba* and thus affirm the things they have in common' (Barber 1997: 355–6).[42] The multiaccentual and factious propensities of sonic–social interaction described in the previous section are therefore matched by a contrasting dynamic: by the capacity of music and sound to promote affective unities, with the potential to overcome difference or disinterest through aesthetic mutuality and common attachments. Such processes are fostered by a crucial property of music: its capacity to create 'affective alliances' (Straw 1991: 374), engendering collectivities – musically imagined communities (Born 1993: 283) – that are irreducible to, even if they are traversed by, prior forms of social identity. This bears out a co-constitutive mediation theory: music producing its own aggregative and affective identity effects, its own modes of possession (Candea 2010: 9); and yet music also mediating pre-existing social formations. As is apparent today in music's prominent role in social media and online networking, music seems to be ever more powerful in its generation of musically imagined community.

What is curious, then, is that the socialities immanent in musical publics can take diverse and even opposed forms. In Marilyn Strathern's terms, while they are constituted by the making of relations, this process can be oriented either towards 'de-pluralisation', the elimination of difference and creation of social unities, or, on the contrary, towards the establishment or maintenance of social differences or heterogeneity (Strathern 1988: 13 and Chapter 1; cf. Strathern 1990). Barber demonstrates this point, emphasising with reference to research on African publics that the nature of the social fabric constituted by both co-present and mediated publics cannot be known in advance. If, in Europe and the West, the modes of address that imagined audiences as 'publics' rested on principles of homogeneity and of the equivalence of human beings, she proposes, in Africa the same disciplines were imported by the colonial state but were 'overlaid upon a deeply heterogeneous mass, united and divided by religion, occupation, language, family, place of origin and degree of education, and often by philosophies of irreducible human difference' (Barber 1997: 350). To understand the nature both of co-present and of mediated African publics is therefore to analyse how the socialities of performance and the virtual socialities of musically imagined community, both animated by musical attachments, refract such

---

[42] Barber is commenting here on James 1997.

a nexus of prior social relations. If musical publics engender collectivities, they are 'variably construed, emergent and continually undergoing redefinition' (1997: 355).

Previous research on musical publics suggests a further distinction. On the one hand, music can be drawn in to buttress the constitution of national, regional, ethnic, religious or other cultural or political publics or public spheres. In these circumstances music amounts to just one medium of articulation of such publics, albeit one that has enormously powerful expressive reach and affective resonance; music performs this work, again, both in performance and in mediated form. Philip Bohlman (1993) exemplifies these processes when he examines the transformation of public space in American cities (in this case Chicago) by rap musicians in the early 1990s at the time of the LA riots: 'The city's el-trains became stages for rappers, who jumped on trains and performed for the riders … then disembarked before taking the next el. In this way, rappers reconfigured the public spaces of the entire city … with the politically charged news' (Bohlman 1993: 413). The cultural geography of modernity can be written, he suggests, by making music a metaphor for an increasingly multicultural public sphere of political speech. On the other hand, music and sound can themselves form the bases for public spheres. Ana María Ochoa Gautier (2006), in a piercing analysis, argues that the constitution of Latin America's 'highly unequal modernity' has centred on the elaboration of an aural public sphere through a series of socio-spatial operations, notably the escalating national and transnational circulation, recontextualisation and relocalisation of 'traditional' musics over the course of the twentieth century, a 'sonic transculturation' accelerated by electronic and digital media. Such processes were accompanied by an epistemological 'purification' of these musics by folklorists, composers, anthropologists and other intellectuals based in folklore institutes, radio stations and state cultural organisations (Ochoa Gautier 2006: 814). Thus, music mediates politics; but politics – in Ochoa Gautier's case, nationalist politics and the politics of knowledge – also mediate music.

Of particular interest for this book are the co-present musical and sonic publics animated by the socio-spatialities of performance, participatory audio event or sound installation site – a process described in several chapters. In them we encounter three types of co-present musical or sonic publics, which extend the analysis of the mutual mediation of music and politics. The first is that agentive, solidary and politicised musical public forged in part with the aim of effecting through musical participation, or through changes to the boundaries of the performance space, a larger, non-musical political transformation.[43] A second type is that intimate musical public, sometimes involving a collective withdrawal or separation from the world, that constitutes a zone of musical or sonic consociation that is intended to engender either an integration or a transformation of participants' social identities.[44] The transformative potential of this kind of co-present musical public is confirmed by ethnomusicological studies. It is found in Jocelyne Guilbault's (2010) analysis of live soca performance in Trinidad as it creates socialities – 'public intimacies' – among performers and audience that both 'reiterate identities' and allow 'new points of connection [to be] developed (for example among artists and audience members of different ethnicities, nationalities and generations, and across musical genres)' (2010: 17). It is evident in Marina Roseman's (1984) account of how the musical performances and attendant cosmologies of the aboriginal Temiar people of peninsular Malaysia enact alternatives to, and invert, the hierarchical gender relations that characterise the society at large. Here, the autonomy of the first plane makes possible transformations in the third plane: a co-present musical public prefigures or portends potential wider social change. A last, minimal type of musical public is that fragmentary group constituted by synchronous participation in performance or sounding space, an aggregation that is, however, traversed by resilient social differences or by the individuation favoured by auditory self-enclosure in headphones: a participation, we might say, that does not amount to affiliation.[45]

What is remarkable about the first and second types is that, even when they are not ontologised, these forms of co-present musical or sonic public are held to *matter*: they are credited with powers either to reaffirm existing boundaries of political affiliation or social identity formation, or to initiate or catalyse their reconfiguration – although no such change can be assured. Particularly audible today are those sonic publics enlivened by the prominent use of sound in the performance of political protest – when sound, noise and/or music are employed to enhance the efficacy, presence and consociation of a political public. Such tactics are apparent in actions such as the Cambridge 'defend education' occupation described at the start of this Introduction and the Montreal-based 'casserole' movement of May 2012, which involved protestors banging on pots and pans in

[43] See the chapters by Ouzounian, Bohlman and Cook (in regard to the West–Eastern Divan Orchestra).

[44] See the chapters by Dueck, DeNora and Cook (in regard to the Society for Private Musical Performances).

[45] See the chapters by Gopinath and Stanyek, and Eisenberg.

the streets as they marched, and which grew in reaction to the introduction by the Quebec provincial government of a controversial law aimed at curtailing student protests over tuition fee increases.[46] Similar tactics are apparent on a wider scale in the 'sonic amplification of dissent'[47] that characterises the transnational 'Occupy' movement in its diverse local manifestations. From drumming circles to the 'people's microphone', a practice of call and response that developed in reaction to a 'prohibition against using electric sound amplifiers in public without a permit', both of them prominent in Occupy actions, sound tactics have become a means both of occupying, politicising and re-sounding urban space and of reshaping these movements' microsocialities. As an 'Occupy' activist explains, a key feature of the 'people's mic' is reciprocity: 'it not only attenuates the hierarchy usually exerted by one amplified person over the soundscape, but it also fosters the pursuit of accord within the group ... because the method's very functioning relies so heavily on the crowd's ongoing willingness to participate'.[48]

It is notable that the inventive political and social potential of such modes of participatory and agonistic performance has been recognised by writers concerned with the cultivation of democratic publics from the social sciences (Amin and Thrift 2002: Chapter 6) and political theatre (Boal 2000). These perspectives resonate with Hannah Arendt's use of performance as a model for the pluralistic, participatory and agonistic qualities that she takes to be fundamental to political action in the public realm. In the words of Dana Villa, Arendt's performance model 'emphasizes the embeddedness of action in the "already existing web of human relationships" while stressing its phenomenality, its need for an audience ... [Indeed] Arendt directly links the meaning-creative capacity of initiatory action to its "futility, boundlessness, and uncertainty of outcome"', where 'boundless' implies the creation of 'myriad new relationships [and] unforeseen constellations' (Villa 1996: 84–5 citing Arendt 1989 (1958): 190–2, 184). For Arendt, it is the autonomy and the anti-teleological premise of political action, its 'essential initiatory power' (Arendt 1989 (1958): 47), that fuels emergence – and her insights

---

[46] On the Montreal 'casserole' protests see www.guardian.co.uk/world/2012/may/26/montreal-casseroles-student-protests (last accessed 18 August 2012); and on the putative roots of the movement's use of pots and pans in Chile's '*cacerolazos*' protests of the 1970s and 1980s, www.globalmontreal.com/quebecs+cacerolazo+protests+stir+memories+in+chilean-montrealers/6442649486/story.html (last accessed May 2012).

[47] Quotation from the discussion of 'sound publics' on http://kaleidophonic.wordpress.com/2011/12/11/occupy-sound-studies/ (last accessed 18 August 2012).

[48] See the blog written by Ted Sammons, soundstudiesblog.com/?s=people's+microphone, a contribution to the site 'Sounding Out!': soundstudiesblog.com/ (last accessed 18 August 2012).

can be returned by analogy to the emergent political properties of musical or sonic performance.[49]

## Music, sound and the socio-technical mediation of subjectivity

The changing constitution of subjectivity, as we have seen, is a central element in the history and anthropology of musical privacy and publicness, and it is also a theme of this book. In his account of the development of the literary public sphere, Habermas emphasises its origins in 'experiments with subjectivity' in the intimate form of letter exchange, diary-writing or communion with the domestic novel, a privacy nested within the encompassing privacy of the conjugal family. These practices, he says, involved the individual communicating with herself or himself about the nature of humanity, the soul, self-knowledge or empathy: 'the psychological interest increased in the dual relation to both one's self and the other' (Habermas 1989 (1962): 49). More recently, Ulrich Beck's theory of institutionalised individualism, addressing the 'second modernity' (Lash 2002: vii) ushered in from the second half of the twentieth century, identifies a simultaneous individualisation and standardisation of lifeways. The individual, Beck contends, is confronted by the paradox of increasingly reflexive, enforced and precarious 'choice' associated with liberation from and the de-normalisation of traditional roles: 'the individual must become the agent of his or her own identity-making and livelihood' (Beck and Beck-Gernsheim 2002: 203). While such normative accounts of the formation of the modern individual are illuminating, they lack consideration both of the encultured nature of subjectivity and of its mediation by those 'socio-technical systems' (Lash 2002: xiii) – foremost among them music and audio media – that, as we have seen, have been employed for centuries, and with intensifying sway since the phonographic revolution, in 'identity-making' through the cultivation and care of the self (DeNora 2000: 46).

Three seminal empirical studies of the use of music and audio media contribute greatly to our understanding of these processes. Each casts light on the mutual mediation between listening subject, on the one hand, and music or audio media, on the other. Tia DeNora, in her compelling sociological study of the consumption of music in everyday life, argues that music

---

[49] For a fuller version of this Arendtian analysis, applied to an art–science public art work, see Born and Barry 2010: 112–16.

is a 'technology of self' in that individuals 'engage in musical practices that regulate, elaborate and substantiate themselves as social agents' (DeNora 2000: 47). Music, woven into the rhythms of life, becomes 'an ordering device … a means for creating, enhancing, sustaining and changing subjective, cognitive, bodily and self-conceptual states' (2000: 49); it serves as 'a resource for modulating and structuring the parameters of aesthetic agency – feeling, motivation, desire' (2000: 53). She demonstrates how music is mobilised in the choreography of both memory and identity, not only consciously but in non-conscious, corporeal and micro-behavioural ways (2000: 74). Where DeNora focuses on individuals' self-creation through musical resources, Michael Bull in his research on personal stereo users in London in the 1990s probes 'the nature of a technologized form of … experience' (Bull 2000: 157). Personal stereos, he argues, favour the privatisation and 'monumentalisation' of experience (2000: 181) along with a withdrawal from urban public life. He charts the aestheticisation of everyday life effected by the solipsistic zoning of listening through the erection of a technological 'barrier between the subject and the exterior world' (2000: 156–7). Bull notes users' paradoxical desire for greater experiential control and a denial of contingency along with intensified dependence on audio media. He observes their 'minimalization of the social through [an] "imaginary" social inhabited within personal stereo space', their production of 'non-places' (Augé 1995) from public space, and their 'narcissistically orientated' disposition towards the 'other'. In this way he etches the limits or 'outside' of the 'atomistic subjective expressiveness and instrumentalism' (Bull 2000: 194) of users. Considered together, and despite their quite different orientations, twin tendencies stand out from the analyses given by Bull and DeNora: an intensified affective semanticisation of music, along with an intensified narcissistic individualism.

The work of DeNora and Bull inaugurated research on musical experience in the present. Following on, there is a pressing need for further research both on the encultured nature of acoustic experience and acoustic environments and on institutionalised soundworlds. Such studies should encompass not only evolving music and media, but the varied and changing forms of subjectivity brought to these processes (Born 2009b: 80–1). They should analyse the materiality and thus the subjective affordances of particular musico- and sonic–social–technological assemblages; they should examine how subjectivity responds to the recursive interplay between private and public; and they should attend to the affective constitution of modes of subjectivity by music and sound without assuming that it promotes the self-communion of the liberal subject. Resisting the universalisation of notions of the sovereign individual in the way advocated by postcolonial and anthropological critiques,[50] future research should interrogate the mutating character of the ensounded liberal subject in the manner of DeNora and Bull, but set this alongside analyses of the alternative forms taken by the imbrication of music or sound, subjectivities and socialities.

Exemplifying these ambitions is Charles Hirschkind's (2006) study of ethical self-formation through cassette-listening in Cairo, which, by bringing culture into the analysis and elucidating alternative modes of subjectivity, portrays a quite different articulation of selfhood and mediated soundscape. Hirschkind's focus is the popular practice of listening to cassette sermons – devotional and contestatory vocal performances – by adherents of *da'wa*, an Islamic movement that claims moral leadership while decrying the state's failure in this role. Hirschkind stresses how these practices and the subjectivities they engender exist in tension with secular–liberal values, notably any presupposition of individual autonomy or of the normative separation of public and private life. Played in the street and buses, shops and cafés, the Qur'an cassettes reshape the 'moral architecture' of the city (Hirschkind 2006: 124) such that ethical interiority and discipline are resoundingly made public. 'As opposed to the private reader, whose stillness and solitude became privileged icons' for the bourgeois imaginary, he says, 'it is the figure of the ethical listener – with all of its dense sensory involvements – that ... inhabits the [Islamic] counterpublic I describe here' (2006: 107). Hirschkind depicts an alternative sonic–social ontology to that portrayed by Bull and DeNora, one that productively defamiliarises the late liberal subjectivities – replete with 'agency', 'self-identity' and 'choice' – that they describe. Through the distinctive articulation of private and public embodied in Cairene cassette-listening, he reminds us that technology is not ontology and that subjectification is not reducible to the affective interiority of the liberal subject. Without this corrective it might be tempting to naturalise the twin tendencies identified above – tendencies that are the more significant for not being naturalised.

Several chapters in this collection respond to the challenges set out in the paragraph before last. They offer a nuanced vista for music and sound studies when addressing the constitution of subjectivity, one that augments the sonic–social phenomenology advocated in this Introduction. Some

---

[50] For critiques of the universalisation of the liberal individual see Strathern 1988, Chakrabarty 1992: 9, and Barber 2006 and 2007. Barber's research on the constitution of the self through the proliferating forms of writing in colonial Africa pointedly counters a series of Habermasian assumptions (e.g. Barber 2006: 6–12).

chapters show how music, sound and audio media can be mobilised to humanising, creative or ludic ends in shaping subjectivity and engendering affect,[51] as well as identifying multiple dimensions of the expansion of aesthetic experience galvanised both by audio media and by performance, installation and sound works.[52] Other chapters testify, in contrast, to the ways in which sound, music and audio media can be deployed to problematic or malign subjective or psychological ends, whether by systematising the individuation attested to by earlier research[53] or in being oriented to the very obliteration of subjectivity.[54] In either direction – humanising or malign – music, sound and audio media are credited precisely with being mediators: agents of the voluntary or involuntary transformation of subjectivity. Moreover, whether in the extremes of 'sheer acoustical energy' meted out in the sonic bombardment of prisoners in interrogation centres of the 'war on terror',[55] or in the sounding room that figures not as 'object' or 'context' but as an evolving, 'breathing' subject in a Yoko Ono composition,[56] or in the sense of proximity conjured up by recorded music's spatialisation in a Goldfrapp track as it evokes intersubjective and psychic states:[57] it is the affective, post-representational *materiality* (Bennett and Joyce 2010: 5) of musico- or sonic–social–technological assemblages and their subjective affordances that are at issue in these chapters.

Two further points arise. Repeatedly, the authors show how the musical or sonic orchestration of boundary transformations occurs through the mobilisation of affect and its subjective traces. This can take a number of forms. It is evident in the way that the boundaries between religious communities – Islam, Judaism and Christian Europe – were reconfigured in the late eighteenth century through the opening of 'internal sacred space to public performance through music'.[58] It can take the form of changes to the boundary between the privacy of the self and public space, music's powers to effect 'an intense exteriorisation of intimacy' (Connor 1999: 22), as when the ballad singer, apparently engulfed by personal emotions, projects and universalises them in public performance.[59] It is apparent in the intensification of sonic individuation and denial of auditory coevality fostered both by headphone-enabled mobile music players and, more acutely, in the severe psychic isolation effected by acoustic harassment – when sound itself

---

[51] See the chapters by Dibben and Haake, Dueck, Cook and DeNora.
[52] See the chapters by Ouzounian, Clarke, Sterne and Middleton.
[53] See the chapters by Sterne, and Gopinath and Stanyek.
[54] See the chapter by Cusick.     [55] Cusick p. 288.
[56] Ouzounian p. 78.     [57] Clarke p. 108.
[58] Bohlman p. 212.     [59] See the chapter by Middleton.

becomes 'a force field of power'.[60] But such an infolding of self is matched by music's capacity to forge connections across the permeable membrane between self and collectivity, in this way auguring the reconstruction or redemption of damaged subjectivities or flawed biographies, or the over-coming of emotion-laden subjective and social divisions.[61] As we will see, for aboriginal Manitobans country music jam sessions express a common social peripherality while setting in dialogue 'a range of ethical and affective perspectives regarding the stigmatised social practice of drinking' that so afflicts aboriginal subjectivities.[62] More routinely, as certain chapters attest, music and sound are employed to negotiate the borders between subjectiv-ity and social relations, as well as to create zones of interference between the distinctive planes of sociality, with concomitant subjective entailments.[63] Thus, aboriginal Manitoban country sessions amount also to 'interstitial zones: sites of intimate [social] interaction' that are articulated to dual social imaginaries – the national public sphere and the rueful, ambivalent collect-ivity that is aboriginal public culture.[64]

The second point follows on: it concerns the role of affect and entrain-ment in these and other experiments with subjectivity afforded by music, sound and audio media. It is perhaps unsurprising, given music's hyper-affective propensities, that it engenders the formation of social bonds or what I have called aggregations of the affected (Born 2012: 262), a potential manifest in both the first and second planes of music's social mediation: the intimate socialities of performance and musically imagined community. Recent social theory offers new understandings of these processes since rhythm, dance, bodily proximity and corpor-eal experience, all associated with music and performance, are thought to promote the intensification of affect and the creation of affective alli-ances (Brennan 2004; Thrift 2008: Chapter 6). One source for these ideas is the rediscovered work of Gabriel Tarde, in which the fabric of the social is portrayed as resulting from collective flows of affect, a logic of semi-conscious imitation and suggestion (Barry and Thrift 2007; Borch 2007). Tarde's thought is predicated on a rejection of two foundational dualisms: the distinction between psychology and sociology, as well as that between individual and social (cf. Ingold 2000a: 171). In their place he advocates an inter-psychology attuned to how 'subjects [are] open to

---

[60] See the chapters by Gopinath and Stanyek, and Cusick p. 276.
[61] See the chapters by DeNora and Dueck.        [62] Dueck p. 240.
[63] See the chapters by Dibben and Haake, Rice, Eisenberg, Cook and Dueck.
[64] Dueck p. 256.

affecting and being affected' (Blackman 2007: 576). A similar perspective comes from the neo-Spinozist philosophy of Moira Gatens and Genevieve Lloyd in their concern with how 'the awareness of human collectivities ... of bodies in relation – is not a merely cognitive awareness ... [but] shot through with emotion ... Sociability is [therefore] inherently affect-ive [and] the incorporation into collectivities which determines our indi-viduality involves affective imitation – dynamic movements of emotional identification and appropriation' (Gatens and Lloyd 1999: 77). A third influence is Teresa Brennan's (2004: Chapter 3) development via entrain-ment of the work of crowd theorists and group psychoanalysts on the transmission of affect. Brennan aims to transcend another dualism, that of the social and biological, by pointing to physiological mechanisms that underlie affective contagion (Brennan 2004: 49), and she locates them in transmissible hormonal changes triggered by particular 'atmospheres' and social environments. In Brennan's compelling, anti-neo-Darwinian account, 'certain biological and physical phenomena themselves require a social explanation. While its wellsprings are social, the transmission of affect is deeply physical in its effects' (2004: 23).[65] Entrainment, in turn, is increasingly invoked in research pursuing connections between music, affect and social processes (DeNora 2000: Chapter 4; Borgo 2005: Chapter 6), including ethnomusicological studies of links between physiology and sociality in musical performance (Clayton, Sager and Will 2004).[66] Here synchronisation as well as rhythm, movement and embodied experience come to the fore when addressing such questions as: 'Since certain degrees of entrainment between individuals seem to be associated with positive affect, is it the case that particular patterns, periodicities, hierarchies or intensities of entrainment afford particular affects? Could positive affect be associated with a greater degree of self-synchrony as well as closer syn-chrony with a social group?' (Clayton, Sager and Will 2004: 21).

Extending the discussion of entrainment in music, however, some of the chapters that follow are concerned with its mundane or negative modalities. On the one hand, we encounter its healing potential in the capacity of clients of music therapy to discover, through pleasurable entrainment to song and to the microsocialities of performance, a path between subjective states of

---

[65] For an overview of recent developments in theorising affective transmission, including Brennan's work and a variety of alternative contemporary readings of Spinoza, William James and Gabriel Tarde, see Blackman 2008.

[66] The ethnomusicological discourse on entrainment builds on earlier models of the connection between rhythm, movement and musical socialities in the work of John Blacking, Alan Lomax, Charles Keil and Steven Feld (Clayton, Sager and Will 2004: 19–20).

illness and well-being.[67] We learn of office workers' use of the entrainment afforded by headphone-listening to reduce distraction and aid concentration.[68] On the other hand, we confront runners' instrumental entrainment by music and thence their enrolment in 'experiential marketing' through the use of the Nike+ Sport Kit apparatus to optimise their running performance;[69] and, with reference to the somatic experience of sympathetic vibration, we witness the violent sonic attacks on prisoners in the military camps of the 'war on terror' effected by their subjection to involuntary bodily vibration when forcibly entrained to the overwhelming sounds played by their captors. Unequivocally, the contributors to this book demonstrate that entrainment is a mechanism the social, political and ethical telos of which cannot be adjudged in advance: it is at work in techniques and disciplines of subjective and social regulation or domination through music and sound[70] as much as in practices of self-regulation.

It follows, as I have argued throughout this Introduction, that music, sound and audio media are not invariably employed to generate positive affect or create social unities. They also animate and configure practices and spaces in which are played out social and cultural differences and divisions (Born 2009a), and they refract an array of modes of power. Entrainment must therefore be reconceptualised in this light: it can form part of an apparatus of subjection; and even entrainment – like the flow of affect, or the network (Strathern 1996) – has boundaries or limits that become apparent when music fails to attach potential entrainees, boundaries that are definitively socio-cultural in derivation. This is where Brennan's resistance to biological determinism is salutary: rather than entrainment stemming from physiology, which stimulates affect, with social results, her arguments suggest that these processes are bidirectional. That is to say, social and cultural experience, which may include entrenched or emergent differences and antagonisms, can orient the transmission of affect, which need not be unifying but may be heterogeneous in its distribution and will have physiological entailments. Together these findings recall Feld's portrait of the fluid, ambiguous boundaries between individual and collective experience and between emotional, aesthetic and symbolic modalities in Kaluli sonic and musical life. They vindicate a sonic–social phenomenology attuned to

---

[67] See the chapter by DeNora.
[68] See the chapter by Dibben and Haake.
[69] See the chapter by Gopinath and Stanyek.
[70] Although he does not make use of the concept of entrainment, this is also a message of Goodman's 2009 study of the 'vibrational force' of sonic experiences as they are mediated by wider fields of power (Goodman 2009: 189–90).

the relational nature of ensounded subjectivity and sociality, individual and collectivity (cf. Gatens and Lloyd 1999: 78–9).

## Sound, music and the private and public modalities of power

A final perspective arising from this volume responds to the Lefebvreian challenge to rejoin the enlarged sonic–social phenomenology elaborated up to this point with a critical analysis of modern forms of power. A number of chapters indicate how the spatialised modes of sonic and musical experience being depicted do not appear *ex nihilo* or exist in isolation, but derive from specific social and historical conditions. This opens a rich seam of scholarship and represents a rejoinder to those writers – whether from sound studies, anthropology or music studies – whose ontology of sound and music stops at the phenomenal. For the bidirectional mediation at work in the musico- and sonic–social–technological assemblages presented in this collection calls for an analysis of how power is operative in a variety of ways – more and less decentred or 'microphysical' (Foucault 1977: 26) – in reconfiguring the nature of public and private experience. The social and historical conditions addressed in the chapters that follow range from dimensions of the capitalist cultural economy, through forms of state and military power, to other governmental and disciplinary formations; they straddle, in other words, the private and public writ large.

The chapters address these issues with reference to diverse institutional sites. One perspective comes from the micropolitics of sound and the ensounding of social relations in British public hospitals. They are evident in the exteriorisation of interior bodily sounds, experienced by patients as a disturbing confusion of the boundaries of inner and outer self as well as a potentially devastating loss of privacy and autonomy; and in the dominion of a medical regime of truth in which the circulation of knowledge is hierarchised and privatised, excluding patients from discussion of their own conditions.[71] More violently, power is operative in the extremes of acoustical, physical and psychic suffering at the heart of the biopolitical, carceral regime of US military interrogation camps, emblematic of the complex sonic and political zoning of territory under the 'state of exception' (Agamben 2005; Elden 2009: 55–61).[72] For in an obscene, parodic inversion of the affective interiority of iPod-listening, the camp oversees

[71] See the chapter by Rice.
[72] On the etymological links between 'terror' and 'territory', sovereign spaces and violence, and thus the inherent 'violence of [state] borders', see Elden 2009: xxviii–xxx.

domination through sonically enforced individuation: an 'ultimate violence that batters prisoners' bodies, [shattering] ... the capacity to control the acoustical relationality that is the foundation of subjectivity'.[73] The micro-political role of musical and sonic practices of worship in reconfiguring the contours of 'public religion' are apparent in the evolving historical articulation between the sacred spaces of religious community and urban public life, producing in different eras more or less cosmopolitanised or culturally and religiously zoned modes of urban experience.[74] Further perspectives come from chapters touching on relations between aboriginal groups and the state, in particular their deployment of sound and music to orchestrate either cohabitation or confrontation with the state. Thus aboriginal Manitobans, as we have seen, create through country music sessions spaces of affective and entrained consociation that renew collective feeling against the opprobrium of a racist state; musical performance and its circulation on national radio engender musically imagined community and thence a subaltern counterpublic. While the overtly politicised subaltern counter-public produced by Rebecca Belmore's 1991 site-specific sound installation, which responded to a land dispute between a Mohawk community and the Canadian government, fuelled 'alternative modes of [public] social and political exchange' both within the Mohawk community, whose participation it solicited, and between the community and the state.[75]

Two chapters address, finally, the evolving, synergistic relations between music's deepening commodification and related branches of knowledge: science, engineering and marketing as they foster 'a tendency to classify human beings in terms of data' and a 'biologisation of the consumer profile'.[76] Together these chapters give insight into the proliferating and expansive forms of commodification and reification of listening in the present day. One focuses on the design and development of the most ubiquitous digital audio format, the MP3; the other on a consumer audio accessory, the Nike+ Sport Kit, developed through inter-corporate links between Nike and Apple: a running-attuned, sensor-enabled iPod that generates realtime and sonified biofeedback, drawing users to a website on which they post personal data that can then be commodified.[77] If the MP3 format affords digital music's accelerating spatial and intersubjective mobility, the Sport Kit embodies the continuing inter-corporate mining of profitable elaborations

---

[73] Cusick p. 276. On the connections between music and violence, see Johnson and Cloonan 2009.

[74] See the chapter by Bohlman.

[75] Ouzounian p. 87.     [76] Gopinath and Stanyek p. 145.

[77] See the chapters by Sterne, and Gopinath and Stanyek.

of the mobile music player – now compounded by a burgeoning 'biocapitalism'. Both amount to contemporary emanations of the genealogy of a desire, encountered earlier in Leppert's (1998) account of aristocratic listening in early modern Europe, for a type of musical sovereignty: the desire to command music into existence by cultivating a zone of privatised consumption, thereby intensifying the pleasurable affectivity of being subjectified by music. In part these software and hardware innovations respond to dynamic conflicts between sectors of the capitalist music and music technology industries thrown up by the dual processes of digitisation and convergence (Hesmondhalgh 2009: 58); but they also partake in wider tendencies in the marketisation – and 'musicalisation'[78] – of consumption.

Research on the media industries reveals clear parallels in the responses by the music, film and television industries to the threats to profitability posed by digitisation and downloading. To understand them it is necessary to be alert to two complementary properties of contemporary capitalism identified by economic anthropology: the performativity of economics, market analysis and forecasting, their capacity to bring about the very futures they imagine and project (Born 2007; MacKenzie, Muniesa and Siu 2007; Muniesa and Callon 2007);[79] and the dynamic framing of markets. Together they highlight a last way in which music is deployed to reconfigure the boundaries between private and public in the guise of the rationalities of powerful economic actors as they experiment with reshaping everyday experience. As Timothy Mitchell has argued, property arrangements are never static; forms of property proliferate. One of the main ways that commercial actors ensure expanded profitability is by extrapolating new kinds of consumption via the commodification of that which previously lay outside or resisted commodification; this entails continuous efforts to reorganise the boundaries between market and non-market, private and public, boundary transformations that are the 'scene of political battles' (Mitchell 2007: 247–8). 'The starting point of [these transformations] … is to render [former] ways of life defective, almost dead … Since their defectiveness is what makes accumulation possible, it is an outside on which the … inside [of capitalist markets] depends' (Mitchell 2007: 268). Under this dynamic, in the present we see the extrapolation of long-standing commercial strategies, their roots in the nineteenth century, as Sterne (2003) shows

---

[78] See the chapter by Gopinath and Stanyek, esp. p. 145.
[79] Callon 2007, Mackenzie, Muniesa and Siu 2007, and Muniesa and Callon 2007 show that experimentation is a permanent and dynamic feature of institutionalised economic life, characterised by the performativity of the diverse modes of research and forecasting or 'future-making' (Born 2007) involved.

in his archaeology of auditory media: new property relations attached to new physical and immaterial commodities, new distribution platforms, and new modes of musical experience segmented in terms of time, space, place and sociality. Commercial strategies attempt to incorporate both non-commoditised musical experience and non-musicalised spatial, temporal and embodied experience, coining novel kinds of aesthetic experience: both a temporal aesthetic of digital music's mobility and fluidity, its openness to remediation and circulation (as in the MP3 file), and a spatial aesthetic of the simultaneous, multiple or montage: music *and* movement *and* place *and* sound (as in the Sport Kit). The drive to proliferate music's mediatised consumption multiplies both the spaces and activities colonised by consumption (the bedroom, car, bar, mall, bank queue, underground …; walking, jogging, travelling, eating, waiting …) and the aesthetic modalities proffered by these media (cf. Hosokawa 1984), yielding new articulations of private and public experience. With regard to time, the industries' strategy is to carve out and exploit more and more temporal 'windows' of consumption of the same musical object, tiered into a hierarchy of more and less exclusive, premiere or archival releases.

In short, what we encounter is a doubled privatisation: a segmentary calculus engaged in dividing up and individualising the spatial, temporal and social experience of music to be sold. However, the effect is to intensify *both* the individualising *and* the distributed and aggregative modes of musical experience: both iPod-listening or Sport Kit-jogging and musico-social networking via SoundCloud or Facebook as they feed practices of music-sharing and diversifying sites of performance. Indeed as relentlessly as the individual is instated and reinstated, so the individualising imperative is deflected or finessed as the iPod, mobile phone and laptop become means of crafting novel musical socialities.[80] We see how ceaselessly inventive has been the experimentation undertaken by engineering and capital with the privatisation and public-isation of music: with hailing us both as interiorising 'self-identity' projects and as nodes in networks of dispersed sociality. It is these inventive propensities of musical capitalism – by which I refer to the particular sectoral and intersectoral qualities and dynamics of late capitalism as it is mediated by music (Toynbee 2000: 19–25; Hesmondhalgh

---

[80] Alexandrine Boudreault-Fournier, for example, in her fieldwork on post-hip hop subcultures in Montreal, identifies a number of socialities cultivated by practices of music-'sharing' through iPod, laptop and other digital devices. One is 'cypher', when a laptop is used sequentially among a group of friends at a party to play song after song: as one informant put it, 'My laptop just passes hands like that in the cypher all night' (Boudreault-Fournier 2011: 8).

2009)[81] – in its expansive redesign of the infrastructures of musical experience that are touched on in the two chapters mentioned.


## The chapters

### Part I: The design of mediated music and sound

The first section of the volume focuses on the production or design and
the materiality of mediated music and sound, and through this the nature
of the experiences that they afford. Rather than musical capitalism, the
opening chapters by Gascia Ouzounian and Eric Clarke address aesthetic
and perceptual issues, exploring the spatialised nature of, respectively,
the sonic–social and musical assemblages of sound installation art and
of popular music recordings. Ouzounian traces a genealogy of the field
of sound installation art through its evolving problematisation of a series of oppositions: sound and music, space and time, and aesthetics and
ethics. She charts the field's emergence in the 1960s and 1970s in the
interplay between a series of art movements: new sculptural and architectural practices, conceptual art, performance art and public art. Drawing
out its changing conceptions of space, as well as its experimentation with
novel audience relations, she analyses the evolving material, aesthetic and
ethico-political bases of sound installation art. Ouzounian's genealogy
finds a point of departure in Varèse's *Poème électronique* (1958), which,
although influenced by the emerging practices of *musique concrète* and
*Elektronische Musik*, surpassed them in the scale of realisation of spatial
music composition. *Poème électronique*, Ouzounian suggests, offered an
immersive listening experience more ambitious than its precursors as well
as the experimental electronic music of Cage, Tudor, Brown, Feldman and

---

[81] In coining the term 'musical capitalism' I intend to highlight that capitalism is not a
monolithic but a protean entity, and that late capitalism as it is mediated by music – hence
musical capitalism – has specific properties and potentialities linked to music's socio-material
qualities, a number of which are identified in this section. The term responds to ongoing
ambivalence in the political economy of music and culture as to whether music's imbrication
with capitalism can be reduced to prior terms – concentration, cultural imperialism and so
on – or whether it exhibits particular trajectories and even innovations that in some ways
depart from these general processes. For an example of such ambivalence see the discussions
in David Hesmondhalgh's study of the cultural industries of individualisation (2002: 101–2),
largely attributed (as in this Introduction) to innovation in music technologies, of resistance
to concentration via independent production (2002: 149–51), attributed also to innovations
in music, and of cultural imperialism (2002: 195–6), portrayed by Hesmondhalgh as a general
process exemplified by world music. For a similar argument in favour of anti-essentialist
accounts of capitalism that attend to the specificity of the material, see Mitchell 2002.

Wolff. The reigning model of space for the Western musical avant-garde in this period was Euclidean: the concert hall was conceived as an 'empty container', and sound's movement through it could be determined and controlled through its segmentation and serialisation. Yet a radical departure was marked by the introduction of space as a compositional parameter, for certain composers were compelled to supersede the Euclidean model by a burgeoning commitment to the perspectival nature of sound in space and thus to the irreducible difference of each listener's experience. Ouzounian argues that this led to a counter-practice, indeed a counter-ontology, of spatial sound, one that valorised the multiplicity of audience experience and the ineluctable participation of audiences in the event, as well as the non-inert, temporal and material contribution of the site or space itself. This departure was evident in such works as Fluxus event scores, which promoted an 'everyday aesthetic', in works by Yoko Ono and LaMonte Young, and in the extended ritual performances of Joseph Beuys and Terry Fox, in which sound became a tool 'with which to connect objects and transform spaces' (p. 81).

But it is Max Neuhaus who coined the term 'sound installation' to describe sound works that were situated in space rather than organised in time. In the mid-1960s Neuhaus began to facilitate listening walks with audiences in order to refocus 'attention on sounds that we live with everyday'. Neuhaus was insistent on transforming the public for contemporary music: henceforth it was to be 'anyone who listens', and he demanded of this broader public that they must become attuned to their aural environments. The chapter culminates in a discussion of the work of two contemporary sound installation artists, the Finn Heidi Fast and the Anishnabe Canadian Rebecca Belmore, both of whom create site-specific sound works oriented to the participation of particular, localised publics. Belmore's 1991 installation *Ayumee-aawach Oomama-mowan: Speaking to their Mother*, for example, set out to intervene in a major land dispute between First Nations communities and the government by mobilising a group of Native Canadians to speak through a giant megaphone to the disputed land, which, by virtue of this address, Ouzounian argues, was constituted as a living entity rather than merely an object to be owned. The installation not only effaced the line between aesthetics and ethics, but reconfigured the space of politics, asserting the sound of political speech and its ability to 'bypass dominant modes of political containment' while reclaiming 'the political worth of marginal (and marginalised) places' (p. 88). Ouzounian contends that by drawing attention to space as social production, sound installation art of this kind constitutes 'spatial sound practice … not only as a poetics, but as a politics … Such a critical spatial–sonic practice does not merely "happen in" space, but is poised radically to transform the very terms of its constitution' (p. 74).

A quite different analysis of the materiality of spatialised music and its subjective affordances is given by Eric Clarke. Clarke traces the development of research on the capacity of musical sound to specify motion and space, both the physical spaces in which it is performed and the virtual spaces that it can seem to occupy. Rather than adopt a cognitive framework concerned with the musical representation of space, he builds on principles to do with how listeners perceive auditory cues about space and movement from their environment. Focusing on recorded sound and its capacity to specify spatial forms, movements and transformations, Clarke's approach integrates ecological perceptual theory, Lakoff and Johnson's conceptual metaphor theory and the theory of proxemics. With these resources he addresses how spatial–musical effects seem to proffer modes of subjectivity and intersubjectivity, indeed can evoke or partake in psychic dramas or narratives. Recording and its techniques have historically formed a central dimension of the aesthetics of popular and electroacoustic musics, and the use of spatialisation in recording has been particularly important in both spheres. Yet by contrasting two recordings of Berlioz's *Symphonie Fantastique*, Clarke shows how spatialisation has also been prominent in classical music recording and points to the tensions in these recordings with either upholding or departing from a sonic–spatial realism.

Clarke's main focus, however, is on two examples of spatialisation in British popular music. On the one hand, he charts the virtual spaces figured sonically in Pink Floyd's track 'Echoes' (1971), in which a central episode portrays what Clarke interprets as the vast, inhuman and empty physical spaces of an imaginary landscape. On the other hand, he analyses a track by Goldfrapp, 'Deer Stop' (2000), to illustrate the dramatic spatialisation and movement conjured up by its treatment of the singing voice, through which means are conveyed a tantalising and sensuous intimacy and emotional instability. Clarke argues that despite or perhaps precisely because of the 'barely decipherable, and semantically opaque' nature of the lyrics, the human voice's capacity to conjure up intersubjectivity and empathy becomes more pronounced. The track swoops between intensely corporeal effects – a sense of engorgement, of having 'been taken apparently almost inside the body [or throat] of the singer' (p. 108) – and episodes in which the singer's voice is felt to traverse space, rushing from an immense distance towards the listener. Clarke proposes that through such spectral transformations of the voice, a definitively non-realist, almost uncanny sense of spatial relations is evoked, relations that are at once intersubjective relations and that 'seem to demand interpretation in a different type of domain – a metaphorically related psychic space' (p. 108). Noting that such interpretations rest on a reading of the material properties of recorded sound, Clarke points to the methodological correlate: that the semantic affordances he has highlighted, and their implications for listeners' experiences of subjectivity and intersubjectivity in recorded music, must be rooted in turn in an analysis of wider cultural historical developments with which audiences are familiar – notably the semantic and aesthetic intertextualities stemming from the interrelations between twentieth-century Hollywood film sound, video games and recorded music (p. 110).

The next chapters zoom in on two prominent components of the redesign of the infrastructures of musical experience by musical capitalism, two pervasive digital audio technologies: the MP3 format (Sterne) and the Nike+ Sport Kit (Gopinath and Stanyek). In both cases the conditions for the emergence of the technologies take centre stage, and it is in these conditions that answers are sought for the distinctive form taken by the complex and recursive articulation of privacy and publicness.

Taking the design of a ubiquitous audio technology as its theme, Jonathan Sterne's chapter asks how it is that the MP3 digital file format has become the most commercially successful such technology in global history. Sterne notes that the development of the MP3 was an episode in the ongoing clash between rival sound reproduction formats, driven by competing corporate economic interests as well as by the commercial need to identify common standards that would enable a new phase of convergence and consolidation between emerging digital audio and computing technologies. What these interests necessitated in turn was close attention, through systematic research, to the optimal representation of acoustic music in the form of digital code, and its optimal reduction so as to achieve the immense benefits of small size. Sterne's particular focus is on the nature and role of the industry technique known as the 'listening test' in the design of the MP3 format. Effectively, the practice of listening tests entailed an instrumentalisation of psychoacoustical research; the result was to reify and standardise musical subjectivity in the guise of a specific digital codec (or coder–decoder): the MP3 format. It is the 'radical reduction' in size of the MP3 format compared, say, to the .wav format used by the CD that enables its extreme portability and intensive digital circulation, which in turn fosters affective contagion and ensures the format's omnipresence. As Sterne observes, the MP3 points to the ways in which 'contemporary media forms strive at once for some form of universality … even as they allow for the irreducibility of private, subjective experience' (p. 113).

Four intriguing paradoxes run through Sterne's account. The first is between the universalising scientific claims of the listening test and the highly particular demographic profile of its experimental subjects, such that, as he contends, any potential challenges that may have been posed to the format's model of listening by cultural and social difference were simply unaddressed. The second is between the anaesthetic perceptual models that originally prevailed and the growing recognition of a timbrally inflected, aesthetically imbued mediation by the format. The third is between the tendency for the format to become inaudible and to disappear in listening, and the historical process whereby listeners appear to become increasingly attuned to the format precisely as a mediation that is itself the bearer of an aesthetic – what we might call an aesthetic of the format. And the fourth is between the normative perceptual model of listening immanent in the format and the actual multiplicity of listening. Hence the reification of subjectivity immanent in the digitally encoded model of listening in the MP3 format, while it is envisaged as universalistic and as subsuming difference, encounters the heterogeneity of living individuals and particular subjectivities participating in the assemblage. Each – normative model, particular ears – mediates the other. But a further paradox is also worth noting: how the material properties of the MP3 format have enabled convergence and corporate expansion while also affording the busting of commercial controls through 'piracy' – indicating that the technical architecture of the MP3, as with that of certain earlier analogue and digital music formats, escapes its embedding in corporate economic interests. It is because of its immaterial materiality as code and thus its ultra-portability, suitability for instantaneous replication and circulation, and flexibility as an element in multiple musical assemblages – its qualities as 'a format designed for casual users, to be heard in earphones on trains or on the tiny speakers of a computer desktop, to be sent in emails, instant messages and through file-sharing programs' (p. 125) – that the MP3 is generative and proffers a host of non-corporate and public creative possibilities.

The last chapter in this opening section addresses another contemporary emanation of the corporate commercial mining of auditory practices: the Nike+ Sport Kit, an apparatus resulting from an alliance between Nike and Apple that enables runners to 'tune their run' to the iPod- or iPhone-relayed sounds of voiced biofeedback, as well as playlists and mixes of well-known bands. Sumanth Gopinath and Jason Stanyek begin their anatomy of the Sport Kit by describing its critical location at the centre of the 'Human Race': a spectacular, participatory global marketing event staged by the Nike Corporation in the late 2000s in twenty-five 'global cities'. The 'Human

Race' itself magnifies, almost parodies, this book's themes: in it a million runners were propelled synchronously through urban space by their entrainment to the Sport Kit vocal feedback and audio track, in this way propagating a transnational spatial constellation of dispersed yet unified corporate–athletic publics; while runners who were not present in any of the partner cities could participate in real time as members of the virtual public hailed by the event and the technology. At the same time, the Sport Kit engendered collectively in the 'Human Race' runners a voluntary auditory self-enclosure via the multiple soundtracks and individuated biofeedback narratives fed to each participant. As Gopinath and Stanyek show, the mass entrainment afforded by the Sport Kit – the individual athletic body tuning in to music's motions, and through this individual tuning in the formation of an aggregate – indicates a doubled hailing of the musico-athletic subject: what might be called the 'aggregate-individual'.

Gopinath and Stanyek locate the Nike+ Sport Kit within a series of historical developments, foremost among them the Nike Corporation's adoption in the wake of its well-known branding operations of 'experiential marketing'. This is a strategy that utilises consumers' willingness to submit themselves to a participatory consumerism through modes of affective and sensory labour, which the authors link in turn to the exponential growth in athletic capitalism. It is evident in the co-introduction of real-time biofeedback to the runner, voiced through the earphones, along with the extension of the runner's temporal connection to the apparatus through a website that encourages him or her to engage both in personalised preparations and in post-run, cumulative archiving of personal biofeedback data. The runner is thus hailed both as a satellite moving through urban public space and as a node in an online network, while the website enables personal data to be mined for market analysis and sold on by Nike. The authors contend that the biofeedback data thus permit Nike to traffic 'in the production and commodification of extensive data sets that define human beings'. Together these processes fuel 'a practice of capital accumulation built upon the extraction of value from the *bios*' itself (all p. 135). For Gopinath and Stanyek, the integration in the Sport Kit of, on the one hand, consumer surveillance via the sensor-enabled mining of intimate data and, on the other hand, the athletic goods and music industries, 'brings together two crucial tendencies marked by the decline of state and individual autonomy from capital during the neoliberal era' (p. 134). The Sport Kit therefore positions itself at the intersection of four vectors of privatisation: that of Nike's proliferating inter-corporate synergies; that of intensifying market analysis through commercial data mining; that of the body under athletic capitalism and an encompassing biocapitalism; and that of the experience of urban public space via auditory consumer-individuation and sonic self-enclosure. As Gopinath and Stanyek convey, the 'publics' generated by the apparatus are dwarfed by these privatising vectors.

## Part II: Space, sound and affect in everyday lifeworlds

The next three chapters examine how sound and music are employed in everyday situations in the creation of spatiality, and in particular to mark, construct, contest or transform the boundaries between what is deemed to be private or public experience. Nicola Dibben and Anneli Beronius Haake outline the results of research on music-listening in contemporary work-places. They chart the changing nature of music's role in regulating work and negotiating its demands, as well as the individuation of mediated musical experience in the workplace, in contrast to the prevalence in earlier decades of broadcast music in work settings. Their findings point to music-listening as a practice that commonly results in a nesting of the private auditory space of individual earphone use within the public soundscape of the office. However, by comparing two office settings with quite different architectural and spatial characteristics, and with reference to earlier research by Michael Bull and others, the authors argue that individuated listening is not used simply to create 'aural cocoons' or 'auditory bubbles' in the workplace, but engaged more subtly and variably to respond to situational contingencies in their subjects' working lives. They highlight the contradictory affordances of music in the workplace, used both as a pleasurable distraction and yet also as a means of blocking out other distractions, particularly in open-plan offices. The use of music, the authors find, is significantly correlated with the particular physical features of the workplace.

Dibben and Haake propose that 'It is the very capacity of music to make attentional demands that workers turned to their advantage when the music lay within their control' (p. 156). On the one hand, music-listening enables employees to aid their own concentration by avoiding interruptions and managing interactions with colleagues, dissuading people from making contact when desired and affording temporary zones of psychological privacy. On the other hand, music use is informed by a sense of professional responsibility as well as by ethical concern for the welfare of co-workers and an awareness of the negative effects of imposing one's music habits on others. Managers, in particular, may engage in 'one-eared' listening in order to monitor and be responsive to the wider office environment; while the playing of music or radio through loudspeakers may be calibrated temporally and spatially so as not to disturb others, with radio being seen as a relatively 'neutral', more socialised medium than the personalised iPod because it is one in which no single individual's tastes predominate. The authors point out that in the post-Fordist, 'funky offices' of today's knowledge economy, the presence of music blurs the boundaries between work and leisure, symbolising the 'responsible autonomy' of the contemporary office worker. Yet the exercise of this autonomy, epitomised for many respondents by music-listening, is felt by others to threaten professionalism and to risk a deterioration in the quality of work. The result of these countervailing forces is a complex and shifting soundscape in which music is employed to achieve a sonic–spatial nesting and zoning, listeners carving out their sonic territory within the office while also remaining aware of and acknowledging the territories of others.

Drawing on ethnographic research in two British hospitals, Tom Rice portrays the potentially acute emotional effects of everyday soundscapes in his account of patients' experience of the sounds of hospital life. A feature of hospital soundscapes, particularly of public wards, is how the sounds of intimate and involuntary bodily processes – associated with pain, birth and death, diagnosis and treatment – are broadcast ignominiously to the world. Sounds transgress the attempts to create zones of privacy manifest in the 'swish' of the drawing of the 'privacy curtain' around patients' beds, a screen that affords no sonic segregation. Aware not only that they are overhearing their neighbours' suffering but that their own indignities are being overhead by others, patients are subject to a 'sonic incontinence' in which bodily sounds leak uncontainably into public awareness. Moreover, Rice suggests, sound complicates the boundaries of the body, transmitting even its interior spaces – those physiological processes and functioning organs magnified by diagnostic or monitoring technologies – into public acoustic and discursive space. He describes how heart monitors produce a constant beeping on the cardiothoracic ward, a background noise that magnifies the rhythm of patients' hearts, and thus an 'auditory reminder of [patients'] vulnerability' (p. 180). Privacy is undermined through these sounding technologies. Independently, patients in both hospitals employed the same aphorism about hospital life: 'the first thing you lose is your privacy, the second is your dignity and the third is your sanity' (p. 170). Sound was heavily implicated in these potentially devastating losses, and tactics were developed to mitigate them; the hospital radio station was widely listened to, for instance, because of its capacity to occlude the ward soundscape.

Rice argues that the hospital soundscape also makes audible a distinct field of power relations manifest in the professional control of knowledge about and discourse on a patient's condition to the exclusion of the patient, as well as the public disclosure of intensely private information. Details about patients' illnesses and treatment processes were transacted by medical professionals such that intimate matters were experienced as uncontrollably the substance of medical discourse, subject to the preoccupations of the experts. The information generated by the investigation of a patient's illness 'circulated through the "network" of the care system' (p. 175), objectifying that individual. Medical discourse was sometimes revealed in ward rounds; yet in the main it was confined to 'backspace' areas. In this way a strict zoning of discourse prevailed. Occasionally, acute anxiety could be caused when medical discourse was overheard, allowing a patient or relative to hear a truth – the failure of a procedure, the deterioration of a condition – that had carefully been withheld. What is at stake in Rice's material, then, is not only how sound is employed to mark the boundaries of private and public, but sound's agency in disturbing and confusing these boundaries. Sound is experienced as exteriorising or broadcasting the inner recesses of the body, crossing the boundaries between inner and outer, autonomic and conscious aspects of self, as well as self and other. But upsetting sound, in the guise of the uncontrollable circulation of objectifying discourses or sonic diagnostics, also produces an interiorisation, stimulating anxieties and psychic fantasies. The result is repeated incursions into patients' psychic and corporeal integrity, even if such incursions can be mitigated by the professional ethic of care. Rice argues compellingly, with reference to Annemarie Mol (2002), that sound and listening – given their perspectival and sensory nature, and their multiplicity – are centrally involved in producing what she calls the 'body multiple'.

The following chapter, by Andrew Eisenberg, pursues the ethnographic revelation of the multiplicity of sonic–spatial dynamics and their potentially disjunctive and conflictual nature. Importantly and tellingly, it foregrounds culture in this analysis. Eisenberg brings together a focus on the affective and embodied nature of experience with the notion, adapted from Vološinov, of the multiaccentuality of space. He is concerned with two aspects of quotidian urban existence in the predominantly Muslim Old Town of the coastal Kenyan city Mombasa. He addresses first how urban space in the Old Town is engendered in and through sound, particularly through the 'polyphony of cantillated (Arabic) calls to prayer [emanating] from the rooftop loudspeakers' (p. 190), along with weekly broadcasts of Arabic and Swahili sermons, which together produce an 'Islamic soundscape'. This sonic constitution of urban space is matched by a host of other multisensory practices – sights, aromas, Arabic and Indian-inflected *taarab* music. But Eisenberg suggests that it is the repeated sounding of the call to prayer, the *adhān*, and the habitual, affect-laden vocal and gestural responses that it evokes from listeners that interpellate a community of believers through a form of Muslim–Swahili subjectification. Indeed, the embodied responses index 'a lifetime of ethical practice', while sacred sounds and embodied responses together orchestrate a sanctification of urban space. This participatory sanctification of the space–time of Mombasa Old Town, Eisenberg suggests, produces 'communitarian privacy': a term previously applied to the physical and architectural features of Islamic cities, but which he argues is also applicable to their acoustical forms.

Eisenberg contends, however, that the ensounded communitarian privacy of Old Town cannot be understood simply in these terms. Rather, it has to be interpreted in light of the normative liberal–democratic conception of the public/private distinction and of the role of religion in public life espoused by the Kenyan polity. According to these liberal norms, urban public space is a neutral arena 'in which even sacred sound may be marked as noise and any subject may address any other without regard to minority norms of social intercourse' (p. 197). Against this backdrop Eisenberg's second theme comes to the fore, through the question: what does it mean 'for a resonant Muslim sanctuary – Mombasa Old Town – to be constantly superposed on the public spaces of Kenya's heterogeneous "second city"'? (p. 196). With reference to ethnographic material – such as an incendiary and well-publicised dispute that arose outside a mosque when a non-Muslim female resident angrily complained about the pre-dawn *adhān*, which led to her being physically assaulted by the imam – Eisenberg charts a clash of logics, a 'constant struggle between Islamic–Swahili and broadly liberal–democratic understandings of publicity and privacy' (p. 188) threaded through daily life. Emphasising the 'acoustemological *multiplicity*' (p. 187) of urban space on the Kenyan coast, he proposes that the dynamics of sonic–spatial competition and disjuncture fuel nothing less than 'an "ontological politics", "a politics over what there is and who/what can know it" (Verran 1998: 238)' (p. 197) that simmers mostly unignited beneath the surface of cosmopolitan cohabitation. Ultimately, Eisenberg proposes, what is revealed by a focus on the potentially conflictual multiplicity of sounded space in the Old Town is not a politics of publicity and privacy sited *in* urban space, but an ontological politics about the very nature *of* urban space.

## Part III: Music, identity, alterity and the politics of space

The third section of the book pursues the role of music, sound and space in animating the politics of identity and of musical socialities. Music's relation to urban and architectural space, as well as musical and sonic boundary crossings – movements between private and public, inside and outside – are highlighted on a vivid historical scale in the chapter by Philip V. Bohlman. In it such boundary crossings appear in the form of musico-spatial transformations that augur large-scale social transformations. Bohlman opens with the momentum evident at the outset of post-Enlightenment modernity in late eighteenth-century Europe towards religious tolerance. Such tolerance was enacted through a reconciliation of the sacred and secular, itself manifest spatially in the entry of religion into the public spaces of the modern city, of which Berlin was paradigmatic. Music had a prominent role in this reconfiguration of urban space, as 'worship and the music of worship moved from the sanctuary to the public square, sometimes in gradual stages, but often through the dramatic modulation of public soundscapes' (p. 207). As a result sacred and secular communities commingled. Bohlman's chapter draws an unsettling arc, arguing that 'the secular Europe formulated at the end of the eighteenth century is reformulated as a post-secular Europe at the end of the twentieth century' (p. 208). In the early nineteenth century Bohlman charts simultaneous transformations in the architectural and urban–spatial characteristics of the European synagogue and mosque. Both saw changes in which the sacred interior was opened on to the outer, public spaces of urban life; both cantorial music and the *adhān* performed such transformations. Not only urban landscapes but soundscapes were altered: 'The historical evidence … argues strongly for a historical telos unleashed by the Enlightenment that leads increasingly to the opening of internal sacred space to public performance through music' (p. 212).

Bohlman finds that the dialectic between inside and outside, private and public that he has identified architecturally and in urban space can be traced analogously in music. Asking, 'When does the outside – the public space of European music – overwhelm the inside – the private space of difference, of appropriated otherness?' (p. 217), he charts these dynamics in the formal structures of Western music. Bohlman proposes that musical fragments facilitate the reconfiguration of musical insides and outsides, whether in the development section of sonata form or the bridge in many popular musical forms. Fragments enable musical border crossings and the entry of the musical periphery into the musical centre; indeed 'fragments destabilise form, enhancing mobility, the in-betweenness of genre' (p. 217).

Coming to the present, Bohlman foregrounds the tensions of cosmopolitan coexistence, showing how politics and power mediate the zoning of urban and religious soundscapes. He observes that not only contemporary Islam, but also Pentecostalism, the American 'megachurches' and German Catholicism foster a provocative spilling of the sacred spaces of religious discourse into secular public space. Bohlman traces the increasingly conflictual dynamics between religious and secular urban soundscapes in Germany and Switzerland, epitomised by the 2009 Swiss ban on the construction of minarets on mosques. But he closes with the destabilisation of territorial and social borders in the aftermath of the 1985 Schengen Agreement, which created a borderless space of 'silent in-betweenness … a space between inside and outside where the problem of religious tolerance continues to be unresolved' (p. 223).

In a similarly wide-ranging contribution, Nicholas Cook explores the plural and overlapping ways in which music both defines and marks space and movement, while also affording changes in spatial and social boundaries. Since at least the early nineteenth century, and culminating in Heinrich Schenker's paradigm, Cook argues, music theorists have pointed to the 'inherently musical spaces' created by 'music as structure in motion' (p. 206), spaces that more accurately amount to a compound of time and space. Theories of tonality, he points out, have encompassed not only temporal models but pronounced topological and social metaphors in which the contrast between tonic and non-tonic keys is commonly interpreted in the dualistic terms of 'home' and 'foreign' or 'self' and 'other'. At the same time, through a kind of 'tonal cartography' (Taylor 2007), tonality has been employed as a musical means of effacing these very dualisms. Yet inherently musical spaces are constructed not only by musical systems such as tonality; they are also realised, Cook suggests, by the corporeal gestures and socialities of live performance, and by the virtual spatialities of recording. For Cook, in its capacity to reshape space, music augurs a politics of space. He charts this politics, first, in the way that music can generate spatialised modes of musical experience that are detached from place – from the 'private communion' proffered in the early nineteenth century by Beethoven's music, to today's iPod-listening. It is, Cook proposes, the existence of 'inherently musical spaces' that affords both this detachment and its corollary: the 'frequently contested yet undoubtedly historical autonomy of music' (p. 231).

Cook proceeds to address the politics of musical space in the expanded terms of music's ability to fabricate spaces of intersubjectivity and social interaction, which he portrays as a key dimension of music's autonomy.

He offers three case studies: first, *fin-de-siècle* Vienna, where the musical cartography developed by Schenker portrayed the 'German logic of music' as the centre of a supranational entity that was at once musical and political. It was in reaction against music's enrolment in such problematic ideological work, Cook contends, that Schoenberg founded the Society for Private Musical Performances. By staging a withdrawal from public life, the SPMP at the same time instituted an intimate, micro-musical public, one that resonates nostalgically with both earlier and later notions of intimate music making – notably chamber music – as a 'space for a lost sociability' (Leppert in Adorno 2002a). Cook's second case comes to the present: the classical music concerts staged in the online world, Second Life. He suggests that these concerts have a complex, multiple socio-spatial existence, constructing for their audiences a type of community that is not only virtual or 'in-world', but entails a real and transnational sociality. Finally, Cook addresses the socio-musical interactions engendered by the 'inner space–time of performance' in the work of the West–Eastern Divan Orchestra. Cook argues that WEDO performances engender socialities that are autonomous in the sense that they are 'not simply an epiphenomenon of the world beyond music' (p. 237). He notes how these socialities are taken by some commentators to augur in microcosm a reconciliation that can be transposed on to the larger historical plane of the Israeli–Palestinian conflict (an interpretation that remains controversial).[82] Music, he concludes, is Janus-like, favouring autonomy and reification and yet also – through the tuning-in afforded by its inner motion – enabling transformations in the spaces of, and boundaries between, public and private experience.

The idea expounded earlier in this Introduction that the space of musical performance is one of intimate socialities, socialities that may be transformative of both subjectivity and social identity, is central not only to Cook's contribution but to the two following chapters. Drawing on ethnographic research among aboriginal people in the city of Winnipeg in Manitoba, Canada, Byron Dueck focuses on their attendance at two kinds of music venues, core elements of aboriginal public culture: 'wet' or drinking establishments, and 'dry' gatherings where alcohol is banned and which are also spaces of Christian worship. Varieties of country music prevail in both arenas, musical styles that 'allow Native musicians to speak about their social peripherality' (p. 240). Dueck notes that these clubs, bars and rooms exist at the intersection of two kinds of sociality: on the one hand, the intimate socialities constituted by face-to-face socio-musical

---

[82] See, for example, Etherington 2007 and Beckles Willson 2009.

interactions; on the other hand, forms of imagined community or 'stranger' publics (Warner 2002). Through music performances and their circulation as radio broadcasts, aboriginal music venues, the musicians who perform in them and their clientele build an aboriginal public culture embodied in common musical, cultural, social and moral practices and codes. But this aboriginal public culture is itself encompassed and monitored by a national public culture that has often condemned indigenous sociability – in particular, for the destructive repercussions of widespread alcohol abuse. It is against the backdrop of a moralising national public discourse that aboriginal musicking in wet venues is understood as a 'flawed form of civility', a perspective internalised by indigenous Manitobans. Citing Michael Herzfeld's (1997) concept of cultural intimacy, Dueck notes that performances at wet venues become sites of 'rueful recognition' among aboriginal people that the dominant culture perceives their lifeways as problematic.

In light of the 'sharp and morally freighted divisions between wet and dry events' for aboriginal Manitobans (p. 251), Dueck uncovers surprising aspects of these apparently opposed spaces of aboriginal sociality. For it proves to be difficult, in reality, to draw distinctions between dry and wet, sacred and secular musico-social occasions. Artists and repertoires, harmonic, melodic and formal languages cross easily between them, muddying the apparently inviolable social and moral boundaries. The soundscape is in fact a common one, although in performance musicians may make reference to the 'other' side of aboriginal culture through humour, parody, playful transgression and so on. The common soundscape is made possible, Dueck explains, by country music's mass-mediated ubiquity and in particular by the commonplace nature of its musical tropes, which themselves afford intimate musical publics – in the sense that aboriginal strangers can and do come together and play and sing for hours on end, fluently and without preparation. But in addition, the shared musical language and the migration of musicians between genres and spaces allows artists 'to be both sinners and saints, lyrically and indeed biographically', as well as enabling 'sounds, lyrics and public personas [to] have multiple, mutually enriching sacred and secular associations' (p. 254). Country music therefore engenders spaces of conviviality in which are enacted forms of conciliation that traverse what is otherwise deeply and painfully polarised. In effect, the intimate, rueful socialities and soundscapes of country music sessions appear to perform the redemptive work of producing a relatively undamaged and unified aboriginal (musical) public.

## Part IV: Music and sound: torture, healing and love

Drawing on an ethnographic study of community music therapy in a mental health centre (BRIGHT), Tia DeNora's chapter also concerns the potential identity effects of musical performance – in this case transformations in individual subjectivities. With reference to the music therapy clients' 'creation and negotiation of shared musical-aesthetic space' (p. 259), and taking her cue from Erving Goffman's *Asylums* (1968 (1961)), DeNora examines how, through musical performance and the solidarities and socialities thereby generated, and by halting but continuous steps, a transfiguration of the clients' identities can be effected: from illness to well-being. Asylum, she suggests, should be conceptualised as those 'situations, moments or environments which, albeit fleetingly, permit individuals to flourish, to have respite from a troubling world and to have space … that can be appropriated for self-development … [in part through forging] connections to others' (p. 262). The BRIGHT music therapy sessions, she proposes, proffer 'temporary "asylums"' of this kind. 'Musical activity, to the extent that it confronts individuals as a medium that stands outside of but as a resource for the self, offers a means for creating selves and collective identities. In this way it facilitates individuals' progression along what Goffman … terms "moral careers"' (p. 262). In the therapy sessions, 'the elements of performance style … become proxies for identity, signs of embodied and tacit dispositions that shoot through and structure social action' (p. 264). Music making at BRIGHT therefore amounts to the performance both of a song and of a self – a self that is the cumulative and fragile outcome of repeated alliances between particular song repertoires, performance events and responsive reception.

Critically, the projection of self in BRIGHT musical performances – self as mediated through the adoption of the persona required by a particular repertoire – can catalyse and be harnessed to a desired shift in subjectivity and personal identity. DeNora conceives of this process as a path-making activity achieved by what she calls 'taking a stand' (p. 267). BRIGHT sessions are structured on the expectation that their clients will take a stand, a requirement for action that demands the mobilisation of publicly available musical materials to illuminate subjective or inner psychic space. Moreover the sessions require clients to 'pull themselves together' (p. 267) in public: for the duration of the session, and particularly for the duration of performance, this entails stepping outside the boundaries of the 'sick role' dictated by the standard therapeutic encounter and the culture of mental health institutions. In the space–time of the BRIGHT sessions, and in the pathways forged over time between the sessions, DeNora suggests, individuals' capacity to navigate but also to enhance and extend the socio-musical topology that they inhabit furnishes them with wider resources that can also be mobilised for health. The music therapy sessions offer a site in which clients garner musical and cultural resources, and are thereby enabled cumulatively to negotiate the passage from 'illness-identities' and social isolation to 'health-identities' and social connection. Through the example of BRIGHT, DeNora shows how the space of musical performance can also be a space of psycho-social healing. Music, she contends, can be a powerful medium for psychological and social change.

If DeNora offers a revelation of music's potential to (re)construct subjectivity, the next chapter charts the obverse; indeed, the contrast between the two chapters issues a shock effect to readers and a radical conceptual challenge. On the basis of dialogues with four individuals who experienced imprisonment by American authorities in recent years as a consequence of the 'global war on terror', Suzanne Cusick analyses their subjection by loud (Western) music and other highly disturbing manipulations of the sonic environment: a practice of 'harsh interrogation'. Through the experiences of the four men, Cusick draws a harrowing portrait of the variety of ways in which loud music and noise, as well as ubiquitous acoustical surveillance, were employed to effect nothing less than the destruction of the prisoners' subjectivities. She draws on recent scholarship on Anglophone security forces which unearthed evidence that these practices form part of a larger pattern of interrogation techniques focused on sensory manipulation. Cusick's analysis of the nature of the interrogation and imprisonment techniques centres on two arguments. The first is that such extreme manipulations of the acoustic environment achieve their intended results through the disruption of 'ordinary relationality'. Cusick places this relationality at the core of an account of human subjectivity in which, through the reciprocities and dialogics of language and other human sonic and musical interactions, we 'turn space into place, and place into intelligible, navigable worlds' (p. 278). She connects this perspective in part to the Lacanian idea of subjects' interpellation through language into the symbolic order, and thence into social relations. But she links it also to fundamental tenets of liberal humanism: the ability to engage in sounding human relations and sounding reciprocity with others, she argues, 'is the premise for liberal claims both to the privacy of our individual thoughts (our right to remain silent) and to the universal right to share those thoughts freely in a public sphere' (p. 278).

A second argument running through Cusick's chapter is that the particular destructive power of the 'music programme' in interrogation stems from a physical property of the connection between sound/music and the body: that acoustical vibrations in the sonic environment always produce 'the somatic effect of sympathetic vibration' (p. 276). In this light, the prisoners subjected to 'acoustic harassment' could not prevent their very bones from vibrating to the sounds; as Cusick puts it, they involuntarily 'become, themselves, the characteristic sounds of their captors' (p. 276). This amounts to an ultimate violation since it denies the first relationality she has identified, itself dependent on the maintenance of difference, separation or spacing. Instead, subjectivity is effaced along with the victim's sense of the proper boundaries between corporeal and psychic interiority and exteriority; bombardment by loud music 'blasts away all sense of privacy, leaving in its place a feeling of paradoxically unprivate isolation' (p. 276). In this way music 'becomes not a metaphor for power, but power itself' (p. 288). Cusick holds this analysis up against Jean-Luc Nancy's post-liberal philosophy of human sociality, of 'being singular plural', which envisages 'an environment dense with … the "re-soundings" *by* all the vibrating entities in a space *of* all the vibrating entities in that space' (p. 278). Given evidence of the significance attributed by US authorities to acoustical interrogation in the 'war on terror', Cusick argues that the acoustemology of detention points to the 'dystopian political possibilities' immanent in Nancy's 'vibration-centred' metaphysics. Acoustical interrogation produces 'prison populations … who do not hear, vocalise and co-create with each other an acoustical environment characterised by relationships of reciprocity between self and other, individual and collective, private and public'. Rather, an extreme, sonically enforced isolation denies prisoners both 'the privacy-based right to silence and the public right to free speech' (pp. 290–291).

The final chapter, by Richard Middleton, might be understood as forging a philosophical path between the contributions by DeNora and Cusick. It also returns to the territory set out by Clarke – constructing an arc across the volume, while confounding any symmetry. Like Clarke, Middleton addresses the psychic affordances of popular music recording; but rather than in recording's virtual spatialities and perceptual dimensions, he locates them in the phonographic medium and expands his analysis to the psycho-social body. In a bravura exposition, he moves between an analysis at the outset of Rufus Wainwright's 2007 cover of Judy Garland's 1961 Carnegie Hall performance of the Gershwins' ballad 'How long has this been going on?' and, at the end, a reflection on the African American comedian, composer and singer Bert Williams's 1906 recording of the ballad–blues song 'Nobody', which Williams performed in blackface. Cutting a swathe through an old debate, that of the authenticity, fidelity or truth status of phonography, Middleton interweaves two core ideas. The first is that 'the antinomy between the longing for "authenticity" and its Derridean deferral structures modern thought as a whole' (p. 296), and he takes phonography and the repeated deferrals enacted by the 'cover' to epitomise this antinomy. The second idea stems from Richard Sennett's (2002 (1977)) account of the decay of the public sphere and the elevation of psychic existence on to the public stage. The result is 'the reduction of the key lineaments of the social body ... to the dynamics of a purely private sphere, which at the same time are generalised as the only available building blocks of mass society' (p. 293). In this condition, 'private desires and traumas [are] performed out in public', while psychological qualities of personality, charisma and star quality are magnified, projected as a 'gigantic image of universal emotion' (p. 293), filling the public sphere.

Noting that Sennett says little about phonography's place in this history, Middleton affirms Barbara Engh's (1999) thesis that phonography, in its splitting of the human voice from embodied consciousness, which 'formerly had been thought to be so coterminous as to virtually define each other', amounts to 'an anthropological revolution in human history' (p. 294). It is the phonographic medium that favours the projection into the public sphere of the most intimate qualities of human life and love. Thus, of Wainwright's performance: 'Here is someone, shaken to the marrow by the most personal, intimate emotion, choosing to shout about it in public' (p. 292). And yet deferral and loss are always present: 'the moment of origin is definitively lost – indeed, in the modern studio recording regime, it may never have existed ... Despite the signs of live performance embedded within Wainwright's CD, these are symptoms of disavowal: we aren't there, we never were, and we don't even hear Wainwright; we hear the ghostly simulacrum offered by a machine... as recorded voice refuses the boundaries of any given body' (p. 294). Given the potential for deconstruction immanent in the intimate vocalisations transposed by popular music recordings into the public sphere, the fidelity or truth promised by phonography is, for Middleton, indeterminate, 'a utopian "as if"'. Phonography proffers an 'ethical *undecideability*' (p. 296) such that 'the question becomes: who speaks, to whom, from what bodily location and with what authority?' (p. 300). From a reading of 'Nobody' as part-blues – where blues offers a 'dystopian treatment of love, which, however, always stands metonymically for ... the trope of *fraternity*'(p. 307) – Middleton concludes with an affirmative reading of Nancy. Such recordings, he argues, have the potential to invoke a 'community of those without a community' (Bataille), one that is akin to Nancy's 'being-with', in which singularity and plurality always imply each other (pp. 309–10).

The contributions to this book, as the final section makes dramatically clear, cannot resolve long-standing and often polarised debates over the creative or destructive social and political entailments of the evolving transformations of musical and sonic experience. Rather, they insist on complexity by putting in dialogue new analytical perspectives on the relations between music and sound, space and time, subjectivity and sociality, opening up the terms of debate and unsettling any complacent closure. If this dynamic six-term constellation, introduced earlier, might be thought to be at risk of reifying its component dualisms, it is the mutual mediation between the six terms that is constantly at stake and interrogated in the chapters that follow. With the addition of technological mediation, it has been necessary to coin an ungainly epithet – musico- or sonic–social–technological assemblages – to indicate the multiple, non-linear vectors of mediation at work in the material presented. The chapters provide evidence as to the astonishing array of transformations of public and private experience, as well as the sonic and musical agencies animating them and the heterogeneous forms of sociality and subjectivity enlivened by them. Moreover, the volume expands the critical framework in which these changes are understood, as well as the analysis of their social, cultural and historical conditions. If this framework and the ideas and material reported in this book can be more than an exercise in analytical encompassment by sparking recognition among practitioners of the arts of music and sound – perhaps prompting experiments with the terms it sets in motion, stimulating new and inventive directions – then it will have contributed to another welcome and ongoing development: destabilising the separation of academic research from creative practice in the rich and fertile borderlands between music, sound, space and the social.

# PART I

# The design of mediated music and sound

# 2 | Sound installation art: from spatial poetics to politics, aesthetics to ethics

GASCIA OUZOUNIAN

In a perceptive essay on Robin Minard, a Canadian artist who creates sound installations for public spaces such as subway corridors, the musicologist Helga de la Motte-Haber suggests that the development of sound installation art 'marks the 20th century'. She writes (1999: 41):

With [the] new availability of [electro-acoustic] sound material an art form congealed that overstepped traditional boundaries. The development of this art form marks the 20th century. Visual artists no longer had a monopoly on structuring space, just as musicians were no longer the only ones concerned with the aspect of temporal change. New forms of art arose that lay claim to simultaneous existence in space and time. Located beyond the realms of the traditional art world, installations created a new consciousness of our perception of reality. Here, the public was also granted a new authority.

The emergence of sound installation art in the second half of the twentieth century reflects fundamental shifts within multiple arenas: conceptions of space and space–time; the ascendancy of site within the aural imagination; the extension of music and sonic arts into expanded sculptural and architectural models; and the role of the public in relation to aesthetic experience. Perhaps owing to its liminal position between more established disciplines, however, sound installation art remains under-recognised within historical accounts of twentieth-century art and music, even as it marks this history through such shifts, extensions and ruptures.[1]

Parts of this chapter are adapted from my Ph.D. dissertation, *Sound Art and Spatial Practices: Situating Sound Installation Art Since 1958* (University of California, San Diego, 2008). I am grateful to my dissertation advisers George Lewis, Jann Pasler and Anthony Davis for their guidance during the early stages of this research, and to Georgina Born for her guidance in developing the current work.

[1] Studies by Nyman 1974, Lander and Lexier 1990, Kahn and Whitehead 1992, Augaitis and Lander 1994, Wishart 1996 (1985), Kahn 1999, Schulz 2002a, Drobnick 2004, LaBelle 2004; 2006; 2010, Licht 2007, Kim-Cohen 2009 and Voegelin 2010 have made significant contributions to the historical and theoretical understanding of sound art. Much of the current literature on this subject remains focused on composition, recording, transmission and performance practices, however, with installation practices receiving less attention by historians and critics. Writings by artists, exhibition catalogues and artist monographs are an important resource, and make up the bulk of the literature on sound installation art.

This chapter begins by tracing a genealogy of early sound installation art, examining its precursors in 1950s electro-acoustic spatial music composition, and its inception within emerging interdisciplinary models in the 1960s and 1970s. Here, examples are chosen that highlight evolving concepts of space and spatiality and propose new modes of audience interaction. This previews a discussion of two contemporary artists whose sound installations and site-specific sound works place new pressures on constructs such as 'space', 'site' and 'public'. The first of these, the Finnish sound artist Heidi Fast, creates works that employ the public voice in enacting new modes of community within shared urban environments. My second example, Rebecca Belmore, engages what Lucy R. Lippard (1997: 19) has described as 'an activist art practice that raises consciousness about land, history, culture, and place [and serves] as a catalyst for social change'. Belmore's 1991 sound installation *Ayumee-aawach Oomama-mowan: Speaking to Their Mother* raises critical questions about the potential of site-specific sound to reorder dominant political narratives and re-situate political discourse within marginalised spaces.

Sound installation art, what Brandon LaBelle (2004: 7) has described as work in which 'sound [is positioned] in relation to a spatial situation, whether that be found or constructed, actualised or imagined', has undoubtedly recovered and reoriented the sonic–spatial imagination. What is in doubt is whether or not this imagination is critically located or able to engage with a public in meaningful ways. My claim is that it can, when it is founded upon conceptions of space that take into account not only physical geographies, but social and political geographies as well. When space is understood not in abstract or absolute terms, but as socially and politically constituted, a spatial sound practice can emerge not only as a poetics, but as a politics, not only as an aesthetics, but as an ethics. Such a critical spatial sonic practice does not merely 'happen in' space, but is poised radically to transform the very terms of its constitution.

## Music projected into space

Audiences at a sound-and-light spectacle at the 1958 Brussels World Fair, where the predominant theme was nuclear disarmament, were overcome by the feeling that they were being bombarded by sound. Electronic whines, human shrieks, moans and sirens assaulted them from every point inside a fantastical building whose walls were lined with hundreds of loudspeakers. Edgard Varèse, the composer of this unearthly music, claimed that for the first time in his life, he could 'literally hear [his] music projected into space!' (Strawn 1978: 141). Someone in the audience described the experience as a 'modern nightmare' (Trieb 1996: 217).

*Poème électronique*, the name given to this eight-minute-long electro-acoustic assault, was the musical component of a multimedia work conceived by the architect Le Corbusier for the Philips Corporation. This work combined architecture, film, hanging sculptures, automated lighting schemes and spatial music in telling a 'story of all humankind' that depicted the evolution of human societies from prehistoric to modern times. The music was recorded onto multi-track tape and diffused via an eleven-channel sound system to an estimated three to four hundred loudspeakers along nine 'sound routes' (see Trieb 1996). For Varèse, this work represented the culmination of a lifelong pursuit to add a 'fourth dimension' to music: the spatial projection of sound. He saw this spatial dimension as liberating Western music from its stationary perspectives, and envisioned its coming-into-being in singularly grandiose terms: as a 'journey into space' (Varèse 2004 (1936): 18).

The journey, however wondrous, was not without its detractors. One critic suggested that *Poème électronique* was sending 'lethal beams of sound' to unassuming fairgoers (Cabrera 1994: 80). Another wrote: 'the intense spine-tingling reverberations overwhelm you as the sound impinges on you from all directions at once, only to numb you in turn with extremely high shrieking, whistling eerie echoes' (Gernsback 1958: 47). The transcendent potential of the immersive listening experience figured in this work, however, was not completely lost. A third critic wrote of *Poème électronique* that 'one no longer hears the sounds, one finds oneself literally in the heart of the sound source. One does not listen to the sound, one lives it' (Ouellette 1968: 201–2).

Despite its mixed reception, *Poème électronique* was perhaps the most ambitious of post-war spatial music projects, which included the efforts of composers working within burgeoning *musique concrète*, Elektronische Musik and experimental electronic music traditions. Watershed moments in this early history include Pierre Schaeffer and Pierre Henri's *Symphonie pour un homme seul* (1950), which made use of the *pupitre d'espace* in routing monophonic *objets sonores* between five loudspeakers positioned around and above listeners;[2] Karlheinz Stockhausen's *Gesang der Jünglinge*

---

[2] Pierre Schaeffer's assistant Jacques Poullin developed the *pupitre d'espace* (also called *potentiometre d'espace*) to route sound from five-track tape to five loudspeakers. Four tracks were assigned predetermined routes, while that belonging to the fifth track was improvised by a performer who manipulated the device live in concert.

(1955–6), which serialised the spatial parameters of a five-channel tape piece using serial operations to determine the location and movement of sounds (Fishman-Johnson 1993–4: 16–17);[3] and the works of composers associated with the Music for Magnetic Tape Project – John Cage, Earle Brown, Morton Feldman, David Tudor and Christian Wolff – who between 1952 and 1954 experimented with octophonic tape composition. For Cage, space represented another frontier in musical indeterminacy. He wrote, '[Sounds] enter the time–space centred within themselves, unimpeded by service to any abstraction, their 360 degrees of circumference free for an infinite play of interpenetrations' (Cage 1961: 59).

In conjunction with developing new sound spatialisation technologies, the Western musical avant-garde thus developed a new vocabulary of space in relation to musical forms and processes during the post-war period. This poetics was firmly grounded within Euclidean and Cartesian models of space, concerned with such elements as: the location of sound objects within three-dimensional space; the movement of sounds along sound routes or *trajectoires sonores*; the segmentation of (absolute) space for the purposes of serialisation; and the idea of time–space as an empty container wherein sounds can develop.

Here, the listening public was not necessarily imagined in active or productive terms, but more typically as receivers of spatial music, in line with conventional models of concert listening. However, the use of space as a compositional parameter drew attention to the fact that every listener has a unique experience of a given work depending on his or her position in the auditorium, and that a work cannot be fully appreciated outside of the particular, contingent situations of hearing. This awareness compelled compositional methodologies that accounted for many individual listeners instead of a single 'body' of listeners. The composer Henry Brant alluded to this in a 1955 article for the *American Composers Alliance Bulletin*:

Spatial music must be conceived in accordance with the premise that there is no one optimum position in the hall for each listener … Spatial music must be written in such a way that the composer is able to accept whatever he hears as a listener, regardless of his position in the hall. (Brant 1955 cited in Brant 1967: 224)

Such an approach was contrary to dominant practices and discourses in electronic and computer music of the 1970s and 1980s, which considered

---

[3] According to Fishman-Johnson, Stockhausen 'devised a detailed spatial plan, which plotted out from what side of the hall the sound would come, how many loudspeakers would play at once, how sound would rotate, and if sound would travel or stay still' (Fishman-Johnson 1993–4: 16–17).

the concert hall as a single 'aggregate' space of experience (in the Euclidean sense of space). Similarly, although notions of public participation or audience interaction were not yet common in Western art music of the 1950s, for some composers the spatial distribution of sounds as a key compositional device could require them to account for the multiplicity of listening perspectives. This was an important step towards locating the value of a musical work not only within the abstracted medium of the score, but in the actual, experiential dimensions of listening.

## Fluxed forms

The experimental thrust of the 1960s provided fertile ground for extended spatial imaginings within music; it coincided with the extension of music into intermedial forms that invited new relationships with audiences, especially the repositioning of audiences as co-creators of music. Cage's course on Experimental Composition at the New School for Social Research in 1958–1959 brought together future Fluxus luminaries – George Brecht, Dick Higgins, Allan Kaprow, Toshi Ichiyanagi and others – who proposed audience-interactive works that typically embraced an anti-elitist, everyday aesthetic. Minimalist Event scores transmitted instructions that could be realised by non-trained performers using commonplace materials, and often included audience participation in their scope:[4]

*Concerto for Audience by Audience*

The audience is invited to come to the stage, take instruments that are provided to them, sit on the orchestra seats and play for 3 minutes. If the audience does not respond to the invitation, instruments should be distributed to them. (Ben Vautier, 1965)

*Fluxus Instant Theater*

Rescore Fluxus events for performance by the audience. A conductor may conduct the audience-performers. (Ken Friedman, 1966)

In breaking down composer–performer–audience hierarchies Fluxus works also brought external, 'unwanted' sounds into the rarefied spaces of the concert hall. The instructions for Richard Maxfield's *Mechanical Fluxconcert*, for example, indicated that microphones should be placed 'in the street, outside windows or hidden among audience and sounds are amplified to

---

[4] These Event scores are reprinted in Friedman 1990.

the audience via public address system'. Thus, the sounds of the every-day environment, including sounds made by an 'everyday public', spilled into the auditorium, while commonplace activities with everyday objects carried out by non-specialist performers replaced specialised techniques, instruments and musicians as the tools for musical production.

Artists associated with Fluxus also spearheaded the conceptual turn of art and music in the 1960s, which ushered in extended concepts of space and spatiality. Yoko Ono's *Tape Piece II: Room Piece* from 1963, for example, stands a universe apart from tape music of the previous decade. Its score reads:

*Tape Piece II*
*Room Piece*
Take the sound of the room breathing.
1. at dawn
2. in the morning
3. in the afternoon
4. in the evening
5. before dawn
Bottle the smell of the room of that particular hour as well.

Here, Ono imagines a room as a living, 'breathing' element, the subject and source of the musical work rather than merely its context or setting. She asks the performer to listen to the room, not in order to ascertain its acoustic properties, but to hear (and capture) its breath, to document its existence as it unfolds over the course of a day. *Tape Piece II: Room Piece* proposes that space is not a static, absolute or empty construction, but that it evolves and has a 'voice' that also changes over time; the focus in this 'tape piece' shifts from the evolution of sounds inside a space to the evolution of the space itself.

The composer La Monte Young, who was associated with Fluxus in its early stages and who curated concerts of experimental music at Ono's loft during this period, similarly conceived of the *Dream House* (1962–ongoing) as having the potential to become a 'living organism with a life and tradition of its own' (Young and Zazeela 2000 (1968)). In its earliest incarnations the *Dream House* was a space wherein musicians (notably the Theatre of Eternal Music) could play continuously for extended periods of time. In its current manifestation it is presented as 'a time installation measured by a setting of continuous frequencies in sound and light' (see Young and Zazeela 2010). This environment is made up, in part, of magenta-coloured lights and hanging mobiles by the artist Marian Zazeela, as well as a dense, synthesised drone composed of multiple sets of frequency intervals (all sine waves). According to one reviewer (Farneth 1996):

Each sine wave vibrates in different parts of the room, so that the chord you hear changes as you move through the room. I like to sit on the floor in modified lotus position, tilting my head slowly back and forth, from side to side, to create my own melodies and sound textures. The visitor with an acute ear can actually 'play' the room like an instrument: explore the sound close to the wall, close to the floor, in the corners, or just standing still. Or lie on the floor and allow the sound to float you to heaven, slide you into hell, or transport you wherever you want to go.

Although the aural components of *Dream House* never vary, every turn inside the room results in a profoundly dislocating shift in the listener's perception of sound and space owing to the action of the room upon an otherwise 'static' sound. Again, the room is not an afterthought but a critical element of the composition, the source and place of the 'life' of the work.

## Sound is sculpture

The influence of Fluxus upon emerging traditions of Performance Art and Conceptual Art is well known (see Lippard 1973; Friedman 1998; Higgins 2002); its footprints can also be found in the work of 1970s Bay Area artists whose work challenged traditional dichotomies between performance and sculpture. From December 1979 to February 1980 the San Francisco Museum of Modern Art hosted one of the first major exhibitions in the United States in which works with sound were prominently displayed or, rather, documented. *Space/Time/Sound: Conceptual Art in the San Francisco Bay Area, the 1970s* collected the work of twenty-one prominent Bay Area artists, tying together a number of practices under the common banner of conceptualism: site-specific installation, sculpture, performance and events. This was a daunting task, considering that most of these works no longer existed by the time of the exhibit's unveiling.

In her introduction to the exhibit catalogue, the curator Suzanne Foley (1981: 1) wrote that the SF MOMA 'had decided to include works of a temporal and ephemeral nature, [considering them to be] worthy of recognition'. Paradoxically, many of the works that Foley felt warranted this disclaimer had developed within sculpture traditions, although they closely resembled Fluxus performance. Some sculptures were particularly ephemeral, consisting of actions so incidental or brief that they would hardly warrant being framed as art under typical circumstances, much less as sculpture. In

Tom Marioni's 1969 *One Second Sculpture*, for example, the artist released a tightly wound piece of measuring tape into the air. The tape made a sound as it unfolded and landed on the ground in a straight line.

Other temporal sculptures lasted much longer, actions turned into ritual through their continuous repetition or extended duration. In his 1972 *Action for a Tower Room*, Marioni's frequent collaborator Terry Fox played the tamboura for six hours a day on three consecutive days, 'filling the space of a small, square, stone room at the top of a tower reached by winding stairs with a continuous, circular sound' (see Fox 1972). Fox claimed that the 'spatial sound' produced through his actions influenced the movement of a candle flame and made vibrations in still water.

When Foley gathered such works for *Space/Time/Sound*, her role shifted somewhat from curator to archivist since most of these works could only be shown through their residual documentation. A common criticism levelled at the exhibit was that there was 'no art there'. Charles Shore's review of the exhibit for the *Oakland Tribune*, for example, took issue with 'art which happens and then disappears. Except for its documentation' (Shore 1980: G32).

The most pertinent historical link between these Bay Area artists and Fluxus is perhaps Joseph Beuys, who participated in the proto-Fluxus concert *Neo Dada in Der Musik* in Dusseldorf in 1962, and who subsequently abandoned more traditional forms of sculpture in favour of ritualistic performances, *Aktionen*, many of which took shape as sound works. In a 1963 performance at the Galerie Parnass in Wuppertal, Beuys 'played the piano all over – not just the keys – with many pairs of old shoes until it disintegrated'. He claimed that his intention 'was neither destructive nor nihilistic. "Heal like with like" – *similia similibus curantur* – in the homeopathic sense. The main intention was to indicate a new beginning, an enlarged understanding of every traditional form of art' (Beuys 1990).

In 1967 Beuys co-founded the German Student Party, which was renamed Fluxus Zone West the following year. Like Cage, Beuys attracted an international group of students and artists to Dusseldorf, where he taught sculpture at the Kunstakademie. Fox learned of Beuys's activities through Fluxus publications and travelled to Dusseldorf in 1970. In David Ross's account (1992: 10), 'much of Beuys's work, like Fox's, had to do with energy transfer through the artist's ritual interaction with materials. Fox learned from Beuys that the residue of a ritual action could retain the aura of the event'. Upon Fox's arrival in Dusseldorf, the two artists collaborated on an impromptu work, *Isolation Unit* (4 October 1970), in a storage room at the Kunstakademie. As Fox (1982: 30) tells it, they worked 'simultaneously, although independently, but frequently came together, particularly in relation to sound'. Over the course of six hours, the two used acoustic energy to 'connect' found objects:

Beuys, clothed in a hat and felt suit, wandered around the room with a dead mouse in his hand. Later he spun the mouse on the spool of a tape recorder and used a silver spoon to eat a passion fruit, whose seeds he dropped with a bright, resounding tone into a silver bowl between his feet. Along with an electric light bulb, a candle, and a cross … Fox had two metal pipes of different lengths, which he banged against the floor and against each other, producing bell-like, pulsing sounds. He also knocked the pipes against the four panes of a dismantled window unit; by observing the resulting resonances, he found acoustically dead spots in the glass. Then, one after the other, he smashed the panes. Now he could reach through the window, grasp the candle behind it, and place it in the middle of the room. He tried to influence an open candle flame with the sound waves from the pipes. (Osterwold 1998: 17)

Through his interactions with Beuys, Fox came to understand his actions as 'plastic works that, extended in the temporal dimension, sculpturally form a situation and charge a space with energy and emotion in such a way that the visitors perceive its qualities as changed' (Osterwold 1998: 17). In Fox's performances, sounds are not considered musical but sculptural: tools with which to connect objects and transform spaces. Fox proposed that 'sound is sculpture', and stressed that his performances were geared towards discovering 'the limitless sculptural possibilities of sound' (Osterwold 1998: 18–19).

## Sounds placed in space

The disciplinary transgressions proposed by Fluxus artists and conceptual artists working within expanded models of sculpture and performance were critical to the emergence of sound installation art, an intermedial art form that began to develop between music, sculpture, architecture and other disciplines from the late 1960s.

In 1967 an American percussionist named Max Neuhaus installed a series of radio transistors along the side of a non-descript road in Buffalo, New York. People who drove on this road found themselves privy to a rich combination of sine tones that emanated from their car radios for no apparent reason. The amplitude, frequency and duration of these tones changed according to weather conditions, the time of day and other environmental factors. In describing this work, which he called *Drive-in Music*, Neuhaus coined the term 'sound installation', distinguishing the genre from music by indicating that in sound installations, sounds are 'placed in space rather than in time' (des Jardins 1994: 130).

Neuhaus's sound installations partly grew out of his experiences as a professional musician specialising in contemporary music:

> As a percussionist I had been directly involved in the gradual insertion of everyday sound into the concert hall, from [Luigi] Russolo through Varèse and finally to Cage who brought live street sounds directly into the hall. I saw these activities as a way of giving aesthetic credence to these sounds – something I was all for – but I began to question the effectiveness of the method. Most members of the audience seemed more impressed with the scandal than the sounds, and few were able to carry the experience over to a new perspective on the sounds of their daily lives.

In attempting to merge the newly adopted concert aesthetic of 'real-world' sounds with listeners' everyday experiences of these sounds, Neuhaus carried out a series of public listening walks between 1966 and 1976, which he called *LISTEN*. Audiences would arrive at a designated location, and Neuhaus would stamp the word 'LISTEN' on their hands and lead them outdoors to explore their everyday aural environments. Neuhaus explains that his interest in these walks was to 'refocus attention on sounds that we live with every day. I felt that perhaps the way to do this was not to bring the sounds in but to take the people out' (Neuhaus and Loock 1990).

Through these listening exercises Neuhaus hoped permanently to alter listeners' relationships to their everyday environments, by introducing them to a focused mode of listening that they could integrate into their daily lives. Neuhaus characterises his mode of listening during these walks as being so 'intense' that it transformed other listeners' own habits of hearing; he also imagined that this act of focused listening would result in hearing 'sound' rather than 'noise' and, concomitantly, transform a meaningless 'space' into a meaningful 'place'.

Neuhaus's listening walks emerged in parallel with, and are in some ways reminiscent of, similar practices associated with soundscape studies as proposed by R. Murray Schafer and others in the context of the World Soundscape Project. However, Neuhaus's concerns were primarily aesthetic, while the WSP emerged out of ecological concerns to do with documenting aural environments, raising awareness about noise pollution and preserving acoustic ecologies; the WSP concerns only later developed into a compositional practice (Schafer 1994 (1977)).

Neuhaus's sound installations grew out of his 'everyday listening' projects, which he extended into more permanent forms by installing sound works in everyday environments, often as anonymous interventions in public spaces. In his best known work, *Times Square* (1977–92; 2002–ongoing), synthesisers housed in a chamber beneath a subway grater on a traffic island in Manhattan's Times Square produce a continuously evolving, multi-frequency drone.[5] There is nothing to announce the work; instead, Neuhaus hopes that listeners will accidentally discover it, and through their discovery find a new point of connection to a potentially impersonal cityscape.

Neuhaus explains that his first sound installations were created for a public at large: 'They were about taking myself out of the confined public of contemporary music and moving to a broader public, [I had] a deep belief that I could deal in a complex way with people in their everyday lives' (Neuhaus and Loock 1990: 58–9). Neuhaus thus reimagines the listening public as 'anyone who happens to listen' rather than those who seek out (and gain access to) specialised listening experiences. This has aesthetic consequences for Neuhaus, who must conceivably create meaningful listening experiences for an audience that is not limited to an elite or pre-selected group with predictable or aligned expectations; it also has consequences in terms of public engagement, since listeners must be attuned to their aural environments in order to notice or appreciate the work.

## Listening bodies, social spaces

Since the late 1960s sound installation artists have increasingly incorporated listeners into the scope of a work. Some have even created works in which the listening body becomes the 'site' of a sound installation or sculpture. In Laurie Anderson's *Handphone Table* (1978), for example, sound is conducted through a listener's elbows, transmitting a barely audible recording directly into the body. Artists such as Maryanne Amacher and Bernhard Leitner have similarly created sound installations that position the body as a resonant space, inviting a 'full-bodied hearing' that challenges neutral or disembodied modes of listening (see McCartney 2004). Some of Amacher's installations produce what she calls a 'third-ear music', in which 'ears act as instruments and emit sounds as well as receive them' (Amacher 1999):

[My audiences] discover music streaming out from their head, popping out of their ears, growing inside of them and growing out of them, meeting and converging

---

[5] See www.diacenter.org/sites/main/55 (last accessed 18 August 2012).

with the tones in the room … Tones dance in the immediate space of their body, around them like a sonic wrap, cascade inside ears, and out to space in front of their eyes, mixing and converging with the sound in the room.

The Austrian architect and sound artist Bernhard Leitner imagines that the 'boundaries of sound spaces can [go] through the body' and that 'space can extend into the body' (Schulz 2002b: 82). Leitner began investigations into 'body-space' and 'sound-space' relationships in the late 1960s, conceiving of their merger as an 'acoustic-haptic' space:

In October 1968, I laid down the base for my Sound-Space work: Sound itself was to be understood as building material, as architectural, sculptural, form-producing material – like stone, plaster, wood. The invention of spaces with sound, formerly inconceivable as a readily available material, was the central artistic motive. Sound and its movement define space. A new type of acoustic-haptic space. (Leitner, as cited in Ouzounian 2008: 187)

In Leitner's 1976 *Sound Chair* a listener rests on a reclining chair fashioned with speakers that project sound to different points along the body; de la Motte-Haber has commented of this work that 'space seems to be a movement that emanates from your own body, or flows through it' (de la Motte-Haber 1998). Leitner's 2003 CD *Kopfraüme (Headscapes)* presents sound sculptures (heard through headphones) that appear to form inside the space of the listener's head, as though that space was an empty geometrical volume. For Leitner, 'entirely new concepts of space open up through extended hearing, through bodily hearing' (Schulz 2002b: 82), a comment that illustrates the idea that spatialities and modes of perception are inextricably tied. In the case of body-based sound installations, not only are new modes of listening and new spatialities imagined, but the location of the work also shifts to the individual listener herself, since these works cannot function outside a listener's particular engagement with them.

This model of body-as-site is an important step towards critical models that account for the listening body as a productive element of space, where space is understood not only as a physical quantity but also as a production that includes the body and social action within its scope. Until the 1970s the term 'space' was used almost exclusively in order to describe Cartesian and Euclidean space. With *La production de l'espace* (1991 (1974)), the French Marxist philosopher Henri Lefebvre helped to launch a notion of space as a social construction. He wrote (1991 (1974): 2):

Not so many years ago, the word 'space' had a strictly geometrical meaning: the idea it evoked was simply that of an empty area. In scholarly use it was generally accompanied by some such epithet as Euclidean, isotropic, or infinite, and the general feeling was that the concept of space was ultimately a mathematical one. To speak of 'social space', therefore, would have sounded strange.

Lefebvre outlined a 'conceptual triad' underlying the production of space: *spatial practice*, 'which embraces production and reproduction, and the particular locations and spatial sets characteristic of each social formation'; *representations of space*, 'tied to relations of production and to the "order" which those relations impose'; and *representational space*, 'embodying complex symbolisms, sometimes coded, sometimes not, linked to the clandestine or underground side of social life, as also to art' (Lefebvre 1991 (1974): 33). Lefebvre famously encouraged clandestine spatial practices such as squatting and illegal immigration, practices that support the 'right to space' of all people regardless of social status. Perhaps most critically, Lefebvre's writing embraced the idea that spatial practices can be constructed and deconstructed, reflected upon and resisted through social action, and that artistic practices could also operate within this model.

## Critical spatial practices

Many contemporary discourses on 'spatial sound', including those common in computer music, continue to privilege Euclidean and Cartesian conceptions of space and are focused upon the technical aspects of locating sound within three-dimensional space. However, a number of sound installation artists have challenged this model, inviting audiences to consider Lefebvre's proposition that space is a social product and not an absolute or hegemonic quantity that exists outside of material reality or lived experience.

In developing critical spatial practices, sound artists have imagined new interactions with their publics, creating works for specific audiences who have particular relationships with, or interests in, the places in which these works reside. Such works are not only site-specific in terms of their physical or geographical location; they are also specific to the publics who engage and interact with them, and are intended for a 'localised public' whose social composition is as central to the work as any other compositional element.

The Finnish artist Heidi Fast, for example, has created several 'social sound sculptures' for communities in different parts of Helsinki.[6] In *A Nightsong Action* (2006) she invited the residents of apartment buildings surrounding Hesperia Park, a sprawling urban park, to join her in a 'vocal course'

---

[6] An in-depth reading of the work of Heidi Fast appears in Ouzounian 2009.

through the park. Her hand-delivered letters of invitation instructed residents to meet her at a specified time and place and walk with her through the park while making vocal sounds, in order to 'diversify human voice in our common, public urban space' (Fast 2006):

I will walk along Hesperia Park and sing a long and even tone. Answer me with your own voice, from your window or balcony (or your neighbour's) when you hear my voice, or come down to the street and sing with me! Sing with your voice until you no longer hear the others, or continue for as long as you wish.

The point of *A Nightsong Action* is not to strive for the clarity or beauty of the voice. You can (and should, if you wish) join it with very hoarse or clear singing, with whispers or shouts that 'become' from your throat.

Approximately a dozen people participated in the walk, while others joined in with vocalisations from their apartment windows or simply watched. For Fast this work did not have any 'special meaning or function … it was an un-function in a way'; she recalls that participants were at times self-conscious in that the action 'did not involve singing collective songs, but just making [meaningless sounds]'.[7] The work's 'un-functionality' was part of its critical perspective, in that it offered a radical view of how collective song might emerge within a public forum. The sounds of *A Nightsong Action* were not the patriotic songs that are typically heard in public gatherings, songs that serve to further a dominant conception of national identity. Instead, they were non-linguistic sounds that were not necessarily coherent and could not be reduced to a single model of collective identity.

In another work from 2006, *Song of the Dwellings*, Fast invited the residents of an apartment building to vocalise with her while walking up and down the building's central staircase. About thirty people participated, including residents who opened the doors to their apartments during the event. In a way that recalls Neuhaus's *LISTEN* project, *Song of the Dwellings* invited audiences to form new relationships to familiar places through a renewed connection to sound. Fast's work extends Neuhaus's proposition by asking participants not only to listen to their everyday environments, but also to create sounds in and through them, an act that draws attention to the 'voices' of the places the participants inhabit and to their roles in constructing these voices (and by extension, places). Fast considers her work to be 'political', although in a way that entails only 'small displacements'. The use of sound is critical in this context:

---

[7] Interview with the author, unpublished, 2008.

The voice – or sound in general – is not divisible into parts that can be controlled or quantified. Sound is not easily delimited. This is political, even though it may not be visible. My essential goal is to establish small islets that deal with multiplying the power in us, or in a nonhuman world. That is, to resist the violent praxis in society through intensities other than strong or powerful resistances: to ruffle and round the edges between interior and exterior, to open up the in-between. (Fast 2007)

The Anishnabe Canadian artist Rebecca Belmore has similarly used sound and voice in articulating a critical spatial practice, one that presents alternative modes of social and political exchange within public forums. Much of Belmore's work, including her 1991 sound installation *Ayumee-aawach Oomama-mowan: Speaking to Their Mother*, holds particular weight for the Native Canadian communities who were its intended audience.

Belmore created *Ayumee-aawach Oomama-mowan* in response to the Oka Crisis, a much-publicised land dispute between the Canadian government and the Mohawk community at the Kanesatake settlement near Oka, Quebec. The stand-off, which lasted through the summer of 1990, was triggered by a bid by the town of Oka to develop a golf course over native burial and sacred grounds and the rejection of a land claim filed by the Mohawk community. Belmore's installation consisted of a giant, two-meter-wide megaphone that was designed to carry the voices of native speakers directly to the land; she claimed, 'Protest often falls upon deaf government ears, but the land has listened to the sound of our voices for thousands of years' (Lippard 1997: 15). Belmore describes the genesis of this work as follows:

During the summer of 1990, many protests were mounted in support of the Mohawk Nation of Kanesatake in their struggle to maintain their territory. This object was taken into many First Nations communities – reservations, rural, and urban. I was particularly interested in locating the Aboriginal voice on the land. Asking people to address the land directly was an attempt to hear political protest as poetic action. (Belmore 1991)

Belmore's project to 'locate the Aboriginal voice on the land' is striking in that it creates room for marginalised voices to emerge within a contested political sphere, and allows these voices to embody the tensions figured in the conflict itself, by engaging directly with the land. The 'audience' in this installation is not the typical one for political protest (i.e. the government), or even the communities that are invited to interact with it; it is the land itself, which, through the mere act of 'being spoken to', is reconstituted as a living entity and not an object that can be owned or occupied.

In one instance, Belmore installed *Ayumee-aawach Oomama-mowan* in a meadow in the Rocky Mountains, as part of the exhibition *Between Views* at the Banff Centre (an arts institution in Alberta, Canada). Lucy R. Lippard (1997) describes this exhibit in her excellent treatise on site-specific art, *The Lure of the Local: Senses of Place in a Multi-Centered Society*:

> For an exhibition about nature and tourism, Belmore organized an eclectic gathering of Native Canadians – leaders, writers, poets, social workers and activists – who spoke to their mother earth from an alpine meadow in the Rockies. The huge megaphone symbolized public address, carrying amplified Native voices far and wide. Self-determination and land rights were primary themes, but they were couched in the empowering language of celebration ... Mowhawk Elizabeth (Toby) Burning said through the megaphone: 'You are our reason for continuing our resistance against development, and standing up for our language and for our past, because we are you.' Belmore's work is a way of healing assimilation, her forced estrangement from her own culture. A place in culture is a place to speak from. (Lippard 1997: 15)

*Ayumee-aawach Oomama-mowan: Speaking to Their Mother* shifts the location of a public forum from the centres of power to remote areas, and as such reclaims the political worth of marginal (and marginalised) places. The installation draws attention to the uneven modes of exchange that determine who speaks, who listens and where; it shows that the place of political exchange is integral to that exchange, that the positions of political actors cannot be divorced from the 'place(s) from which they speak'.

The curator Jolene Rickard, who later included *Ayumee-aawach Oomama-mowan* in an exhibit at the Smithsonian's National Museum of the American Indian in Washington DC, wrote that she found it to be 'one of the most significant expressions of sovereignty beyond political boundaries' (Rickard 2006). I would support the idea that the very scope of 'political boundaries' is redrawn in Belmore's installation: not only is the place of politics multiplied and diversified, and the boundary between the powerful and the marginalised complicated, but the dimensions of political communication are no longer limited to the sense of language. Here, the sound of political speech is as important as meaning, as is the unique ability of sound to bypass dominant modes of political containment and confinement.

Charlotte Townsend-Gault has described Belmore's work as blurring the distinction between 'an aesthetics and ethics':

> Native artists in Canada over the past two or three decades have been expected to be embodiments of tradition, seers, perfect spiritual beings, and all-purpose spokespersons for the moral high-ground. This proved an untenable guide for reading

native art and the hermeneutics has moved on. Yet it is exactly the precariousness of their position, caused by the tangle of aestheticised politics and desire, which certain artists of native ancestry like Belmore ... contrive to make compelling ... [It] becomes evident that for her there is no sharp divide between aesthetics and ethics. (Townsend-Gault 2002)

The spatial practice that is embodied in Belmore's work is at once poetic and political, aesthetic and ethical, drawing upon marginalised social histories and voices in creating alternative expressions of place and public space.

## Conclusion

Sound installation artists have profoundly reconceptualised the meaning of 'spatial sound' and its ability to reflect multiple dimensions of social and political life. In the 1950s electronic spatial music projects were predominantly concerned with articulating sonic geometries within three-dimensional space: routing sound objects along Cartesian grids at different speeds and angles, positioning masses and planes of sound within Euclidean space. Since that time, myriad influences ranging from experimental music and conceptual art traditions to expanded forms of sculpture and architecture have contributed to what has become a critical sonic–spatial practice: one that is concerned not only with the 'composition' of acoustic space, but with the confluence of acoustic, political, social and public spaces.

As sound installation traditions move from articulating poetic to critical concerns, theoretical discourses must also reflect these shifts. Rather than investigate the location of sounds within three-dimensional space, our questions should extend towards critical realms: how are spaces constructed, socially and politically? How do spatially organised sound works reflect and resist these constructions? What is the role of the public in shaping these forms? In developing such critical perspectives, the sonic–spatial imagination is reoriented from absolute to experiential realms, from universal to particular ones, with social identities and political histories newly implicated in creating alternative spatial expressions and relationships to place in and through sound.

# 3 | Music, space and subjectivity

## Intro

Music theory, the aesthetics of music and the psychology of music have all tended to treat music as if it were a phenomenon radically separate from the rest of the auditory environment. But music is inextricably bound up with that wider auditory world, since it sounds within it, incorporates environmental sounds into its own material, and (with the development of recording, broadcast and listening technologies) takes on fluid relationships with the physical and social spaces that it occupies – from practical and normative to provocative and paradoxical. A powerful attribute of music, though relatively neglected until recently, is its capacity to specify space and motion – both real (the actual spaces in which performed music takes place) and virtual (the fictional spaces that it can seem to occupy or afford). This capacity is further intertwined with twentieth- and twenty-first-century developments in the ways in which music is distributed, delivered and technologically mediated: from massively social to intensely private means, and across a rapidly changing range of fixed and mobile technologies. Using principles of ecological perceptual theory, this chapter explores the ways in which sound and music specify various real and virtual spaces, types of motion, and senses of agency and subjectivity. After establishing some general principles for the perception of space in sound and music, a framework for the perceptual meaning of musical space is proposed, based on a combination of ecological theory and Lakoff and Johnson's conceptual metaphor theory. Three extracts of music are discussed, concluding with the track 'Deer Stop' from the album *Felt Mountain* by Goldfrapp, which demonstrates a number of perceptually salient transformations of virtual space, understood as the components of a psychic drama or narrative enacted across 'inner' and 'outer' spaces.

## Sound, music and the auditory environment

As has been widely discussed, music has generally been studied in abstracted and disembodied terms, as if it were a form of philosophy or writing. The consequences of this within musicology have been broadly debated, and there have been significant changes brought about by the influence of ethnomusicology, performance studies, popular musicology and the study of recordings. In the psychology of music the situation began to change with the publication of Albert Bregman's *Auditory Scene Analysis* in 1990, which tackled a variety of auditory phenomena – with music prominent among them – within a single perceptual framework that took sound and the auditory environment as the central topic. I have also (Clarke 1999; 2003; 2005) made the case for understanding supposedly abstract properties of music in terms of general perceptual (and more specifically auditory) principles, and it is arguably for those aspects of music that are least easily read from a musical score – timbre, texture, space – that this approach has most to offer. Expressed concisely, the argument is this: since a single auditory system is involved in our understanding of everyday sounds,[1] speech and music, it is inescapable that certain general auditory (or even more generally perceptual) functions play a role in all three domains. It seems, typically, to have been assumed that these more general functions are of little or no consequence for 'interesting' aspects of music perception – in part because the usual approach to the psychology of perception[2] is one that indeed seems to offer little scope for such a possibility. By contrast, ecological perceptual theory offers powerful ways to understand a variety of musical phenomena based on a radically different outlook: it takes the perceiver/environment relationship as central; understands perception in relation to action; rejects the dominant metaphor of internal representation and focuses instead on perceivers' acquired sensitivities to environmentally available information; and sees cultural systems as outgrowths from (and continuous with) natural opportunities. The most important thing for a perceiving organism is to know 'what is going on and what to do about it', encapsulated in the term 'affordance' coined by the psychologist James Gibson, and used to refer to the (action) opportunities of the environment in relation to the capacities of the perceiver.

Applying these broad principles to music brings a shift of emphasis away from abstraction and representation, and back to a careful and ecologically appropriate analysis of the information available to a perceiver. In a pair of papers, William Gaver (1993a, 1993b) took an important initiative in this

---

[1] Music cannot be distinguished from other kinds of sound in simply sonic terms, but I use the term 'everyday sound' to identify common or garden sounds (such as the sounds of cows and clocks and cars) heard in non-musical circumstances.

[2] A shorthand for this approach might be the information-processing or cognitivist paradigm (see Still and Costall 1991).

direction in relation to sound (and to a lesser extent music), providing the basis for an ecological acoustics that still remains to be properly developed. Gaver's central questions of 'what people hear' and 'how they hear it' can be transposed directly into the questions of space perception that are the concern of this chapter: what kinds of space do people hear in music, and how do they hear them? And rather than considering these questions as leading to cognitive issues of the *representation* of space, my aim is to explore them in more directly perceptual terms.

## Perceiving auditory space

A first step in understanding space in music in terms of general features of auditory perception is to consider the general principles by which listeners pick up auditory cues for space and movement from the environment. Because our visual system is so well adapted to spatial perception, it is easy to overlook how finely attuned to the perception of space the human auditory system also is. Human visual spatial acuity vastly exceeds auditory spatial acuity under optimal conditions (good lighting and no occlusion), but there are nonetheless plenty of circumstances in which we rely heavily on auditory space perception: in darkness, fog, dense smoke, forests, blizzard – and of course for blind or visually impaired people. So what are the auditory cues that enable people to pick up the position and movement of objects in space?

In broad terms, there is a good understanding of the psychoacoustics of human space perception (the relationship between the physical signal and the perceptual consequence), for instance as described by Brian Moore (2003). The localisation of sound sources can be reduced to the detection of distance and direction, perceived and expressed in terms of three dimensions of space in relation to an observer: left/right; in front/behind; up/down. Left/right is the most acute of the three, with listeners able to detect a shift in angular position of as little as one degree. The ability to do so stems directly from time and intensity differences between the acoustical signal as it reaches the two ears. In simple terms, a sound source to the left of an observer will give rise to a positive intensity difference in the left ear (due to the 'shadowing' effect of the head for the right ear), and the waveform will reach the left ear marginally before it reaches the right ear. It is the detection of this Interaural Level Difference (ILD) and Interaural Time Difference (ITD) that specifies the position of a sound source for a listener. For relatively continuous sounds ITD is detected not in terms of a difference in arrival time at the two ears (a steady state sound does not 'arrive' since it is always already there), but in terms of the phase difference[3] between the signals at the two ears. Because low frequency sounds are diffracted ('bent') around the head, reducing the shadow effect, intensity-based discrimination is poor or non-existent below about 500–800 Hz; and phase differences become ambiguous above about 1,500 Hz – although in both cases acuity improves with the dynamic cues that come from moving sources and listeners' own head movements.

The front/back and up/down positions of a sound source are much less acutely judged – particularly for stationary sources and immobile listeners; and are less well understood in terms of detailed mechanisms. These aspects of spatial position seem to be mainly specified by changes in the spectral properties of sound (i.e. the specific frequency/intensity distributions). The complex ridged shape of the pinna (the external ear-flap) has the effect of filtering sounds, some frequencies being reflected into the ear canal with little or no loss, while others are diffused or absorbed. An external sound source that has a relatively flat spectrum, with all frequency components more or less equally represented, is differentially reflected/absorbed by the pinna so that the spectral pattern at the eardrum shows peaks and troughs, and this spectral pattern changes as the sound source changes its position. For a source that lies behind a listener, for example, the entrance to the ear canal will be more in the shadow of the pinna than for a source in front of the listener; and sound sources at different elevations in relation to a listener will reflect off, and be absorbed by, the convoluted and differentially hard/soft surface of the pinna in distinctive ways.

The account given so far deals with the angular location of a source in three planes, but how does a listener know how far away a sound is? One obvious cue is simple intensity: because sound dissipates in the environment, the intensity of the signal that reaches a listener will be greater for a source that is nearer than for the same source when it is further away. But, by analogy with the size/distance relationship in visual perception, this simple and direct relationship is undermined by the problem that the distance of a source from the listener cannot be distinguished from the intensity of the source itself. How do we know how much sound a source radiates in the first place, and how do we distinguish a quiet sound nearby from a loud sound far away? In the absence of other cues we cannot, but the

---

[3] In simple terms, phase difference is the relationship between the peaks and troughs of two waveforms: if the peaks of one exactly coincide with the peaks of the other, then they are perfectly in phase; and if the peaks of one coincide with the troughs of the other, then they are exactly out of phase.

situation is disambiguated by a number of other features. First, different frequency components are dissipated or absorbed in the environment at different rates, with high frequencies attenuated more quickly than low frequencies. The acoustical 'signature' of a sound source will therefore sound more bassy, as well as having a lower overall intensity, when distant than when close. Second, the signal for a close source will be stronger in relation to background noise than for a more distant source. And third, the relationship between the directly received signal and reflections of the signal from environmental surfaces will similarly be greater for nearby sources than for more distant sources: noticeable echo and reverberation relative to the signal specify a more distant source.

Echo and reverberation are also important cues for the size of the space within which listeners perceive themselves to be: long delays between direct sound from a source and the arrival of one or more echoes specify larger distances to the reflecting surfaces than do shorter delay times. Similarly, longer reverberation times specify larger spaces, although there is a potential confound here with the materials of the environment: a space lined with acoustically absorbent materials will have a short reverberation time even if it is large, and a small but acoustically reflective space can be relatively reverberant – the classic 'bathroom' acoustic. Finally, empty spaces such as plains, deserts or snowfields will have little or no echo or reverberation at all – despite being very large.

In summary, there is a rich array of perceptual information that specifies the position of sound sources in the environment and the volume of the space in which a listener is located. These include: intensity differences between the ears – specifying left/right position of source; time and phase differences between the ears – specifying left/right position; changing spectral properties – specifying elevation, front/behind position and distance of source; signal-to-noise and signal-to-reverberation ratio – specifying distance of source; echo delay – specifying distance of object and volume of space; and reverberation time – specifying volume of space. With static sources and immobile listening conditions, most of these cues are individually indeterminate: as is generally true of human perception, convergent information that changes over time specifies much more clearly what is going on. For example, a combination of increasing intensity, spectral shift towards higher frequency components, increase in signal-to-noise ratio and no change in ILD or ITD specifies the approach of a sound source to the listener in a straight line – even if each one of these cues on its own is spatially indeterminate. Note that the auditory scene as described here is identical for a source that moves towards a stationary listener and a listener that moves towards a stationary source – though listeners will usually know whether they are stationary or moving from visual, kinaesthetic and proprioceptive information.

Finally, before turning to the perception of space in music, it is important to recognise the distinction between real and virtual spaces. Perceivers noticing the size of room in which they sit, or the distance of a police siren, are detecting real spatial attributes by virtue of the available auditory (and visual) information. Listeners at home hearing the size of a recorded space or position of a voice are detecting the attributes of a *virtual space* – a space specified by the same perceptual attributes as a real space, but which is not physically present at the time. That virtual space may or may not have ever existed, and certainly has no literal reality at the time of listening: it could be the product either of a 'high fidelity' recording of just such a real space or of studio techniques used to transform a recording made in a space of quite different dimensions and attributes. It is the ability of recorded music to specify these virtual spaces, and their attributes, that is the central concern of this chapter.

## Space in recorded music

Until recently, musicology and music theory have had little or nothing to say about space in music, for a combination of reasons connected with their focus on the score, their comparative lack of interest in recordings and their intense focus on pitch and rhythm to the exclusion of almost everything else. In his *Aesthetics of Music*, for example, Roger Scruton (1997: 12) argues that although listeners locate sounds in space, the focus on sounds themselves that he characterises as musical listening causes this feature to be 'refined away' so that space 'plays only an attenuated part in music'. He cites the dialogue between the oboe and cor anglais in the third movement (*Scène aux champs*) of Berlioz's *Symphonie Fantastique* as 'not a dialogue in physical space, even if it *uses* our perception of physical space, in order to remind us of the sense of distance. Musically speaking, there is no distance at all between the oboe and the cor anglais, both of which float in the same musical empyrean' (Scruton 1997: 12). Scruton's tacit appeal to the idea of 'primary' and 'secondary' parameters of music (pitch and rhythm being primary, space being secondary) might be true of a narrowly confined consideration of Western art music, though even here it neglects a whole variety of ways in which that music, from medieval times to the present day, makes use of the specific spaces for which it was conceived. From Machaut's Mass to Stockhausen's helicopter string quartet, the varied spatial and acoustical affordances of cathedrals, theatres, concert halls, salons and opera houses have played a significant if relatively unsung role in Western art music. And in recordings of the classical canon space takes on a much more critical role, particularly in opera recording where the relationships between the real space of the recording studio, the space of an actual or imagined opera house, the fictional space of the operatic drama and the virtual space of the recording can present conductors, performers and producers with all kinds of opportunities and challenges. The classical record producer John Culshaw was one person who relatively early on grasped the opportunities that changing studio technology offered to create a 'virtual world' within his operatic productions on record (Patmore and Clarke 2007).

Taking two of the numerous recordings of Berlioz's *Symphonie Fantastique*, the *Scène aux champs* mentioned by Scruton is realised on the recordings in significantly different ways. Rather like an opera, the *Symphonie Fantastique* invokes fictional dramatic spaces, so that the *Scène aux champs* is conceived as taking place outdoors in a rural setting: Berlioz's programme for this movement starts 'Finding himself one evening in the country, he hears in the distance two shepherds piping a *ranz des vaches* in dialogue',[4] with the oboe part initially marked '*derrière la scène*', followed by an instruction to rejoin the orchestra at bar 21. Colin Davis's recording from 1974 for Philips with the Amsterdam Concertgebouw Orchestra was recorded in the Concertgebouw hall, while Roger Norrington's 1988 recording for EMI with the London Classical Players was recorded in the No. 1 studio at Abbey Road. A studio would seem the more likely venue for a recording that exploits the spatial possibilities suggested by Berlioz's score and programme, but actually it is the Davis recording that is the more spatially distinctive. At the start of the movement in the Davis recording, the opening cor anglais melody is recorded slightly to the right of centre in the stereo field, at some distance from the listening point (perhaps five or six metres – since there is little detectable sound of either the instrument's keys or the player's breathing and embouchure) and in quite a reverberant acoustic space. The answering oboe is clearly very much further away, or possibly outside the main space of the recording hall in an antechamber: the sound is much quieter, the signal to reverberation ratio is much smaller and higher frequencies are noticeably attenuated (particularly the

---

[4] 'Se trouvant un soir à la campagne, il entend au loin deux pâtres qui dialoguent un ranz des vaches.' A *ranz des vaches* is an unaccompanied melody used for herding animals in alpine pastures.

attack components of individual notes, which have almost disappeared), as if the instrument was more like fifteen or twenty metres away. When the two instruments overlap in the next pair of melodic phrases, these dynamic and spectral differences mean that the cor anglais melody almost obscures the oboe's answer. In the Norrington recording, by contrast, the cor anglais is placed left of centre in the stereo field,[5] a little closer to the listening point than in the Davis recording, and the answering oboe is located slightly to the right of centre and only slightly further away than the cor. There is little sense of the instrument being in a different space from the cor anglais (when the two instruments overlap, both remain distinctly audible), and the whole room acoustic suggests a distinctly smaller spatial volume than that of the Davis Concertgebouw recording.

What are the consequences of these different recorded characteristics as far as a listener is concerned? Davis's recording sounds more 'picturesque' and evocative of a context that contains real distances (from hill to hill, or field to field) than does Norrington's – though of course the acoustic of the virtual space is completely wrong for a truly outdoor scene. The long reverberation time of the Concertgebouw successfully conveys large spatial volume, but if this cor anglais and oboe were really out in the fields there would be little or no reverberation at all – a contradiction that listeners seem happy to accept. Arguably, then, Davis's recording adopts a more realist approach to the work's programme, coming closer to creating a sounding space that conveys the drama of physical distance; while Norrington's, arguably in keeping with its 'historically informed' claims and the conductor's rather strident comments on his adherence to the score,[6] is much closer to an attempt to capture a historical concert performance – located though it is, ironically, in the Abbey Road studio.

If there is this much to say about one small section from two recordings of the *Symphonie Fantastique*, then there is a great deal more to be said about those kinds of music for which the recorded medium is more integral

---

[5] The liner notes for the Norrington recording include a relatively detailed description of the layout of the orchestra for the recording – based on Berlioz's own preferred arrangement. The woodwind are indeed described as being on a 'tiered block to the conductor's left at the rear of the first violins' (Murray 1989: 8), corresponding to where the cor anglais sounds in the recording. There is no mention of where the off-stage oboe is located – but its position slightly to the right of centre suggests that it has been placed behind the 'trumpets, trombones and ophicleides [which] were similarly positioned to the right-hand side of the orchestra' (Murray 1989: 8).

[6] 'First of all, we try to play the *score* (of course with all its repeats). Since it is immensely detailed and the work of a genius, it does not seem necessary to add all sorts of extra speed changes or to alter those that Berlioz prescribes' (Norrington 1989: 5; original emphasis).

to their aesthetic world – pop music and electroacoustic music. Trevor Wishart (1996 (1985)) and Luke Windsor (1995, 2000), among others, have written in important ways about space in electroacoustic music, Wishart being among the first to use the term 'virtual space' in recorded music and to discuss the ways in which all manner of real spaces (concert spaces, outdoor spaces from field recordings, the interiors of drainpipes, caves and termites' nests), as well as synthesised and perhaps impossible spaces, can be projected into what he calls the 'virtual acoustic space' (Wishart 1996 (1985): 73) of the loudspeaker. In writing on pop music, too, there has been a steadily developing literature on space in pop music recordings, including important work by Allan Moore (1993, 1998; Moore and Dockwray 2008), Lacasse (2000), Albin Zak III (2001), Peter Doyle (2005) and Nicola Dibben (2009).

Moore's approach to space in music is the first serious attempt to describe in explicit terms the layout of the instrumental and vocal sources in pop music recordings, using the idea of a four-dimensional 'sound-box' (three spatial dimensions and a fourth dimension of temporal continuity). His approach is oriented primarily towards establishing the style norms of sound-box layout: for example, the aim of Moore and Dockwray (2008) is to establish a taxonomy of spatial distributions in rock recordings from 1966 to 1972 and to discuss why one particular distribution (a 'diagonal mix') came to dominate. Similarly, Zak (2001) provides numerous descriptions of the spatial layout and use of echo and reverb[7] in a wide range of rock tracks, but stops short of suggesting what the perceptual or interpretative consequences of the properties might be for listeners. Lacasse (2000) presents a broad account of what he terms the 'staging of the voice' in popular music, the term capturing both the physical elements (size of stage, proximity of stage, place on stage) and the dramatic elements (persona, style of address, narrative) of what it is to 'stage' a voice.[8] His approach considers how these stagings are achieved and what they might mean for listeners' interpretations based on broadly semiotic principles, text–music relationships and three aspects of spatialisation: environment (the volume and type of space), stereo location and distance. Dibben (2009) pursues similar aims but bases her account (which is focused specifically on the music of Björk) on an ecological approach.

---

[7]  Zak uses the term 'ambience' rather than reverb.
[8]  In a somewhat different vein, Wishart 1996 (1985): 136–47 provides an extremely interesting and wide-ranging 'description in terms of sound objects' (p. 136) of the possibilities of human utterance.

Peter Doyle's (2005) book on echo and reverb is the most sustained treatment of space in recorded music to date and builds significantly on the earlier work by Moore, Lacasse and others to provide a rich account of space in recorded pop music in the period up to 1960.[9] Both echo and reverberation are phenomena based on acoustical reflection – echo being distinguished from reverb by the identifiability of one or more discrete replications of the original sound at a noticeable time delay, while reverb consists of a large number of overlapping sound reflections none of which are specifically identifiable. Doyle's explanatory framework for the specifically spatial consequences of echo and reverb combines loosely perceptual principles and more culturally convened associations. As Doyle reveals, considered in the light of twentieth-century manifestations of echo in a whole variety of domains (music, film, narrative), the Greek myth of Echo and Narcissus is a fascinating repository of persisting cultural meanings.[10] Given this heterogeneous hermeneutic framework, it is not surprising that Doyle resists any attempt 'to "read" echoic and reverberant sound effects back to a single stable, bedrock meaning – the actual maternal womb or the prehistoric oceanic home of our evolutionary ancestors' (Doyle 2005: 19). Nonetheless, the two principal sources for his 'readings' are the associations of everyday auditory experience and the specific uses (and ultimately conventions) of echo and reverb in Hollywood film soundtracks, where the two effects are heard in a whole variety of visual and dramatic contexts: big empty spaces with hidden or otherworldly presences; evening or night scenes; the drowsy (or, more strictly, hypnagogic) state of a fantasised Hawaiian paradise; and situations of threat/anxiety or mental instability.

All of this writing – Doyle, Lacasse and Dibben – brings home the powerful ways in which the virtual spaces of the recorded voice, and the singer's subjectivity, interrelate. On-mic or off-mic; with or without reverb; filtered or unfiltered; whispered or belted out: these and many other properties, some achieved by virtue of the singer's actual spatial relationship with the microphone, others using studio production methods, specify both innumerable spatial relationships with the listener, as well as a relatively narrow range of specific communicative contexts (intimacy, aggression, fear, secrecy, disengagement) for each 'staging' by virtue of the particular kinds of communication that such circumstances afford in a given cultural

---

[9] Doyle concludes his account at that date, since in this pre-stereo period spatial effects are mostly achieved with echo and reverb.

[10] Echo is: female, transgressive, voluble, punished by being rendered only responsive/passive (unable to initiate) and disembodied, and as a consequence 'uncanny'.

context. Dibben (2009: 147–8) gives just such an account in relation to the track 'Cocoon' from Björk's album *Vespertine* (2001):

In this track ['Cocoon'] the lead vocal is recorded close to the microphone, with seemingly little treatment, placing the listener in close proximity to the singing voice. The vocal tone is a timbrally unstable whisper: in places the melody is barely sustained and on the verge of becoming an un-pitched whisper. It is as though the listener is being told a secret, appropriate to the intimacy of the lyrics.

Not all that Dibben describes is reducible simply to space, but virtually all of it depends upon the close proximity that the sounds specify. As the literature on non-verbal communication demonstrates, and the theory of proxemics most obviously (Hall 1969), the spaces between us contribute powerfully to our intersubjective relationships. Recorded sound has the capacity to specify a great range of 'proximities', with all the consequences for the experience of subjectivity that ensue.

## Virtual space in Pink Floyd's 'Echoes'

The theoretical framework within which to tackle space in recorded music, as has already been shown, is heterogeneous and diverse. In order to indicate the potential of a primarily perceptual approach, I will start by considering Pink Floyd's twenty-three-minute track 'Echoes' from their 1971 album *Meddle*, which is an object lesson in that exploration of virtual space that characterised much of the psychedelic progressive rock from around 1968 to 1975. The track opens with a sound like a sonar signal (produced by putting the sound of a grand piano through a Leslie rotating loudspeaker),[11] with a long reverberation time but no echo. Over the subsequent minute the empty space specified by the isolated sonar is slowly, and at first sparsely, filled with widely spaced single piano notes played through the Leslie speaker, and a sustained organ pad – all treated with moderate amounts of reverb, spread across the middle and right of the stereo field, and gradually increasing in dynamic level to a more robust and established sound at 1:08, when the lead guitar enters. Just before that entry, and as the dynamic

---

[11] The sound was the serendipitous discovery of Pink Floyd's keyboard player, Rick Wright – as documented by Mason 2004: 153. Leslie loudspeakers have motorised rotating treble horns and bass baffles, which create a highly distinctive sound by virtue of the rapidly oscillating dynamic and timbral effects that are caused by the masking/filtering (amplitude modulation) and Doppler-related (frequency modulation) consequences of the rotation.

level starts to rise more quickly, a number of distinct echoes can be heard from some distance (specified by the low dynamic level) and on the right of the stereo field. It is at first not clear whether the Leslie-treated piano notes, which have a glassy and timbrally unstable quality, will turn out to be figure or ground, but as the texture fills the overall perceptual effect of this opening minute is to define and populate an acoustic space that functions as an environment for the lead guitar in the role of agent. The guitar, placed left of centre in the stereo field and a little more forward than any of the sounds so far, is underpinned at 1:31 by an equally forward bass guitar and at 1:50 by the kit, and with its unhurried bluesy melody leads – like a voice – to the entry of the actual voices (Dave Gilmour and Rick Wright) at 2:57. These voices occupy a central and forward position in the mix, and are relatively close-miked (the sounds of their mouths and intake of breath are clearly audible), but with a low-energy delivery and degree of reverberation that gives them the same disengaged and emotionally neutral quality that has characterised all the music so far. The lyrical content of the verse is similarly disinterested and descriptive, but with a strongly spatial quality, conjuring up images of motionless seabirds hanging in the air, labyrinthine caves under a rolling sea, and the distant sound of the tide coming echoing across the sand.

A chorus immediately follows, and from this point on (incorporating a second verse and chorus) the track establishes a fuller and more conventional rock texture, though the continuing reverb and echo that are applied to elements of the mix maintain the large-space, otherworldly and remote quality of the opening. A low-key and undemonstrative guitar solo rises to a climax that increasingly incorporates artificial echoes (at 7:00), leading to a more rhythmically taut and harmonically static section with a second more 'unbuttoned' guitar solo in occasional dialogue with the Hammond organ. The bass, kit and Hammond organ all occupy a comparatively dry acoustic, though spread across the stereo field, while the guitar sound becomes progressively more reverberant, loaded with feedback and distorted/noisy in quality. The overall effect is to give a sense that the guitar is becoming increasingly unhinged until (at around 10:28) it finally cuts loose and floats off.

The rest of the band slowly fades out, ushering in the ensuing central episode of the track (from around 11:00 to 16:00), featuring wind-like and slow pitch drone effects combined with long high-pitched cries/calls that echo and respond to one another in a highly reverberant and very sparsely populated space. To begin with the sounds are not recognisable as natural sounds, but from around 12:40 the sounds of wind and the clearly identifiable calls of crows can be heard. The effect of this central section is of a huge (highly reverberant), inhuman (absence of recognisable human musical evidence – voices, instruments, pitches or rhythms) and empty space, inhabited by alien (unrecognisable) and/or sinister (crows) creatures.

Preceded by the return of the opening 'sonar' sound (just after 15:00), a long slow crescendo of static harmonic pulsation starts (signs of human agency), which, transformed into a fully-fledged and rhythmically active repeating sequence in B minor, brings back the full band. This third section of the track is a loose retrograde of the first in terms of its general textures and structures, culminating in a final verse and chorus (at 19:11–19:57) with Gilmour's and Wright's vocals phased or flanged[12] – paradoxically close (clear sounds of mouth and breath) but at the same time remote (as if through some kind of acoustic 'veil') by virtue of the mobile filtering of the phasing/flanging. The track concludes with a quiet coda consisting of answering melodic phrases between the guitar and piano over Hammond organ, bass and kit, fading into (or being engulfed by) an eternally ascending quasi-vocal chorus.[13]

## Subject-position and 'psychic space'

As described so far, the spaces in 'Echoes' are primarily of a physical kind – albeit virtual: the sounds specify certain kinds of spatial volumes, together with the relative distances of sound emitting or reflecting bodies in those spaces. But those spatial properties also contribute to the specification of a subject-position (Clarke 1999) and the listener's involvement in a psychic space, and it is to these properties of the track that I now turn. The work of Lacasse (2000), Doyle (2005) and Dibben (2009) has already been mentioned as different variants of one way in which literally spatial properties (echo, reverb, spectral features and the audibility of the body) contribute to vocal staging. A complementary conceptual framework within which to understand the consequences of perceived space for the experience of subjectivity is the conceptual metaphor theory of George Lakoff

[12] Phasing and flanging are two closely related sound treatments that create cyclical spectral transformations of the signal, experienced as distinctive changing timbral patterns.

[13] The technique of creating eternally ascending scales, using octave harmonics, a constant spectral 'envelope' and discrete scale steps, was the discovery of the psychologist Roger Shepard (1964) – subsequently developed into eternal glissandi using similar principles by the composer Jean-Claude Risset.

and Mark Johnson (Lakoff and Johnson 1980; Johnson 1987). Lakoff and Johnson's theory can be summarised in highly simplified and condensed form as follows.

1. The primary way in which we know and 'have a world' for ourselves is through the body.
2. Sensory-motor engagement with the world generates, and is in turn mediated by, schemata – patterns of action, perception and conception that 'emerge as meaningful structures for us chiefly at the level of our bodily movements through space, our manipulation of objects, and our perceptual interactions' (Johnson 1987: 29).
3. Building upon this developmentally fundamental embodied experience, all our knowledge and understanding is conceived in terms of generalisations from, and extensions of, that primary contact.
4. These generalisations and extensions are conceptual metaphors, not because they necessarily have a linguistic component (though many do), but because they all involve a mapping of properties from a source domain onto a target domain: 'A metaphor in this "experiential" sense, is a process by which we understand and structure one domain of experience in terms of another domain *of a different kind*' (Johnson 1987: 15; original emphasis).
5. The primary and overwhelmingly prevalent source domain, for almost every target domain that we encounter, is bodily experience: experience is deeply and pervasively embodied.

Johnson and Larson (2003) use conceptual metaphor theory to analyse and understand how it is that music moves, and in what kind of space it moves, by mapping from the source domain of physical (bodily) motion onto the target domain of musical materials – harmonic, melodic and rhythmic processes, motivic sequences, instruments, registers and textures. In what follows, I do something a little different, which is to map a perceptual experience of auditorily specified space onto the target domain of the psyche. Having recognised that principles of proxemics establish one set of strong relationships between spatial properties and psychological states, conceptual metaphor theory provides a framework within which to understand a wider set of relationships between space and the psyche.

I will start by considering briefly how these principles work in Pink Floyd's 'Echoes', to allow my discussion to move beyond the merely physical sense of space presented so far. It is risky to suggest how others hear this music, but I am going to propose that the prevailing subject-position specified by these sounds is that of observation rather than identification, primarily by virtue of their spatial qualities. As a listener to the track, I auditorily explore, or am auditorily presented with, an environment whose size and 'density and style of habitation' I experience through the spaces, textures and events of the music. The rather abstractly sonic and instrumental character of the track, and the comparative absence of voices (only 10 per cent of the track duration contains vocal sounds), mean that this sounds like a space not much inhabited by humans.[14] The three-part arch structure outlines the following trajectory:

1. Emptiness ('sonar' alone), acquiring an increasing sense of agency (lead guitar, closer in the mix) and subjectivity (voices and guitar solos at the front of the mix), leading to dissipation and disappearance (reverb, echo and fade) (0:00–11:00).
2. An unfamiliar and empty 'space-scape' (sparse sounds specifying few objects), of very large extent (very reverberant, long echo delays), observed and navigated by the listener (11:00–16:00).
3. Loose retrograde of part 1: return of agency/subjectivity (slow but steady rhythmic/harmonic approach) to a final verse and chorus, phased/flanged voices indicating some kind of transformative/revelatory experience; final word of chorus ('sky-y-y-y-y-y …') dissipating/dissolving; coda finally engulfed by 'eternal ascent' mixed with original 'sonar' (back to the eternal present of the start) (16:00–end).

In brief terms, then, this indicates how various kinds of sounding space relate to qualities of agency and subjectivity in 'Echoes', but for a more developed discussion of those relationships I now turn to a track in which spatial attributes align with the powerful sense of subjectivity that derives from the audible presence of a singer-songwriter at the front of the mix.

## Space, embodiment and subjectivity: Goldfrapp's 'Deer Stop'

'Deer Stop', from the album *Felt Mountain* by Goldfrapp (2000), is a track that uses a variety of striking auditory spatialisation effects, primarily in relation to the vocal part, in a way that engages powerfully with questions of subjectivity. The track has a fairly straightforward verse structure, as indicated in Table 3.1, though the surface manifestation of this structure is

---

[14] Instrumental sounds can also specify the presence of human beings, of course, but in a less direct and incontrovertible manner than when voices are present.

**Table 3.1** Goldfrapp 'Deer Stop': schematic structure

| | |
|---|---|
| 0:00 | Instrumental intro |
| 0:16 | Verse I |
| 0:16 | Part 1 (i, with Phrygian inflection) |
| 0:47 | Part 2 (iv i alternation) |
| 1:18 | Part 3 (iv V i) |
| 1:50 | Verse II |
| 1:50 | Part 1 (as in verse I but voice absent) |
| 2:20 | Part 2 (as verse I) |
| 2:52 | Part 3 (as verse I) |
| 3:27 | Coda (based on part 3) |
| 4:02 | End |

somewhat disguised by the absence of the voice at the start of the second verse (1:50–2:20).

The discussion of space and subjectivity that follows focuses almost exclusively on the voice, since it is this component that demonstrates the most interesting spatial attributes. The simplest way to identify specific moments or sections of the vocal track is by reference to the lyrics, a 'quasi-phonetic' transcription of which appears in Table 3.2 using Goldfrapp's printed lyrics as a rough framework or prompt.[15] Subsequent references to the voice will be made in terms of the line numbers (#1–#12) from Table 3.2, or in track time (min:sec).

First, a brief word on the instrumental sounds: the instrumental introduction (0:00–0:16) consists of string bass and vibraphone recorded centre field and very forward in the mix, with the slightly claustrophobic quality of a confined space, joined soon afterwards (0:04–0:16) by a high string sound, right of centre and with the spaciousness that comes from a moderate level of reverb. At 0:31–0:47 a string quartet is added to the texture, with a less reverberant and more forward position, the whole instrumental sound replaced at 0:47 by a Fender Rhodes piano playing alternating bass notes[16] and chords in a manner reminiscent of Erik Satie's *Gymnopédies*. These elements in various combinations remain the instrumental resources for the whole track, against which Alison Goldfrapp's voice is projected.

Let me start by considering the more literally spatial properties of the voice. The first vocal entry (#1) is recorded significantly forward of the

---

[15] The lyrics to the track are in many places very hard to decipher, and the transcription provided here (made by the author) functions principally as a means to locate and identify specific moments in the music.

[16] Doubled by string bass.

Table 3.2 'Quasi-phonetic' transcription of the lyrics to 'Deer Stop'

| # | Transcription | Start (min:sec) |
|---|---|---|
| 1 | And I long to go, love started here, | 0:16 |
| 2 | Shoot your star, feel like a star | 0:32 |
| 3 | Don't you call, deer stop bottle in a shell | 0:47 |
| 4 | Shoot your thousand stars over me | 1:03 |
| 5 | Who above, who disturbed? To scream, she came home ... | 1:18 |
| 6 | You've arrested a knight. | 1:39 |
| 7 | Say my name, whisper it – don't ever turn | 2:20 |
| 8 | I'm deliciously wired, I'm falling in a cloud | 2:36 |
| 9 | Don't you ... skies are dark, she changed | 2:52 |
| 10 | Shoot your thousand stars over | 3:07 |
| 11 | Ay ee ai ee ai ee ai ee ai ee ai yah, Ya ya ya, ya-hah, lai-ha | 3:27 |
| 12 | Say my name, whisper it. | 3:53 |

instrumental sound, and phased or flanged (see note 12) so that it has a filtered and hence somewhat remote quality, as well as a regularly varying spectral quality that gives the impression of sounds heard through some kind of moving or changing material. Line #2 is recorded even more forward, and with that sense of enlargement, 'super-fidelity' and proximity that comes from a voice recorded extremely close to the microphone: there are clear sounds of the singer's mouth and breath, and a feeling of the voice so far forward in the mix as to be leaning right into the space of the listener.[17] Lines #3 and #4, coinciding with the change in instrumental texture, and presented in an even more exposed manner, repeat the spatial treatment of lines #1 and #2. The overall effect of this first part of the verse is of a heightened reality, with Alison Goldfrapp's voice alternating between the forward but slightly veiled quality of lines #1 and #3 and a kind of 'hyper-real' forwardness in lines #2 and #4, but combined with an audibly low-energy delivery that conveys sensuous intimacy.[18] By contrast, the voice at line #5 is quite strongly and narrowly band-pass filtered – a sound that Lacasse (2000) calls 'telephone effect' – giving it a hollow and remote quality, the diction very indistinct, and for the first time more distant in the mix than the instruments. As the line proceeds, the filter becomes more high-pass,

---

[17] Doyle 2005 draws a distinction between concave and convex recordings, the former drawing the listener into the space of the recording, while the latter – of which this is a powerful example – projecting elements of the recording into the space of the listener.

[18] Explained in proxemic terms: the singer is heard to be very close – almost impossibly close – and yet relaxed, confiding, physically unguarded.

bringing the voice forward as though extruded, though the reverb applied to it paradoxically also continues to specify distance – or remoteness. As the end of the line is reached, the voice is treated with filter and reverb of a kind that give it a peculiar quality as of drops of water in a reverberant space, like a cave. The disconcerting or puzzling effects of these acoustic transformations, applied to Alison Goldfrapp's already drawn-out delivery of the elusive words, are largely 'resolved' when line #6 restores the more intimate and stable sound quality of lines #2 and #4, and a degree of articulacy is restored.[19]

At the start of the second verse (1:50) the voice is absent for the equivalent of lines #1 and #2, but a number of sounds that have residually vocal qualities are overlaid on the same instrumental sounds that were used at the equivalent place in verse 1: the first is a low and swooping pitch, like a continuously variable oscillator, placed right of centre in the mix, and which moves slowly around in a growling or humming manner until it is replaced at 2:00 by a much higher frequency glassy, whispery sound – highly variable and unstable, and located to the extreme right in the mix. At 2:07 this in turn disappears to be replaced at 2:12 by a sound with a rubbing/scraping/metallic/glassy quality, and with prominent descending harmonic series components. All three of these superimposed sounds have elements of vocality about them (continuously variable pitch, harmonic series, noisy/breathy/articulating sounds), though with the components taken apart and rendered unstable. Rather like the arrival of line #6 after the heavily treated line #5, the forward-sounding physical presence of lines #7 and #8 provides a stabilising and physically sensuous grounding after the unstable and obscure sounds of the preceding passage.

Lines #9 and #10 constitute the sonic and dramatic focus of the track, the voice treated with a variable filter that has instabilities similar to the glassy, hollow qualities at 2:12.[20] As line #10 proceeds, the filter progressively attenuates the high frequencies in a manner that suggests that the voice is sucked into an occluding space – as if it is being swallowed by the singer herself. The human voice is a powerful channel for intersubjectivity and empathy,[21] and the distinctive 'engorging' character of the vocal line gives

[19] This more familiar reality is also the consequence of the much more natural and clear delivery of the words of that line – free of the stretched and opaque phonemes of line #5 – however semantically anomalous the line nonetheless seems to be.

[20] Alison Goldfrapp's musical collaborator, Will Gregory, confirmed that this, and many of the other filtering effects applied to the vocal part, is achieved by feeding the vocal through a VCS3 synthesiser (personal communication).

[21] There is a burgeoning literature on the central significance of empathy and intersubjectivity in human development (e.g. Stern 2004; Bråten 2007), much of it focused on the mouth

it a pronounced corporeal quality, strongly focused on the throat.[22] Having been taken apparently almost inside the body of the singer, the voice at line #11 takes a dramatically different turn, with a wordless melisma (Ai-ee-ai-ee … 3:27–3:51) that emerges from nothing, in a reverberant space (as if miles away) and rapidly approaching the listener – rushing forwards while simultaneously becoming spectrally fuller and richer. The sense of release or outpouring reaches a climax at 3:44, as the voice releases its breath with a 'Ha' on the metrical downbeat and cadential tonic. The final line #12, quiet now and already fading away, brings the track to an end with the reassuring familiarity of an untreated voice articulating the recognisable words, reiterated from the start of the verse: 'Say my name, whisper it'.

The barely decipherable and semantically opaque lyrics of 'Deer Stop', delivered with the sensuous intensity that has been described here, present the listener with an urge to understand what this curious and elusive musical utterance means. The sounds seem to specify significant events, and a powerful component in that sense of significance comes from the spatial properties of the vocal part, which in turn specify changing conditions of subjectivity and intersubjectivity. First, principles of proxemics determine that the singer's variable distance from the listener (between extremely distant at 3:27 and extremely close at 0:32, 1:03 and elsewhere) is heard as varying relationships of remoteness and intimacy. These spatial relationships are specified by spectral attributes, as described above in the section on space perception, and by virtue of the audibility or not of the mouth and breath of the singer. Second, the more unusual spectral transformations of the voice, at 1:18–1:39 and 2:52–3:27, seem to specify peculiar and unfamiliar spatial relationships that are not easily accommodated in a simple *physical* space – real or virtual. They seem to demand interpretation in a different type of domain – a metaphorically related psychic space. The apparently spatial and material attributes of the voice (its hollowness, glassiness, fragility, extrusion, engulfment) are mapped onto a psychic domain,[23] such that hollow sounds specify emptiness and lack of substance, glassy sounds specify brittleness/vulnerability and engulfing sounds specify the experience of being overwhelmed. What these sounds afford for any individual listener cannot be definitively stated, since it arises out of complex

---

and voice. A common experience is for listeners to feel the need to clear their throats empathetically when listening to a speaker who needs to cough.

[22] Cf. Roland Barthes's 1985 focus on Charles Panzera's throat in his essay 'The grain of the voice'.

[23] Lakoff and Johnson 1980 and Johnson 1987 discuss a number of manifestations of the 'container' schema and its associated metaphors, many of them relating to emotional states.

interdependencies between detailed attributes of the sounds themselves and the particular sensitivities and circumstances of each listener. Even the apparently simple proxemics of sound can be significantly multivalent, as the potential interchangeability of the proximity of intimacy with the proximity of threat demonstrates. But these attributes are certainly not unconstrained or arbitrary, and a detailed consideration of material properties on the environmental side of the perceiver/environment dialectic – as has been attempted here – plays a crucial role in the larger and more complex project of understanding music's affordances.

## Outro

The various kinds of spaces – real and virtual – specified by musical sounds have until recently remained relatively neglected and unanalysed compared to other attributes of music. In this chapter I have proposed that a fruitful way to tackle such spaces is by means of ecological perceptual theory: musical sounds, like other sounds, specify the various spaces from which they emanate, and well-established psychoacoustic principles, framed in ecological terms, provide a framework within which to understand how that happens. In live musical performance, when seeing and hearing converge on the manifest realities of people, instruments, physical layouts and venues, it may be easy to overlook the latent virtual realities that the sounds also afford – though even here, as the informal evidence of listeners who speak of being 'transported' or 'blown away' demonstrates, other spaces are within reach. But in acousmatically presented music,[24] particularly pop and electroacoustic music created specifically for the recorded medium, there are dramatic opportunities for the specification and exploration of a great variety of virtual spaces. Those spatial components of musical experience are compelling and powerful in their own right, and they also have significant consequences for listeners' experiences of subjectivity and intersubjectivity in music, as I have argued here. A number of factors contribute, including spatial and other material attributes of the auditory scene as specified by the musical sounds, and the extension of those immediate properties into the other domains opened up by conceptual metaphor theory. Equally, it is important to recognise that while the spatial possibilities opened up by sound recording are little more than 100 years old, aesthetic conventions

---

[24] Music presented over loudspeakers or headphones, away from the sight and physical presence of the sound sources.

that stretch, transform and codify the affordances of everyday reality have emerged from the complex and overlapping relationships between film sound, video games and recorded music. The spatial sounds of music afford not only their real-world sources, but also the specific cultural contexts with which their audiences have become familiar: the reverberant sound of Hollywood's version of the uncanny or malevolent other; the vocoder voice of the sci-fi cyborg; the close-up sound of the inner voice of fear, doubt or conscience. A consideration of the complex interactions between these and a whole host of more or less mediated relationships between sound and space, and the links between sound, space and subjectivity – understood in terms that range from mirror neurons and ecological theory to social cognition and psychoanalysis – has only just begun.

# 4 | What the mind's ear doesn't hear

JONATHAN STERNE

As of this writing the MP3 is the world's most common storage format for sound. By several orders of magnitude, more sound recordings exist and circulate worldwide in MP3 format than in any other form, whether analogue or digital (Sterne 2012a). The MP3 format's success can be attributed to several factors, but one of the most important is its small size. An average MP3 of a song is about 12 per cent the size of the 'same' song in the .wav file format on a compact disc. So it is possible to fit many more MP3s on a hard drive, on a CD-R or in a mobile phone's static memory than if one were to leave CD files in their original format. The accomplishment of such a radical reduction in size comes from a process called perceptual coding. A perceptual coder is a software program that analyses a CD file, compares the analysis to a mathematical model of human hearing, figures out which parts of the sound are most likely to be unheard and discards those parts. As one might expect, this has led to an ongoing debate regarding sound quality in some quarters, but the fact remains that most of the time, for most people in most circumstances, the differences between MP3s and CD-quality files are not clearly heard or appreciated.[1]

My aim in this chapter is not to consider the MP3 as a technical marvel or achievement. It is, in fact, the result of a major industrial compromise.[2] Instead, I consider the MP3 format as a *political modulation* of private listening experience. By using the metaphor of modulation, I mean to invoke the sense of modulation as one sonic activity affecting the character of another, as when a musician modulates the tone of her instrument through hand technique, a composer changes the key (and therefore the pitch and timbre) of a musical piece or phrase, or a synthesist uses a filter to change

Many thanks to Carrie Rentschler for reading multiple drafts of this chapter, to Emily Raine for some fine editing and to Georgina Born for careful reading and commentary.

[1] For more on the technology behind digital audio, see Pohlmann 2005.
[2] The format was the result of a series of industrial compromises that facilitated the creation of a single international standard. The Moving Picture Experts Group documentation indicates the degree to which it understood itself as mediating industrial competition, with the goal of producing a single, multi-industry and multimedia set of standards that would allow interoperability and transnational circulation (Chiariglione 2003). For more on these processes, see Sterne 2012a.

the tone of a synthetic sound. In each case, one set of practices shapes another, but in an interactive way. The MP3 format can be said to *modulate* private listening experience because the technology both makes use of a specific set of listening experiences and attempts to shape and anticipate future auditory experience in some way. At the same time, the irreducible multiplicity of listening means that the fact of modulation does not result in a necessary or predetermined set of effects. The chapter briefly recounts the use of listening tests in developing and refining the technology behind the MP3 standard. Listening tests are interesting precisely because they cast the subject/object split as a practical problem of sound reproduction: how can an audio format anticipate the private experience of listening and render that anticipation useful to the process of recording, transmitting and playing back audio? In what follows I consider both informal tests by engineers themselves and a set of formal tests conducted by the Moving Picture Experts Group or MPEG, who established the standard that would later be branded as MP3. MPEG conducted three major, intensive listening tests in 1990 and 1991. These tests were designed to accomplish two things. They were to reveal the point at which different perceptual coding schemes for audio would break down, and through that first revelation, provide grounds for MPEG to decide which of four competing perceptual coding schemes should be adopted for use in the forthcoming standard.

At first blush, the listening test appears to be a kind of absurdist scenario. It uses exceptional listeners in exceptional environments and a limited set of recordings to produce numerical data regarding the sonic performance of an audio system. Engineers would call it a worst-case scenario. It subjects an aesthetic question – which system sounds better? – to an entirely anaesthetic situation. But MPEG's listening tests were not just about musical taste or preference or even subjective experience. Their goal was to convert the private experience of listening – a series of small judgments – into a public set of numbers that could then be measured against one another. In converting private experience to public numbers, they hoped to mediate another kind of privacy – private economic interests in adopting one coding technology over another. Testing was the ground through which MPEG thought it would resolve its internal industrial conflicts between competing sets of companies with competing products; but in order for that to happen, the process had to appear as relatively objective and disinterested to participants.

MP3 is a very public format that harnesses and instrumentalises the private experience of listening. In a way, the format is an attempt to dig below the consciousness of its listeners, to render useful the gaps that shape human hearing. By meditating on listening tests and their role in the development of MP3, I hope to elucidate two interesting tensions inherent in the MP3 format. First, the MP3 format has achieved extensive dissemination based on intensive personalisation. There are many meanings of the word 'public', but if by 'public' we mean available, MP3s are the most public form of music in the world. This is only possible because of the model of a private listening subject that is built into the encoder. That leads us to the second tension: the model of listening built into the MP3 encoder has to exist as a set of discrete quantities based on continuous, subjective impressions. Computers have to operate with numbers and the results have to translate from one platform and situation to another – this is the whole point of international standards and protocols (Galloway 2004: 95–6; Fuller 2005: 42). But sonically, this objectification of listening only matters in the moment of an irreducibly private listening experience. No two people can occupy the same exact subjective space. In other words, the format relies upon the measurement of something that can only be approximated: interior listening experience. Neither of these situations are contradictions that must be resolved, transcended or overcome. MP3s work just fine (or they don't, in which case one chooses another option from the alphabet soup of available digital audio formats). But they point to the ways in which contemporary media forms strive at once for some form of universality, or at least translatability, even as they allow for the irreducibility of private, subjective experience.

## Why listening tests?

The original motivation for MPEG's work was to devise a single international standard for VCDs (video compact discs, a predecessor to the DVD standard that encoded video and sound on compact discs); but they were already aware that other kinds of uses would be made of their standard. A large number of companies were working on various compression and perceptual coding schemes, but the few that had been brought to market were not economically dominant enough to become a de facto standard (Chiariglione 2003; Jakobs 2003). MPEG was convened to mediate among major industrial players and to come up with a single standard that could then be licensed for use in a wide range of consumer-level audio technologies. These licences are worth a lot of money, since every time companies design commercially sold hardware or software that encodes or plays back MP3s, they must pay royalties for the right to use the MP3 standard. The major stakeholder in the MP3 patents is a German company called

Fraunhofer IIS. They developed many of the important technologies for the MP3 format and claim credit for its invention on their corporate website.[3]

In an environment where MPEG was seeking to mediate among industrial competitors, listening tests made some sense. Test data have a certain privilege in discourses about the functioning of technology. The goal of a test is to assess whether or not the technology works as intended, but considerably more is at issue in what at first blush appears to be a simple matter of assessment. Although 'test data are usually thought of as providing access to the pure technological realm', or accessing the performance of technologies *as such*, tests are by their very nature made up of contrived conditions. The contrivance itself is the point, since in a testing scenario 'a set of activities is carried out in a circumscribed environment that is designed to produce an outcome that gives us information as to the operation of the technology' (Pinch 1993: 25, 26).

As an idea, perceptual coding is based on concepts from the field of psychoacoustics, the psychological study of human auditory perception. For some time psychoacousticians have tested and documented a phenomenon called 'masking', where one audible sound hides another from the listener's ear. The term masking 'was borrowed from visual concepts, and originally meant simply the failure to recognise the presence of one stimulus in the presence of a second one at a level normally adequate to elicit the first perception – a masking of the first by the second' (Schubert 1978: 63). Frequency diagrams of the ear's masking response were a regular feature of psychoacoustics textbooks, and masking research – which almost always involved listening tests – was an important strain of psychoacoustic studies from the 1940s on. By the late 1970s engineers began to figure out that it ought to be possible to use what was known about masking to save bandwidth in transmissions, because they could use the theory of masking to predict what parts of a signal would not be heard (and thereby choose to discard them).

At first, engineers experimented with simply importing tables of masking responses from psychoacoustics textbooks or in-house experimental data. But these proved insufficient for building technology that would actually process music or speech in such a way that the file was smaller

---

[3]  MP3 may feel like an open standard to end users, but its rights are owned by a consortium that brings in hundreds of millions of Euros each year for its owners. Other standards, such as Ogg Vorbis, are free and open, which means that anyone can freely use them or modify them without paying royalties, but these are a more recent development. As with other types of free software, advocates for formats such as Ogg may make aesthetic arguments for the superiority of their coding, but their main arguments are political in nature (Kelty 2008).

but still listenable, because psychoacousticians had rarely conducted masking research with music or speech.[4] They used sinusoid (sine wave) tones or broad or narrowband noise to do their tests. But these are totally inadequate for perceptual coding. Neither music nor speech – the two holy grails of perceptual coding (especially for commercial sound reproduction technologies) – behave anything like sinusoids or noise bursts. Because the results of prior psychoacoustic research did not neatly map onto the real-world applications of perceptual coding, its developers had to redo some basic research into human hearing, at least insofar as it was relevant to getting a coder to render speech intelligible and music pleasing. The goal of this research was not a universal theory of human hearing or musical pleasure, but simply to create an algorithm that would convert CD-quality audio files into much smaller files with little or no perceived loss of definition.[5]

## How listening tests work

Early perceptual coding algorithms lived in machines called 'codecs' – short for 'coder–decoder'. These boxes would have an input and an output plug, with a microchip and software inside. Run CD audio into the codec, and it outputs perceptually coded audio. Today, a codec more often refers to software that does the coding and decoding process (for instance, a portable MP3 player may also have additional codecs for other formats besides MP3). Early tests in the career of a codec were simple A–B tests. The engineer would play a reference version of the recording and compare it with the version subjected to the coding algorithm being tested. In the early stages problems would be obvious and so there was no need for more sophisticated testing. Although coding problems would be plainly audible, their solutions often were not, as the engineers had to figure out which of dozens of parameters were causing the problems they heard. 'You could change its behaviour completely with a different parameter set … You had so many parameters to play with and so little knowledge of how things would work in the end that it was quite a tricky process.'[6]

---

[4] Unpublished interviews with Oscar Bonello (8 July 2008), Karlheinz Brandenburg (23 August 2006), Joseph Hall (24 October 2008) and J. J. Johnston (22 February 2007).
[5] Algorithms, like recipes, are sets of sequenced instructions that may include a set of ordered actions ('do this, then do this') or if–then statements. Just as one must taste a recipe to see if it works, engineers have to test their algorithms with listening tests (Davis 1965; Wark 2007: 31).
[6] Brandenburg interview, 23 August 2006.

The final tests for what we now call MP3 were done on panels selected by MPEG in July 1990 and May and November 1991. They were 'double-blind triple stimulus tests' – tests where subjects would hear three recordings but only know the origin of one. Listeners would be given a 'known reference', which was the original recording. They would then be given two more 'hidden' recordings, one of which was the known reference, and one of which was the same recording run through a codec. The test was 'double blind' because neither the listener nor the test administrator would know which of the last two recordings was the 'known reference' (Bergman, Grewin *et al.* 1990, 1991). Everything in these tests was carefully calibrated to render the different protocols for perceptual coding as the only meaningful variables. The documentation for the tests provides lists of recordings, names of test subjects, test procedures and deviations therefrom, exhaustive lists of equipment with signal flow diagrams and reverberation times for the rooms in which the tests were held. Diagrams of the studios, tables of reverberation times and frequency responses are all plainly specified (Bergman, Grewin *et al.* 1991; Fuchs 1991). If, after many repetitions of a test, listeners could not distinguish between the coded signal and the known reference with a greater frequency than if they were guessing (more than half the time), the coding was considered transparent. If they could correctly distinguish between the signals, then the level of difference between the signals began to matter. Obvious and annoying differences were more problematic than minor differences, but all differences mattered (Bergman, Grewin *et al.* 1990, 1991).

*Annoying* is a crucial word here, and in a way the whole testing exercise rests upon it. It marks a shift from classic psychoacoustic notions of a relatively anaesthetised listening subject towards a set of aesthetic questions regarding how music and speech ought to sound – what would count as *good-sounding* music.[7] For much of the twentieth century, perceptual tests in psychoacoustics used a scale that ranged from 'threshold of audibility' to 'threshold of feeling' or 'threshold of pain' (e.g. Fletcher 1929). But by the 1980s another scale had come into common use in perceptual listening tests for audio equipment, a subjective quality scale with five different categories: 'Imperceptible', 'Perceptible but NOT Annoying', 'Slightly Annoying', 'Annoying' and 'Very Annoying'. Corresponding to these tests was a 49-point scale (with 0 to 5.0 or 0 to -4.9 in 0.1 increments),

---

[7] Anaesthetic may describe the self-presentation of psychoacoustic research, but the term also conceals part of the field's history. From the moment AT&T took an active interest in the field in the 1910s, very particular notions of 'good sound' came to dominate psychoacoustic testing. I discuss this further in Sterne 2012a.

with 'Imperceptible' given the highest score (Pohlmann 2005: 409). In the terminology of the scale, we can see the cool scientific language of psychoacoustics melt into the warm radiance of aesthetics. Those three adjectives – *imperceptible, perceptible* and *annoying* – speak volumes. The first two provide a means to convert the subjective experience of hearing into measurable units: you can hear a difference or you can't. But since the test is also aesthetic, and since the discourse of beauty in engineering is relatively submerged, beauty's opposite appears: repugnance, or at least its quieter cousin, annoyance.

MPEG audio is processed sound for listeners who live in a processed world. Like the sounds, the listeners – both ideal and real – constructed by the tests might well also be conceived of as processed in their own way. The functional replacement of a 'threshold of pain' with a 'threshold of annoyance' in measurement scales is at one level a matter of practicality since we are talking about musical artefacts and not loudness. But in charting a historical path from pain to annoyance, we follow the well-worn trail of Norbert Elias, whose notion of the civilising process relies on senses that make increasingly fine distinctions, retreating behind an ever-advancing 'threshold of repugnance'. In Elias's account of modernity, as the bourgeois subject becomes more entrenched and actual threats of violence become less and less common in daily life, subtle movements and perceptions take on ever greater meaning (Elias 2000: 98).[8] *Taste* is the name given to the senses so cultivated. Listening tests thus stage the civilising process for audio: they subject different modes of audio signal processing to various 'civilised' sonic sensibilities in listeners. The listening test subjects processes of sonic refinement to subjects' refined sonic judgments, and vice versa.

Although the testing scale measures from imperceptible to annoying, its object is something else: timbre. Audible differences between perceptually coded audio and source recordings are differences of timbre. As these are quite subtle, listening tests can require extensive training. Listeners can be trained to hear audible artefacts of perceptual coding. The Audio Engineering Society, which presents itself as the world's leading body for professional audio engineers, now produces a CD where listeners are

---

[8] The analogy is not exact: one could conceivably argue that modern life continues to present many physical threats to the ear, from the loudness of city life to the incredibly damaging sound pressure levels available on most portable audio players. It is clear, however, that an ear for timbre and for 'sound' has become part of the repertoire of the cultivated bourgeois listener, almost without regard for musical genre or sensibility (though in some aesthetics, such as punk, this 'refinement' is turned on its head). This development has followed the increasing profusion of sound reproduction technologies in everyday life.

instructed in the various kinds of artefacts one might encounter.[9] But in the early history of a codec, even these artefacts may not be immediately apparent to listeners. In a listening test for a new audio technology, it is not always clear what one is to listen for. For instance, one of the first commercially available perceptual coders was developed by an Argentinian team in the 1980s. Oscar Bonello, the team's leader, described their confusion in early listening tests as feeling 'like Adam the first time he saw Eva ... We spent some time in order to learn that this was a different type of distortion'.[10] Bernhard Grill, an engineer with Fraunhofer who was present for the 1990–1 MPEG tests, also questioned his judgment after the fact: while he thought the coded audio streams sounded transparent at the time, he says that he would not think so now. This concern about the limits of testing was well known at the time of the MPEG tests. An account of the tests presented at the 1991 AES meeting in London referred with some anxiety to listeners having a span of thirty years (or longer) to discover artefacts once a system was standardised: 'It can be compared with somebody who moves into a new house. The first time he looks through the window he only sees the beautiful view. After a few days he detects a small flaw in the glass and from that moment he cannot look through the window without seeing that flaw' (Grewin and Rydén 1991).[11]

By the late 1980s it was well established that artefacts of perceptual coding could be heard and reproduced. For instance, one artefact of some perceptual coding is called 'pre-echo'. Already in 1979 Michael Krasner, then a graduate student at MIT's Lincoln Laboratory, had identified a problem with 'onset transients' in coded speech, where distortions of sharp sounds like the letter *t* were quite perceptible to listeners (Krasner 1979: 128). This problem has continued to the present day. Pre-echo smears a sharp transient such as a cymbal hit, so the initial attack has less bite and occurs over a slightly longer period of time than in the reference recording. The recording of castanets used in the tests will still today yield audible pre-echo when processed through a standard 128k MP3 coder. However, the effect is very subtle and bothers some people more than others. While some listeners will hear it right away and be annoyed, others will take years to discover it, never discover it or experience it as part of listening to recorded music, like tape distortion or dust on a record. More to the point, without identifying an artefact, it cannot be tested for. J. J. Johnston

[9]   AES Technical Council, *Perceptual Audio Coders: What to Listen For*, Audio Engineering Society, New York, 2001.
[10]  Bonello, unpublished letter to the author, 26 July 2008.
[11]  As well as an unpublished interview with Grill, 27 May 2008 and letter from Bonello, 2008.

worked for Bell Labs in the 1980s and developed an algorithm for perceptually coding audio as a way of testing a new computer. He recounts of his tests at Bell Labs: 'At that point we didn't know what pre-echo was and we didn't know to have a signal that would cause it to happen, either, so we didn't hear it.' Similarly, because of the way MP3 codes stereo data, the stereo image of the sound can change. For some people with some recordings on some systems, this is very noticeable. For others, it is not perceptible at all.[12]

This is why formal listening tests are actually quite gruelling – they involve a great deal of repetition in order to produce reliable and predictable results. Listeners are given training on the equipment and on what to listen for, and they are given practice so that they become more reliable over time. Louis Thibault, an engineer at the Centre for Communication Research in Ottawa, helped design an international standard for listening tests. For Thibault, 'Our listeners are meters, and if you want a meter to provide a reliable measure you must calibrate it before using it – you do it with volt meters and you do it with human subjects … The goal of the training is that their rating of a given audio sequence will remain the same days or weeks after the initial test.'[13]

Although the testing scenario ostensibly sorts out codecs, it must first sort out listeners. Even with extensive training, a good listening test strains the auditory palette. Karlheinz Brandenburg is often credited as the 'inventor' of the MP3, even though he quickly credits others when asked about it. Brandenburg was heavily involved in the research, design and marketing of the format and spent countless hours in listening tests. He recalled, 'For larger sets of music, it was very tiring because the test subjects had to listen to each test item twenty times. I remember at AT&T at one point in time we had a revolt – people were just refusing to participate in the listening tests [because they were so awful].'[14] Bernhard Grill called the MPEG listening tests 'very hard. If you do listening tests for almost transparent codecs it's really strenuous. Each of the sessions lasts two hours … and you're really exhausted afterwards. It really requires a very high degree of concentration.'[15] This may seem like a circular logic: the test tests the listeners before the listeners test the technology. But it is not entirely circular. Rather, in the testing scenario a series of political modulations occur: subjects become acclimatised both to the peculiar scenario and to the peculiarities of the

[12] Johnston interview, 2007, and Grill interview, 2008.
[13] Louis Thibault, unpublished interview, 9 August 2005.
[14] Brandenburg interview, 2006.     [15] Grill interview, 2008.

technology. Their experiences – within that circumscribed situation – then help to shape the further development of technologies. It is thus a case of mutual influence between subjects and machinery in a very particular set of contrived circumstances. Having detailed the peculiar situation of the listening test, we must now turn to its peculiar subjects.

## Who listens in the MP3?

If it matters how perceptual codecs are listened to in their early development, it also matters who listens to them. If listening tests had a political ideology, it would undoubtedly be republicanism: the subjects of listening tests represent a future public that the codec hopes one day to confront. The test situation is thus not only a worst-case scenario, as the engineers would have it; it is also a moment of listening – and speaking – for others. The first round of listeners for perceptual codecs are usually the engineers themselves, testing the audio on their own ears. These engineers may have a great deal of technical knowledge but may or may not have 'golden ears'. In this sense, the engineer building the codec is not an expert listener or the ideal test subject, but merely an expert who listens. Since early on in the life of a codec audio issues are fairly obvious and technical issues fairly opaque, the argument goes that no other listener is needed. For more advanced tests, expert listeners are often drawn from the ranks of musicians, recording engineers, broadcast engineers, piano tuners and audiophiles, all professions where one must develop an ear for technology, a kind of auditory virtuosity that facilitates careful judgment and the making of finely graded distinctions. In essence, the ideal expert listener functions as an extension of the reproduction system, as a meter for it, measuring the audible performance of the codec and reliably reporting back to the engineers. Anyone who can produce reliable results can be an expert listener, but in practice it is easier to begin the search for expert listeners among populations that spend a lot of time thinking about and listening carefully to sound, and especially to sound reproduction systems. Expert listeners listen for form, not content; they listen to the system, and not the speech or music that it transmits. An expert listener needs a good ear for timbre (specifically, the timbres of different codecs) and must be able to make consistent judgments over time. Many testing facilities have coteries of expert listeners to whom they turn (and whom they pay) for the final testing of equipment, and all of the codecs that made it into the MPEG tests had already been through rounds of testing with expert listeners in their own 'native' corporate environments.[16]

As might be suggested by the list of professions, these listeners make up a highly specialised, relatively elite and strongly white, male and middle-class crowd.[17] The list of participants in the final MPEG tests confirms this. Most of the listeners were engineers who had worked on one or another of the coding schemes proposed for adoption or had some other interest in the standardisation process – they were experts in the technology, regardless of whether they were also actually virtuoso listeners.[18] This is a familiar pattern in the historical encounter between music and psychoacoustics: the assumption that from the cognitive all the way down to the processual level, hearing is the same no matter who you are or where you come from. In Georgina Born's study of the avant-garde computer music research institute IRCAM in 1980s France, she notes that while the psychoacoustic research being developed at IRCAM made strong claims for its 'universal' models of perception, those models were highly specific to the culture that developed them. Thus, much of the research was concerned with pitch and timbre, but there was almost no discussion of rhythm, despite the importance of rhythm in most of the world's musics outside that of Euro-American modernism (Born 1995: 201–2). In the case of perceptual coding, the lack of attention to pre-echo in early testing and coding strategy may further evidence a certain inability to hear rhythm as a central category of musical experience.

It is not enough, however, to note the particularist universalism of psychoacoustic theory and research practices. For it raises the more fundamental question of what difference *difference* might make in the listening tests or in the broader development of MPEG audio. Although researchers repeatedly challenged the existing masking research, they did not question

---

[16] Brandenburg interview, 2006, as well as Thibault interview, 2005.

[17] Professional musicians are clearly a categorical exception here, since one can find among them greater relative representation of women and non-white people, however not so much that it outweighs the heavy biases in the other fields. I had hoped to conduct a more thorough study of test subjects, but despite repeated requests, sources at Fraunhofer, AT&T and the Communication Research Centre in Ottawa did not provide me with any information on the expert listeners used in their tests.

[18] Of the 88 unique participants in the two Swedish Radio tests (60 people took each test), 23 were appointed by Swedish Radio, 24 were appointed by the four development groups whose codecs were being tested, and the rest were appointed by groups such as the European Broadcasting Union and the Audio Engineering Society. No clear demographic data are available on this group, other than that many were employed in one or another audio business; however, all but a small handful of names on the list are recognisably male (Grewin and Rydén 1991).

existing practices of subject selection for psychoacoustic and engineering research. For instance, an article from 1992 by Søren Bech, a researcher for the high-end audio company Bang and Olufsen, sums up the field's common sense regarding the selection of research subjects around the time of the MPEG tests. He argues that subjects should be selected on the basis of who could best produce a reproducible measure (on an appropriate rating scale) of a prespecified aspect of the perceived sound being tested. Demographic and cultural differences such as gender, age, race, class, nationality and language are not directly named in the article or in the literature Bech cites. Test subjects can produce variability in test results, he argues, but these are primarily on the basis of three factors. People with hearing threshold levels that deviate more than fifteen decibels from the norm will produce less reliable results. Training in experimental procedure and protocol also leads to significant differences, since subjects who know how to do the experiments are more likely to operate within their parameters. But a third category, 'previous experience', is of greatest interest (Bech 1992: 591).

'Previous experience' is at first blush just that: prior experience with sound reproduction equipment, familiarity with 'live' sound in concert situations, playing an instrument, critical listening practice, 'and the general aptitude for detecting sonic differences in reproduced sound' (Kirk 1956; Bech 1992: 593). This experience must be obtained, and it could be more or less easy to get depending upon who you are. To begin with, critical listening practice, experience of working with live sound or studios and certain kinds of musical equipment are heavily gendered. Engineering culture is still very male in both number and flavour, as are other relevant areas of musical subcultural practice: from the avant-garde, recording and composition wings of music schools, to musical instrument stores and record shops, to music journalism (Whitely 1997; Sandstrom 2000; Meintjes 2003; Rodgers 2010). Yet for all this, 'previous experience' is an exceptionally desirable quality in a listening test subject. Bech notes that 'there is a positive correlation between the degree of previous experience of a group of subjects and homogeneity of ratings within the group'. This is crucial: people who have more experience with audio technology, who are more inculcated into the culture of working with it, are more likely to produce similar results on tests. The culture's own values overcome differences in the listening test scenario once it is well enough established in the test subjects. This effect – the political modulation of listening towards certain values (and away from others) within an audio-technical culture – was sufficiently pronounced that after finding it, Bang and Olufsen moved to establish a permanent listening team to test their equipment: essentially a panel of professional, virtuoso testers

(Bech 1992: 593–4). Clearly, what are at stake here are the common cultural factors that enable people to be selected for a listening test, and having done so, these subjects' greater amenability to the test scenario itself if they are already used to talking about, working with or thinking about sound. But even if common cultural factors don't bring them to the world of audio equipment, time spent in that world may provide common culture enough.

Another factor may be of even greater significance: aesthetic acclimatisation. A still-cited 1956 study of college students' loudspeaker preferences at Ohio State University found that exposure to a particular sound system over time led students to have a preference for that system; that in general students preferred the sound of 'low-fi' to 'hi-fi' speaker systems; and that the type of music students listened to was correlated with their preferences for the sonic characteristics of speakers (Kirk 1956). Although the author behaves like a good social scientist and cautions against overgeneralising the results, the study has been cited repeatedly in subsequent literature on listening tests down to the present day. Taken together, these various implications of 'experience' explain *both* the bias towards engineering values in the MPEG tests and the preferences among today's university students for 128k MP3 audio over other formats (Ahmed and Burgess 2009). Even though they can be extremely subtle and hard to detect at first (or without instruction), audible differences between MP3 and CD-quality audio have become an important part of mediatic sound culture in the intervening years. For a generation of listeners, MP3 may become 'how the music is supposed to sound' in the same way that cassette tapes, reel-to-reel, vinyl records, tube radios and phonograph cylinders have become defaults in other times and places. Indeed, the worries over the thirty-odd-year lifetime of formats indicated that the test designers considered experience as a problem in the future, and not just in the present. 'Since the use of audio equipment based on audio compression technology (like memory based portable audio players) itself constitutes extensive training, we can expect that over time everybody becomes an expert listener. Therefore, from the beginning, encoders should better be turned to satisfy the quality requirements of expert listeners' (Brandenburg 1999: 9; see also Bech and Zacharov 2006).

It is a cliché to say that technologies reveal themselves and their limits at moments of failure, and best conceal themselves (or at least their technological character) at moments when they succeed. We discover the unusability of equipment 'not by looking at it and establishing its properties, but rather by the circumspection of the dealings in which we use it. When its unusability is thus discovered, equipment becomes conspicuous'

(Heidegger 1962: 102). Yet 'broken' or 'unusable' is not an objective state of a piece of equipment, but rather a question of orientation and relationship. An object is not in itself unusable but unusable for somebody in particular. As Sara Ahmed (2006: 49) writes, '[a] hammer might be too heavy for you to use but perfectly adequate for me ... What is at stake in moments of failure is not so much access to properties but attributions of properties, which become a matter of how we *approach* this object'. Even expert listeners who act like 'meters' (to use Thibault's language) represent a 'for whom' – a referent – of the technology, and not a universal or timeless subject.

I posed the question of difference – in the selection of listening test subjects, and in the range of their experience – to a number of people involved in the development of the MP3 format and received a wide range of responses. Louis Thibault argued that no differences mattered except for the actual regularity of performance on the tests themselves. In other words, if people gave reliable and consistent results, that was good enough. J. J. Johnston asserted the importance of age and experience. As people grow older, they tend to lose some of their hearing – for both natural and cultural reasons – but aging can be mitigated by experience with testing scenarios. In fact, aesthetics can re-emerge as an issue in the case of the very artefacts that test subjects are supposed to note and help eliminate. 'I still hear more coding artefacts than most people. But it helps to have 25 years of doing it. [Even with lots of experience] people actually hear the same thing, but they have very different intense dislikes.'[19] Johnston's account gels nicely with Ahmed's: perceptual coding may fail for *you* but not for *me*.

Other people involved in MPEG also acknowledged that some kinds of difference could matter. Bernhard Grill and Marina Bosi, who represented Dolby in the original MPEG meetings and helped develop a successor codec to MP3, noted that language was important for the speech samples, as non-native speakers had more trouble separating signal from system. Karlheinz Brandenburg said that while they didn't consider issues of cultural difference in the tests, it is possible that it might have mattered. Bosi entertained the idea that women and men may hear best at different frequencies. Given the closed nature of the test, I hadn't expected such a wide range of opinion among people actually involved in developing the technology. Perhaps it is therefore better to consider that, via the category of 'previous experience', the possibility of cultural difference is tacitly acknowledged in the design of the listening test, even as it is officially refused. The listening test seeks

[19] Johnston interview, 2007.

to overcome difference through its own guided particularist strategies; it attends to difference, but primarily by eliminating it as a variable.

## Conclusion

The international success of the MP3 – for countless listeners and musical genres – neither proves the existence of a universal listening subject who stands outside all cultural difference, nor does it prove the bad taste of the masses or the failure of objectivist science. Like good pragmatists, engineers and the communication systems they build do not ask whether something is universally true, but simply if it works. To locate the MP3 and the listening subject it addresses and inscribes, we must move back out from the test to the mediatic world of sound that it inhabits. The MP3 does not only reflect the habitus of its relatively elite and subcultural engineering test subjects. Recall that the listening test is, in engineering parlance, a worst-case scenario: 'difficult' material that is timbrally or temporally complex for the coder, 'difficult' listeners and a listening environment to which few people have access. One might then ask what a better- or best-case scenario for the MP3 would be – and the answer is listeners who are less hung up on sound quality, material less difficult to reproduce, and a sound system and listening environment that are full of irregularities. The more distracted the listening subject, the worse the speakers, headphones or room, and the denser the recording, the better an MP3 will work. MP3 is a format designed for casual users, to be heard in earphones on trains or on the tiny speakers of a computer desktop, to be sent in emails, instant messages and through file-sharing programs. This is not all music for all time; instead the MP3 speaks to the condition of music in contemporary urban life in many places around the globe.

  To put it another way, the shadow of the listening test subject may fail tests for scientific universality, but it achieves a kind of social ubiquity because of the musical and sonic contexts through which MP3s circulate. To the extent that MPEG succeeded in their old ambitions for interoperability and transnationality (ambitions one also finds in the practice of professional recordists, broadcast engineers and mastering engineers), a relatively limited set of sonic aesthetics obtain for an incredibly large and diverse array of recorded media. This is the case not just across musical genres, but across other types of content such as broadcast speech. The sonic referent of the MP3 is a massive, polymorphous, interlaced global network of sonic technologies, practices and institutions. MP3s may confront an almost infinite and unmeasurable multiplicity of listeners, but they do so within a surprisingly limited set of contexts and aesthetics of 'good sound'. A standardisation of sonic aesthetics may suggest a standardisation of musical or sonic subjectivity. But that is not necessarily the case; one can have an infinite multiplicity of listeners even if there are only a handful of important mastering engineers in the world. The MP3 codec's standardised listening subject may serve to modulate real instances of listening, but it is just that: a modulation, an adjustment, and not strictly a determination.

Listening tests turn a historical relationship among ears, technologies and music in upon itself, as an object of manipulation to be sure, but also, as I have shown here, as an object worthy of contemplation. They are not just interesting for their particularity but for the fact that a format born in such specific circumstances, of such a limited and situated set of sensibilities, has travelled so well. The sonic success of the MP3 can be attributed to its mediaphilic qualities: that it is above all else a creature of the mediatic world in which it was supposed to travel. To the extent that MP3s carry with them a sonic signature, this is not the failure of the form. Every recording medium has had a moment in its history where its designers have sought to achieve a transparency, where it would erase itself. The innovation of the MP3 was the quest for perceptual transparency such that the medium would not fully erase itself, but where the mind's ear would complete the Hegelian synthesis. Of course it fails on those grounds – all media do. Like all other formats and media before it, the MP3 is not a transparent conduit (even if lots of people can't tell that it isn't or no longer try to hear whether it is). But its lack of transparency is an index of success, not failure.

As people have spent years with the format, they have come to hear it *as a format*, as a character in the pantheon of sound technologies that populate the contemporary soundscape. Like the hiss of tape or the noise of vinyl records, the artefacts of MP3 sound reveal the format's struggle with its own limits and with human limits. Over time, the MP3's sonic artefacts become historical artefacts marking a moment in the couplings of minds and maths, ears and media that characterise our sonic modernity. Some listeners will listen through the format's artefacts. Others will find them a source of aesthetic sustenance or annoyance. Eventually, the MP3's artefacts will become part of the sound of some music genres, as happened with vinyl and various forms of magnetic tape. In fact, this may already be the case in emergent genres such as mashup.

The MP3 format mutates a public–private split within itself. Every MP3 encoder requires a mathematical model of a listening subject to be used to decide which parts of the audio recording to keep and which parts to discard (and this is true for all perceptually coded formats). When played back, every MP3 has within it the shadow of that imagined ideal listening subject. In the format's psychoacoustic model, the ear is an information device, a sound receiver and part of a digital reproduction system. The format uses the normative listener's body to uphold and lubricate the infrastructures through which digital audio is transmitted, disseminated and circulated: from the internet itself, to individual playback devices, to the legal, semi-legal and illegal markets for physical media that contain MP3s. This process is political modulation at work: the encoder only has access to an imagined, ideal, composite listening subject constructed through listening tests. Yet in making, transmitting, storing and hearing MP3s, real subjects' hearing – and the real limits thereof – are folded into massive communication infrastructures and economies. The MP3 may not be unique in taking advantage of this arrangement, but it is particularly successful. To borrow a phrase from software design, we may experience ourselves as the 'end users' of MP3 audio. We may experience listening as deeply interior, personal and meaningful. But the networks through which MP3s travel also experience our act of listening. For the MP3 and its networks, an act of listening happens in the middle of communication and not only at – or as – its end.

# 5 | Tuning the human race: athletic capitalism and the Nike+ Sport Kit

SUMANTH GOPINATH AND JASON STANYEK

On 31 August 2008 the Nike Corporation sponsored its very first 'Human Race'. This massive, multi-city 10 kilometre contest was billed as the world's largest-ever running event: one million participants, each wearing an orange T-shirt emblazoned with a unique seven-digit bib number and each porting a radio frequency identification (RFID) tag, took to the streets in twenty-five 'global cities', with the first race taking place in Taipei and the last in Los Angeles. The magnitude of the event was befitting of the world's largest manufacturer of athletic footwear and apparel, with almost $20 billion in sales (2009) and a market share of over 33 per cent worldwide (Wikinvest n.d.). Not to be hemmed in by the spatialities of congregated publics, the event's geographies seeped out beyond the twenty-five primary sites: those lacking access to one of the host cities could participate 'virtually' by using the Nike+ SportBand or the Nike+ Sport Kit, a transmitter/receiver set that integrates with Apple products (iPods and iPhones). Both the Band and Kit collect data (run times, distance, speed, calories burned) that runners can access as real-time feedback and upload to the Nike+ website, 'syncing their runs' with other participants – thereby allowing interested consumers to 'run anywhere with Nike+', according to one advertisement. Only the Kit, however, merges data collection with the music-playing functions of Apple's popular devices, a highly successful marketing strategy aimed at appropriating the already existing listening habits of joggers. The Human Race – promoted as a global, feel-good event with humanistic, even humanitarian ambitions – was a prompt for consumers to purchase Nike products (Zarda 2008). Indeed, the 'Human Race' page of the Nike+ website mentioned the 'steps for race day success', with a link to 'get the gear … to track your runs' (Nike Corporation 2009b). The Human Race was clearly a mega-marketing event, with participants serving as both customers and promotional labourers, a veritable 'human billboard for Nike' (Story 2007).

Building on its (in)famous branding practices of the 1980s and 1990s, Nike pursued an innovative 'experiential marketing' strategy in which its

Many thanks to Beth Hartman, Danielle Kuntz, Matthew Mihalka, Aurelie Tu and Georgina Born for their thoughts and suggestions for this chapter.

centrepiece – an award-winning interactive website as much a part of the race as the runners on the ground – converged with more familiar advertising media.[1] A voiceless television commercial, for example, features images of suffocatingly large masses of people running together, swarm-like, through both the iconic areas of Nike's global cities and the nondescript, off-the-race-map locales whose place within the cosmopolitan sphere is seemingly guaranteed by the articulatory magic of the Nike+ website. At the end of the commercial, against a background shot of the planet earth – seen from space with its blue glow accented by a luminescent orange (given off, perhaps, by all the runners in Nike T-shirts darting across its terrestrial continents) – captions tell us to 'Run the Day the Whole World Runs' and 'Join the Nike+ Human Race'.[2]

The triumphant globalism of the Nike+ Human Race had a sound too. Each of the twenty-five cities featured concerts by major artists, including: Moby in London; All-American Rejects in New York; Fall Out Boy in Chicago; Kelly Rowland in Paris; The Pinker Tones in Madrid; Kenan Dogulu in Istanbul; The Fantastic Four in Munich; Yu Quan in Shanghai; Boys Like Girls in Singapore; and a grand finale in Los Angeles with Kanye West.[3] The print ads promoting the event unsurprisingly show some runners with white Apple earbuds and others fiddling with the controls of their iPods. We can imagine what they are hearing, and it is probably not the music emanating from artists on concert stages; these runners principally attend to the sonic worlds crafted and mixed together by the Sport Kit.

The Nike+ Sport Kit system, like the Human Race, is unimaginable without the many different sounds it makes and employs. But the auditory is not the final horizon of the Kit, and for our purposes what is at stake is the way in which sound and music are employed in the service of a broader corporate project, one that also encompasses tightly reticulated marketing practices, the new capitalism's ever more proximate techniques and technologies of the body, and the data-based construction of the human consumer within informational neoliberalism. In what follows, we begin by situating the Sport Kit within contemporary discourses on experiential marketing and the corporate marshalling of the cookie economy in the service of a distinct subsector of the entertainment/leisure industry, an

---

[1] Nike won the Adweek Media 'Best of the 2000s' award for the 'Digital Campaign of the Decade' with its Nike+ website (Morrissey n.d.). On Nike and branding, see Klein 1999.

[2] The video advertisement is found at www.youtube.com/watch?v=KEkrl722niY, (last accessed May 2012).

[3] Music concerts are now frequently combined with long-distance, public-space running events, as in the 'Rock 'n' Roll Marathon' franchise.

'athletic capitalism' inseparable from the broader lineaments of biocapitalism. We then provide a two-part history of the techno-social lineages informing the production and usage of the Nike+ Sport Kit: respectively, the incorporation of biofeedback into athletics training and the adoption of portable music players in a nascent mass exercise culture. Finally, we disambiguate the notion of 'tuning' with respect to the coproduction of data by music and bodies, the broader ramifications of which extend beyond the individual to larger, networked collectivities and the privatised reconfiguration of online publics.

Indeed, it is the concept of 'tuning' – a central trope within Nike's advertising discourse for the Sport Kit – that forms the theoretical heart of our chapter. A fundamentally musical and sonic term deriving from the word 'tone', tuning can allude to feedback and system optimisation (as in tuning an instrument or machine), attentiveness and attendance to sensory stimuli, information and broader social conditions (as in the radiophonic metaphor of 'tuning in'), as well as the making of music and sound itself (as in the now antiquated usage of 'tuning the psalm' or leading a congregation in song).[4] In the case of Nike+, tuning works on multiple levels and scales, from individual instances of running involving the attunement to music and one's own body, to the broader harmonising of large populations in the construction and maintenance of a consumer base sufficient to guarantee returns on corporate investitures. Of course, tuning also implies a degree of agency and requires conscious or unconscious acts of will ensuring the co-ordination of different elements into a functional whole. Tuning is therefore a way of describing a corporate strategy, one positioned somewhat precariously between notions of monopolistic or oligopolistic dominance, on the one hand, and the moments of collaboration that are sometimes described in common business parlance as 'synergy', on the other. (Indeed, the Nike and Apple collaboration considered here is often described as a synergistic business venture.) Hence, seemingly disparate moments of entrainment, syncing/synchronisation and motivation are, in the last instance, a lining up of links within the massively multiple commodity chains that the Nike corporation must continually manage as it exploits the opportunities available within the capitalist world economy as currently constituted. In tuning in to the emergent social tendencies it has helped to produce, Nike amplifies resonances within a system of its own making that can have unpredictable consequences ranging from the demands of unruly consumers to protracted legal battles and other scandals besetting an institution long reviled

---

[4] OED Online 2010.

as a bad corporate citizen.[5] Although we do not tease out all of the broader political and economic implications of the Sport Kit's emergence and rise to prominence, our analysis nonetheless provides a materialist foundation for a more thoroughgoing critique and thereby points to the darkest shadows – and discordant creaks and cracks – cast by the footfall of millions of runners served.

## The Nike+ Sport Kit and the biopolitics of athletic capitalism

Developed by Nike in conjunction with Apple, and released in May 2006, the Sport Kit consists of a pedometric sensor that is meant to be placed in a specially designed space under the insole of a Nike+ shoe and a receiver that connects to an iPod Nano. (The sensor can also be used with an iPhone or iPod Touch.) The receiver contains an antenna that picks up data sent in the form of radio waves by the RFID transmitter in the sensor. The motion-sensing element in the sensor is a piezoelectric accelerometer that detects the amount of time the user's foot is on the ground, converting ground contact time into running speed. In essence, the Sport Kit turns the iPod into a portable running computer that provides information about run times, speed, calories burned and so on. This information is delivered in real time to the user via a graphical display on the Nano's screen that shows elapsed time, distance and speed, and by means of generic voices that periodically provide feedback to the user (for example, 'Halfway point, ten minutes remaining' or 'Activity stopped. Press the centre button to resume your workout'). As the voice enters, whatever music is playing fades down and is brought up to full volume only after the audible data is delivered. Voices of celebrity athletes might also make motivational appearances; at the end of a workout, the world-famous cyclist Lance Armstrong could come on and say, 'Congratulations, that is your longest run ever.' Celebrities also design purchasable playlists of their favourite music, which serve as the backdrop for workout routines that they apparently direct. Sometimes music groups get into the act as well through the creation of Nike-commissioned 'Original Run' albums: 45-minute-long sequences of continuously mixed songs that hew closely to Nike's prescribed tempo progressions (calculated in beats per minute

---

[5] On Nike's egregious labour practices see, for example, Shaw 1999 and Featherstone and United Students Against Sweatshops 2002.

or BPMs).[6] Perhaps the Kit's trademark feature is the PowerSong, which is triggered by the runner pressing the iPod's centre button at a crucial point during the run, suddenly cutting to a new, preselected song with the intention that it will add an extra charge that can enhance one's performance. The PowerSong represents a subtle refunctionalisation of the iPod's architecture, but an important one, as we show below.

When workouts are completed, users can upload the data collected by the Apple device to 'nikeplus.com', an interactive website that synchronises with iTunes. Each user has a personal page on the website and is able to use graphical representations to track his/her workout history or to create competitive 'challenges' with other users. The website also includes a discussion forum and a Nike+ community mile-counter, which in December 2010 was at around the 300-million-mile mark. Of course, Nike and Apple 'gear' can be purchased through the site. In order to sell the Sport Kit, Nike has created a multileveled, integrated projection of its brand, a marketing campaign that vends not only the vastness of the Nike product line (and, not inconsequentially, part of Apple's as well), but also the experience of running itself.

In appraising the Nike+ marketing campaign, we might easily overlook an unassuming advertisement that features the familiar orange background, a single Nike sneaker, an iPod Nano, a Sport Kit in its box, the Nike+ logo and a simple caption telling us to 'Experience Nike+'. *Experience*, here, is the operative term. Not simply a command for customers to purchase and use Nike products, the word issues a call for a participatory consumerism known widely in the advertising industry as 'experiential marketing'. One of its proponents, Bernd Schmitt, describes it as follows: 'In the world in which brands rule, products are no longer bundles of functional characteristics, but a means to provide and enhance a user's experience'. For Schmitt, brands have become rich sources of 'sensory, affective, and cognitive associations' (Schmitt 1999: 10, 21). Erik Hauser, the founder and creative director of Swivel Media, which specialises in experiential marketing campaigns, additionally posits, 'The ultimate medium for marketing is people, and to reach them involves giving them a fantastic brand experience. They then will do the marketing for you' (cited in Lenderman 2006: 7). Nike has long sought to cultivate experiential involvement by consumers, as witnessed in its famously minimalist, imperative-laden television and print ads from the 1980s and 1990s (e.g. 'Just Do It'). Recently, however, the company has

---

[6] Since 2006 Nike has commissioned seven 'Original Runs', by The Crystal Method, LCD
   Soundsystem, Aesop Rock, A-Trak, Cassius, The Hives and De La Soul.

been eschewing traditional, passive-spectator-oriented advertising campaigns in favour of a more interactive marketing strategy as found in the Human Race/Nike+ conjunction (Klein 1999: 15–26). Redirecting copious resources formerly devoted to a mainstream media advertising budget, Nike has developed multiple means of connecting to consumers including its website, organised events ranging from weekly coached runs to the Human Race, stores offering free exercise consulting, and – most importantly for our purposes – carefully designed uses of sound and music appearing on mobile listening devices and elsewhere.[7]

Such sensory enticements provide a way for Nike to extract an unprecedented degree of unpaid labour from its consumers. For Nike+ users do not merely compile their own running data for personal use; they upload it to a Nike-owned proprietary website that allows the data to be stored and used by the company for market analysis purposes. Nike's experiential approach to marketing, then, is a new twist in an older history wherein a consumer's leisure time is transformed into a valuable commodity and wherein labour is implicitly outsourced to the consumer.[8] That twist involves the voluntary donation of labour and production of value by consumers for the companies that advertise products to them, and has perhaps been most effectively realised in the so-called Web 2.0 world of user-generated content and crowdsourcing, in which 'participatory culture' effectively transforms into voluntary *labour* on behalf of media monopolies and venture capital.

The value of the labour that consumers perform for companies such as Nike is rooted in a shift of marketing strategies from a general, undifferentiating approach to a more targeted one that started in the 1970s and 1980s. The end result is a personalised marketing practice in which companies create and make use of individual consumer-produced profiles.[9] But these profiles, when analysed both individually and in the aggregate, are valuable information commodities in and of themselves, and as such are shared between firms or even traded for a price – often unbeknownst to consumers.[10] For example, runners who upload their data to the Nike+ website must adhere to the company's Privacy Policy, which allows for generous use of the information Nike collects. The Policy unambiguously states that

---

[7] As Story 2007 notes, 'Nike increased its spending on traditional media in the United States by 3 per cent from 2003 to 2006, to $220.5 million. But in the same period, it increased its non-media ad spending 33 per cent, to $457.9 million'.

[8] See Smythe 1977 on the construction of audiences.

[9] See Burkart and McCourt 2006: 94–101. On subcultural consumer labour production under contemporary digital capitalism, see Terranova 2000: 39.

[10] Angwin 2010 notes that each individual profile is worth 'a tenth of a penny'.

Nike may utilise data to 'improve' their business and that they may, at will, transfer information to their 'preferred service providers'. Data may also be transferred outside the company in response to 'government request' or 'court order' and 'when required by law'. Additionally, Nike harnesses the analytic power of the cookie economy of the World Wide Web to collect IP addresses, browser types and user names. Pixel tags – tiny graphic images embedded in web pages and email messages (the digital version, perhaps, of the sensor inserted into Nike+ sneakers) – function as collecting agents, sucking up information regarding the conduct of website users (for example, whether they open promotional emails), all in an effort to help Nike 'analyze online behavior' (Nike Corporation 2009a). According to Josh Lauer, the work that the consumer does effectively produces a 'data double' that offers a valuable method of surveillance, one equally utilisable by some companies bent on maximising their sales, by other companies attempting to minimise risks associated with potential clients, and even by state agencies involved in law enforcement cases (Lauer 2008: 49, 41–53). The union of consumer surveillance and the athletic goods industry in the Nike+ marketing system brings together two crucial tendencies marked by the decline of state and individual autonomy from capital during the neoliberal era.

Nike+ thus stands at the leading edge of a constellation that might be termed athletic capitalism, or the hyper-commercialisation of both recreational and professional athletics, particularly within the post-1960s United States. Whereas sport had long played a prominent role in the entertainment economy of the United States in the twentieth century, the emergence of a new Baby Boomer 'fitness culture' helped to bring the commodification of sports more pervasively into everyday life. Thus came into being the two halves of athletic capitalism: a capitalism of professional athleticism and a capitalism of plebeian exercising. Central to this development was the growth of the Nike Corporation from a small operation in the late 1970s into *the* major global athletics goods conglomerate by the 1990s.[11] Given that the human body is the primary object around which this form of capitalism developed, recent critical discourse on the Foucauldian notion of 'biopolitics' becomes relevant. And indeed, in the period under consideration, Foucault took note of the increasing power of corporations in the administration of 'biopower'. Rose's (2007: 32) succinct formulation puts it well: 'biopolitics becomes bioeconomics'. One might even link bioeconomics to the term biocapital, which is usually reserved to describe the capital

---

[11] On factors shaping athletic capitalism, see Lasch 1978, Ingham 1985, Vanderbilt 1998 and Maguire 2008.

invested in and accumulated from the biotech sector (Rajan 2006; Rose 2007: 33). Athletic capitalism is and has long been, at one level, a distinct form of biocapitalism: a practice of capital accumulation built upon the extraction of value from the *bios*. When athletic capitalism comes into conjunction with the close-to-the-body data-extraction techniques of experiential and personalised marketing, as with the Nike+ Sport Kit, it – like biotech and biogenetic firms – traffics in the production and commodification of extensive data sets that define human beings or, indeed, the human race writ large.

## The antecedents of the Nike+ Sport Kit

Immanent in the growth of athletic capitalism over the 1970s and 1980s were two distinct practices that developed through an articulation with miniaturised consumer electronics, one largely pertaining at first to specialist athletes and class elites and the other to the growing mass of exercisers. The former practice is bound up with the historical development of biofeedback and involves a practice of diagnostic listening through bodily sonification, as well as a largely visual implementation of biofeedback technologies for running. The latter practice entailed a form of mobile headphone-listening when the Sony Walkman was first released, at almost precisely the same time as running grew into a mass phenomenon in the United States. As we argue below, the Nike+ Sport Kit effectively amounts to a merging of these two practices and their concomitant technologies. These intertwined historical trajectories are so essential to the understanding of the Nike+ system that they each merit separate treatment.

## Biofeedback, athletics training and diagnostic listening

Defined as the voluntary control of autonomic functions for the purpose of achieving a healthy state of homeostasis, biofeedback emerged as a result of experiments in the late 1950s and early 1960s by the behaviourist psychologist Neal Miller, who demonstrated that rats and humans could, with appropriate rewards, raise or lower their heart rates and blood pressure (Robbins 2000: 37). Two additional developments should be stressed: the 'evolution of [sensitive] electrical instrumentation that grew out of the war effort during World War II', which could measure faint electrical impulses; and 'research on stress and the role it played in illness' (Robbins 2000:

56).[12] The increase in stress management studies and therapies can be traced back in turn to prior research by Claude Bernard (who first coined the term 'homeostasis' in the nineteenth century), Walter Cannon (who first named the 'fight or flight' response of the sympathetic nervous system in the 1930s) and others; it can also be linked to the post-war culture of the 'organisation man', whose daily stresses of conforming to the bureaucratic and managerial requirements of large corporations would make such therapies desirable, particularly to baby boomers seeking to escape the fates of their fathers. By 1969 biofeedback was becoming professionalised, as marked by that year's formation of the Biofeedback Research Society, and the 1970s – when most of the baby boomer generation first sought stable employment – witnessed a distinct rise in publications and organisations dedicated to biofeedback.

The use of biofeedback in sports training first appeared in the late 1970s and early 1980s. According to Wesley Sime, much of the early interest on the part of professional athletics trainers and sports psychologists lay in studying heart-rate variability as a measure of 'emotion and anxiety related to performance' (Sime 2003: 561), with an emphasis on heart-rate and oxygen-intake reduction for the sake of increased efficiency. In a report by the Biofeedback Society of America in 1980, three potential applications for athletes were identified: stress management in performance, sports injury rehabilitation and performance enhancement through training (Sandweiss and Wolf 1985: xi–xii). Central to all of these applications was the facilitation of concentrated attention to the body – particularly in training routines in which 'boredom is a factor', leading to distraction or dissociation (Sime 1985: 59).

Auditory feedback played a significant role in early biofeedback experimentation, the reasons for which might easily be surmised: sound is relatively easy to process while one is focusing on another task, especially when that task is of a visually intensive nature. In addition, redundancy enhances signal perception, and for this reason many biofeedback experiments involve visual and auditory feedback working in tandem. In part, this works because of the simplicity of some sonic signals: the 'auditory culture' of biofeedback therapy is one in which beeps, clicks, oscillator tones and other basic sounds predominate, enhancing perception of bodily activity rather than creating dissociation (which might be caused by more complex sonic

---

[12] Relevant biological measurement technologies include electroencephalography (EEG), electromyography (EMG), electrocardiography (EKG) and galvanic skin response measurement (GSR).

information) (Dozza, Horak and Chiari 2007: 38). In contrast to aesthetic listening, then, biofeedback entrains individuals in a practice of *diagnostic listening* – using sound to identify suboptimal behaviours and prompting measures to correct them.[13] An example can illustrate this process. In 1978 a team of researchers at Pennsylvania State University studied biofeedback training in shooting and archery, noting in one case that:

A world champion archer … had developed a 'bad habit' of tightly squinting his nonsighting eye when the arrow was released. This unconscious squinting continued until the arrow went down range and into the target. Although this only lasted a few seconds, its repeated effect over the course of shooting 144 arrows was to give this shooter a headache at the end of a day of shooting. Suspecting that the squinting might be causing this problem … we placed electrodes adjacent to his nonshooting eye and allowed him to listen, via a speaker, to the sound of his muscle tension. He concentrated on this sound and with each succeeding shot, he was able to reduce what was once a 3–5-sec squint to a single blink of his eye. (Landers 1985: 94)

This example points to another important aspect of biofeedback: it inserts a stage of mediation into the feedback loop between the body and ear. Diagnostic listening is frequently a matter of self-diagnosis (although a clinician often serves as a guiding presence). As such, bio-statistical data is made audible or transformed into sound as communicative information. We might then appreciate that this communicative process is one of sonification, though we tend to associate that term with the transformation of data-rich information into equally data-rich sound; sonification, in fact, exists on a continuum from the simplest mappings of data into sound, on one end, to highly complex sound-production translations, on the other (Barrass, Whitelaw and Bailes 2006).

   The literature on auditory biofeedback, whether in athletics training or in medical–therapeutic contexts, suggests that body-signal mappings and translations orient individuals towards specific spatial positionings and movements. Sound often functions, with proper training, to encourage or discourage certain kinds of bodily movement – as in the archery example above. A distinction then needs to be drawn between the use of biofeedback in precision muscular and motor skill enhancement and its application to the entire motor system in endurance activities such as distance running. In biofeedback training regimens for runners, the representation of bodily signals is typically visual – as in numerical readouts – perhaps in part because

---

[13]  Diagnostic listening is an example of what Jonathan Sterne calls 'audile technique', in which 'listening becomes a technical skill, a skill that can be developed and used toward instrumental ends' (Sterne 2003: 93).

the rhythms of cyclical auditory signals are believed to interfere with the bodily rhythms of continuous, repetitive movement.

Thus, when portable biofeedback devices were first marketed to runners in the late 1970s and early 1980s, they primarily featured visual representations of data. Liquid crystal display (LCD) technology, the product of microelectronic miniaturisation, was critically important, although it did not develop specifically for biofeedback applications but for consumer electronics items such as calculators and digital watches. However, digital watches became very popular among runners partly on account of their stopwatch function – so much so that an entrepreneur, Richard Thalheimer, built a successful specialty firm, The Sharper Image, by marketing the Seiko Realtime watch to joggers. Shortly thereafter, the firm also began to sell pedometers (Russell 2007).[14] Biofeedback training for runners was directly tied to these new miniaturised digital technologies, as in the Polar Electro (1982), the first wireless heart-rate monitor used for running and linked to a digital wristwatch interface. By 1984 another Polar heart-rate monitor, the Sport Tester PE3000, could collect data and sync with a personal computer to keep track of workout information over a longer period of time – thus anticipating the connectivity of the Nike+ Sport Kit. As a critical intervention in biofeedback-based athletics training, the heart-rate monitor would become commonplace in professional and serious amateur athletics, with one expert in exercise training noting that 'Wireless heart rate monitors brought high-tech biofeedback training within the reach of all our athletes' (Burke 1998: vii). By the early 1990s heart-rate-monitor watches, now marketed by larger electronics conglomerates such as Casio, had progressed beyond the specialist clientele for which they were originally developed.[15] This trend has continued over the past two decades, with an ever-greater number of devices – such as portable running computers – being marketed from the early 2000s to ever-larger numbers of the exercising masses.

## Mobile headphone-listening and the running boom

Just as biofeedback was beginning to feature in athletics training, the Sony Walkman first became known to the world. Released in 1979, the Walkman and its history are relatively well known (Hosokawa 1984; du Gay *et al.* 1997). For our purposes, the most important aspect of the Walkman lies

---

[14] See also 'Well healed and wired up', *New York Times*, 2 November 1980, p. 19, col. 3.
[15] See 'New watch takes your pulse', *Report from Japan*, 4 December 1992.

in its contemporaneous articulation with the boom in exercising, particularly running. The same demographic that participated in the convergence of electronic and digital miniaturisation with biofeedback-based athletic training – namely the aging and narcissistic baby boomer cohort, now empowered with growing disposable incomes – also helped to propel the Walkman to great popularity. The Walkman seemed to change the relationship between running and music almost instantaneously. By 1982 a discussion of a fitness centre notes that only a few of its clients 'seem not to be plugged into a Sony Walkman' (Cobb 1982). The Walkman's penetration into daily habits and public space aroused questions about public safety and auditory isolation, questions that were answered at times with rather extreme measures. Thus, reacting to news of a ban against public headphone use in Woodbridge, New Jersey, a columnist offered the following commentary:

I suppose, if I had to finger one culprit, I'd point to what seems an increasing misunderstanding of the value of solitude. These devices, after all, allow you to imagine that you are not alone. 'I am not merely running down this city street or this country lane', says the wired-up jogger. 'I am grooving to my own favorite group. I no longer have to content myself with my own thinking. Ah, no. I am not alone. This is LIFE!' (Kidder 1982)

If the discussion above sounds familiar to those aware of similar debates about the iPod, public safety and social isolationism, it is because the listening practice that the iPod represents has a provenance spanning over two decades, one marked by changing music storage and reproduction technologies: cassettes, compact discs, minidiscs, digital sound files (Bull 2000: 183; Sterne 2006). The practice of running with headphones was, however, altered by the release of the iPod and other portable MP3 players, which came with features suited to exercising. Most obviously, they made running to music much easier: the burdens of switching or flipping cassettes or the (in retrospect) relatively cumbersome interfaces of portable cassette and compact disc players were alleviated. Perhaps even more important is the iPod's multifunctionality, made possible in part through its advanced use of LCD screens; for example, recent iPods incorporate a stopwatch and even a pedometer, the latter making use of the iPod's own motion sensor (Biersdorfer and Pogue 2009: 201–2). Programming playlists allows runners to tailor their musical running experience with a much greater degree of precision, building on the celebrated practice of making mix tapes.

Why did running become so entwined with listening to music on headphones? Popular discourse emphasises music's ability to ward off fatigue and boredom, as well as to provide motivation. But the situation is more complicated than this, and indeed a great deal of sports research has been devoted to whether and how music-listening affects athletic performance. Karageorghis and Priest (2008) summarise previous research and identify five principal mechanisms: 'dissociation, arousal regulation, synchronisation, acquisition of motor skills, and attainment of flow'. They also suggest that runners should utilise a well-chosen sequence of 'a wide selection of familiar tracks'. The implication is that there are specific formal curves – principally mapped around a measured build-up to peak heart rate – that are most advantageous for producing optimal physical states during running. Runners have been intuitively exploiting these curves for years by producing such song sequences (whether in mix tapes or MP3 playlists) that amount to compositional acts, enhancing their running efficiency in ways simply not possible without music piped in through headphones. But only with the release of the Nike+ Sport Kit did a single device enable the sonic affordances of song sequences to converge with the monitoring of vital body signals, combining both into a single sonic flow by turning biofeedback data into auditory information.

## Tune your run

The rhetorical universe of the Nike+ advertising campaign includes a panoply of taglines, none more resonant than 'tune your run'. As mentioned above, the phrase is multivalent, with associations of body tone, mechanical tune-ups, diagnostic 'fine-tuning' and more; but it also highlights the auditory nature of the process – the run, runner and machine as a sonic system to be tuned. Most of the *Original Run* recording booklets include a section called 'Tune Your Run with Nike+', a step-by-step guide for using the Sport Kit in tandem with the iPod/iPhone. While the 'tuning' suggested by Nike precedes the run (i.e. preparing the iPod) and continues after the run has ended (i.e. syncing data to nikeplus.com), the heart of the process happens *during* the run with the pressing of the iPod's 'play' button and the resulting shift in sonic environment seemingly activating the runner's initial motion ('press play and start moving').

Not so apparent in these rather basic directions is that Nike is harnessing two kinds of auditory information: the voices relaying a literal kind of run-time data both at specified intervals and on command, and the music upon which the voices are superimposed. Music, however, functions as a kind of data as well, in the sense that the body, in becoming attuned to various musical parameters (rhythm, textual content, texture and timbre), helps to reproduce it as part of a feedback loop. Perhaps the most common means of attunement in running occurs between physical movement and music's rhythmic–metrical structure, which is frequently conceptualised and measured in BPMs. Runners have long been preoccupied with BPM ratings of music, as can be gleaned from numerous websites presenting a rather precise understanding of how the runner's pace can map literally onto the tempo of the music (using the calculation of steps per minute, SPM).[16] To perhaps state the obvious, running to music involves entrainment: that is, when two or more 'autonomous rhythmic processes or oscillators … "lock-in" to a common phase and/or periodicity' (Clayton, Sager and Will 2004: 2). Human entrainment often involves attentiveness to pre-existing rhythmic processes or patterns, and this can take place in numerous contexts – dancing, musical performance, habituation to schedules and rituals and the unconscious alignment of biological processes, as well as exercise (DeNora 2000: 78–9, 89–102). In entraining their bodies to music, runners are enjoined to apprehend it instrumentally and transform it into a metronome, such that music's qualitative characteristics are reduced – significantly, as we will see below – to a quantitative measure of its rhythmic and metrical structure. The Nike+ website not only produces a graph that plots the run's speed (y-axis) against distance (x-axis), but identifies points during the run when the runner asked for feedback from the Kit.[17] Such moments of human–device interaction are important because they highlight precisely when information affects performance; indeed, one could examine such a graph to determine whether the device queries for run information coincide with significant changes in speed. The runner's triggering of the PowerSong is also identified on the graph; given that the PowerSong is intended, in the words of one Nike+ advertisement, to 'boost' one's performance, one of the features relevant here is, again, the particular BPM marking of that song, which is often slightly higher than that of the average running playlist track.

In this sense, it is BPM – a form of data connecting the epistemologies of music and human bodies – that becomes a crucial link in the articulatory relationship between the sounds that entrain bodies and bodily activity itself, between music's rhythmic anatomy and the rhythms of the human body. A recent (June 2010) alliance between Nike and Polar – the inventor

[16] See, for example, the links on the 'Marathoning Matters' website (Strehlo n.d.)

[17] Other devices and interfaces (such as the Adidas miCoach) developed a more sophisticated global positioning system (GPS) for spatially tracking and mapping a run, causing the Nike+ system in due course to incorporate such mapping as well.

of the wireless heart-rate monitor and a premier manufacturer of portable biofeedback devices for athletes – points to Nike's recognition of the crucial functions of BPM data, which is now the standard measurement for heart rate on most exercise equipment. To state the matter explicitly, both heart rate and musical tempo are measured in BPMs, although runners attend to these forms of information in rather different ways: whereas musical tempo is engaged with at the level of bodily entrainment, heart-rate data is largely cognised through numerical representations (which are rendered as spoken feedback in the Sport Kit). Nike's foray into the world of heart-rate monitors should not be taken as merely another parasitic manoeuvre by a company intent on colonising further outreaches of the athletics marketplace. Certainly, in their mandates to the commissioned composers and artists in the *Original Run* recording series, Nike has been directly involved in linking information about BPMs to a conceptualisation of how running works. But the Nike/Polar alliance (following on Yamaha's BODiBEAT and in relation to other recent BPM running apps for the iPhone)[18] takes a crucial next step towards 'tuning the run', even if the Polar-enhanced Nike+ does not go so far as the BODiBEAT in matching music to heart rate. The + in Nike+, which initially signalled the company's connections with Apple, now indicates Nike's compatibility with the products of other companies, auguring the potential of networked devices in a logic of exponentially growing combinatoriality.

BPM, however, is not the ultimate horizon of a runner's attunement to music. In a 2008 expose in *Runner's World* on 'the perfect running song', author Jeff Pearlman cites disparate features beyond tempo and 'a relentless rhythm' that make a song 'effective' for runners: 'powerful themes' ('lyrics that inspire or inflame the passions'); 'a trancelike quality' (unobtrusive mixes that enable runners to 'forget they're listening' to music while simultaneously distracting a runner's focus from severe bodily stress); and 'uplifting arrangements' ('expansive melodies and sweeping soundscapes that just hold [the runner] up for a while') (Pearlman 2008: 80, 82). These perspectives are generally applicable to headphoned running; but the Sport Kit offers additional ways for runners to interact with music and sound, notably the PowerSong, which, as described earlier, allows the runner to cut immediately to a song pre-chosen to provide an extra 'boost'. Nike, in fact, has produced a rather extensive discourse on the PowerSong, soliciting

---

[18] The iPhone cannot yet calculate heart rate, but BPM-matching apps for runners are becoming increasingly common. As of June 2010, these include 'Cadence' (with the tagline 'Your music. Your motion') and 'Synchstep' ('The beat that follows your feet').

examples from Nike+ users on its website and going so far as to theorise, among other categories, the musically rather unspecific notion of 'energy', which encompasses a large swathe of additional musical attributes such as timbre, volume, genre and texture: 'lyrics are insignificant, but the energy of a song is everything. Jagged guitars and driving beats rule here. The louder the better' (Nike Corporation 2010).

The forum on the Nike+ website is a rich source for learning about runners' thoughts on the PowerSong, which is rarely selected only for its beat-entraining capacity. For example, one runner describes a mimetic relationship between a PowerSong's lyrics and running itself, and cites the line 'feet don't fail me now' from Kanye West and Tupac's 'Jesus Walks' as providing the necessary energy for finishing a run (bellalou 2010). Another forum contributor claims an intertextual link with Bill Conti's 'Gonna Fly Now', from the famous running scene in *Rocky* (1976): 'I don't know why but something about that song gets my legs churning even if I'm at the tail end of a run. I've seen the original Rocky about 10 times so every time I hear it I guess I'm conditioned to push harder' (Dr_Evil_MD 2010).

The central sonic innovation of the Sport Kit, however, lies not in its music-listening capabilities, but rather its capacity to layer prerecorded and synthesised human voices on top of the playlists and tunes heard by iPod users. As we noted earlier, the information imparted by the voices amounts to the crucial moment of auditory feedback guiding the runner during the course of a run. But more is at stake in the discursive content of these vocalised statements. For one, the voices conveying run data in real time appear both at pre-programmed intervals and when invoked during the run, making the run both cognisable and more manageable in a way not dissimilar to how time and progress are marked on an exercise machine. In a sense, these generic voices produce a temporal/spatial plot for the run, segmenting time and space into data that can be attended to audibly. For many runners this is a crucial attribute of the Nike+ system. Writing on the message board of a user website in 2006 (soon after the Nike+ was released), one user responded to another's concern that an early commercial for the device didn't show the iPod screen (and hence the data displayed on it): 'JTS, the updtes [*sic*] are audible! … That's much better than visual. It's darn hard to concentrate on the screen while performance running. I find myself holding my breath or changing pace when adjusting my iPod. That's why they show the runner hitting the nano real quick and getting audible feedback' (Mac Daily News 2006). The other voices embedded into the Sport Kit – those of renowned athletes – appear with less frequency and are designed to be entirely motivational, lending the user the imprimatur of the athletic star's blessing on the proceedings, or functioning as a kind of celebrity coach congratulating a runner while reviewing end-of-run statistics. But it is not merely what the voices say that is important from a sonic perspective. In particular, Nike has developed a kind of smooth mixing practice, wherein the communicative voice seems to emerge from within the fabric of the playlist songs, which then subsume that voice upon the delivery of its message. Smoothness is even characteristic of the generic voice's sound; as one Nike+ user put it, 'As I ran on the treadmill, a sexy, manly voice reminded me of how much time I've ran. I'm freaking loving it, nuf' said' (Cun 2007).

The Nike+ run might therefore appear to be a very individual experience, a rapturous communion between self and sound hermetically sealed in a headphone enclosure. And in many ways, it is. The discourse on running is saturated with accounts of runners achieving a state of ecstasy, an optimised 'flow' generated in part by a taut loop between sound and motion – the phrase 'runner's high', a keyword from the earliest days of the running boom, is entirely apt here. At the heart of this experience is music, which is the central auditory stimulus inducing and maintaining that flow, an aural equivalent to performance-enhancing steroids, perhaps. But Nike's crucial intervention with the Sport Kit was to transform this experience into a three-step process whose purview ranges far beyond the phenomenological scene of the run. First, the run is planned as a sonic event, in which a rough mapping of a musical playlist onto a geographical distance is constructed. Second, statistical data on the run is automatically collected by the Sport Kit, with that data being co-produced by bodily motion and the cumulative effect of rhythmic entrainment, timbral force and communicative messages in song lyrics, as well as voice-prompts relaying biofeedback information and encouragement. And third, that data is uploaded onto the internet and dispersed across a network supervised by the Nike Corporation. Nike is highly aware of its product's ability to collect and upload data, and relentlessly markets this innovative feature of the Kit. From the moment of the release of the flagship Nike+ advertisement, the Nike+ run was conceptualised via a written series of on-screen commands as an activity that went beyond the spatio–temporal boundaries of the run, which now must also incorporate pre-run activities ('Plug the receiver into the iPod Nano' and 'Pick your workout and custom playlist'), linked to during-the-run processes ('The sensor in these shoes/Talks to your iPod Nano', 'Real Feedback in Real Time', and 'Play your PowerSong for an extra boost'), linked in turn to actions that take place after the run ('Sync and track your progress' and 'Tune your run'). Having been redefined as a data set, the runner is now drawn from the run literally and figuratively into Nike's own website.

The irony of this phenomenon is that the noisy plenitude of the Nike+ experience is largely silent once the website becomes the central scene of action. The informational user profiles uploaded from the Apple device to the Nike.com website are soundless, even though sound is so obviously essential to the production of the data and is indeed inextricable from that data once it is uploaded. The site does not provide a readout or translation of the sonic experience of the run; no information shows the way the run intersects with changing tracks on a playlist, the shifts in BPMs of those tracks or changes in volume. The sole exception involves the pressing of the PowerSong, its duration now collapsed into a silent point on the website's graph of the run. But we should not be surprised by all this. Although Nike cannot do away with sound, given that sound is quite literally what the Sport Kit user runs on, the corporation, in the end, is not interested in consumers' experiences, despite the rhetoric of its experiential marketing campaign. Its goal, instead, is to collect data for the production of consumer profiles for the purpose both of honing its selling strategy to individual consumers and of trading consumer profiles as profitable commodities. The site, then, merely has to maintain sufficient involvement on the part of users such that they continue to contribute valuable information and data to it.

This incorporation of dynamic user profiles is not unique to Nike. Since the early 2000s a cornerstone of an emergent internet economy has been its growing dependence on the availability and sophisticated processing of highly specific information about consumers. Indeed, if consumer profiles are increasingly being used to define the human, Nike occupies a leading role in the biologisation of the consumer profile; in this sense, it is at the forefront of a tendency to classify human beings in terms of data, with bio-genetic and medical profiles being particularly important in this process. However, in following Apple and other firms using music-preference algo-rithms, Nike is also centrally involved in the *musicalisation* of the consumer profile. Unlike these other firms, Nike has found a way to measure a quo-tidian music use that also gives some insight into how the human body works, providing information that could conceivably be of immense use to corporations specifically targeting the body. And in undertaking a form of digital harvesting while the body engages in a specific combination of listening and movement, Nike taps into a much broader and more signifi-cant dynamic in contemporary capitalism: the blending of production and consumption which, while not unprecedented, is taking place at a much finer grain and wider scale than ever before.

## Conclusion: hear how Nike runs

The Human Race no longer exists. Writing on the Nike+ website in early October 2010, 'Nike+ Pro 16' (AKA 'Clover'), a discussion board contributor whose more than 7,000 posts belied his or her status as a company representative, announced that the Nike-sponsored race had 'gone to the great 10k course in the sky' and would 'not be held this year'. Responding to the queries of Nike+ users, 'Clover' thanked them for their 'loyalty' and apologised for any 'disappointment' the Nike Corporation may have caused (Nike+ Pro 16 2010). Perhaps this outcome was to be expected: the organisation of such a massive event was costly and, in the end, surely outstripped its value to the company. In a sense the event was a redundant sonic spectacle, given that runners were encouraged to promote the Sport Kit by listening to it and, therefore, themselves, rather than ambient performed music. We might infer that the presence of the Human Race served as an inconvenient reminder of the importance of human proximity, which the Nike+ Sport Kit claims to obviate and replace with its online community.

Of course, the *human race* still does exist, but it is now embodied within the informatics of multinational capital. As a mass actant within the Sport Kit system, humanity's presence is found primarily as agglomerations of data, whether on Nike's corporate website or in its hoard of lucrative consumer profiles. Nike+ presents the experience of a lifestyle and ideology built around the self-production of bio-data and its voluntary submission to a proprietary web portal and consumption vehicle that produces a networked global community of exercisers, motivating those runners in part through a unique articulation of sound and music – one that entails the production of an entire mediasphere, complete with artistic commissions and relentlessly diversified advertising and marketing campaigns. This is, in the most general sense, what Nike means when it exhorts consumers to 'tune your run'.

The ramifications for the normalisation of this kind of tuning – which, at its broadest, can be understood as everyday productive consumption under the sign of a sonically infused corporate digitality – are vast. Taking place during a historical period of expansive privatisation of once-public goods, the relationship between public and private appears to be thrown out of balance, so much so as to render this pair of terms inadequate: state and capital, maintaining their relative autonomy in liberal theory, are increasingly interconnected in ways far more favourable to capital in a period of depressed productive accumulation. The correlative effect concerns the subject, even the human: once historically divided as consumer, worker, citizen, leisure seeker, the human becomes a merged entity, one for which these earlier classical categories are blurred together by capital. What replaces these categories, the bedrocks upon which capital was once able to secure a certain guarantee of returns, is a smaller set of particles – motions, data sets, psychic states – whose synchronisation must be repeatedly effected in order to produce surplus value. The individual runner on a Nike+ run – at once fitness enthusiast, consumer of athletic gear and paraphernalia, corporate labourer (as marketer and data producer) and, importantly, listener and composer – is tuned to capital within a new kind of enclosure, one that subsists on a number of radical alignments between bodies, sounds and data. Thus, when Nike ends its flagship ad with the imperatives 'Sync and track your progress' and 'Tune your run', it signals a process vastly more complex than the mere act of uploading data to the website in an effort to optimise the individual body. In particular, Nike harnesses the irreducible gap between data input (digital music and sound from the Sport Kit) and data output (digital run information) from which all of the Sport Kit's reifications must ultimately emanate. The utopian zone of the run is characterised by 'flow experience' or 'pure presence', produced by the interanimations of music and sonified biofeedback data; without this zone, this gap, the Nike+ experience would be a mere process of data conversion. The irreducibility of the run provides the pretext for consumers' agency in the production of value: they are precorporated into a system in which they willingly, even enthusiastically, help to write the protocol, and in which the protocol is the run itself.[19] Yet the powerful feedback and control systems that Nike has put in place to monitor and maintain information flows through the 'black box' of the human-as-runner are by no means perfected; they constitute an attempt to compensate for the vicissitudes of a capitalism without guarantees.

It would be a mistake to suggest that these consumer-labourers remain immersed in an endorphin-induced haze, tricked into de facto unpaid employment positions within the Nike+ network. Instead, the digitisation of athletic capitalism – as with digital capitalism in general – has produced a conundrum that compounds and confuses the logics of the commodity fetish: experiential or personalised marketing's tightly wound feedback loops between consumers and corporations have transformed the way that consumers understand their very relationship to capital. No longer appearing as the big Other to labour, capital forms a veritable second skin around

---

[19] On precorporation – 'the pre-emptive formatting and shaping of desires, aspirations and hopes by capitalist culture' – see Fisher 2009: 9.

the consumer, mirroring the consumer's consciousness – or, more start-lingly, anatomy – in unprecedented ways, such that capital's interests seem far more congruent with consumers' interests than ever before. The head-phone enclosure of what has been called the 'bubble', so central to mobile music-listening, is therefore not a matter of isolation, but rather of the extreme propinquity of capital and consumer such that, tuned to the same frequency, they almost seem to fuse into a single entity. Disarticulating this conjoined entity would seem to be a central task for a critical analysis of the present conjuncture. The Gordian knot, however, cannot be so easily cut when found on a pair of tied shoelaces.

# PART II

# Space, sound and affect in everyday lifeworlds

# 6 | Music and the construction of space in office-based work settings

NICOLA DIBBEN AND ANNELI B. HAAKE

In contemporary workplaces, employees have more opportunity to listen to self-selected music in offices than ever before. This is due to the availability of mobile listening devices, enhanced storage capacities on computers and the preponderance of desk-bound work. This chapter reports an empirical investigation of the way in which music is used by individuals to demarcate space, project themselves within it and establish or blur boundaries between the public and the private. Our focus on music at work is part of the broader direction in research on music in daily life that conceives of music as an 'aesthetic technology' that can structure the social order and enable people to self-regulate (DeNora 2000).

Music's history in the regulation of work has been characterised in terms of four periods (Prichard, Korczynski and Elmes 2007: 7). Prior to industrialisation, manual labour was often accompanied by singing, which functioned to pace and co-ordinate work as well as to provide stimulation, aesthetic pleasure, a resource for expression and to educate novice workers in the tasks at hand. Music often had a direct relationship to the work itself through such features as its rhythms, tool sounds and physical movements, as illustrated in Robertson, Pickering and Korczynski's (2008) study of the pre-industrial textile industry. During the industrial period, the mechanisation and regulation of work within the factory system diminished the need for music to pace and co-ordinate labour, and the noise of machinery made singing impractical. Moreover, the imposition of industrial 'discipline' by management included attempts to ban singing, although these were not always successful, nor universally applied (see, for example, Korczynski *et al.*'s (2005) account of female factory workers during the Second World War). Korczynski and Jones (2006) have shown that during the period of Fordist industrialisation in twentieth-century Britain and the USA, music was reintroduced into the workplace in the form of broadcast music. This top-down initiative was part of the trend for scientific management of work, epitomised by the theories of Frederick Taylor (1911), in which rational control of the labour process was paramount. Notably, subsequent research into the effects of music on productivity and morale focused on the use of music to combat the boredom and lack of meaning in the Taylorised workplace rather than on changing the character of the work itself. In the industrial context, music comes from outside work rather than having a direct functional relationship with it, and the distinction between the place of work and the place of leisure that characterises industrialisation is to some extent bridged by music.

In the contemporary post-industrial context, epitomised by motivated professionals engaged in project-based mental work, music is often consumed individually by workers or broadcast in service settings. Many of the studies of music in the contemporary workplace focus on music's capacity to influence worker morale and performance, as well as consumer spending, product choice and queuing behaviour. Such research often bears the shadow of the concerns of scientific management because it focuses on ways in which managers can improve their control over the behaviour of workers and consumers. This contrasts with the more sociologically informed approaches of Thorsén's (1985) study of Swedish factory workers, DeNora's (2000) research on female music listeners, Korczynski's (2007) ethnographic study of British factory workers and Bull's (2007) interview-based research on iPod users, all of which, in common with our study, take a qualitative approach focused on worker experience.

Individualised listening by office workers appears to be very common, yet relatively little research has been directed at this population. A recent study showed that 77 per cent of British workers listened to music at work, for a third of their working week on average, and workers in computer-based office environments listened to significantly more music than people in other workplaces (Haake 2010). The functions of music in this post-industrial context differ from those of the factories studied in the mid-twentieth century. Taking findings from only those studies that included individualised listening in office settings, workers claimed that music improved focus, blocked out unwanted noise, prevented interruptions, improved concentration and creative flow, and regulated mood (Thorsén 1985; DeNora 2000; Bull 2007; Haake 2010). Music was not used to pace work or communicate about the work itself (both aspects of the uses of music in work settings prior to post-industrialisation), nor did it function to express the worker's experience of labour, contrary to Korczynski's (2007) observations of shared music-listening in a factory. The perceived importance of music for office workers appears to arise from the way it helps to reconfigure the work environment by making the experience of work more pleasurable and the work itself more effective.

One reason why music may be particularly important within offices is that it offers a means to cope with some of the perceived difficulties of open-plan and shared workspaces, such as a lack of control over the environment (McCarrey *et al.* 1974), lack of privacy and confidentiality and increased disturbance from co-workers (Sundstrom, Burt and Kamp 1980; Ding 2008). The construction of boundaries and of self-identity in the workplace may be particularly important in open-plan offices; being overlooked in the workplace has been shown to diminish self-perceptions of importance (Baldry 1997: 370), and a scarcity of opportunities to display distinctiveness through personal possessions can undermine self-identity (Brown, Lawrence and Robinson 2005). Music-listening in offices can be seen as a behaviour through which listeners mark their own territories, while also respecting and/or trespassing on those of others. It is this use of music as a means to control experience of the place and space of work that forms the focus of our study.

In this chapter we consider how space is reconfigured through the use of self-selected music in offices using qualitative data gathered from interviews with workers in two companies: a research institute and an architectural practice, both located in the north of England.[1] These two work settings afforded individualised music-listening because job roles involved desk-based computer use and limited customer communication. The workplaces differ from the types of work settings previously investigated because they both involve relatively highly skilled workers within organisational systems of 'responsible autonomy' (Friedman 1977): to some extent the employees were able to decide what to do (including listening to music). The research institute received funding from government research councils and commercial operations. The majority of the 500 employees had either scientific, administrative or managerial roles. The institute had in the past been a teacher-training college and resembled a campus building, with long corridors (Figure 6.1), private offices and shared workspaces (Figure 6.2). The architectural practice employed 120 people in open-plan spaces within a converted church. The office had a large shared ground floor space (Figure 6.3) and workspaces located on balconies, with almost no private offices.[2]

Three main themes emerged from analysis of the interview data and they are dealt with in turn below: management of the auditory environment to serve the 'internal' needs of the individual; the use of music to mark identity and territory in relation to the needs of others; and the nesting of private and public spaces.

---

[1] The qualitative data used in this chapter is from a larger research project exploring the role of music-listening in workplaces in the UK (Haake 2010).

[2] Semi-structured interviews were carried out with eleven employees from each company, and the data was analysed using a grounded theory approach (Corbin and Strauss 2008). The names of informants are pseudonyms, used here to ensure the anonymity of participants.

**Figure 6.1** A typical corridor leading to private offices in the research institute

## Managing the auditory environment

One of the most striking aspects of the way in which music was talked about by workers was its contradictory characteristics: at times interviewees described music as interrupting work, referring to it as a 'distraction', yet on other occasions it was referred to as a way to 'block out distractions', and even as a 'welcomed distraction'. Such apparently conflicting functions of music were also observed by DeNora in her study of female music listeners (2000: 59). However, these functions of music are only contradictory if one believes that music's 'effects' lie solely in intrinsic properties of the music, rather than, as DeNora argues, from music's contexts of use. Hence, in our study, whether music was perceived as a distraction was dependent on the capacities of the person for the task they were carrying out, in

**Figure 6.2** A shared office in the research institute

**Figure 6.3** View over the open-plan ground floor and balcony space in the architectural practice

relation to the attentional demands of, and the degree of control over, the music. It is the very capacity of music to make attentional demands that workers turned to their advantage when the music lay within their control: interviewees often talked about music as an aid to managing other kinds of distraction in their working environment, and thereby as assisting concentration. Hence, the apparently paradoxical status of music as both a distraction and an aid to concentration is a reflection of the contextual uses and meanings of the attentional demands it offers.

Drawing on Fisher's (1993) distinction between different types of distraction, music is used to manage both the internal environment of the individual (for example, an individual's mood and attentional focus) and the external environment of the workplace (for example, interruptions from colleagues and office noise). When interviewees were doing a task with which they felt very familiar and confident, this tended to coincide with feelings of greater attentional capacity, which in turn led them to feel bored more easily and resulted in internal distractions such as daydreaming:

The job that I do is … well, not tedious; it is repetitive. And your concentration can wander if you don't have some form of stimulus. And I find that the radio provides that. (John: administrative officer, research institute)

Music reduced these distractions for John by providing a focus and stimulation, which kept the mind from 'wandering'; music became a 'welcomed distraction' that both kept his mind 'in place' and provided 'stimulation'. The same experiences were noted by Bull's (2007) and DeNora's (2000) informants: music provided an 'aesthetic environment of "working"' and boundaries to 'where the mind can go' (DeNora 2000: 60).

The office environment also presents external interruptions, such as noise from colleagues, phones and other events, which workers often tried to mask with music:

For me, there's a certain comfort zone that is created by music. And that blocks out people yacking in the next office and people shouting at each other in the corridor, and other peoples' problems and vehicles arriving outside. It does filter those distractions out, I think. It is giving me total control of my aural environment … I find myself concentrating, and focus more. (Patrick: research and development workshop manager, research institute)

Using music to mask other sounds is a simple way in which individuals can protect themselves from sounds otherwise perceived as interrupting. Bull (2007), in his study of iPod users at work, conceptualises these same functions of individualised listening in terms of cognitive control. However, whereas Bull conceives of this as a process of shutting out the external environment and minimising contingencies, our study suggests this use of music can additionally be understood as a way to substitute external distractions with a familiar auditory environment.

As found by Bull (2007) and Thorsén (1985), listening to music provided a means to take greater control over interactions with colleagues, as the presence of music in the workplace was widely understood as a 'do not disturb' sign. In our study this sign was both visual, in the case of using headphones, and/or aural, in the case of listening via speakers:

Sometimes you do it if you are particularly busy and you need to get something done, to dissuade people. It is like that old trick of pretending you are on the phone, or something like that. So yes, it is perhaps a statement to other people, 'look I want to get this done at the moment'. (Peter: associate director, architectural practice)

Headphone use, or playing music through speakers, therefore acts as a public display of attention and, as noted by Birnholtz, Gutwin and Hawkey (2007), is part of a larger set of practices through which workers afford themselves periodic privacy and mitigate the lack of control over interactions that results from open-plan offices. Privacy serves a number of functions for workers: it affords an optimal level of stimulation and freedom from distractions, it signifies status and it helps to create personal boundaries important to a sense of self-identity (Sundstrom, Burt and Kamp 1980). Sundstrom's questionnaire study shows that the sense of psychological privacy – the amount of control one has over how accessible one is, over distractions and interruptions, and spoken privacy (Brill 1985) – is highly correlated with architectural privacy – the visual and acoustic isolation provided by a workspace. Put simply, people working in private offices have more control over their accessibility to others. Furthermore, both types of privacy – visual and acoustic – are associated with increased job satisfaction and satisfaction with the workspace. Music-listening can provide a degree of psychological privacy by providing control over accessibility to others, and architectural privacy by providing sound isolation. In other words, music-listening provides a means for workers to reconfigure their working space so that it conforms more precisely to ideals of privacy and individuality. For Bull (2007: 109), this 'auditory privatisation' constitutes 'the power of the listener to define his or her own space and interaction', and leads to a sense of invulnerability. However, as discussed further below, this is not always the case: informants in our study sometimes perceived the insulation to be negative as it reduced the possibility for useful interaction with other colleagues.

A key aspect of music use in our findings is the way in which listening practices were shaped by the particular physical characteristics of the office space. This was most notable in the architectural practice, which inform-ants experienced as having idiosyncratic acoustic properties:

Our [office] is open plan, but with a nice big acoustic … it is designed to have acoustic spread. So I can hear diagonally up, right across the office to the top bal-cony, and right down below. But you couldn't hear someone sat about two foot to the right or two foot to the left … And I think that's quite strange, and that's why people tend to shut themselves off in there. (Charlie: project architect)

The auditory characteristics of the architects' workplace were unusual because they featured attenuated acoustics nearby yet acoustic overstimula-tion across the whole space. This informant believed that these characteris-tics caused people to use headphones so as to engender a greater degree of auditory privacy and control. Music-listening therefore becomes a way to manage the lack of privacy resulting from open office designs.

In summary, music at work was seen as either a negative distraction or a welcomed diversion and a way to block out other interruptions, whether those be external distractions arising from the workspace or the internal distractions of intrusive thoughts or daydreaming. In each case music can be understood as a tool by which people reconfigure their auditory envir-onment, here that of the open-plan office, to meet their needs more closely. In DeNora's (2000) terms, music is used as a 'technology' to 'care' for the self at work. In the workplace, as in the other realms of everyday life discussed by DeNora, individuals use music to constitute and maintain the self, to modulate mental and bodily states, and in our study it is the appropriation of music to construct and maintain appropriate levels of energy and focus at work that comes to the fore.

## Music, territory and identity

As well as managing the internal needs of an individual as they relate to work, three further themes emerged in the interviews, which can be understood in terms of music-listening's capacity to respond to 'external needs': the welfare of the organisation, the welfare of others and auditory awareness.

The use of music was mediated by consideration of the welfare of the organisation. This included policies forbidding music-streaming (due to its detrimental effects on IT bandwidth) and music-sharing (due to copyright legalities), and revealed perceptions of music as the personal within the public space of work. One place this latter issue was evidenced was in policies on storage of music files: both companies restricted storage of music files to the desktop computer rather than to shared servers or networks. According to David, the IT manager at the architectural practice:

No personal information, including music, is saved to the server. The local disc on their machine, we say 'that is your space, and if you have got anything private you save it there and it is your personal responsibility to back it up'.

Music files were therefore designated as private, 'personal' and separate from work. However, the boundaries enunciated by these practices were contradictory: employees' computers were seen as semi-private, and music files as private, yet music-listening software was perceived to be the responsibility of IT staff. These paradoxical policies can be understood as produced within the larger context of the changing nature of work, where the boundaries between different life realms are also becoming increasingly blurred (Lewis 2003), an issue we return to below.

A second way in which listening practices were shaped was by consideration of the welfare of others, namely the avoidance of evoking negative feelings among colleagues through imposing music on them. This involved showing respect for people and their working environment and avoiding difficulties that might arise due to a particular listening behaviour:

A lot of people in this organisation still have their own offices. And so they tend to have their music playing quite low … But there are some shared offices, and the typical (sic) in those offices is to see people with headphones on. Or, unless people are all having the same kind of taste, they might have the radio on, or something like that. Because, obviously, you can't upset your colleagues. (Benjamin: IT security manager at the research institute)

In shared workspaces there were unwritten rules about who could control the music. In the research institute laboratory there was a common understanding that whoever was spending the most time there in a day would put their music on. On those occasions in which employees found it hard to compromise they chose to listen to the radio, as it was perceived as 'relatively neutral' because they did not 'have any control over' the content. Other strategies for managing music played over speakers in shared spaces included voluntarily turning music down or off, negotiating with colleagues or using headphones to block out unwanted music with one's own music.

As well as highlighting the role of music in the construction of sonic–spatial territories, these modifications to music in the workplace have the effect of shrinking and expanding personal space by turns, as this example from Mark, a manager at the research institute, illustrates:

As soon as I get in at half six, quarter to seven, the music goes on. And my first member of staff arrives at half past seven. And in that first hour, or three quarters, I am rocking! This is up very loud … I am not disturbing anybody else. I don't believe I am disturbing myself, and I still manage to plough through my work. After that it will go down a bit. Again, that member of staff doesn't actually work directly outside my office, just along the corridor, so once she has come and gone it goes up again until two other members of staff come in at about twenty minutes past eight. And then it will go down to a reasonable level.

When Mark was alone, he felt that he widened his personal space through music so that it reached the whole of the office, and when someone else entered he reduced the volume, thereby changing his sonic claim to work territory and moderating his incursion into that of others. This behaviour shows how sound transmission can demarcate territorial boundaries. Sterne's (1997) study of the use of broadcast music in an American shopping mall describes the way in which boundaries between the hallways of the mall and individual retail units were articulated through distinct types of broadcast music. The difference in the case of music in offices is that the listener can choose to alter the boundaries of his or her sonic space at any moment; such behaviour involves both a claim to a particular space in the workplace and a recognition of the right of others to space.

Territoriality in offices is partly connected with the idea of psychological ownership; it states 'This is my office and not yours' (Brown, Lawrence and Robinson 2005: 579). But irritation from involuntary listening to 'increasingly portable noise in increasingly densely packed spaces' (Cloonan and Johnson 2002: 31) is potentially exacerbated by the personal meanings and emotional characteristics attributed to music in contemporary culture. Frith (2002: 46) puts it like this:

It is because music is now used to mark out private territory that it can also 'invade' it; it is because music has become so deeply implicated in people's personas that it can be 'misused'; and it is because music is now so widely employed as an emotional tool that its misuse is genuinely upsetting.

Music-listening behaviour in offices can therefore be seen as a process through which listeners mark their own territories, while also acknowledging and respecting others' territories, which may or may not be marked by music.

Listening to music also impacted on work relationships in other ways: for example, wearing headphones to listen to music was a way to manage interruptions, but could have the detrimental effect of cutting the listener off from the social world of the workplace:

It is a solution. It is also a problem. You know, you can be sort of aware, you hear a conversation and know [a colleague] is on the phone and dealing with something. And in putting headphones on you kind of isolate yourself from what is going on around you. But it is also a way of isolating yourself if something is going on around you that is distracting you. Like my 180 decibel drum and bass (laughs). (Bethany: analytical geochemist, research institute)

Reduced auditory awareness in the workplace was problematic for some. For example, Adam's job as an associate director in the architectural practice involved monitoring his team and their work conversations, and it was important for him to be able to do so even while listening to music. For others, the perceived withdrawal of headphone users from the workplace was sometimes seen as negative because it became difficult to have a 'casual conversation', and required a speaker to enter their colleague's visual space or physically touch them to capture their attention. Lack of auditory awareness therefore impacted on the perceived potential for informal learning within the workplace, as well as socialising with colleagues:

There's this one guy who listens to big, full-on headphones and he probably doesn't learn a lot. He probably doesn't know an awful lot about people sitting around him either. Not just in terms of projects, just in terms of the person as well ... I wouldn't say it detracts from people's work, because I don't think that's fair to say ... But to do with your actual learning experience, I think it is fair to say that would be a criticism of listening to music in general. Music in headphones, rather than music necessarily. (Charlie: project architect)

Notably, it is not the sounding music per se that was seen to detract from informal learning, but listening via headphones. Bull (2007: 119) interprets similar experiences described by his iPod users at work as a use of music to shut out the office environment 'through the creation of a hermetically sealed aural bubble', thereby absenting themselves from the auditory world of the office. In contrast to Bull's description, many of our interviewees purposefully avoided this 'auditory bubble', possibly because the type of work they were carrying out required more attentiveness to others than that of Bull's informants. Workers in our study used a 'one-eared' listening technique to preserve auditory awareness of the office environment:

Often when I listen to music I only have one earpiece in … That works brilliantly, so that I can listen to music and I can keep tabs on if someone talks to you or whatever, or you can hear a conversation … [But] if I am trying to concentrate, or I know that I am not going to be needed, then it's both earpieces in and turn the volume up. (Adam: associate director, architectural practice)

Adam's desire to have auditory access can be understood as arising from his managerial role; and in a previous study it has been shown that many managers wish to have visual control over the entire workplace (Ding 2008). By using only one earpiece, Adam was able to keep the other ear 'open' towards the rest of the team, allowing a compromise between his individual desire to listen to music in order to manage interruptions and the requirement to be aware of colleagues' interactions. Charlie described a similar approach when listening to a radio, which he positioned facing one ear with the other ear facing the office, so as to hear interactions around him. He also selected music and volume levels which he felt allowed office sounds to penetrate: 'Stuff like Damien Rice and Ray Lamontagne … Stuff that I can actually hear people over the top of as well. Not really loud music.' Interviewees in our study therefore adopted strategies to maintain auditory contact with the office; the construction of an auditory bubble was not always seen as suitable or as something to strive for.

To summarise, the use of music in the workplaces we studied was mediated by external considerations such as the welfare of the organisation and of other colleagues. In offices where awareness of surroundings was required, headphone use caused irritation and frustration among some colleagues as it was perceived to obstruct spontaneous verbal communication, informal learning and socialisation. Bull (2010) argues that the experience of insulation that headphone-listening permits leads to a sense of invulnerability, which makes people feel empowered. On the one hand, the results of this study confirm the importance for workers of being able to manage interruptions, while the lack of this opportunity could lead to negative experiences. On the other hand, the feeling of insulation could also lead to negative consequences, including potential conflicts with colleagues. The reconfiguration of space through music-listening by our interviewees was not simply the replacement of public space with private, individualised space, but the overlaying of the one by the other in a way that responded to the contingencies of the situational context of their working lives.

## Music as private space within the workplace

The themes identified above point to the place of music-listening as a symbolic and material practice that creates what Born has termed a 'nesting' of private space within the public space of the workplace (see the Introduction to this book). One aspect of this nesting is practical, as described above: music blocks other potentially distracting sounds and discourages interruptions. The listener is able to use music to create a preferred auditory environment conducive to work. A second aspect of the 'nesting' is symbolic and requires rather more explanation. With industrialisation came a distinction between the 'disciplined' time and place of work – in which workers laboured in fixed locations, performing repetitive activities for specific periods of time monitored by managers – and the rest of life (Thompson 1967). Notions of work and leisure became conceptualised as binary opposites: the realm of work was deemed to be one of rationality and discipline from which music was excluded, whereas that of leisure was characterised by irrationality and freedom (Korczynski 2007: 255). Within disciplined industrial capitalism, music's symbolic status is as 'leisure' activity and therefore it forms part of the 'private' space of the individual within the public realm of work. This positioning of music within the work/leisure binary continues to mediate attitudes to music in the workplace, as revealed in our study: the presence of music (a leisure activity) within the workplace was seen either as benign or disruptive, depending on the individual's conception of work, as we will show.

Some informants described the ability to listen to music at work as a benefit and a 'privilege' that symbolised the 'care' of the organisation for its employees, signalling an attempt by the company to distance itself from Taylorist principles of managerial control in favour of some degree of autonomy for employees. One informant spoke about the tolerance of music-listening in this way:

I suppose because the practice sees itself as a reasonably open-minded and creative place, so [tolerance of music-listening] does send out quite a strong message that people can do that if they want. They are not just plugged into their CAD-machine to draw buildings; they are here to do something slightly less formal, a bit more creative, and the ability to do what they want really, to a certain extent. It is not a call centre or something that's mechanical or, there is a bit more freedom, or a more liberal atmosphere to the place. (Peter: associate director, architectural practice)

Peter identified here the many different meanings that the presence of music in the architectural practice communicated for him – 'open-minded', 'creative', 'less formal' – illustrating that auditory stimuli can contribute to the social construction of the office space, just as has been previously acknowledged for visual signs and symbols (Baldry 1997). Peter's characterisation of his organisation differs radically from a Taylorist model, in which labour is divided among a deskilled workforce under strict managerial control; the employees in both companies studied here were skilled professionals who had some degree of control over their work. Nonetheless, as Peter hints above, the character of the work carried out by architects and technicians had the potential to dehumanise ('plugged into their CAD-machine'), a potential that was defused partly by the freedom to listen to music at work. Some similarities with music in the Fordist work-settings of the early and mid-twentieth century remain: for example, Jones and Schumacher (1992) argue in relation to broadcast music at work that music is a 'gift' bestowed by the company and an embodiment of the company's care for the employees. The difference in the context of the post-Fordist companies we studied is that it is the opportunity to listen to self-selected music that is the 'gift' of the company to its employees, rather than the direct provision of music. The freedom to choose music is the corollary of the 'responsible autonomy' afforded to employees in the post-Fordist work-settings of our study.

By contrast to those who viewed music as a benefit and in keeping with an organisational structure based around responsible autonomy, the status of music as leisure meant that, for some, music-listening at work was associated with a lack of professionalism:

I wouldn't be happy with people in Personnel listening to music. I would just see it as a distraction, and not very professional, really. That's my view. You know, everybody sat around with music blaring away … to me it wouldn't give the right impression of what we were about. (Will: personnel manager, research institute)

Whereas Peter saw music at work as a symbol of the architectural practice's valuing of autonomy, Will perceived music to signify a lack of commitment on the part of employees. As 'leisure' activity, music was perceived to be inappropriate at work. Will's remarks are reminiscent of the attitudes to music found among management in the industrialised workplaces of the nineteenth and twentieth centuries in which work and music were separated. Korczynski *et al.* (2005: 208) have noted that the decline of singing at work can be partly attributed to the belief among management that it was bad for discipline and distracted from work, which led many employers to ban or at least discourage singing. Will's remarks attest to the power of this historical belief system to shape contemporary attitudes to music in the workplace.

As these examples illustrate, the status of music as 'leisure' within the workplace arises from a conceptual framework in which work and leisure are distinct and separate domains. Yet the presence of music in the workplace blurs the boundaries between the two. One aspect of this is technological: as Thorsén (1987) points out, individualised sound reproduction technologies mean that people can listen to the same music anywhere, thereby bridging the geographical gap between the place of work and the place of leisure. Moreover, the design of contemporary listening technologies embodies the fluidity of work/leisure domains; Bull (2007: 110–11) points out that the iPod allows multiple uses and functions including transporting work files, photographs and contacts, as well as music listening. A further aspect of these blurred boundaries arises from practices of music use: for example, Bethany, an analytical geochemist at the research institute, described how listening to loud drum and bass at work on Friday afternoons provided a 'bridge' into the weekend because it expressed her tastes and blurred the boundaries between work and leisure time.

The blurring of boundaries between work and leisure through music-listening at work is part of a more widespread trend (Lewis 2003), evident in the emergence of what van Meel and Vos (2001) call 'funky offices'. These types of workplace incorporate facilities more usually associated with time and space outside work, such as a domestic living room (as in the UK headquarters of the manufacturer Dyson) and an indoor helter-skelter to take office staff between floors of a building (as in the Electric Works building opened in Sheffield in 2009). Innovative office designs such as these aim to project a brand identity and foster employee creativity to enhance competitiveness, but they also blur the distinction between work and leisure, public and private lives. Some have argued that such blurring of boundaries between public and private time and space represents a colonisation of the private individual by the public world of work, which detracts from quality of life (Moore 1963; Hochschild 1997). For example, the regulated work-time nap can be seen as an extension of the public realm of work and social discipline into private space and time (Baxter and Kroll-Smith 2005). To what extent music-listening at work crosses the boundaries of private and public space is a question we consider further below.

The discussion so far has considered music-listening practices; but what of the specific music chosen by listeners in the workplace? Does the music heard have any distinctive characteristics? Most interviewees stated that they listened to the same music at home as at work. As Patrick put it: 'Anything that I would listen to at home I would be happy to listen to at work.' However, not all music listened to outside work was listened to at work; the kind of music that interviewees listened to depended on what music they felt helped them to achieve particular goals in particular situations (e.g. awareness, concentration, consideration for others). Previous research indicates that workers who use individualised listening at work tend to prefer music that is 'background' and 'non-interruptive', although what this constitutes differs from one person to the next (Bull 2007: 112–13). Similarly, Thorsén (1985) in his study of Swedish factory workers found that the type of music workers chose to listen to was determined by the type of sound environment, the type of work and the concentration needed, all of which would often change for individuals over the course of a day. As Bull (2007: 112–13) remarks: 'It is not the type of music listened to that is significant but the role that music plays in the auditory ecology of the user'. Nonetheless, certain sonic characteristics are more or less likely to afford certain uses. For example, our informants remarked that unchanging dynamics and familiar music were more likely to aid concentration. These are both characteristics of programmed music for workplaces. In addition, the desire for 'auditory awareness' of the workplace meant that music with a thinner texture was deemed more appropriate. Music selections were often spontaneous and pragmatic rather than the result of planning, and in this respect the choice of music at work differs from the carefully programmed selections made by people in other listening contexts. In summary, no particular music was prioritised in the context of work; music was instead weaved into the demands of the working day. This emphasises the importance of context-specificity for understanding music preferences in daily life (DeNora 2000; North, Hargreaves and Hargreaves 2004; Dibben and Williamson 2007).

## Conclusion: reconfiguring the space and place of work

This study reveals the way that workers use music to structure the boundaries between the public and private spaces of the workplace. Listening practices are shaped by the 'internal needs' of the individual, such as the need for stimulation, focus and auditory privacy in offices, and the 'external needs' of the company, colleagues and job demands. In this context music is a tool to manage the needs of the individual within the public realm of work; in DeNora's terms, music in our study was a 'technology of the self' – used to 'care' for the individual by modulating states of attention and energy, and enabling 'performances' of identity. In auditory terms the acoustic space of the workplace is overlaid by a different (virtual) acoustic space provided by music. This new acoustic environment is guided by broad criteria that provide contextually appropriate levels of diversion and familiarity. The effect is to replace the acoustic ecology of the shared, public space of the workplace with music from a personal selection often heard privately by the individual. In other words, music-listening in the workplace allows the acoustic environment of the public workplace to be reconfigured as a private realm.

Individualised listening, and the private space it constructs, may provide a strategy by which to cope with close and prolonged proximity to other people. At its most extreme, headphone-listening creates a place 'cut off', a 'bubble'; it 'shuts a door' and 'puts up a wall', suggesting a hiving off or nesting of private space within the larger public space of the workplace. However, just as Beer (2007) argues that use of MP3 players in urban environments allows listeners to prioritise the music overlay and 'tune out' of the cityscape rather than 'control it' through total exclusion, so the experiences of informants in this study show that this apparently private space is permeable by the day-to-day demands of the work environment and, moreover, that listeners adopt strategies to avoid the isolation from the shared physical space of the workplace that headphone listening affords. These strategies are mediated by the acoustic ecology and constraints of the workspace: when headphone-listening within open-plan offices, informants adopted 'one-eared listening'; when listening through loudspeakers in individual or shared offices, the radio provided a depersonalised taste culture.

There were few attempts by employers to regulate music use in the workplace beyond adhering to copyright legalities and maintaining IT capacity. In that sense music-listening was not a clandestine activity nor a private 'rebellion' against work discipline, but was a common strategy for self-regulation. Music-listening was frequently legitimated and normalised within the workplaces we studied because it was viewed as enhancing productivity and work satisfaction (a remedy to the problem of distractions in the workplace), and because the freedom to engage in this private and individualised behaviour fitted with the post-Fordist labour being undertaken (employees were engaged in skilled mental labour, often on project-driven tasks, where there was a high degree of trust and internalised discipline). Thus, there is a relationship between contemporary uses of music in the regulation of work and the organisational structures of post-industrial workplaces: office workers carry out 'responsible listening' commensurate with the 'responsible autonomy' they have within the workplace.

Viewed from this perspective, the presence of music listening in the workplace can be seen as a positive activity in which the construction of private space within the public workplace, and the blurring of boundaries between public and private, are part of a post-Fordist ideal – one in which high-status workers on project-driven tasks use time as they see fit to get the job done. Nonetheless, this research highlights a contemporary work culture that has the potential to co-opt and transform a 'non-productive', private activity of music-listening into a public (but often individualised) behaviour.

# 7 | Broadcasting the body: the 'private' made 'public' in hospital soundscapes

TOM RICE

Hospital wards can be noisy places, crowded with sound (Grumet 1993; Rice 2003; Bharathan *et al.* 2007; Dalziel 2008). Numerous people undergoing treatment in close proximity to one another, a high intensity of staff activity, machines giving out signals, tones and alarms: these sources can combine to produce a cacophony of illness. Some medical professionals are rightly concerned that excessive (and largely preventable) noise on wards might negatively affect patient health and recovery times (e.g. Bharathan *et al.* 2007). But while discussions of ward 'noise' capture the irritating or even overpowering nature of some sonic environments within hospitals, the term 'noise' can lead us to think somewhat reductively, overlooking the meanings and associations that soundscapes can hold for those who are immersed in them. This chapter teases out some of the experiential detail of ward soundscapes. Specifically, it illustrates how, for some hospital patients, sounds present a challenge to the creation and maintenance of private space.

The chapter brings together observations from two different research periods. The first took place in 1999 at the Edinburgh Royal Infirmary in Scotland. Here I conducted a short ethnographic study into patients' experiences of hospital soundscapes. The second was carried out between 2003 and 2004 at St Thomas' Hospital in London. Based on the wards of the Cardiothoracic Unit, the research (for my Ph.D. thesis) focused on the ways in which auditory knowledge is used and applied by doctors in their practice. Spending time on the wards of the Unit, however, also allowed me to deepen my understanding of how sounds affected patients in that environment.

In her contribution to this volume, Suzanne G. Cusick describes the use of sound and music in the detention camps of the 'global war on terror'. Inmates relate their experiences of a kind of 'acoustic dystopia', where loud music is used strategically to disorient, demoralise and even debilitate. The present chapter is concerned with a different 'sonics of suffering' (Gunaratnam 2009: 3) from a different kind of 'total institution' (Goffman 1968 (1961)). But in the contexts described in both Cusick's chapter and this one, sound becomes notable as an agent or vector of discomfort and anxiety, its dynamics even presenting a challenge to the preservation of normal subjectivity. In both contexts, too, a distinct field of power relations becomes audible.

Cusick suggests that, in some detention camps, loud music is deliberately used to articulate a crude power differential. Its palpable, physical force is designed to underscore the relative omnipotence of the captor and impotence of the captive. Efforts by detainees to block or escape from the music, or even to make sense of their prison environment through normal listening practices, can be understood to constitute quiet acts of resistance. Power relations within the hospital are undoubtedly subtler. Nonetheless, like detainees (and for that matter the inmates of other total institutions such as conventional prisons), patients, once admitted to hospital, become subject to a more or less stringent set of institutional rules and routines. At the same time, the wards they enter are managed by medical professionals who are trained to follow detailed protocols, producing for patients what Goffman (1968 (1961): 11) terms 'a formally administered round of life'. Patients must, to some extent at least, accept and submit to the regime of the hospital and the authority of those who staff it.

Significantly, on entering hospital, patients are no longer able to exercise control over the physical and social proximity or distance they maintain in relation to others. In public hospitals in particular, patients are often obliged to spend each phase of their daily existence (sleeping, eating, etc.) in the company of relative strangers (both patients and staff) sharing a managed communal space. In both of the institutions where I spent time, patients remarked that upon being admitted to hospital, 'the first thing you lose is your privacy, the second is your dignity and the third is your sanity'. Their usage of this exact phrase made me think that it had been passed between patients and hospitals across the country and could perhaps be aligned with a distinct patient culture. But it is certainly easy to see that for a person committed to hospital, privacy is difficult to preserve. He or she must share space with others, being almost constantly under the gaze and within earshot of those others and of medical staff.

For the patients to whom I spoke, sounds played a key role in the loss of privacy that they identified. Many found they were unable to escape the sonic detail of the suffering of their ward neighbours. Sounds would infiltrate and pervade both patients' immediate physical environment and what they tended to describe as their 'mental' space. At the same time, most patients were acutely conscious that they themselves could be overheard by those nearby. It was difficult for them to control or restrict the dissipation of sounds.

While in hospital, patients are generally obliged to occupy a relatively passive position at the centre of a system of medical work. They become the objects or recipients of a range of diagnostic, management and treatment practices. These practices, like the inhabitation of shared space, often necessitate the invasion or compromise of privacy. A patient might have to undergo examinations or procedures that involve physical exposure and intrusion. He or she might even depend on staff for intimate bodily care. Also, within the clinical environment more generally, bodies are scrutinised such that their surfaces, recesses, structures, tissues, fluids and processes are made subject to inspection, analysis and discussion.

For my patient interlocutors, sounds were implicated in these processes of 'opening out' the body. The signals, tones, sonified data and alarms produced by medical technologies conveyed information about bodily events not only to medical professionals but also to the patients themselves and beyond, across the ward. Most patients found that they occupied a position of relative powerlessness – that they were rendered undiscriminating and inexpert listeners amid the audible interactions of specialists and their machines. They were obliged to overhear snatches of sound generated by what, following Latour (1999), we might describe as the 'network' of human/technological relations through which care is organised. At the same time, diagnosis and treatment involved confidential discussions in communal spaces, so that patient bodies were articulated but also distributed and dispersed through sound in the form of verbal exchanges. The intensely private spaces of the body and its interior were allowed to enter more public zones of acoustic and discursive space. Sound, then, complicated bodily boundaries. As I explain below, the patients' perceived loss of control over this sonic reconfiguration of the private body in relation to the public spaces of the hospital could create feelings of humiliation, anxiety and even fear.

## Overhearing

It quickly became apparent during my first period of research that patients were deeply affected by the distinctive soundscape that surrounded them in hospital. Ward soundscapes were characterised by the activity and work of care: the conversations and footsteps of nurses, the rattling of medicine trolleys, the rasp of privacy curtains being drawn around beds, telephones ringing, pagers sounding and so on. Overlapping and interweaving with these noises were sounds produced by the patients themselves: talking and moving around, but sometimes also coughing, vomiting, sobbing, emitting cries of pain or of delirium. Unable to move far from their bed, many patients found themselves to be a 'captive audience' to the sounds that were constantly being broadcast across the ward and which invaded their physical and perceptual space (Kittay 2008).

In the hospital environment, certain gestures are made towards securing or preserving a vestige of *visual* privacy for patients. For instance, curtains are often pulled around the beds of patients undergoing examinations and procedures or receiving care. Even if all other patients on the ward are well aware of what is taking place behind it, the privacy curtain ensures they are spared the visual details. The curtain also functions as a sign that advises or even warns the onlooker: 'You should turn away' or 'For your own good, you should try not to register what is happening behind here'; after all, curtains are pulled around the beds of patients who are dying or have recently died. The privacy curtain alerts those who see it to redirect their attention, and performs a kind of theatre of respect for privacy and individuality. But sound is no respecter of the privacy curtain. Sounds move under, over and through these screens. They escape the temporary area of visually 'private' space the curtain constructs, seeping or radiating out into the ward and the auditory space of others.

Sometimes the sounds coming through the curtain could be harrowing for patients. One lady I spoke to grimaced as she described the whimpering that had come from behind the screen as her neighbour used a bedpan for the first time since undergoing a bowel operation. Another had had to endure prolonged cries of agony from nearby as a man underwent an unpleasant procedure hidden from view. She looked exhausted and upset as she related what had clearly been an ordeal for both of them. A man named Gordon, who had recently been discharged, described how during his stay in hospital his ward neighbour had suffered a heart attack late at night. Nursing staff had been quick to help and had pulled the privacy curtains around all the beds. A resuscitation team had been called and Gordon had been obliged to listen to the dramatic sounds of their attempts to save the man's life. Eventually he had heard them agree that their efforts had failed and after the necessary preparations had been made he heard the body wheeled away. 'I was shattered for days by these horrible noises', Gordon said. This violent eruption in the hospital soundscape, associated in this case with death, had been deeply disturbing for him.

When listening to sounds issuing from behind a privacy curtain, patients are effectively involved in 'acousmatic listening' of a very literal kind (Schaeffer 1966). This term is derived from the Greek word 'akousmatikoi', used to refer to the pupils of Pythagoras who were required to listen to their teacher delivering his lectures from behind a veil or screen so that they might better concentrate on his teachings. Schaeffer suggests that in acousmatic listening, auditory attention is focused on sound alone as it becomes disconnected from its (hidden) source. These patients certainly achieve a specific focus on auditory information. Rather than hearing the sounds as disconnected from their source, though, they seem to be involved in an intense imaginative engagement with frightening, hidden-yet-vividly-evoked procedures and events.

During my research at the Edinburgh Royal Infirmary I was introduced to a man named Zafer. He explained that he had been admitted to hospital in the UK when, as a 17-year-old, he had been suffering from leukaemia. His condition had quickly worsened, and he was soon transferred to a ward where it became clear to him (judging by the condition of the people in neighbouring beds) that he was expected to die. He told me: 'I realised there were two ways out of this ward: the first was to be wheeled out as a corpse, the second was to walk out having made a recovery and essentially beaten the disease.' He prepared himself to 'fight' the disease and save his own life. But the hardest thing to do in preparing his mind and creating a positive outlook, he said, was to shut out the terrible sounds from the patients who were suffering in the beds around him. 'Sounds can kill you', he told me. They threatened fatally to undermine his concentration on his recovery. He described himself as actually having to preserve what he called a 'space' inside his head where he was determined the sounds should not reach and where his morale could remain unaffected.

In everyday discourse we frequently draw a distinction between an exterior 'physical' and an interior 'mental' space. Suzanne Cusick describes the detainees in her study attempting to escape from excessively loud sound by retreating into an interior 'mental place'; and there is a sense that sounds of all kinds can readily permeate this interiority, influencing mood and affect or, in the case of excessively loud sound, disabling or destabilising subjectivity altogether (Cusick in Chapter 13, this volume; Ellman 1993: 101). Zafer describes his being forced actively to police and reinforce a boundary between the exterior 'pain-scape' of the ward and the resolved and positive interior space of his own mind (Ellman 1993: 101). His success in eventually shutting out the sounds had been integral to his recovery.

Not all patients to whom I spoke managed to block out the soundscape so well. 'It creeps into your headspace', said a lady who had been in hospital for ten days following a valve replacement operation. Her reference to 'headspace' again indexes a simultaneously physical and mental interior: 'I even hear the ward in my sleep', she added. There was a sense that sounds crept into her consciousness surreptitiously or at a time when she was incapable of offering resistance, percolating into the interior, private space of her thoughts.

During my fieldwork the Edinburgh Royal Infirmary had its own radio station called *Red Dot Radio*. The station broadcast to patients, as it does at the time of writing, for three hours each weekday evening and two hours each evening at weekends. Patients could listen through headphones connected to sockets in the wall. Speaking to patients, it became clear that *Red Dot Radio* was popular because it provided a few hours of relief from the ward soundscape every day. It enabled those who so wished to temporarily immerse themselves in an alternative soundscape. The ability to escape into a technologically mediated sound world is something generations familiar with personal stereos and MP3 players perhaps take for granted. But the patients I encountered during both research periods tended to be elderly. Few owned personal stereos or were familiar with using them to 'manage' and control their involvement in an external sound environment (Bull 2000). *Red Dot Radio*, however, allowed them to exercise a degree of control over their immediate, private auditory space, or at least it enabled them to consume a different kind of mediated public soundscape.

While the hospital radio, and occasionally televisions on the wards, could sometimes provide an auditory distraction, most of the time there was little else for patients to do but listen to the ward around them or do their best to turn a deaf ear. One day as I walked down a ward, a patient being attended to behind a curtain could be heard vomiting profusely. The lady in the adjacent bed was sitting up, turning the pages of a magazine. She held a fixed, bland smile as she pretended to be oblivious to the sounds that were loud and plain. Of course, she had little choice but to do exactly this. Unable to escape the sound, she was obliged to tolerate it as best she could. I felt her facial expression encapsulated the effort made by many simply to put up with the sounds, however invasive, irritating or distasteful. This attempt to remain unperturbed could be understood as a way of managing the auditory environment. Like Zafer, patients tried to create privacy through the application of a particular attitude or mental approach, this time one of studied unawareness or indifference (which we could perhaps visualise as mental headphones or earmuffs).

As well as being conscious of the sounds those around them might be making, many of the patients to whom I spoke were acutely conscious that they themselves were contributors to the hospital soundscape. They could not only be heard moving around, talking or coughing, but were also obliged to endure more embarrassing forms of auditory exposure. Culturally specific norms of bodily privacy are instilled in people from an early age. In the West it has come to be regarded as inappropriate for other people to see and hear, for instance, certain bodily functions such as hiccuping, burping, farting, being sick or using the toilet. We monitor our own behaviour carefully in this regard, acting in anticipation of listening ears all around us. There is a 'panaudic' principle in play here (a term I adapt from Foucault's use of the term 'panoptic') (Foucault 1977; Rice 2003). But hospital patients could do little to guard their acoustic privacy. Intensely 'private' sounds inevitably spilled over into public space. There was a leakage or seepage of body sounds into spaces occupied by other people (Lawton 1998; Gunaratnam 2009: 7). Patients experienced an unpleasant kind of sonic incontinence.

Privacy, then, is partly compromised through patients being constantly within earshot of other people. Of course, being audible could be reassuring. Patients knew that if they needed help, they could call or cry out and someone would hear and come to assist them. But they resented the fact that they could not remove themselves from being in the auditory presence of their neighbours if desired. Not only did they have little control over what sounds intruded into their immediate private acoustic space, but they were also limited in their ability to restrict how their own bodies projected into the public acoustic space shared by others.

## Reluctant confidantes

'It's amazing how many people know about you in here', said a patient I was chatting to one day. 'Yesterday a doctor I'd never seen before came up to me and started telling me all about myself. In fact he literally knew more about me that I did.' As suggested above, during hospitalisation patients are subjected to a range of examinations and investigations that generate information about them. This information, obtained through a variety of techniques and technologies, is circulated through the 'network' of the care system, medical professionals acting on different elements according to their role (Latour 1999; Mol 2002). Knowledge about a patient, then, is both collected in and disseminated through the hospital. Most patients I spoke to were perfectly aware of this and knew that information they might once have considered private was circulating in a more public discursive zone shared by hospital staff. 'In a way they're all talking about you behind your back', a lady awaiting a valve transplant told me. 'But there's no point in being precious about it', she conceded. 'It's got to happen if anything's going to get done.'

There is a sense among doctors, too, that in their comparative vulnerability, patients need to be protected from 'raw' medical discourse about their conditions and treatment. They need to be cushioned from the brutality of medical facts and the style of detached clinical objectivity in which those facts are often discussed. In a sense, while in hospital, patients' bodies need to remain confidential to doctors, rather than being made known to patients themselves. Information circulating in the zone of clinical discursive space should not be allowed to flow (unfiltered) back to the patient, or into wider zones occupied by the non-medical public. Indeed, although legally entitled to do so, patients I met during fieldwork were not encouraged to view their medical notes usually held at the nurses' station, or to read other documentation relevant to their cases that was being exchanged between medical professionals. Most doctors to whom I spoke felt it was best that patients be protected from all but absolutely necessary information about their own cases. They argued that patients would be unlikely to understand medical language, its intricacies and implications. 'A little knowledge is a bad thing', I was told, and would do patients 'more harm than good'.

Discussions among doctors about patient treatment and care, then, tended to take place away from the wards. They were confined to 'back-space' areas – offices and meeting rooms out of sight and earshot of patients (Goffman 1971). These might be regarded as the 'corridors of power', the places where medical decisions are made and courses of action planned (Snow 1964). During my fieldwork I was able to spend a lot of time in these back-spaces. For instance, I attended the Cardiothoracic Unit's weekly meeting where doctors would present cases that had proved particularly interesting or unusual. All those present were doctors and so there was no need to exercise the diplomacy necessary when patients were in the vicinity. There would be occasional jokes about patients, but more striking were remarks that had a straightforward and rather brutal honesty. I am not suggesting these to have held any kind of malice. They were merely statements of plain, if sorrowing, fact. For instance, 'This man's going to die fairly soon, isn't he?' In this particular case the patient was a 36-year-old man. It was often strange to meet patients on the wards having overheard conversations of this strangely intimate kind about them.

At times, clinically 'private' conversations would spill out of the separate, bounded zone of professional discursive space and into more 'public' spaces within the hospital. This was a danger of which the hospital management were aware and which they were keen to prevent. In a number of the lifts inside St Thomas' there were signs warning doctors not to talk about patients there lest they be overheard by the patients themselves or by concerned friends and relatives. The risk involved in having clinical discussions in inappropriately public spaces was underlined on one occasion when I was with a group of medical students in an empty bed bay. They were working on case notes they were due to present next day, but, distracted from their immediate task, had begun a discussion in which one of the students was criticising cardiothoracic surgeons. His argument was that these people became highly specialised and expert at one particular procedure or stage of the treatment process. As a consequence, as long as they felt themselves to have done their own work in a satisfactory manner, they did not mind if the patient thereafter lived or died under someone else's care. Of course, what the student said was not fact, and indeed, was not necessarily a view to which he held firmly. I think he was saying this because one of the surgeons had spoken to him harshly in a teaching session the day before and, angered and humiliated, the student wanted to find a way of attacking him in return. However, the group was standing perhaps 15 metres from a bed where a patient was sitting up talking with a visitor. As the student finished speaking the visitor got up and approached us. 'Excuse me', she said, 'but my husband has just been told his recent heart bypass operation was unsuccessful. Would you mind having your conversation somewhere else?' After apologising profusely, the group left.

As the students recognised, their behaviour had been inappropriate. They had not, in this particular case, been discussing a patient, but had nonetheless been making unprofessional remarks about the hospital system. To the listening couple the student's words might well have been profoundly upsetting. He had indirectly inferred that the hospital's cardiothoracic surgeons had no interest in the man's long-term well-being. In all likelihood the student had further undermined the couple's already shaken confidence in those responsible for the surgery. The students belatedly acknowledged the importance of containing their conversations within appropriate conversational zones, not just away from authority figures, but also away from the ward and from patients who might be adversely affected by overhearing what was said.

Of course, doctors would often be required to talk to patients on the wards. At times the subject was not difficult or sensitive and there was no need to speak in confidential tones. But when serious matters had to be discussed the curtain would be drawn around the bed and the doctor(s) would get close to the patient, speaking in a lowered voice, conscious of the need to attempt to generate a zone of private auditory space in a public environment. Their efforts were not always successful. Words and phrases describing particular conditions, giving diagnoses and detailing prognoses were often still audible to other patients. At the time of my fieldwork, the principle that a patient's details should remain confidential to everyone except those immediately involved in his or her care was one of the central tenets of medical practice; sounds (as vocalisations), though, tended to find their way around, under or through this principle, so that private information was once again made public.

The difficulty of creating areas of private conversational space was well recognised by patients, who sometimes found themselves having to have serious discussions with friends and relatives while in hospital. If mobile enough, they would tend to take visitors to the TV room, the landings immediately outside the ward or even to the hospital café to get away from those who, albeit unintentionally, might eavesdrop. But patients knew that their neighbours would inevitably overhear a great deal of personal information. A retired army captain I spoke to told me: 'Everyone here is in the strange situation of being a reluctant confidante. They know things about you that you'd rather they didn't, and you know things about them that they'd rather you didn't.' An elderly lady I interviewed nodded towards her ward neighbour and said: 'I know what's going on in her heart just as she knows what's going on in mine.' Patients were conscious that on the ward, just as in the back-space zones of the medical profession, information about their bodies was broadcast, circulated in acoustic and discursive space. This was poignantly illustrated when, as I interviewed a man recovering from bypass surgery, the privacy curtain was pulled around the patient in the bed diagonally opposite his. 'I'm not surprised', my interviewee said to me in a low voice. 'I heard him being told yesterday that the heart muscle's badly damaged. He hasn't got long.'

## Sounds and disquiet

During my research at St Thomas' I studied the ways in which doctors use and apply auditory knowledge in their day-to-day work. One auditory technique that was frequently adopted during examinations was stethoscopic listening or auscultation. I was struck by the ways in which sounds from, for instance, the heart and lungs were brought into the perception of the doctor through the technological mediation of the stethoscope. The bodily interior underwent a process of sonic exteriorisation.

Modern medical practice involves the use of other technologies that mediate and externalise internal bodily events through sound. On the Cardiothoracic Unit at St Thomas' patients were almost invariably suffering from heart problems. Electrocardiograph machines (sometimes known as heart monitors) were in frequent, if not constant, use. At the time of the research, all patients on these wards received 15 minutes of electrocardiography twice a day and some were monitored for much longer periods. The repetitive beeping sound produced by the machines was noticeable. One patient described it as being 'the heartbeat of the ward', a sonic leitmotif of life there.

In electrocardiography a set of sensors are placed at specific points on the patient's chest. These sensors pick up the electrical activity produced by the heart as it beats. The information is then relayed to a unit where it is converted to appear as a set of lines on a paper printout or computer monitor. The nature of the data produced by the electrocardiogram is too sophisticated to discuss in detail here. Suffice it to say that, by looking at the output, the doctor is able to assess numerous aspects of the heart's condition and functioning. Electrocardiograph machines are usually set to give an alarm tone if the heart rate exceeds or drops below a particular number of beats per minute, and a fault tone may be produced if sensors become detached from the cables connecting them to the monitor. The characteristic beep that the electrocardiograph produces, however, coincides with systole (the point at which the ventricles of the heart contract). The sound does not convey complex data, but as it forms a sequence through time, gives basic information as to the rate and rhythm of the heart. This signal sequence of the electrocardiograph is usually of little use to the doctor, who can if necessary consult the screen for a numerical reading of the patient's heart rate; besides, he or she is generally more interested in the detail of the heart's functioning as displayed on the printout or monitor. The beeps are, however, useful to nurses, who, through a kind of monitory listening, are able to carry out other tasks some distance from the patient while keeping the tones at the periphery of their attention. If there is a rapid speeding up or slowing of the beeps, or if they cease altogether, the nurses will notice and can make appropriate checks or interventions. The purpose of the electrocardiograph's beep, then, is to broadcast information about the heart across the ward. The heart's activity is exteriorised through sound.

There was a consensus among patients to whom I spoke that the near-constant pulsing of the electrocardiograph was irritating. The sound was high-pitched, persistent and rarely out of earshot: 'Can't they turn the wretched thing off from time to time?', one lady wanted to know. It seemed not. 'Sometimes it makes me want to scream', said the person in the bed adjacent to hers. But patients' attitudes to the sound tended to become more complex when relating to *their own* monitoring sessions. Some remarked that they liked being able to hear their own hearts beating away and found it reassuring. But more felt that it was frightening. Suffering from heart problems as they were, they preferred not to think about what was going on inside their bodies at all. As the former army captain introduced above explained: 'I know somebody has to know about my heart, but I'd just rather not and this way I have to.' He didn't like the auditory reminder of his vulnerability that the electrocardiograph produced. 'It sometimes sounds to me like the thing is counting down', said a patient named Colin. 'You don't know how many pips you've got left.' 'When it's you connected up, you're always waiting for the next beep, worrying that it's not going to come', added his ward neighbour. By broadcasting a sonic representation of the patients' heartbeats, the electrocardiograph could simultaneously reinforce a sense of their lives being in jeopardy. Medical dramas and films with emergency room scenes, of course, exploit this quality of the electrocardiograph's beep. The action often culminates in a spell of silence with the sudden resumption of the beep signifying a life narrowly saved. Alternatively, there is also the now rather clichéd continuous tone or 'flat line' (though cardiologists I have spoken to assure me that the continuous tone is never actually heard, as a stopped heart produces no beat and therefore no tone at all).

Another technological sound that could often be heard on the wards of the Cardiothoracic Unit was that of the echocardiograph. In echocardiography or cardiac ultrasound, the operator directs ultra high-frequency sound waves at the heart using a kind of probe known as a 'transducer'. These ultrasound waves (which are too high-frequency to be audible) are reflected back to the transducer and are converted so as to create a two-dimensional visual projection of the working heart that appears on a monitor. Echocardiography is a powerful technology that generates detailed real-time images of the heart as it beats, producing valuable diagnostic information. But in addition to creating images of the heart, echocardiography also involves the use of Doppler ultrasound. Here, a phenomenon known as the Doppler effect is used to make assessments as to whether blood is moving towards or away from the transducer, and to gauge the relative velocity of that movement. This can be particularly useful when assessing, for instance, the leakage of blood across damaged or malfunctioning heart valves. Doppler ultrasound is not crucial to carrying out an echocardiogram, but most sonographers prefer to use the sounds to guide their visual inspection of the heart and consolidate their interpretation of the images.

The sounds produced during echocardiography can be loud. Unlike those heard through the stethoscope they are audible not only to the person operating the technology but also to the patient and even others some distance away. Certainly, in the ultrasound sessions I observed, patients were often captivated by the character of the sound produced by what they usually referred to as the 'echo'. One patient to whom I spoke likened it to the rhythmic swishing of a washing machine. Another suggested that it was 'like a ship sinking' with water 'gushing and pouring'. Still another likened the sound to 'water spilling through caves', capturing its swooshing, liquid quality.

Following Mol's (2002) assertion of the importance of keeping practices at the centre of efforts to understand disease, we might consider the use of electrocardiography and echocardiography as clinical activities through which heart disease is both sounded and enacted at St Thomas' Hospital. These technologies (among others) enable technicians and clinicians to produce information about patients' hearts. At the same time, by interpreting and sharing this information, doctors and technicians enact what Mol (2002: 84, 115) describes as particular 'versions' or 'variants' of heart disease. These clinical 'versions' differ in nature and quality from the versions of the disease that are enacted by patients through their lived experience of illness and descriptions of that experience, but Mol asserts that these distinct versions of the disease (and of the patient body) are able to coexist simultaneously. In a hospital, she argues, there is not just a single patient body, but rather many versions of the same body: the body is multiple and disease is composite – an entity produced through different versions of the disease and of the body, more or less comfortably, 'hanging together' (Mol 2002: 84).

What becomes clear from the accounts given above is that sounds, too, are involved in the production of particular 'versions' of heart disease. There are the sounds of the electrocardiogram that allow the acoustic production of a heart's rate and rhythm in beeps that are heard by the nurses. There are the sounds of the echocardiogram used by the technician to guide his analysis of hearts as they appear on a monitor. But these sounds are also heard by the (generally less medically educated and clinically skilled) ears of patients. They constitute part of patients' experience of being ill, so that sounds and listening become involved in what Mol (2002: 27, 20) describes as 'lay ways', as well as professional ways, of 'doing' disease. Within the hospital, then, distinctive sonic 'versions' of the body become audible, which themselves have different consequences for the interlocutors engaged in practising Mol's 'body multiple' (2002: 84).

Like the beep produced during electrocardiography, the auditory information generated by the echocardiograph projects into perceptual space. Echocardiography was not used as frequently as electrocardiography on the wards in which I conducted my research. When necessary, patients were often transported to a special suite of rooms where a number of echocardiograph machines were located. But enough examinations took place on the wards using a mobile echocardiography unit for its sounds to become a recognisable feature of the soundscape. Patients did not tend to identify the sounds as nuisance noise. Their striking character meant that patients tended to find them 'weird', 'strange' or 'unnecessary' rather than annoying. But again, as with electrocardiography, patients' reactions to the sounds produced during *their own* scans tended to be more complex.

When undergoing a cardiac ultrasound examination the patient is usually asked to lie facing away from the monitor. This is not necessarily so that he or she does not see the images (though that may be an advantage of the patient's being in this particular position), but because it enables the technician to move the transducer more easily over the chest, generating images of the heart from the desired angles. However, the patient can still hear the sounds produced. The technicians to whom I spoke told me that they tended to advise patients that the sounds were unimportant and that no notice should be taken of them. But the patients could not help listening and inferring their own meaning from the sounds. They tended to interpret them as a direct amplification of events taking place inside their own bodies. For instance, one young man I spoke to was in hospital for an infection that had damaged the mitral valve of his heart. He took the sounds produced during the echocardiogram to be an amplification of a 'murmur' made by his blood as it leaked through the damaged valve (he had heard the doctors referring to this 'murmur' during previous examinations). 'It sounded pretty loud', he told me. 'I'm glad they've decided to do something about it' (by which he meant operate and replace the valve). An elderly lady I spoke to on several occasions had received a number of echocardiograms over the years in order to monitor a leak in her aortic valve. 'On the echo you can actually hear it and it's not very nice. You can actually hear what's going on inside your body. That was something I'd never heard before. You don't normally realise what's going on in there.' The technologically mediated sounds offered patients a way to hear inside themselves, or at least to imagine what was taking place inside their own bodies. The sounds were interpreted in the light of existing clinical knowledge that patients had acquired about their conditions.

Above I suggested that one dimension of the erosion of privacy that patients experience during hospital stays can be linked to unwanted exposure to sounds from other patients. Privacy can also be threatened when patients lose control over the ways in which their own sounds project into the auditory space occupied by others. The technologies described above present additional challenges to the patients' sense of auditory control over their own bodies. Electrocardiography and echocardiography have the effect of exteriorising what are perceived as internal bodily events, projecting them across the ward in unfamiliar acoustic forms. The body becomes acoustically distributed: an 'unbounded' or 'boundless' entity (Lawton 1998; Rice 2008). Its internal events seep and leak into public perception.

The historian Jonathan Sawday (1995) has identified an enthusiasm for dissection of the human body among medical men and scientists during the early modern period. He considers that the consequent rapid accumulation of anatomical knowledge during this era created a major advance in scientific understanding. One consequence of this advance was that the population in general (i.e. even people who were not medical men by profession) came to develop a detailed understanding of the functioning of the body. Although potentially empowering, this development was unsettling too. Through a familiarity with dissected corpses, people were able (at only a slight remove) to perceive their own insides – an unnerving situation because, Sawday (1995: 15) writes, 'the interior recesses of the body are not merely private to others but peculiarly private – that is, expressly forbidden – to the owner or inhabitant of the body'. Indeed, he suggests that there is a 'taboo' against gazing inside one's own body (1995: 15). For patients with whom I conducted fieldwork, the sounds of electrocardiography and echocardiography could create a sensation of sonic disquiet. With an understanding that the sounds corresponded to events unfolding inside them, many patients received an often unwanted opportunity to engage acoustically with that 'peculiarly private' space that is one's own bodily interior.

## Conclusion

In the present era, the terms 'public' and 'private' have particularly strong resonance in relation to hospitals in the UK, in the sense that they also reference and contrast publicly and privately funded institutions. Typically better resourced than public ones, private hospitals tend to differ in terms of design. Where public hospitals (like those mentioned in this chapter) generally have large, open wards, private hospitals tend to have smaller wards or even individual rooms. There is a less 'public' performance of the illness role and less exposure to the presence of other patients. Unlike many public hospitals (including both the Edinburgh Royal Infirmary and St Thomas'), private hospitals are also rarely used in the teaching of medical students and so patients are unlikely to become involved in the 'public' arena that tuition sessions represent (Sinclair 1997). That illness in a private hospital is a comparatively 'private' experience would doubtless be reflected in the soundscapes of these clinics.

In the comparatively public spaces of the public hospital in which my fieldwork took place, sound has been shown to create a variety of problems around patient notions and experiences of privacy. There were threats to bodily boundaries and bodily control, anxieties over embarrassing acoustic presences, fears over forms of exposure and an acute awareness of the need for concealment or quietening. There was also a real concern over intrusive sounds. Cusick suggests that the detainees in her study attempted to find refuge from the loud sounds to which they were subjected by retreating inside themselves. They might put their fingers in their ears, trying to seal off and preserve some vestige of physical and mental space. In the surveillance-intense setting of the detention centre, the only privacy available to detainees seems to have been inside this mental space, which was invaded and at times even annihilated by the intensity of the loud music. In a similar way, some patients in my study emphasised the need to preserve an interior 'headspace' while on the ward. They stressed the difficulty of doing so in an environment in which they were in such uncomfortable sonic proximity to others.

There is a sense, then, in which we can loosely index the bodily interior and exterior to categories of 'private' and 'public' space respectively. Privacy seems to involve the ability to control and manage the extent of one's own bodily presences within space, to govern and police one's own bodily boundaries. It also implies a capacity to manage intrusions into a zone of intimate or close 'personal space', while at the same time having some ability to manage the volume and dynamics of (one's own and other peoples') auditory presences within the wider spatial field represented by the ward. It seems, then, that we can imagine roughly concentric zones of auditory space radiating away from the body, each carrying a relative (and culturally particular) charge reflecting a sense of personal ownership and occupancy. But living within the institutional setting of the hospital (in particular the Cardiothoracic Unit) and being subjected to the routines and practices in place there, many of the patients to whom I spoke clearly felt that the integrity of the body as a core private space was, at times, challenged. The body could no longer be understood as being located at the spatial centre of a set of concentric rings. Indeed through sounds, bodily interiors were exteriorised in many ways on the wards, and these exteriorisations were re-internalised through different sets of listening ears such that it became difficult to be certain any more where bodily boundaries (and thus related zones of 'owned', 'occupied' or 'controlled' space) began and ended. The diagrammatic concept of concentricity might still be useful, but the body cannot always be understood to be firmly at its centre because, as the body is sonically broadcast, it becomes dispersed and dissipated. Indeed, sounds – words, whispers, coughs, cries, beeps, whooshes – encourage us to reflect on the multiplicity of sonic forms in which the body, and information about the body, can travel. In an institution such as a large public hospital, we might say, sound makes the materiality of the body both multiple and transmissible across spatial, social and moral boundaries; 'flows' of these sounds draw our attention to the constant shifting and morphing of bodily space. They emphasise in turn the fragility and fluidity of public and private space as constructed and experienced by patients.

## 8 | Islam, sound and space: acoustemology and Muslim citizenship on the Kenyan coast

ANDREW J. EISENBERG

As the site of an ancient Muslim 'mercantile civilization' (Middleton 1992) of the Indian Ocean world, Kenya's Muslim-dominated 'Swahili coast' has always held a problematic place within the Christian-dominated Kenyan postcolony. Viewing the region in the light of its history of Omani Arab rule and movements for political autonomy, up-country Kenyans typically see it as 'neither completely African nor, by extension, Kenyan' (Prestholdt 2011: 6). Meanwhile, coastal Muslims, viewing it in the light of their marginalisation in the postcolony, often see it as having been 'colonized' (Brennan 2008) and 'looted' by up-country Kenya (Mazrui and Shariff 1994: 154; cf. Yahya 2000). These competing narratives amount to an ongoing symbolic struggle (Bourdieu 1989) over coastal Muslim citizenship in Kenya, a struggle over understandings of how coastal Muslims have been treated, what they deserve and how they fit within the Kenyan nation. Scholars have taken a renewed interest in this struggle in recent years, as debates over the status of Islamic courts and Kenya's entanglement in the 'global war on terror' have opened the possibilities for new forms of oppositional politics among the coastal Muslim population, including separatism and Islamism (Brennan 2008; Goldsmith 2011; Kresse 2009; Prestholdt 2010, 2011; Seesemann 2007). Recent scholarly interventions have done much to historicise and demystify the symbolic struggle over coastal Muslim citizenship in Kenya. But they have largely left untouched the essential problem of how this struggle inheres in Kenyan coastal Muslims' quotidian, visceral experiences of being (subjectified as) Kenyan citizens.[1]

Recognising the centrality of ritual sounding and listening practices for Muslim subject-formation (Qureshi 1996; Hirschkind 2006), this chapter approaches the subjective dimension of the symbolic struggle over coastal Muslim citizenship in Kenya through a 'sounded anthropology' centred on 'the soundscape and the politics of aurality' (Samuels et al. 2010: 339). Drawing on eighteen months of fieldwork on the Kenyan coast (2004–6), I take an 'ethnographic ear' to affective (i.e. pre-discursive), embodied spatial

---

[1] An exception is Kresse 2009, who reflects on the Kenyan coastal Muslims' (subject) position on the 'double periphery' of the Kenyan postcolony and the global Muslim *umma*.

practices through which denizens of the coastal city of Mombasa negotiate the literal and figurative place of a Muslim community within the bounds of a heterogeneous Kenyan metropolis.[2] My primary concern is with the architectonics of Islamic vocalisations that every day resound in the public spaces of Mombasa's historic Muslim–Swahili Old Town. Working in dialogue with other anthropological work on Muslim subject-formation (Hirschkind 2004, 2006; Mahmood 2005; El Guindi 2008), I argue that this 'Islamic soundscape' recruits a set of bodily practices through which Muslims in Mombasa Old Town transform the ostensibly public spaces of their neighbourhood into de facto private spaces of a Muslim–Swahili community.

Steven Feld's (1996) 'acoustemology of place' in Papua New Guinea provides a model for my approach to the dynamics of the Islamic soundscape in Mombasa Old Town. As with Bosavi auditory practices according to Feld, I argue that Muslim auditory practices in Mombasa Old Town serve as ways of understanding and enacting the material environment as a place-in-the-world. I depart from Feld, however, in focusing heavily on acoustemological *multiplicity* and *contestation*, phenomena that are likely more common in postcolonial African cities than in the rainforest setting of Papua New Guinea. While I do hear a relatively coherent Islamic–Swahili 'acoustemology of place resounding' (to borrow Feld's phrase) in Mombasa Old Town, my interest lies with the ways in which this acoustemology interacts with competing acoustemological commitments, particularly those fostered by the Kenyan state's broadly liberal–democratic logic of urban public space. My aim is to reveal something of the subjective dimensions of Muslim citizenship on the Kenyan coast by asking how such acoustemological disjuncture shapes Muslim denizens' visceral understandings and experiences of being 'Kenyan'.

The approach I am outlining stands in tension (productive, I hope) with the influential work of Nilüfer Göle and her academic interlocutors (see inter alia Göle 2002, 2009; Göle and Ammann 2006), who also explore Muslim belonging in contemporary societies with an empirical focus on

---

[2] Affective, embodied spatial practice has become a major concern in human geography in recent years, particularly with the turn to so-called 'non-representational' (or 'more-than-representational') theory (e.g. Lorimer 2005; Anderson and Harrison 2010). In writing this chapter I have garnered a great deal of insight and inspiration from geographers' recent attempts at mapping 'how life takes shape and gains expression in shared experiences, everyday routines, fleeting encounters, embodied movements, precognitive triggers, practical skills, affective intensities, enduring urges, unexceptional interactions and sensuous dispositions' (Lorimer 2005: 84).

'concrete' public space.[3] In the first place, my approach challenges Göle's emphasis on Islam's public 'visibilities', an empirical bias that is problematic in light of the many, high-profile public and legal–juridical debates over the electrical amplification of the Islamic call to prayer in recent years.[4] But this chapter ultimately offers a more radical challenge to Göle's approach than simply a methodological exhortation to 'listen'. My focus on acoustemological disjuncture makes audible something that gets lost in Göle and her interlocutors' approach to concrete public space as a 'space of appearances' (Arendt 1989 (1958)): namely, that contestations in concrete public space may also be contestations *of* concrete public space, driven by (epistemological) disagreements over how space can be known to be public or private and (ontological) disagreements over what constitutes public or private space in the first place. In contrast to Göle and her interlocutors, I approach concrete public space as something that is enacted, and potentially enacted in multiple forms (cf. Mol 2002; Hinchliffe 2010), in everyday life. Concrete public space on the Kenyan coast, as I will argue, is deeply 'multiaccentual' (Vološinov 1986 (1973)) by virtue of the constant struggle between Islamic–Swahili and broadly liberal–democratic understandings of publicity and privacy. It is my task here to *listen in* to the practices and politics of this multiaccentual public space to hear the conditions of Muslim citizenship on the Kenyan coast.

## Mombasa Old Town and its Swahili context

Like other surviving 'Swahili stone towns' of the Kenya–Tanzania littoral, Mombasa Old Town was a bastion of Islamic urbanism, surrounded by little more than ocean and wilderness, for centuries. By linking the Mombasa area to the African interior by rail, British colonialists fostered the growth of a 'New Mombasa' at the turn of the twentieth century – a new urban settlement with a new mix of inhabitants, including labourers from up-country

---

[3] Göle takes the notion of 'concrete public space' from Arendt, who 'insists on the notion of a concrete public space (*öffentlicher Raum*) rather than an abstract public sphere (*Öffentlichkeit*)' (Göle 2009: 291). I use 'concrete' in this chapter also with Henri Lefebvre's abstract/concrete distinction in mind. For Lefebvre, 'concrete space is the space of gestures and journeys, of the body and memory, of symbols and sense' (Elden 2004: 189).

[4] Debates or disputes over the amplification of the call to prayer have received scholarly and/or journalistic attention in Singapore (Lee 1999); London (Eade 1996); Hamtramk, Michigan, USA (Weiner 2010); Cairo, Egypt (Smith 2005); and to a lesser extent (but apropos the present work) Kenya, where the passage of anti-noise legislation in 2009 provoked a brief uproar from Muslim organisations concerned that the move was aimed at silencing mosques.

as well as the Indian Ocean world – just outside the bounds of (what then became) the Old Town. Today, Mombasa Old Town's tight assemblage of 'Swahili'- and 'Indian'-style buildings abut a sprawling metropolis populated by nearly one million Kenyans of various geographical, ethnic and religious backgrounds. Remarkably, however, the ethnic character of the neighbourhood has changed little, save for the introduction of significant numbers of Somalians following the Somalian civil war in 1991 (MCP 1990: 43–55). The northern section is still dominated by the same Swahili-speaking Shāfi'ī Sunni Muslim clans that are thought to have settled the area as far back as the fourteenth century; the southern section is still home to a mix of coastal communities and Indian Ocean diasporants: Swahili, Arabs, Baluchis, South Asians (Hindu and Muslim), Somalians and a small number of African Christians.

While diverse in regard to ethnicity and sect, Mombasa Old Town's Muslims share a common language of everyday intercourse (Swahili) and a social imaginary grounded in a distinction between their own civilised Islamic urbanity (*uungwana*) and the supposed barbarism (*ushenzi*) of others (Kresse 2007: 55–6). These cultural connections, which Kai Kresse (2007) refers to as the 'Swahili context', determine shared 'patterns of speech and behaviour, greetings and terms of status and emotional states of being', as well as sartorial, culinary and musical practices (Kresse 2007: 55–6).

The most important unifying factor for Mombasa Old Town's Muslims, however, is *place*. Their neighbourhood and its surroundings provide them with shared sensory experiences while reaffirming 'the bitter reality of their political marginalization' in contemporary Kenya (Mazrui and Shariff 1994: 155). The constantly expanding city of Mombasa reminds them of their shared history of dispossession: every major stage in the development of New Mombasa was accompanied by a move towards the economic and political downfall of those in the Old Town. New Mombasa's emergence in the late nineteenth century coincided with the dismantling of slavery, an institution that had propped up Mombasa Old Town's Arab and Swahili patricians (Salim 1973: 100–1). The city's first growth spurt, in the 1920s, then saw the relocation of shipping activity from the Old Port to the other side of Mombasa Island (De Blij 1968: 41; Willis 1993: 146–7). Finally, New Mombasa's postcolonial boom saw an influx of newly empowered up-country Kenyans, among whom were 'men … hand-picked by President Kenyatta to ensure the incorporation and integration of the coast (remote, exotic, and largely Muslim if viewed from Nairobi, and certainly a former [opposition] stronghold) into the mainstream of Kenya's economic and social life' (Yahya 2000). Thus the urban spatial practices that every day reproduce the Swahili context are inherently political, reflecting and refracting the larger symbolic struggle over coastal Muslim citizenship in Kenya. Most of these practices are not *overtly* political, however. Only when Mombasa Old Town residents actively defend the cultural/moral character of their neighbourhood – for example, when male residents decry the 'immodest' dress of young Christian women who enter the bounds of the neighbourhood – do we find an overt politics. In this chapter, however, I detail a subtler but ultimately more significant spatial politics in Mombasa Old Town – one that proceeds in and through sound.

## An Islamic soundscape

Mombasa Old Town is every day awash with electrically amplified male voices delivering Islamic devotional and moral texts in Arabic and Swahili. Five times a day a polyphony of cantillated Arabic calls to prayer emanates from the rooftop loudspeakers of dozens of neighbourhood mosques, its 'soaring yet mournful, almost languid harmonic webs' (Hirschkind 2006: 124) somewhat harshened by the crackling of overstressed or substandard sound reproduction technologies.[5] The constant rhythm of this key 'soundmark' (Schafer 1994 (1977)) is further punctuated each week by the polyphony of Arabic and Swahili sermons that emanate from many of these same loudspeakers. Between these periodic sonic events, a random assemblage of radios and computer speakers in local shops and homes supply the neighbourhood's private and semi-private spaces with layers of Qur'anic recitations, sermons in Arabic, Swahili and sometimes English, and religious songs in Swahili and Arabic (Swa. *kaswida*; Ar. *qaṣīda*) – producing a continuous (e)merging of vocal performances that I refer to as an Islamic soundscape.

Though most of its constituent elements involve a recitation of, or reference to, a key text (the Qur'an), an Islamic soundscape is less an intertextual field than an architectonics of audible events resounding in local spaces and sensibilities. As will become clear, what makes the Mombasa Islamic soundscape a coherent entity is not its intertextuality but rather its 'inter-practicality': the ways in which its sounding and listening practices relate to each other and to the originary Islamic 'recitation', the Qur'an.

---

[5] Mosques throughout Africa, the Middle East and Asia commonly employ loudspeakers. The electrically amplified *adhān* came to Mombasa Old Town in the 1970s, after years of creative attempts by local muezzins to compete with the increasing volume of the city by using other makeshift technologies, including horns cannibalised from gramophone players.

Above all, an Islamic soundscape must be understood as deeply implicated in processes of subject-formation; it is an *apparatus*, 'a machine that produces subjectifications' (Agamben 2009: 20). At the simplest level, the Islamic soundscape *qua* apparatus recruits those within earshot as particular types of inhabitant–subjects (residents, visitors, etc.). The call to prayer, or *adhān* in Arabic, is key: as a literal act of hailing a community of believers (*umma*), its role in demarcating the space of a Muslim community is always at the forefront (Lee 1999). Indeed, the *adhān* is one of the primary '[subliminal] cues' that enable both residents and visitors in a heterogeneous city to recognise a 'Muslim quarter' (Abu-Lughod 1987: 160). In Mombasa, the sound of the *adhān* marks the Old Town as a 'Muslim quarter', even though the neighbourhood is not the only part of the city in which the call can be heard. This is because outside of the Old Town, Mombasa's *adhāns* are simply part of the urban din. In the market area, for example, though *adhāns* ring out from powerful loudspeakers mounted atop the high minarets of the large, Saudi-funded mosques, their sounds get lost in an urban din of rumbling cars and trucks, popular music soundtracks of *matatu* taxi-vans, and voices of touts and peddlers. In the Old Town, meanwhile, a thick polyphony of *adhāns* easily reaches the ears of anyone present. Since Swahili-style mosques typically lack minarets, the voices are close to ear level; moreover, they are relatively unfettered by the rest of the acoustic environment. Some of the humanly produced sounds that could potentially compete with *adhāns* in the Old Town (shouts, laughter, music, etc.) give way as pious Muslim residents receive the call; others, such as the throbbing *matatu* soundtracks, are simply absent in any case (*matatus* ply no routes through the Old Town's narrow streets).

In its guise as a 'subliminal cue', Mombasa Old Town's Islamic soundscape is not just an apparatus but also a sign-vehicle. For outsiders, especially, the Old Town's Islamic soundscape is part and parcel of a multisensory tableau that ties together the neighbourhood's other typical sights, sounds and smells: Indian-style wood doors, women in black purdah robes, Arabic- and Indian-inflected *taarab* music, aromas of incense and coconut rice and so on. Mediated by narratives of the Kenyan tourism industry, this tableau reflects the 'Arabian Nights ambience' (MacDonald 1956: 13) that has long been marketed to foreign tourists and is now increasingly marketed to middle-class up-country Kenyans as well. But for some Kenyans this tableau signifies something more repellent and frightening: a number of Mombasans not from the Old Town (including one Muslim) informed me that they avoid the neighbourhood for fear of being harmed or seduced by genie magic, homosexual practices or transnational jihadism, all of which are rumoured to be common among the Old Town's Arab(ised) inhabitants (Porter 1995; McIntosh 2009: 89–126).


## An Islamic acoustemology

The subject, according to Georgio Agamben (2009: 14), 'results from the relation and, so to speak, the relentless fight between living beings and apparatuses'. It is in this more energetic sense that the Islamic soundscape serves as an apparatus for the production of *Muslim* subjects – only what Agamben describes as a 'relentless fight' Muslims describe in quite different terms, as *sacred obligation* (*farḍ*) and *submission* ('*islām*).

The Islamic soundscape's apparatical character is most apparent in its attendant practices of 'reception' (a somewhat imperfect term in this context). Consider the *adhān* once again. Unlike the Christian church bell, which is also a 'call to prayer' in the most literal sense, the *adhān* hails its subjects by initiating a participatory 'communicative practice' (Fennes 2010: 79). Proper audition of the *adhān* implies an active process engaging not only the ears but also the entire body, including the voice. Upon hearing the first line, pious Muslims repeat the first words '*Allahu Akbar*' (God is Great) quietly to themselves, along with other prescribed responses to subsequent lines (El Guindi 2008: 135). The obligation to respond in this way to the *adhān* is laid out in the *ḥadīth*s, the authoritative narratives of the Prophet's words and deeds. But the idea of a vocal response is also embedded in the institution of the *adhān* at a more basic level, as the text includes the *Shahāda*, the testimony of faith ('There is no god but God, and Mohammed is his messenger'), the enunciation of which is the first 'pillar' of Islam. Pious Muslims who do not engage in such vocal responses (the question of whether women are obligated, or even allowed, to do so is actively debated in many parts of the Muslim world) typically respond with an attentive, otherworldly silence and, if necessary (and it often is), silencing actions: the muting of televisions and radios, the silencing of unruly children and so on. Women, meanwhile, adjust their headscarves. All these actions are habitual, undertaken with a 'calm serenity' (El Guindi 2008: 138) and 'a spontaneity analogous to the reflex adjustments of the muscles of a driver approaching a curve' (Hirschkind 2006: 125).

The *adhān* is not unique in demanding a particular form of participatory listening from Muslims. Sermon-listening also calls for habituated bodily techniques. Charles Hirschkind (2001b, 2006) describes Islamic sermon audition in Cairo as an 'ethical performance', which 'demands a particular

affective-volitional responsiveness from the listener … while simultaneously deepening an individual's capacity to hear in this manner' (2001b:
624). Habituated responses to the Islamic soundscape therefore index a lifetime of ethical practice: 'These are the motions of the heart, limbs, and will
… as they continuously accommodate themselves to the familiar demands
of a sonorous moral acoustics' (Hirschkind 2006: 124). Accordingly, pious
Muslims place a great deal of emphasis upon the acquisition of pious listening habits in the earliest stages of physical and social development. In
many parts of the Muslim world parents quietly perform the *adhān* and
*iqāma* (the echo of the *adhān*, recited in the mosque) into the ears of their
newborn children (Trimingham 1980 (1964): 126). Two influential works
of Swahili autoethnography, Mtoro bin Mwinyi Bakari's nineteenth-century
work *The Customs of the Swahili People* (1981: 8) and Hyder Kindy's *Life
and Politics in Mombasa* (1972), attribute great importance to this practice,
citing 'a belief that children who do not experience [it] when they are born
will go astray and become bad characters' (Kindy 1972: 5).

In the context of contemporary social theory, a discussion of shared bodily dispositions evokes Bourdieu's (1980) theory of the habitus. But as some
anthropologists of Islam have argued in recent years, Aristotle's theory of
the habitus, which has left a strong mark on the writings of Islamic philoso-
phers such as Ibn Khaldun, provides a more powerful theoretical perspective on Muslim subject-formation (see inter alia Starrett 1995; Mahmood
2005: 136–9). Unlike Bourdieu's theory, which stresses the unconscious and
ineffable nature of embodied dispositions ('body *hexis*'), '[habitus in the]
Aristotelian tradition is understood to be an acquired excellence at either a
moral or a practical craft, learned through repeated practice until that practice leaves a permanent mark on the character of the person' (Mahmood
2005: 136). In other words, it is a *cultivated* bodily orientation, which 'does
not simply express the social structure but also endows the self with particular capacities through which the subject comes to enact the world'
(Mahmood 2005: 139). Armed with this Aristotelian notion of habitus,
we begin to see and hear how habituated modes of sounding and listening
are also acoustemic capacities that enable Muslims in Mombasa Old Town
to actively transform, or 'convert' (El Guindi 2008), the physical spaces of
their neighbourhood.

Understanding how Muslims call upon their acoustemic capacities
to enact the world requires an understanding of the Islamic ontology of
the divine word. Muslims regard the Arabic text of the Qur'an as God's
*ipsissima verba*, his very words, which were revealed to the world through
the Prophet Mohammed's (mantic) recitation and were thereafter 'intended

to be rehearsed and recited' by all believers; the Qur'an is literally 'the reciting' [al-quran] (Graham and Kermani 2006: 115). In an Islamic cosmology,
sounded sacred words link the material world to the immaterial realm of
God. In the process of forging this connection, sacred sound creates sacred
space. A Swahili interlocutor in Mombasa directed me to a *ḥadīth* passage (from Al-Bukhari, one of the most trusted collections of the Sunni
canon) that beautifully illustrates this sonorous process of spatial sacralisation. 'When the Imam comes out', the Prophet is reported to have said,
'the angels present themselves to listen to the *khuṭba* [the Friday sermon]'
(Al-Bukhari 1997: 23). The image here is one in which angels literally make
themselves present within the space and time of the *khuṭba*'s sounding (the
Arabic root used in the passage, ḥ–ḍ–r, connotes physical presence in space
and time). That is to say, heavenly beings listen to the *khuṭba* not through
some mystical mode of hearing but by temporarily joining with human
beings in the profane world (*dunyā*). Sound thus becomes a material tendon linking sacred and profane realms, thereby transforming (sacralising)
the latter; or, better, sound becomes a *potential* tendon linking the sacred
and the profane, as human beings also play an essential role in this sonic
sacralisation of space.

In a boldly panoptic ethnographic study of spatiotemporality in Islamic
cultures, Fadwa El Guindi (2008) outlines the effects of this spatial sacralisation on the concrete spaces inhabited by Muslim individuals and communities. She describes a 'rhythm of Islam', which is grounded in pious
subjects' periodic 'movements … out of ordinary time and space and into
sacred time and space and back' (2008: 134). Such movements, El Guindi
contends, may be effected by individuals or by groups: they are 'effected
singly' in the act of prayer, when a 'Muslim, stripped temporarily of worldly
identity, is in a sacred state'; they are 'effected collectively' in contexts of collective ritual practice, such as 'the mosque during Friday noon prayer and
the annual pilgrimage to Makka' (2008: 136). In Mombasa Old Town, as
in other Muslim places, the constant movements 'out of ordinary time and
space and into sacred time and space and back' are effected to a significant
extent in and through the acoustemic capacities associated with the Islamic
soundscape.

## A resonant privacy

Mombasa Old Town's Muslim denizens' constant movements 'into sacred
time and space and back' effectively transform, or 'convert' (El Guindi 2008),

the neighbourhood as a whole into something of a sanctuary. As in the Arab world, the notion of 'sanctuary' in the Swahili context is a concept that 'connects sacred places, like mosque and pilgrimage centre, house of worship and house of learning, [and] also applies to women, women's quarters, and family' (El Guindi 2008: 150). Another way to understand this sanctification is as a kind of 'communitarian privacy' (Ammann 2006: 98–110), understanding 'privacy' in the Arab/Swahili sense, which 'does not connote the "personal", the "secret" or the "individuated space" [but rather] two core [social] spheres – women and the family' (El Guindi 1999: 82).[6]

In the literature on the 'Islamic city', communitarian privacy is classically described as a function of architectural form: winding streets and mazes of courtyards make public space 'defensible' (Abu-Lughod 1987: 170) by fostering multiple '[gradations of] private, semi-private and semi-public space' (Ammann 2006: 102). But to the extent that a Swahili stone town counts as an 'Islamic city', it suggests that Islamic communitarian privacy may be acoustical (or acoustemological) as well as architectural. Indeed, in the Swahili context a sanctuary is inherently *resonant*. Take, for example, the ideal-typical Swahili sanctuary, the domestic sanctum (*ndani*). As Swahili architecture scholar Linda Wiley Donley (1982) describes, the traditional house of a Swahili stone town is constructed not only with stones but also with sounds. Donley (1982: 72) offers the example of the elite Swahili ritual *kutolewande*, in which a forty-day-old infant is introduced to the house that will become her 'very cosmos for several years'. In this ritual the mother and other female members of the household make audible the differences between the various rooms of the house, making each room vibrate with its own didactic songs (1982: 70).

In the Swahili context, humanly produced sound can also turn public (i.e. extra-domestic) spaces into sanctuaries. Indeed, for centuries residents of Swahili towns and villages have used sound to distinguish their settlement from a surrounding wilderness, or one moiety within the settlement from the other. Until the late twentieth century, along the coast, Swahili Muslims performed a yearly ritual of spatial demarcation and purification in which a sacrificial bull was led counter-clockwise around the town or moiety to the sounds of *siwa*s (decorated side-blown horns of ivory, brass or wood which historically served as symbols of power in Swahili towns) and

---

[6] Neither Arabic nor Swahili (the latter of which borrows much of its philosophical lexicon from the former) has a word that adequately expresses the classical Western notion of 'privacy' as the domain of an individuated subject (on Arabic, see El Guindi 2008: 147–50). El Guindi glosses 'privacy' in Arabic with reference to three intercalated cultural categories of 'sanctity–reserve–respect' (El Guindi 1999: 77–96).

verses from the Qur'an were recited (see inter alia el-Zein 1974; Ghaidan 1975: 69; Bakari 1981: 189–90).


## A multiaccentuality of space

While the question of whether or not Kenya counts as a true liberal democracy is hotly debated today, it is nevertheless clear that the Kenyan state espouses a broadly liberal–democratic conception of the public/private distinction and the role of religion in public life, treating physical public spaces (at least in urban areas) as embodiments of the 'arena of "neutral principles"' on which it can justify its policies towards individual citizens and communities (Mitchell 1997: 165–6). What does it mean, then, for a resonant Muslim sanctuary – Mombasa Old Town – to be constantly superposed on the public spaces of Kenya's heterogeneous 'second city'? To approach the question, I want to move briefly away from Mombasa, to an area just north of the city.

In July 2006 the quiet, verdant area of Kikambala played host to a highly publicised dispute between a local imam and a female member of the coast's foreign expatriate community.[7] The trouble started soon after the imam's mosque had been fitted with new rooftop loudspeakers that happened to be aimed in the direction of the expatriate's nearby home. Early one morning, the expatriate made her way over to the imam's mosque to register her consternation at being jolted out of bed by the pre-dawn *adhān*. She arrived outside the mosque while the elongated tones of the sacred recitation were still sounding, and began to shout her complaints towards the edifice. The imam soon emerged to investigate the disturbance. Upon finding an angry woman vocalising a dissonant counterpoint to the *adhān*, he offered what he would later calmly describe as the only appropriate response: he punched the woman squarely in the eye.

The imam's response (that is, attack) was received with general approval from Kenyan Muslims. Leaders of Kenya's national Muslim organisations were soon standing shoulder-to-shoulder with him in hastily organised press conferences, arguing that his violent response, however regrettable, was carried out in accordance with Islamic law as well as common sense. The local community of worshippers offered a similar defence, only more

---

[7] The woman, who was of apparent East Asian extraction, was described as 'Chinese' in local news reports. In interviews she demonstrated knowledge of Swahili, indicating that she was a long-time resident.

performative in nature: in the gaze of television news cameras, a group of male worshippers constructed a stone wall to block the footpath that the expatriate had used to reach their mosque. Given that it was only wide enough to block the footpath, the wall was clearly a message meant to communicate that the expatriate's actions were an attack of an equivalent brutality to what she herself had suffered at the hands of the imam.

The story of the imam and the expatriate in Kikambala makes visible and audible the presence of competing logics of public space on the Kenyan coast, which is the essence of what I call the 'social multiaccentuality' (Vološinov 1986 (1973)) of public space on the Kenyan coast. In both the formulation and delivery of her complaint, the expatriate situated herself within the ostensibly 'neutral' public space of a liberal democratic republic, a space in which even sacred sound may be marked as noise and any subject may address any other without regard to minority norms of social intercourse. The imam's response, meanwhile, was grounded in a different logic of public space, an Islamic–Swahili logic, which bears its own rules of conduct and address.

V. N. Vološinov's (1986 (1973)) heuristic concept of multiaccentuality captures the *ontological* nature of the competition between logics of space on the Kenyan coast. By resisting the false dichotomy between representations and 'concrete material reality' (1986 (1973): 65), Vološinov reveals that the multiaccentual sign – whether it be a stretch of urban public space or a verbal utterance – 'does not just exist as part of a reality – it reflects and refracts another reality' (1986 (1973): 10). An active competition between logics of space thus marks an 'ontological politics', 'a politics over what there is and who/what can know it' (Verran 1998: 238; Mol 2002; Law 2010; Born forthcoming). By acting upon (and thereby enacting) divergent logics of public space, the imam, the expatriate and any others who became involved in their dispute were waging just such a politics.

Ontological politics, it must be stressed, is about more than the conflicts and clashes that arise from ontological disjuncture. Subjects can and do engage *strategically* with multiple, discrepant ontologies. The idea of a multiaccentuality of public space allows for the fact that subjects may strategically navigate and negotiate multiple logics of public space. This is particularly important for the context of the African postcolony (Hecht and Simone 1994; Mbembe 2001), whose subjects often 'learn to bargain in [a] conceptual marketplace' of multiple, 'entangled ... logics' of public space (Mbembe 2001: 104). In the case of the imam and the expatriate in Kikambala, it is possible the disputants may have been engaged in active, self-reflexive negotiation of multiple ontologies of public space. Indeed, the fact that both primary parties to the dispute sought recourse to public opinion through the national media suggests that one or both may have been strategically refusing to recognise the underlying logic of their adversary's actions.

To bring this discussion back to Mombasa Old Town, some Muslim residents may comprehend the communitarian privacy of their neighbourhood *doxically*, as 'the way of the world'. Others, recognising the political power of communitarian privacy as an alternative to Kenya's dominant liberal–democratic logic of public space, may comprehend it as a provocative collectivist variation on the liberal–democratic theme of the individual right to privacy (i.e. a group of individuals claiming their right to be 'left alone', together). These two possibilities are not necessarily mutually exclusive.

## A sonorous ontological politics

The multiaccentuality of public space in Mombasa Old Town thus engenders a sonorous ontological politics. I want to get deeper into this politics by attending to the Old Town's weekly polyphony of electrically amplified Friday sermons, or *khuṭbas*. Delivered by an imam or designated preacher, a *khuṭba* is an essential component of the all-important Friday midday prayer (*Jumuʿa*). The highly structured sermon is always delivered in Arabic; however, in East Africa most (though not all) preachers include a Swahili portion (technically speaking, it is a separate sermon). While it is ostensibly meant to provide a translation or explication of what is conveyed in the (sacred) Arabic sermon, the Swahili sermon is often the lengthier of the two.

At first blush, there is a bit of irony in my using the *khuṭba* to discuss politics in Mombasa Old Town, as *khuṭbas* in the Old Town are understood locally to be far less 'political' than *khuṭbas* in other parts of the city. A number of Mombasa's preachers attached to newer (mid-twentieth-century) mosques outside of the Old Town have received their training at Islamic universities in Saudi Arabia, Iran or other Muslim countries on scholarships. Their preaching, influenced by Salafi reform movements, often draws upon the rhetoric of global political Islamism, condemning Western values and Jewish Zionism. In contrast, the 'traditionalist-' or 'sufi-'style *khuṭbas* delivered by the locally trained preachers of the Old Town tend to focus on general ethical concerns (though references to the Israeli–Palestinian conflict are not uncommon). It would seem, then, that *khuṭbas* broadcast by preachers at mosques outside the Old Town are far more 'political' than those broadcast by preachers in the Old Town. But this is only true 'on paper', and the *khutba* is not primarily a written genre. My argument here is that *khutba*s in the Old Town are deeply political because of the ways in which they resound in the neighbourhood's multiaccentual public spaces.

The political timbre of the Old Town's *khutba*s becomes audible upon considering the question of audience with respect to the Swahili portions. The fact is that the Old Town's electrically amplified *khutba*s bear the potential to reach a broad and diverse audience that includes many Swahili-speaking Christians who reside, work or simply pass through the neighbourhood each day. On Fridays there are even more non-Muslims in the Old Town than on other days, because Friday is the day for Muslims to distribute charity (*sadaqa*) to the poor. Needy Mijikenda and Kamba women, many of whom are Christians, flood the city with children strapped to their backs to make their rounds after the prayer. Not all of these women are highly competent Swahili speakers, but their aural comprehension of the language is likely to be fair. Intended or not, they are a potential audience for the Swahili portions of the neighbourhood's *khutba*s.

When I asked Mombasan preachers and imams from within and without the Old Town about the significance of non-Muslims hearing a broadcast of the Friday *khutba*, some allowed that a non-Muslim may be able to learn something from lessons (Swa. *mawaidha*) in the Swahili sermons, but all averred that the words of the Friday *khutba* are not meant for a non-Muslim's ears.[8] A *khutba*, I was reminded, is a *sacred* oration mediating the relationship between the audience and God (Hirschkind 2006: 39). While Muslim preachers may speak directly to non-Muslims or expect non-Muslims to listen while preaching in a public park or in a radio broadcast, this is not the case when they are preaching in or from the mosque during Friday prayers. When I asked why the *khutba* is then broadcast on loudspeakers into public space, the answer was once again unanimous: all my interlocutors mentioned the homebound Muslim women, insisting that electrical amplification is a practical solution to address the fact that pious women wish to (and are encouraged to) listen to the *khutba*, but Swahili mosques do not have women's sections that would allow them to attend in person.

This characterisation runs contrary to the opinion I heard from some up-country Christians in Mombasa, who asserted that the *khutba* is most likely broadcast in Swahili precisely so that it may reach the ears of non-believers.

---

[8] I conducted formal interviews and informal conversations with a number of Islamic leaders and intellectuals in Mombasa. Two consultants who can be named are Sheikh Abu Hamza of Sparki Mosque and Sheikh Mohammed Dor of Mbaruk Mosque. The latter is General Secretary of the Council of Imams and Preachers of Kenya.

This belief is understandable given the growing number of preachers out-side of the Old Town who use their Friday Swahili sermons 'as a platform for communicating with other communities as well when necessary' (Topan 2000: 102). It also conforms to a liberal–democratic logic of public space, which is operative (if not always dominant) in Mombasa. To some extent any public broadcast in the Old Town is a true *public* broadcast, which must '[abandon] the security of its positive, given audience' (Warner 2002: 113). 'Public discourse', Michael Warner writes (2002: 113), 'promises to address anybody. It commits itself in principle to the possible participation of any stranger. It therefore puts at risk the concrete world that is its given condi-tion of possibility.'

Discrepant understandings of the publicity/privacy of the broadcast *khuṭba* occasion ontologico-political struggles over public space every Friday afternoon in Mombasa Old Town. I first became aware of these strug-gles by committing a faux pas (a time-honoured ethnographic method). One Friday, early on in my research on Mombasa Old Town's Islamic sound-scape, I set out to make an audio recording of an amplified *khuṭba* from a window of the flat I had rented in the neighbourhood. Though I was trying not to be conspicuous, neither was I attempting to hide what I was doing, naively confident in the knowledge that neither Kenyan law nor my profes-sional ethics dictated that any permission was necessary to record a 'public broadcast'. As I later learned, some congregants who noticed me with my microphone expressed concern and called a meeting to discuss possible ways of preventing me from making any further recordings. Fortunately, friends of mine who were respected members of the Old Town's Swahili community caught wind of the developing situation and helped to defuse it by arranging for me to meet with the mosque's imam to explain my (purely academic) interest in their *khutba*s.

When I first learned that something I had done had stirred suspicion among some local Muslims, I was not entirely surprised, given that Kenya's entanglements in the 'global war on terror' had given coastal Muslims rea-son to suspect any white stranger who is not a tourist of being a spy (see Prestholdt 2011). I wondered, however, how my act of recording a public broadcast could be seen as threatening? A Swahili friend – I will call him Ahmadi – helped to answer this question, and in the process opened my eyes and ears to the nature of the Old Town's sonorous ontological politics. Ahmadi asked me to consider the case of Mbaruk Mosque in the Old Town, which is situated across a narrow street from Mombasa's Central Police Station, a building occupied by up-country Christians who literally embody the authority of the Kenyan state. 'You know', he said, 'those *polisi* hear every word of the *khuṭba* while just sitting there in their station. But if just one of them would stand outside like this' – he crossed his arms and puffed up his chest, imitating a police officer's posture – '*listening!*', he stressed, and then he completed his thought with a characteristically Swahili '*eh-heh*', meaning 'just you see!' In other words, according to Ahmadi's hypothetical narrative, Mbaruk Mosque's leaders and congregants understand, and perhaps even accept, that their weekly *khuṭba* is audible to agents of the state; but if an agent of the state should suggest, even through a simple bodily gesture, that he or she had the obligation to make sure the *khuṭba* accorded with the laws and regulations governing urban public space in Mombasa, this would be taken as an attack against or transgression of the communitarian privacy of the Muslims of Mombasa Old Town.

Ahmadi's ethnomethodological thought-experiment reveals a constant process of negotiation (or mediation) in Mombasa Old Town, a kind of social choreography whereby Muslims and non-Muslims with conflicting acoustemological commitments respond to the Islamic soundscape accord- ing to a shared set of normative behavioural expectations. Missteps are constant in this negotiation, but they are usually small and subtle, such as (to take one example from my field notes) when an old Muslim woman bluntly informed a young non-Muslim woman that the ostensibly public setting in which a traditional *maulidi* recitation was being delivered for the annual commemoration of the birthday of the prophet Mohammed was 'no place for infidels'. Such micropolitical controversies are part and parcel of the seemingly impalpable 'social tensions' (Prestholdt 2011) that obtain between Muslims and non-Muslims on the Kenyan coast. As such, they set the conditions for larger 'blow-ups' (Göle 2002), like the one involv- ing the expatriate and the imam in Kikambala, or the one that might have resulted had no one intervened on my behalf after I was spotted recording a *khuṭba*.

## Conclusion: communitarian privacy resounding

I have described a sonorous production of Islamic communitarian privacy in the public spaces of Kenya's major coastal city. As a palpable alterna- tive to a liberal–democratic social imaginary, this communitarian privacy bears a powerful resonance for struggles over notions of coastal Muslim citizenship in Kenya. Much of the scholarly work on coastal Muslim citi- zenship in Kenya focuses more heavily on another resonance, however – the resonance of the past. Historian James R. Brennan (2008: 859–60), for example, stresses the 'surprising resonance' of coastal Muslims' memories of their unsuccessful struggles for political autonomy during the late colonial era; and Jeremy Prestholdt (2011: 6–9) writes of 'histories of alienation' whose mnemonic resonance feeds tensions between coastal Muslims and the Kenyan nation state. While the resonance of the past is always central to debates and struggles over coastal Muslim citizenship in Kenya, the communitarian privacy that resounds in Mombasa Old Town and other Muslim-dominated spaces of the coast has taken on equal, if not greater, significance since the run-up to the final referendum on the new Kenyan constitution (enacted in 2010). During these debates, coastal Muslim activists and politicians raised the quixotic yet highly provocative idea of complete political autonomy for the coastal strip (Ndurya 2009). While the idea of coastal autonomy is partly grounded in particular interpretations of historical events (Brennan 2008), it is certainly given impetus by the model of communal autonomy provided by the Islamic communitarian privacy that resounds daily in Mombasa Old Town. Enacted through affective, bodily practices of ritual sounding, listening and responding, the Old Town's Islamic communitarian privacy supplies a model of communal autonomy that does not need to be recollected from the past. It is a *living* model, experienced, bolstered and defended every day through sonorous ontologico-political struggle.

# PART III

# Music, identity, alterity and the politics of space

PHILIP V. BOHLMAN

## 9 | Music inside out: sounding public religion in a post-secular Europe

## On tolerance: parable and paradox

With the telling of a parable, itself a retelling of a myth, Gotthold Ephraim Lessing calls a secular Europe into being as the eighteenth century is eclipsed by the German Enlightenment (Lessing 1779). In the seventh scene of the third act in Lessing's 1779 *Nathan, der Weise*, the play's eponymous protagonist, Nathan, regales his friend, Sultan Saladin, with the 'Ring Parable'. The ring in the parable had inestimable worth and belonged to a wise man of the East. With its opal radiating a hundred different colours, the ring had the magical power to make anyone who bore it pleasant in the presence of God and human beings.[1] Because of its magnificent beauty and mystical powers, the ring had passed down from father to son through many generations. Until, that is, the father in one generation was blessed with three sons, all of whom pleased him equally. To resolve the dilemma the father turned to a great artist, who made two more rings, each like the original in the smallest detail. Upon the death of the father, each son laid claim to the real ring, without, however, proving the claim. Upon turning to a wise judge, the sons were forced to recognise that, because of their failure to realise the love borne by the ring, the only resolution to the dilemma would follow from the judge's pronouncement that the original ring must have been lost.

The three rings in the parable, of course, were the three Abrahamic faiths – Judaism, Christianity and Islam – none of which, in Lessing's play, could plausibly claim to be the true faith. The historical meaning of the parable, as well as the entire play, was and remains transparent. Nathan, the Wise was a dramatic realisation of Lessing's friend, the theologian and philosopher, Moses Mendelssohn (1729–86). Throughout the play the distinctions between Judaism, Islam and Christianity disintegrate. Even Nathan's daughter, Recha, turns out to be Christian, in fact the long-lost sister of the

---

[1] Der Stein war ein / Opal, der hundert schöne Farben spielte, / und hatte die geheime Kraft, vor Gott / und Menschen angenehm zu machen, wer / in dieser Zuversicht ihn trug (Lessing 1779: lines 1913–17).

# Nathan der Weise.

Ein

Dramatisches Gedicht,

in fünf Aufzügen.

Introite, nam et heic Dii sunt!

APVD GELLIVM.

Von

Gotthold Ephraim Lessing.

1 7 7 9.

**Figure 9.1** Title page of G. E. Lessing, *Nathan, der Weise* (1779)
Epigraph: Introite, nam et heic Dii sunt! (apud Gellium)
'Enter into this place where there are also Gods!' (from Gellius)

Christian with whom she has fallen in love, but, it follows in conclusion, she cannot marry her own brother.

This literary moment from the Enlightenment marks a transformation from myth to history – Lessing wrote in a letter to his brother (11 August 1778) that he took the parable from a variant of the third tale in volume one of Giovanni Boccaccio's *Decameron* (1350–53), and it is equally likely that he was aware of the related folk tale-types circulating in oral tradition, which would be classified as Aarne–Thompson 972 (Aarne 1961). I have chosen to begin with the Enlightenment enunciation of a secular Europe because it illumines the differences between sacred and secular, private and public identities at the onset of post-Enlightenment modernity. The ring parable symbolically recognises the possibility of reconciling the sacred and the secular by endowing European history with a new teleology, the momentum of which depends entirely on its entry into and passage through the spaces of religious tolerance, to which I refer as public religion in this chapter. Moses Mendelssohn, like the allegorical role he plays as Nathan, enters the Enlightenment as a Jewish theologian journeying from Dessau to Berlin, the modern city whose public spaces promised tolerance.

Lessing himself underscores this enunciation with his own epigraph, 'Enter into this place where there are also gods' (Gellius). The play itself sets in motion ways to think about the public spaces of Christian European culture from the standpoint of Jews and Muslims entering them and discovering, in essence, that multiple identities already exist. Multiple religions converge in European history as multiple religious enlightenments, forging modernity from a sacred secularism (Sorkin 2008). The identities of this secular world inhabited by gods are constituted and reconstituted through fragments, using these then to enter the history of modernity that has become crucial to Jürgen Habermas's notion of public space, *Öffentlichkeit*, among others (Habermas 1989 (1962)). In *Nathan, der Weise* nothing appears as it is. Religion is love; love is religion. Lovers become siblings, thus they must love in a different way. Jews are Christians are Muslims, and history has deemed that they live in the same, not different, spaces. Spaces and the identities of those occupying them are turned inside out. With the new stage in modernity unleashed by the religious enlightenments at the end of the eighteenth century, worship and the music of worship moved from the sanctuary to the public square, sometimes in gradual stages, but often through the dramatic modulation of public soundscapes. Moses Mendelssohn's grandson, Felix, would compose in a style in which the Jewish and the Christian were indistinguishable because they were one, and in this common style they would influence nineteenth-century sacred and secular music, Jewish and Christian, equally, realising musically the ring parable placed allegorically in his grandfather's mouth by Lessing.

Beginning allegorically, the narrative arc of this chapter will proceed in a broadly historical direction, which is to say, towards the modern and post-modern notions of publicly producing and experiencing sound that have led to the reformulation of private and public spaces that shape the subject of the present volume. The secular Europe formulated at the end of the eighteenth century is reformulated as a post-secular Europe at the end of the twentieth century. The search for Nathan's lost ring, or rather the faith in its existence, returns as faith shapes the spaces, private and public, in which the music of public religion is sounded. With the twenty-first century, however, the question of the ring's identity, seemingly unified through the multiple allegories of its perfection and the possibility of music in a multicultural, multireligious Europe, is raised again as the very vastness of the common spaces in a unified Europe once again defer retrieval of a ring gone astray.

## Post-Enlightenment reconfigurations of public and private space: the emergence of public religion

The Enlightenment project was one in which private spaces became reconfigured as public. Religious space that was previously private similarly became public, so that the spaces defined by congregational worship were opened so that sacred and secular communities overlapped and intersected. The Enlightenment reconfiguration of space did not, in fact, eliminate religion by making it secular, as it ushered in a transformation that broadly goes under the name of public religion. A post-Enlightenment shift in history and historiography emerged from the rise of public religion in Europe, for example in the theories of the natural sciences (e.g. Alexander von Humboldt), mathematics (e.g. Carl Friedrich Gauß) and industrial social formations (e.g. Karl Marx).

It was hardly surprising that history's rerouting through public religion resituated musical practice in new spaces, occupied by both the sacred and the secular. There were specific ontological issues about the space of German music, for example, that arose from post-Enlightenment theology. Johann Gottfried Herder (1744–1803) and folk song are perhaps the most obvious case of these theological formulations. It was no accident, of course, that Herder was himself a Lutheran pastor and that his considerable writings on music drew together theological and philosophical perspectives. His coinage of the word *Volkslied*, folk song, might seem at first glance a secular formulation, but Herder's writings on folk song throughout his life bore clear witness to a moral imperative (see, e.g., Herder 1778–9).[2] The musical signifiers of religion simply did not disappear. In the course of the nineteenth century the formal structures of the chorale tune were used again and again to signify public religion, whether in Wagnerian opera, the German national anthem, the 'Deutschlandlied', or the closing use of 'Ein' feste Burg' in the great opera from the concentration camps, Viktor Ullmann's *Der Kaiser von Atlantis* (1943). There is another ontological question coupling otherness and religion in geography and discourse in post-secular Europe. Sacred spaces are publicly identifiable in attacks against others: synagogues, even those no longer used for worship, are the most frequent targets of neo-Nazi graffiti, and mosques, especially those newly built, are no less targets of desecration. The history of Kristallnacht (9 November 1938), in which musical instruments and music itself were desecrated and destroyed, is not simply a matter of the past.

Sacred music had to re-enter the modern history of public religion, and it did so, significantly, *as music*. The space of public sacred music making changed dramatically at the beginning of the nineteenth century, Jewish music providing a case in point. Spaces inside the synagogue became public in new ways, not only within the Jewish Reform movement in northern Germany, but for the growing liberalisation of city synagogues in the rapidly urbanising Jewish communities across Europe and the Americas. The urban synagogue was a place of gathering for Jews from different ethnic and historical backgrounds. Jewish music accommodated the public nature of the new synagogues by providing a vehicle for vernacular language, polyphony and instrumental music. The organ was increasingly present, mixing Jewish and non-Jewish sounds, in a post-Enlightenment sense remixing them as Jewish. Professional musicians, *ḥazzanim* (cantors) and choir directors turned outward to public spaces as liturgical music became cantorial music, performed on the *bima* of the synagogue and in the *Bühne* of public concert life.[3]

---

[2] This moral imperative increasingly dominated Herder's writings in the closing years of his life, particularly beginning in *c*.1790, when his criticism of Kant's theories of will became sharper. In the Appendix of new songs for the edition of his *Stimmen der Völker in Liedern* and *Volkslieder* that would only appear posthumously in 1807 Herder included a new section of songs from Madagascar, which openly criticised the impact of European colonialism and missionary culture on the people of the island (Herder 1998; cf. Bohlman 2007).

[3] The Yiddish *bine* (etymologically derived from *Bühne*, stage) is a more common designation of the space of the altar in front of the Torah ark than the Hebrew *bima*, which also bears the meaning of theatrical stage (as in the Zionist and later Israeli national theatre, Habima (lit., 'the stage')).

The expansion of public religion further led to the reconfiguration of sacred architecture throughout Europe. Mosques moved from the secluded spaces of the 'rear courtyard' – *Hinterhofmoscheen* was the common designation in the German-speaking lands – to the street, and they announced their presence through the erection of minarets, from which the *adhān* sounded across non-Muslim public spaces. Synagogue construction, too, moved to the centre of the city, with grand structures built directly on the main thoroughfares of the city and taking their names from those streets, for example, in the case of the Dohány utca Synagogue in Budapest – Europe's largest synagogue – and the Oranienburgerstraße Synagogue in Berlin. Figures 9.2 and 9.3, the interior and exterior of the Oranienburgerstraße Synagogue at the time of its dedication in 1866, illustrate this movement between the outside and the inside, the secularisation of sacred space in nineteenth-century public religion. Paradoxically, Figures 9.4 and 9.5, both images of the synagogue from unified Berlin, reveal the continued play of spaces that characterises the everyday of the synagogue. The postcard puzzle makes it possible not only to construct, reconstruct and deconstruct the synagogue's spaces, but to send them to acquaintances throughout the world. The construction evident in my photograph from 2005 accompanied the transformation of Oranienburgerstraße itself, which had become a stage for local and itinerant klezmer bands, particularly during Friday and Saturday Sabbath, and one of the most important zones for clubs featuring electronic dance music.

The architecture of European mosques and synagogues bore witness to the rise of public religion in still other ways: the two religious spaces came to resemble each other. The Oranienburgerstraße Synagogue displays all the aesthetic attributes of the modern mosque, notably a surface covered with arabesque designs and two minarets dominating the spaces of central Berlin.[4] For both mosques and synagogues arabesque aestheticised the orientation of worship towards the East (Mecca and Jerusalem), whereas minarets served as symbols of soundscapes that ritually gathered worshippers to pray together and participate in the common auditory experiences of listening to Qur'an and Torah recitation. Sacred space, therefore, undergoes another reformulation, which Monica Sassatelli, writing about post-unification forms of European identity, sees in the shift from a culture of 'monuments' to 'landscapes', or for our purposes, soundscapes,

---

[4] Only the façade of the synagogue, now generally called the 'Neue Synagoge' or New Synagogue, survived the Second World War after the sanctuary fell during a bombing of Berlin, but that has sufficed for tourist posters and postcards alike, which frequently frame the synagogue as one of several symbols of unified Berlin and Germany.

**Figure 9.2** Berlin, Oranienburgerstraße Synagogue (Neue Synagoge; interior, dedication 1866) (*London Ill. News*)

which more capaciously include the practices of Europeanness (Sassatelli 2009: 168–92). The transformation of the synagogue and the mosque, therefore, was critically about the sound of worship and music, above all the enhancement of their audibility in the spaces of public religion (see Beinhauer-Köhler and Leggewie 2009: 9–40).

**Figure 9.3** Berlin, Oranienburgerstraße Synagogue (Emile de Cauwer, 1866)

Public religion is the space of the private that is opened through music, coming from outside-in. The historical evidence I muster for this chapter, therefore, argues strongly for a historical telos unleashed by the Enlightenment that leads increasingly to the opening of internal sacred space to public performance through music. The American megachurch

**Figure 9.4** Berlin, Oranienburgerstraße Synagogue (photo © Philip V. Bohlman, 2005)

or European megamovements, such as Taizé and Pentecostalism in Eastern Europe, are among the most recent instances. Pilgrimage and klezmer return the musics of religion to the European street. Islam in post-colonial and post-industrial Europe increasingly shifts prayer and liturgical practice from the inside to the outside, with the mosque and especially the minaret signifying the sonic limits of tolerance.

The shift in Muslim practice, moreover, is no less historical a symptom of postmodernism than the reformulation of other major religions. Cologne, the German city with the most contested claims on sacred private and public spaces, is a powerfully symbolic case. Cologne Cathedral is the largest Gothic cathedral in Europe, with a historical claim on dominating the city skyline. The Catholic pilgrimage to Cologne is based on the belief that the relics of the three Magi lie in the cathedral. The orientalist claim to traces from the nativity of Christ, however, is now challenged by the competing claim for one of the most architecturally significant mosques in Europe, Paul Böhm's plan for a mosque in the suburban area of Köln-Ehrenfeld (see Figure 9.6).[5] German Muslims are making their claim on the public spaces of a post-secular Germany in increasingly transformative ways.

---

[5] The vernacular designation is 'Großmoschee' ('large' or 'great mosque') rather than 'Zentralmoschee' ('central mosque'), for the building would not be in Cologne's city centre.

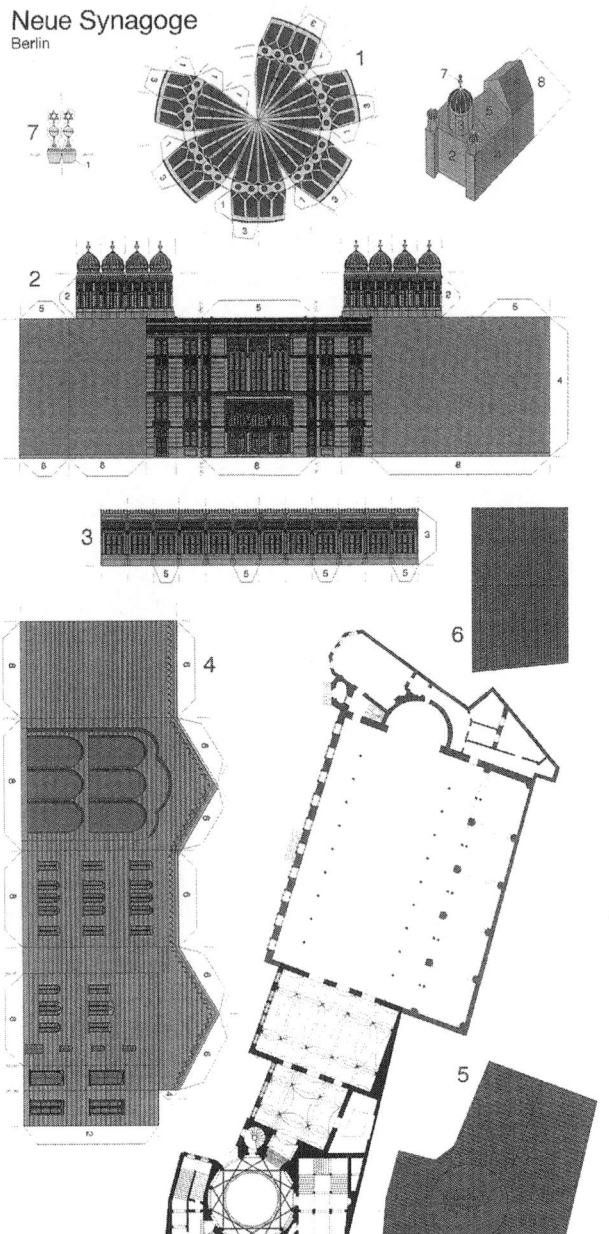

**Figure 9.5**  Berlin, Neue Synagoge, paper cut-out model on postcard (2008)

**Figure 9.6**  Paul Böhm's architectural design for the Cologne Mosque (Köln-Ehrenfeld)[6]

In the two decades since the reunification of Europe and the spread of the European Union, the sacred spaces of Muslim communities in Germany are more contested than ever, for the growing populations of Germany's Muslim communities, whose residents are also entering the second and third generations after immigration, increasingly seek recognition for their faith and worship in public spaces. Mosques, orientalised and hidden, have a history of several centuries in Germany, but prior to the rebuilding and reunification of Germany after the Second World War and the fall of the Berlin Wall, mosques were not thought to threaten public spaces. The threat to Germany's public spaces has assumed two forms, both of them aesthetic, at least on their surfaces. First, mosques should not disturb the skyline of German cities. Ironically, the most controversial mosque project, Paul Böhm's design for a mosque in Cologne, is only one-third the height of Cologne Cathedral, and when built it would be only the seventh tallest building in Cologne.[7] Second, the use of the call-to-prayer, *adhān*, projected into the spaces around a mosque, is claimed to disrupt and Islamicise the German soundscape. If Muslims make sound when praying, reciting and worshipping, it should be contained. The aesthetic dimensions of *adhān* are even more complicated by the fact that it is normally sounded from the minarets, the tallest parts of the mosque structure.

The struggle over mosques in contemporary Europe, no less than struggles over synagogues, sharpens our questions about sacred spaces and sacred

---

[6]  I have exhausted all possibilities to find the copyright source for Figure 9.6, which circulates widely in the public domain.

[7]  For a schematic representation of the Köln-Ehrenfeld mosque in comparison with the Cologne skyline see Beinhauer-Köhler and Leggewie 2009: 147.

music in the struggle over public religion. The struggle itself has acquired modern and postmodern dimensions just as they find their way into public religion, because there is considerable evidence that the Abrahamic faiths share some attributes of a historical *longue durée*. Etymologically, the common Semitic root is s–j–d (as in the Arabic *masjid*), and historical evidence recognises moments when the different religions shared the same spaces.[8] In Islam, Sura 22, 40 contains fairly unequivocal evidence of space common to community and worship, a space whose sacred character results from otherness vis-à-vis secularism:

Sura 22, 40. They were evicted from their homes unjustly, for no reason other than saying, 'Our Lord is GOD'. If it were not for GOD's supporting of some people against others, monasteries, churches, synagogues, and masjids, where the name of GOD is commemorated frequently, would have been destroyed. Absolutely, GOD supports those who support Him. GOD is Powerful, Almighty.

In the soundscape around Cologne Cathedral sacred traditions could not be more visible and audible. Processions and pilgrims fill the surrounding square, and the cathedral's own bells are, of course, meant to reach believer and non-believer alike. The cathedral is the space of sounding belief in multiple forms of music, and as the largest cathedral in Europe, Cologne Cathedral commands its own soundscape entirely. The last time I spent a Sunday morning in Cologne at the cathedral (September 2007), it was, in fact, the gathering point of Rhineland hunting and shooting societies, with their individual brass bands and men's choral ensembles. The mixture of individual ensembles and the bells chiming across the cathedral square, connecting Cologne's central train station to the masses in the cathedral itself, was nothing short of cacophonous. Under no circumstances would a *muedhdhin* in distant Köln-Ehrenfeld be audible or would his call-to-prayer penetrate the carnivalesque practices of Rhineland Catholicism that define Christian public religion in Cologne. Such celebration, mixing the secular with the sacred, would be denied to the large Muslim community of Cologne, which claims 120,000 Turkish Germans alone. For them, music must open spaces within the music itself.

## Fragments and the movement between outside and inside

My examination of private and public space in the context of this volume arises also from my theoretical treatment of the ways these spaces exist in

---

[8] It needs to be stated that the European prejudice and hatred against Muslims and Jews are more similar than different (see Bunzl 2007).

sounded music itself. What locates music on the inside, what on the outside? When does the outside – the public space of European music – overwhelm the inside – the private space of difference, of appropriated otherness? Surely, the reformulation of one of the most familiar of all Enlightenment musical projects, the Turkish March in the final movement of Beethoven's *Ninth Symphony*, provides evidence for the ways such questions might be answered. In Beethoven's treatment, the Turkish March bears witness to the pre-Enlightenment encounter between Christian Central Europe and the Muslim Ottoman Empire. In Herbert von Karajan's textless reworking of the Beethoven/Schiller 'Ode to Joy' as the 'European Anthem', however, the Turkish March is silent, the symbolic centre of the European Union purged of Turkish and Islamic history (Clark 1997).

Several explicitly theoretical points assist my explanation of the ways in which I seek to connect spaces in music to those spaces outside music. The internal section of Western formal structures in music – the B-section – is the site of difference. Movement between internal and external sections is facilitated by the agency of fragments. We might understand this even in the post-Enlightenment mobility signalled by fragments reconstituted in the development sections of sonata form. Or in the trajectory of popular-song forms – the use of a bridge – that stretches from Thomas Moore's *Irish Melodies* through blackface minstrelsy to Tin Pan Alley to rock music.

Critical to the relation of musical structure to public space are the ways the fragment – and of course the ways fragments coalesce musically as larger forms – make it possible to move between inside and outside. Fragments of insides are used throughout wholes that emerge in the Enlightenment. My epigrammatic opening with *Nathan, der Weise* makes this clear, because Lessing constructs it by quite literally moving fragments from one space of Enlightenment modernity to the next. The movement of fragments leads to an aesthetic of music that accommodates intertextuality at borders, for example and above all, between inside and outside.

Considering fragments, we also realise that not everything fits. Fragments destabilise form, enhancing mobility, the in-betweenness of genre about which Fabian Holt has written (Holt 2007). This characteristic of fragments reflects the ways in which we see destabilisation between inside and outside. As such, however, it might have led me to substitute my use of the concept of 'reconfiguration' with 'destabilisation'. I recognise that in so doing, however, I should have limited the presence of agency in 'reconfiguration'. In post-secular Europe agency is abundant, as musical fragments are acted upon and made mobile. The orthodoxy of sacralisation becomes the heterodoxy of secularisation. My concern in this chapter is the nature of public religion, which often creates pairs in tension:

Catholicism and the Counter-Reformation
Ecclesiastical architecture and music
Islam and Islamism
Sacred and secular

Ultimately, in the shift from modern to postmodern, secularisation and sacralisation become a single process.


## Public religion and European popular music

The dialectic of centres and peripheries has long provided a narrative trope for the presence of Muslims in and within Europe. When I extend the dialectic inside–outside to Europe's Muslim soundscapes, moreover, I am following a representational practice that began at least as early as the medieval *Cantigas de Santa Maria*, that was inscribed on broadside ballads in early modern Europe in the wake of the *Reconquista*, and that flourished in Central and Eastern Europe after the defeat of Ottoman imperial forces as they laid siege to Vienna in the late seventeenth century. In the twenty-first century, the so-called 'global war on terror' has forced European Muslims once again to reconfigure their presence inside and outside Europe, that is, their safe spaces and dangerous spaces.

As the question of Islam's presence *within* Europe increasingly contests the ways in which European identity is audible in its soundscapes, the distances that such soundscapes have – their in-betweenness – slipped into a discourse that places a burden of change, even conversion, on Muslims. The fundamental question of whether one can be European *and* Muslim is posed to few other religious groups. European discourse about Christianity stresses inclusivity, while the discourse about Islam takes exclusivity as a given. John Bowen asks: 'can Islam be French?' (Bowen 2010), while for Jytte Klausen (2005) 'the Islamic challenge' is all about 'politics and religion in Western Europe'. Islam in Europe forms between 'world politics' and the 'everyday' (Altermatt, Delgado and Vergauwen 2006). Drawing directly on musical metaphors, Julia Gerlach charts the space of Muslim youths in Germany as lying between 'pop music and jihad' (Gerlach 2006). For Islam to become European it must cross religious spaces that are also aesthetic and geographical spaces.

In the sacred domain of sacred music, the mosque's internal and external soundscapes reveal the private and public sides of European Muslim
soundscapes. Prayer and Qur'anic recitation sound within the mosque.
*Adhān*, or the call-to-prayer, is projected outward from the mosque. In
even the most intolerant European societies, the recitation of the Qur'an is
respected, while the *adhān* is rejected. The sonic disturbance of the external
soundscape – the common public space of Europe – has created the greatest problem for European Muslims, causing them to form what Charles
Hirschkind (2006), in writing about the circulation of cassette sermons, has
called 'Islamic counterpublics'.

With this historical context I turn briefly to Eurovision song, to the
internal and external soundscapes in which the musical and political converge. Turning the basic thesis of this chapter towards music, I focus on
musical centres and peripheries, insides and outsides. Eurovision song style,
I should like to suggest, bolsters the outer sections, whereas change – the
aesthetic representation of the political – is located in the middle section,
the site of difference. In order to do the cultural work they are empowered
to do – ideologically and politically, as well as musically – Eurovision songs
move to the public spaces of Europe, where they accommodate European
identities and historical meanings (see Bohlman 2009). For the presence of
Islam in Eurovision entries from Muslim nations such as Turkey, Albania
or Azerbaijan, the aesthetic and political geography of centres and peripheries is particularly important. Similarly, for entries from nations with
a substantial and important Muslim presence in popular music, such as
Bosnia–Herzegovina and France, using the bridge to locate Islam is no less
critical.[9]

Centre and periphery assume many other forms in the articulation of
Islamic soundscapes. The urban and suburban districts in which Muslim
workers live, the French *banlieu*, for instance, ring the city. Filling the
soundscape of the *banlieu* is cosmopolitan popular music, *raï* since at least
the Algerian War, more recently the hybrid forms of French and *Maghrebi*
hip hop. The soundscape of the *banlieu* is European and Islamic, but it is
decidedly secular, all the more so when politicised as Islamist. The point,
here, is that we witness in these soundscapes of Islamic Europe both *lived-in*

[9] The 2006 entry from Bosnia–Herzegovina is a particularly vivid example. Hari Mata Hari's
'Lejla' forcefully claims the borders between Christian and Muslim by filling the public
soundscapes of Mostar with a song that combines two styles, one secular, the other sacred.
'Lejla', the song title, is an Arabic name, also the Arabic word for night, and the designation of a
style of Arabic popular music (*layālī*). The performance style, moreover, mixes *sevdalinka* with
*ilahija*, again realising private (*sevdalinka*) and public (*ilahija*) soundscapes.

and *worshipped-in* spaces. Europe responds in different ways to the claiming of these spaces as Muslim. The *adhān*, as sacred, might be compared to the wearing of the *hijab*, an issue of enormous ideological struggle, even at the level of political debate about integration of Turkey into the European Union.[10] Certain other spaces must remain secular, hence representing the state and its control over citizens. The *banlieu* belongs to the worker and the agent of global and transnational economic production.

## Enlightenment under siege

And one doesn't know, fellow travellers, what's more dreadful: Albion or the merciless Muslims? Freedom without borders or the Islamic yoke? Europe or Asia?! ... Jesus, truly, may we never have to make such a frightening decision.

Andrzej Stasiuk, *Czekając na Turka* (2009: 43)

On 29 November 2009 the people of Switzerland used a national referendum to ban the building of minarets in their country. In practical terms, the implementation of the ban meant that the two minarets scheduled for construction, multiplying the number of Swiss minarets from the existing four to a total of six, would not be built. Of the two minarets in question, the one planned in the city of Langenthal was designed to be five metres tall, surely a modest structure in a nation dominated by the Alps. Just why the international backlash to the Swiss ban on minarets should have been one of amazement and disbelief that a 'Bastion of Tolerance' (Cumming-Bruce and Erlanger 2009: A6) should limit the public religious expression of some 400,000 citizens is itself hard to believe.[11] The Swiss People's Party had, in fact, waged its campaign to ban minarets for two years, and even if the Swiss Government had invested little time and expense in halting the referendum, the campaign received considerable attention from religious groups within the country.

The fight for and against minarets was waged in full public view, especially through the use of posters, which took in all sides of the debate. The right wing used a particularly notorious poster, in which a burqa-clad woman stood amid seven minarets spread across the juxtaposition of the Swiss flag and map, clearly juxtaposing Islam and Islamism (see Figure 9.7).

[10]  Think, for example, about Orhan Pamuk's novels, *Snow* and *My Name Is Red*, indeed about all of Pamuk's writing about the representational differences between Turkey and Europe.

[11]  The total population of Switzerland is about 7.5 million. Islam is the second largest religion in Switzerland.

**Figure 9.7** Poster advocating the ban on minarets in Switzerland

The posters countering the referendum were often the products of religious groups, especially those promoting interfaith understanding, such as Iras Cotis, whose poster depicted the towers of numerous faiths against a skyline with the slogan, 'The Heaven/Sky above Switzerland is Large Enough' (see Figure 9.8).

As the campaign to ban minarets in Switzerland gained momentum, the positions for and against Islam increasingly followed disparate paths. For those advocating the ban, whose eventual vote would be 57.5 per cent of the total, the minaret symbolised global politics and terrorism. Islam had not yet penetrated Switzerland, and the moment had arrived to make sure it would not eventually grow from Swiss soil. For those opposing the ban, the issue was religious tolerance, based on the acceptance that Islam was already a part of Switzerland's multicultural and multireligious society. The parties for and against saw the schism between inside and outside from

**Figure 9.8** 'Der Himmel über der Schweiz ist gross genug' (Iras Cotis)

contrasting perspectives, sacred and secular, Switzerland at the centre of Europe, Switzerland at the very Asian borders of Europe.

The incompatible metaphors of inside and outside have a long history in Switzerland, as in the rest of Europe. The inside space, one of citizenship and participation in Swiss democracy, is attached to the *Rathaus* or city hall, whereas the outside space, one of belonging to the religious community, takes place in the *Moschee* or mosque (Lathion 2006). Cultural and communal spaces accrue to both ends of this continuum. The institutions clustered around the city hall further participation in a Switzerland stripped of religion. In Swiss discourse, the mosque is a space of mixed religious metaphors comprising the family (private) and Muslim social organisations (public). The city hall belongs to all Swiss citizens, and the tolerance that it engenders is, thus, presumably shared by all: the city hall is Enlightenment Europe internalised and modulated for Switzerland. The mosque, according to the Swiss model, makes place only for small groups and individuals: it is anti-Enlightenment in this model, and in the same way anti-Swiss (Lathion 2006: 100). In the Switzerland of the city hall, multiculturalism further takes the form of a patchwork (German, *Flickwerk*), abundantly covered with parts, each bounded in its own way, even as unequal fragments that nevertheless form the fabric of the nation. Tolerance, thus, does prevail, but in the secular spaces at the edge of the *Rathaus* square, also the space in which the Swiss exercise democracy.

There can be no simple conclusion to the Swiss minaret controversy because of the metaphorical slippage between Switzerland as Europe's inside and Turkey and Islam as Europe's outside. Banning the minarets created a public space of silence where there had previously been the sound of Islam. Rather than affirming secular tolerance, the ban destabilised the relation between city hall and mosque. The space of silent in-betweenness has become an ongoing metaphor for the destabilisation of social borders, a space between inside and outside where the problem of religious tolerance continues to be unresolved. It is through religion's presence that the silence of the border zones is again sounded.

Just as it began this chapter, parable epigrammatically closes the chapter, or rather, articulates the public spaces that are easier to open than to close. Andrzej Stasiuk's 2009 play, *Waiting for the Turk*, takes place in a border region at once somewhere, anywhere and nowhere in Europe. For those who inhabited the border region – border guards, smugglers, sex traffickers, refugees, nationalists, a chorus of Europeans – it had been familiar, not least because it buttressed the known against the unknown. In the post-Schengen world of the border region, it has lost all functions and it ceases to exist. It becomes European, just as the chorus sings in a language that all understand and therefore come to fear. There would be no need for Stasiuk's allegorical border culture were it not for 'the Turk' – used in the singular in Polish to stand in for the East, Asia and Islam – of the title, for whom Europe waits, its future no less Godotesque than grotesque. It is the waiting that forestalls conclusion, that transforms the awareness of Islam at the borders of Europe into an anti-parable. Europe remains hopeful that Lessing's ring might somehow be found and reclaimed, and the voice of Islam might confirm the post-secular promise of the Enlightenment.

# 10 | Classical music and the politics of space

NICHOLAS COOK

According to a recent product listing, 'The Mosquito ultrasonic teenage deterrent is the solution to the eternal problem of unwarranted gathering of youths and teenagers in shopping centres, around shops, your home, and anywhere else they are causing problems.'[1] It is inevitable that this device, which exploits teenagers' sensitivity to high frequencies adults do not hear, should be controversial: it is after all an application to people of a technology well established for keeping cats and other unwanted animals out of gardens. But music, it appears, can fulfil the same function more ethically. In 2006 a Local Government Association memorandum advised councils to experiment with what, following its successful use in Australia, is dubbed the 'Manilow method' – dispersing crowds by playing

> songs that young hooligans 'would find almost unbearable to listen to and too uncool to hang around'. An initial list has been drawn up by the LGA. Among the hits recommended as deterrents are 'Things Can Only Get Better' by D:Ream; 'Close to You' by the Carpenters and, of course, Sir Cliff Richard's Christmas number one 'Mistletoe and Wine'. (Woolf 2006)

Retailers had already been experimenting with this approach, however, and not just with popular music. According to a blog from January 2005, 'Co-op, a chain of grocery stores, is experimenting with playing classical music outside its shops, to stop youths from hanging around and intimidating customers. It seems to work well. Staff have a remote control and "can turn the music on if there's a situation developing and they need to disperse people", says Steve Broughton of Co-op' (Patrix 2005). And the blogger makes the point that this is not necessarily a matter of personal taste. 'Teenagers make it a point to run away from classical music', he says, 'and even if they like it, not one would be caught listening to Bach.' The power of such music to clear public and private spaces, then, is based on a percept that is entirely socially constructed: coolness is a matter of how you are perceived by others.

---

[1] See www.cctvdirect.co.uk/products/Mosquito-Mk4-Ultrasonic-Youth-Deterrent.html (last accessed 18 August 2012).

Music not only clears (or, of course, fills) spaces, it defines spaces too. Ever since the youthquake brought teenagers into being, they have used music to create their own space within the family home, just as music is used to create personal boundaries within the visually continuous space of open-plan offices (Dibben and Haake, Chapter 6 of this volume). In shopping malls music marks ownership of space, in the same way as the obligatory curtain of warm air, but through specificity of genre it also brands the space and so acts as a kind of gatekeeper, helping control who comes in and who doesn't. (As is often the case, virtual reality presents such musical constructions of space in a purer form than does real life: in Second Life, the ubiquitous environmental music cuts abruptly from one track to another at the point where land ownership changes.) And the tradition of musical parades now associated with Northern Ireland but in fact part of a wider Celtic heritage transfers such assertion of ownership to the political realm. In all these contexts music demarcates space and figures it with social values, and one reason it does this so effectively is its non-objective nature. One can talk about a sculpture, say, articulating the space within which it is situated, but sound figures or marks space in a much more literal sense. It subsists in the vibration of air molecules, and as air gets everywhere, sound penetrates every last corner. It is what might be termed this consubstantiation of sound and space that explains music's efficacy as a means of appropriating space and policing boundaries.

It can also be claimed that the auditory is a fundamental dimension of space that is frequently overlooked in the ocularcentric culture of late modernism. There is an obvious sense in which not only the theory but also the practice of classical music is delimited by the score, which acts as a kind of information bottleneck, a low-bandwidth carrier through which tradition is forced. And the same applies even more obviously to the architectural equivalents of the score, that is to say the plans and elevations in which space as experienced is schematised in two dimensions, with planning decisions, contractual relationships and possibly architectural prizes being determined on the basis of these highly reduced representations. In short, architecture is diminished to a purely visual practice rather than one that also involves the haptic, kinaesthetic and auditory dimensions of the built environment. Yet the neglected auditory dimensions of space are crucial in terms of its experience and meaning. As Don Ihde pointed out in his book *Listening and Voice* (1976), we can gauge the size of physical spaces from hearing them as well as from seeing them (though it may take a power cut, or curtains being taken down for washing, to make us aware of this), and occasionally there are contradictions between what sight and sound tell us, for instance in a mirrored room or an anechoic chamber – contradictions that may be resolved in either direction.

Experienced space is in this way co-produced by sight and sound. And the same point can be made in musical terms. There is a sense in which Venetian antiphonal music wasn't simply composed for the interior spaces of churches such as Santa Maria della Salute, but actually composed those spaces. It is in the same sense that the magnificent former church, then mosque and now museum Hagia Sophia (Istanbul) might be described as a ruin, even though the fabric has been miraculously preserved: it has outlived its former social, spiritual and musical functions, and has thus survived only in a physical sense. Or to make the point in terms of urban planning, the Vienna Ringstrasse was a design exercise at once social, visual and auditory, a ring or chain of culture whose links were the concert halls, galleries, museums and educational or administrative institutions of the Habsburg Empire. One of those links, the Musikverein, where the Vienna Philharmonic Orchestra still plays, is the place where in the last years of the nineteenth century the concept of structural listening developed, an ideology that combined aspects of architecture, narrative and self-improvement into an institutionalised model that in effect placed musical listening within the public sphere (Botstein 1992).

But there is a further complication to this co-production of experienced space, because music is itself always already spatial. What in this chapter I call inherently musical spaces are constructed through the embedded metaphor of musical motion: as Roger Scruton (1997: 52) says, take away the motion and you have taken away the music, though it is perhaps more productive to formulate the thought in terms of cross-domain mapping between auditory and physical spaces. And the idea of music being inherently a compound of time and space, which is after all what motion means, has been explicitly thought into dominant theoretical conceptions of music. It was Goethe (1850: 146) who, in an 1829 conversation with Johann Eckermann, famously described architecture as 'frozen (*erstarrte*) music',[2] but it was the German-language music theorists of the late nineteenth century who created a system out of the idea of music as structure in motion. Hugo Riemann theorised music in terms of principled movement within a tonal space organised into regular blocks, rather like a contemporary city plan; while in 1894 Heinrich Schenker characterised a fully adequate perception of music (the Viennese structural listening to which I have already

---

[2] In this translation *erstarrte* is translated as 'petrified', but it is in the form of 'frozen' music that the phrase has become well known.

referred) in terms of reaching a point 'somewhere high above the artwork ... from which the spirit can clearly survey the artwork, all its paths and goals, the lingering and storming, all variety and limitation, measurements and relationships, by ear as if by eye':[3] as with Riemann, music is conceived as a kind of formal panorama. And if this version of musical space sounds like itself an expression of ocularcentricity, Schenker (1979 (1935): 6) set the record straight when near the end of his life he wrote that 'every [musical] relationship represents a path which is as real as any we "traverse" with our feet', so anticipating Ihde's point about the phenomenological autonomy of the auditory mode.

To develop this idea, the spatial conception I am talking about is linked with tonality, which has long been fundamental to the Western conception of music in much the same way that perspective has been to the conception of Western art, and shares some of the same features of rationalisation, hierarchisation and point of view. If we separate out the components of movement, tonality is characterised by, on the one hand, a particular temporal model that is generally referred to as teleological, involving the narrative construction of subjectivity epitomised by Beethoven's 'Eroica' (which Scott Burnham (1995: 24) describes in terms of its 'ability to enlist our identification, to make us experience its surging course as if it were our own'); and on the other, a topological distinction between the 'home' and the 'foreign', literally in terms of tonic and non-tonic keys, but easily extended into broader conceptions of alterity, as when Schoenberg satirised xenophobic discourses of his day in his description of vagrant harmonies: 'homeless phenomena, unbelievably adaptable and unbelievably lacking in independence; spies, who ferret out weaknesses and use them to cause confusion; turncoats, to whom abandonment of their individuality is an end in itself; agitators in every respect, but above all: most amusing fellows' (Schoenberg 1978: 258).

Timothy Taylor interprets tonality as a means of constructing centres and consequently peripheries that reflect ultimately colonialist distinctions of self and other: tonal difference serves to represent all other kinds of difference, whether of gender, sexuality, ethnicity or nationality, for (as Taylor (2007: 23) puts it) 'constructions and representations of difference inform one another'.[4] This extremely broad-brush style of social interpretation, which might be traced back through John Shepherd to Wilfrid Mellers, suffers from the same drawbacks as other approaches to musical meaning

---

[3] 'Das Hören in der Musik', in Federhofer 1990: 103 (translation by Lars Franke).
[4] For the general claim about tonality, difference and colonialism, see Taylor 2007: 10, 17–18, 25.

based in homology: it involves highly abstract epistemic categories and is as a result essentially incapable of empirical demonstration. More historically grounded approaches, however, corroborate the general approach. As Thomas Christensen (2008) has shown, the term 'tonality' came into being in the early nineteenth century through the attempt to define contemporary European music in relation to the distinct tonal conceptions of early music on the one hand and non-Western music on the other – that is, in terms of its temporal and spatial others.

Tonality is not simply a means for the assertion of distinctions between self and other, however: it also offers any number of models for bridging or reconciling such distinctions. Built into the concept, then, is the potential to shape or condition the negotiation of relationships of self and other, ranging from the orientalist representation of, say, Alfred Ketèlbey's 'In a Persian Market' to the kind of reverse orientalism exemplified by Henry Cowell's transcultural music with its attempt to embrace the other by redefining the self – not to mention the appropriation of Western tonality by post-colonial and other non-Western countries as a paradoxically efficacious means of national identity construction. All of this might be described (in another of Taylor's (2007: 26) key terms) as a form of tonal cartography. But as with all map-making, more is involved than objective representation. In referring to tonality's 'potential' to shape relationships of self and other, I acknowledge that what I refer to as inherently musical space is not simply an objective property of musical stimuli but rather an experienced quality co-determined by responses to them – responses that are not mandatory but are nevertheless strongly conditioned by traditions of interpretation (Burnham's (1995) 'our' is not simply an exhortation but the description of a once dominant and still widespread practice of listening). The phrase 'inherently musical space' is then shorthand for the ability of certain musical constructs within certain cultural contexts to afford the experiencing of certain spatial qualities.

With its potential for binding and separating, space is in this way built not just into the conceptual fabric of music but into its practice too. Inherently musical spaces are constituted not only through tonal processes but also through the gestural choreography and physical configurations of live performance: it is sometimes impossible to draw a clear line between the literal enactment and the musical symbolisation of communal or hierarchical relationships between participants. (Think of a Balinese gamelan orchestra, or a Beethoven symphony.) Equally conspicuous examples of inherently musical spaces are provided by sound recordings, which can be the traces of actual performances, but more often involve complex temporal and spatial reconfigurations of source materials, resulting in the construction of virtual spaces realised through placement within the stereo image or through reverberation, compression and the other artefacts of record engineering that modify the very fabric of sound space.

I call these spaces 'virtual' since they bear no necessary relationship to the original configuration of the source materials (that is, the former provide no access to the latter). But in this context virtual reality is still reality: adapting what Schenker said about paths traversed by the feet, within the world of record production Phil Spector's walls of sound are as real as any walls we encounter in our daily lives. Indeed there is a sense in which the virtual reality of recorded music is more real than that of live music. Wagner or rock experienced through headphones in a darkened room represent an actualisation of the romantic–modernist aesthetic ideal of music's autonomy and transcendence in a way that could never be achieved by such low-grade anechoic chambers as opera houses or even hi-fi concert halls. There is, then, a sense in which, in music, virtual reality is more real than the real thing.

Let me summarise the story so far. I have described how sounds figure or mark space, and argued that music is a primary facilitator of spatial experience. I have also argued that an inherently musical spatiality inhabits the theory, performing and recording of music, classical and otherwise, and mentioned some links between tonal space and the representation of alterity. I now want to build on these claims in such a way as to more directly address some ways in which classical music can contribute to what, using the word in a broad sense, may be termed a politics of space. The way in which music transforms space by imbuing it with social meaning is easiest to see at the macro level of geographical space, but applies equally at the micro level of personal and interpersonal space. The key to music's efficacy and flexibility as an agent in such transformation lies in its extraordinary ability to retain meaningfulness even in highly reduced forms, as illustrated by sound recordings: music is a powerful connoter of place, yet easily detached from place, when its connotations may or may not remain available for purposes of the negotiation of relationships and identities. To illustrate the extremes, consider on the one hand the extent to which Poland has identified itself with the music of Chopin, or Vienna's self-identification as the 'city of music'; and on the other, the classical music you hear everywhere in Seoul – for instance the snatches of Mozart or Vivaldi that precede underground train announcements – where it carries no connotations of European culture or cultural prestige, but rather embodies an apparently effortless or naturalised international modernism (so illustrating the appropriation of tonal music by non-Western countries to which I referred).

Many controversies over the role of music in today's world, and particularly the effects of new musical technologies, revolve round this ability of music to become detached from place and embedded in new contexts. One obvious example is commercial world music, widely criticised as exploiting third-world cultural property by relocating it within the structures of first-world capitalism; the Irish folk musician Ross Daly (who lives in Crete) turns it into a more personal critique when he complains of 'world music freaks ... surrounded by hundreds of CDs, records, cassettes and DAT recordings, who listen to West African Griots one minute, Japanese Koto music the next and then Bengali music – and ... don't understand the first thing about the music ... they haven't got a clue about the cultural and human background' (Aubert 2007: 55). World music, then, reshapes the world in the same manner as telecommunications and global capitalism. An equally obvious example, but at a more intimate level, is the use of portable music playback devices – the Walkman, iPod, iPhone – to personalise the cityscape, as Shuhei Hosokawa described it as early as 1984. Music is abstracted from its original context of meaning, reduced to a playlist item and interpolated into ordinary life contexts in a manner that may be considered arbitrary, or literally random (if you use the iPod's 'shuffle' function). The result, some claim, is a solipsistic, even alienated experience. 'iPods are antisocial', writes a blogger, 'and I know it. They separate people from other people, make us our own little islands of music that occasionally bump into each other and can't hear the other person say "sorry"' (Dickson 2008).

There is of course another side to the story. 'And yet ...', continues the blogger, 'And yet I have my beloved 80GB Classic plugged into my skull right now specifically so that I don't have to hear the person next to me who has been on their cell phone for twenty minutes telling a friend about their messy divorce proceedings.' Used in public transport, personal stereo carves out a space for personal enjoyment and reflection, for being oneself: private space is 'nested' within public space.[5] Like world music, the iPod reshapes space, or to put it another way, it creates a phenomenological space that is dissociated from physical space. But then, music has done this since long before the development of sound reproduction technology.

---

[5] On the 'nesting' of public and private musical spaces, see Georgina Born's Introduction to this volume.

Eugene Lami's 1840 watercolour 'Upon listening to a Beethoven symphony' is a jumble of seven caricatured figures whose expressions seem completely unrelated: the picture would be unintelligible without the title but, with it, becomes a visual analogue of the new subjectivity Burnham was talking about. Each listener believes himself (they are all men) to be in private communion with the spirit of Beethoven, and there is no more communication between them than between the iPod-wearing passengers in an underground train: the social dimension has been sucked out of the public sphere (in Lami's image, as in Thatcher's Britain, society does not exist). But this is only a roundabout way of saying that Lami's watercolour depicts the detachment from context that, under the name of the autonomy of music, has been a key principle of musical aesthetics since the age of Beethoven. It is of course precisely such consumption of music detached from context – from the contexts of both production and consumption – that Daly ridicules and that gives pause to the iPod-wearing blogger. And in the remainder of this chapter I shall explore the relationship between, on the one hand, this frequently contested yet undoubtedly historical autonomy of music (which I have invoked through my references to inherently musical space) and, on the other, music's ability to create socialised spaces and so facilitate interactions between groups or individuals.

*Fin-de-siècle* Vienna was the centre of a multinational empire riven by separatist tendencies, in which music formed a primary means for the construction of a supranational identity. In 1906 Guido Adler, who occupied the chair of music at the University of Vienna, wrote that 'as the customs of the Austrian peoples are interwoven in the works of the classical composers of music, as the motivic material is taken from the national stores, which the artists … work up into classical structures, so may a higher statescraft join the particularities of the peoples into a higher unity' (Notley 1999: 52). In saying this, Adler was proposing music as a model for political supranationalism. But it was his compatriot Schenker who spelled out how this musical supranationalism might work. In a review of a concert from nine years earlier at the Hofoperntheater, Schenker commented on the way in which Smetana and Dvořák had succeeded in 'bringing their national music into a system', and continued:

The system is naturally that of German art, for this is best able to solve the principal problem of the logical development of a piece of music … [Smetana] simply applied the German system to Bohemian music, and because he understood the German logic of music as it were in its necessity and sensibleness as no other, it was granted to him to present Bohemian music in a perfection which will not be surpassed. Since then Dvořák has also succeeded, always with the German system as a basis.[6]

Schenker is asserting the autonomy and universality of musical logic (or as he puts it, German logic), in other words the spatialised conception of tonal theory in which time is measured by orderly – or sometimes not-so-orderly – transitions from centre to periphery and back again. And this inherently musical space becomes the vehicle for a deeply symbolical reconfiguration of place, in which the individual ethnic traditions of the Empire are embraced within a unified, superordinate structure, rather like spokes radiating out from a hub: it is an exact equivalent of the constitutional structures that were at this time being discussed by the legal and political theorists at the University of Vienna. If this, again, is musical cartography, the mapping of a rationalised system of relationships across the known world, then it is using a projection that places Vienna (or more precisely, German culture as embodied in Vienna) at its centre. Small wonder then that it was here and at this time that the still influential structuralist aesthetic of music developed, which as I mentioned subjected listening to institutionalised criteria; as Botstein (1992) says, music was in this way translated into an object of discourse, something one talked about as one might talk about literature or politics. The experience of music, often figured as purely subjective and ineffable, thus entered into the public sphere: it was private and public at the same time. And as such it became part of the larger political economy that, until the autumn of 1918, held together one of the world's most ethnically and linguistically diverse political entities.

This figuring of music as a public arena for ideological and even political work provides the necessary context for understanding the Society for Private Musical Performances, which Schoenberg founded in the same autumn that the Habsburg Empire fell; as its name implies, the aim was precisely to withdraw music from a public sphere now seen as hopelessly compromised. It is also the context within which to understand the nostalgia that by that time attached to such venues as the Bösendorfer-Saal (demolished in 1913 and hence a perfect symbol of the pre-war world), which was known in Oscar Tueber's words as a '"family space", the scene of intimate music-making … The audience were always aware who was in attendance, bowing and greeting one another, much like a family'. Within this family space – a space at once private and public – 'player and listener

---

[6]  In Federhofer 1990: 361; translation from McColl 1996: 176. I have explored these matters in greater depth in Cook 2007.

alike … could become autonomous individuals, free from the limitations of birth and wealth' (Botstein 1985: 725, 834).

This same nostalgia is reflected in Adorno, who himself moved to Vienna in 1925, and for whom – in Richard Leppert's words – 'chamber music … was a site of momentary refuge, a place of promise, imagination, and perhaps memory, where another kind of individuality might be thought, seen, and indeed heard … a space for a lost sociability … an enactment of musical respect and friendship' (Adorno 2002a (1928): 522). And this potential for the musical reconstruction of a fissured society depended crucially on a further dimension of the autonomy of music constituted by 'German logic', its freedom from words. '[T]he absence of specific meaning within the text allowed meaning to accrue only upon performance', writes Philip Bohlman (1991: 259), 'thus empowering any group – for example, an ethnic community – to shape what it will from absolute music.' He is referring specifically to the practice of chamber music within European Jewish communities in the decades preceding the Second World War.

Jumping to the present, it is plausible to claim that internet technology affords new analogues of the nostalgically imagined musical spaces of pre-war Vienna. If chamber music at the Bösendorfer-Saal allowed the transcending, for a while, of barriers of class, wealth and perhaps most crucially race, then the virtual reality of Second Life is an imagined community that transcends not only these but also physical location, age and gender, since you don't have to reveal your identity to take part in it. Although the majority of the music in Second Life is pop of all kinds, there is also a substantial minority of classical music, most of it promoted by individuals or organisations committed to finding new audiences. Linda Rogers, who lives in Toronto but in the shape of her avatar Kate Miranda organises concerts at the Second Life open-learning community Cedar Island, writes that 'many of those attending classical concerts in Second Life have little or no experience of live classical music. While classical music series are having trouble attracting new audiences to conventional concert stages, it seems that the internet virtual audience is open to the experience of art music' (Rogers 2008). Again, Guy Dammann observes in a blog about the Royal Liverpool Philharmonic Orchestra's high-profile Second Life concert in 2007 (for which they created a virtual replica of Philharmonic Hall) that 'while in the real world our range of activities is tightly policed by all sorts of beliefs about the kind of person we are, how our actions appear to others and whether our friends will laugh at us, the world of Second Life – like much internet life – is considerably less repressed' (Dammann 2007). Perhaps, then, the virtual audience includes teenagers who *like* listening to the music, but who couldn't afford to be seen doing something so uncool in RL (real life), as Second Lifers call the world beyond the game.

Another thing that the promoters stress is the community aspect of Second Life concerts. Writing ahead of the Liverpool Philharmonic's 2007 concert, their marketing and communications director, Millicent Jones, observed that 'what distinguishes this from doing an audio stream via our website is that on Second Life it will be a collective experience. People will be experiencing the watching of a performance within a group of people, and there will be an opportunity to discuss it: it's about creating a community' (Higgins 2007). And Rogers (2008) makes the point in greater detail:

The principal reason for presenting classical music in Second Life, for me, revolves around the quality of the audience experience. Listening to a podcast or recording is a solitary experience. By contrast, concerts in Second Life are joyfully social, audience members are joyfully celebratory in their anticipation and appreciation of the music in a way rarely matched in real life orchestras. Unique to the medium, listeners silently text appreciative comments, hurrahs, and questions that they hope someone more informed will be able to answer. Sometimes Second Life avatars even decide to dance to the music in the manner of small children at a summer concert at the park.

There was no dancing at any of the Second Life concerts of classical music I attended, but the community aspect was certainly there. When you or rather your avatar arrives, you're quite likely to be recognised and addressed by the promoter; it is a virtual recreation of the family atmosphere of the Bösendorfer-Saal. Another community dimension comes from an unlikely source: there are frequently problems with the streamed sound (sometimes solved by toggling the controls), so concerts tend to be preceded by extended texted discussions to establish whether everyone can hear, so reinforcing the sense of real-time interaction between participants, their common investment in the event. The snapshot in Figure 10.1 was taken at a concert held on 12 April 2008 in the virtual recreation of the Santa Maria del Pi Church in Barcelona, as part of the Second Life Bach Festival 2008, and before it began one of the artists, Delia Auer, asked the audience members where they came from: responses included the UK, Spain, Puerto Rico, Mexico and the USA (Denver, Virginia and California). When everything was ready to go the promoter, Tyrol Rimbaud, texted an extended introduction to Bach and to the music to be performed in what might be termed a traditional music appreciation style, and the music began. Audience members texted in appreciative comments as the music played, just as Rogers

**Figure 10.1**  Concert at the Santa Maria del Pi Church, Second Life, 12 April 2008

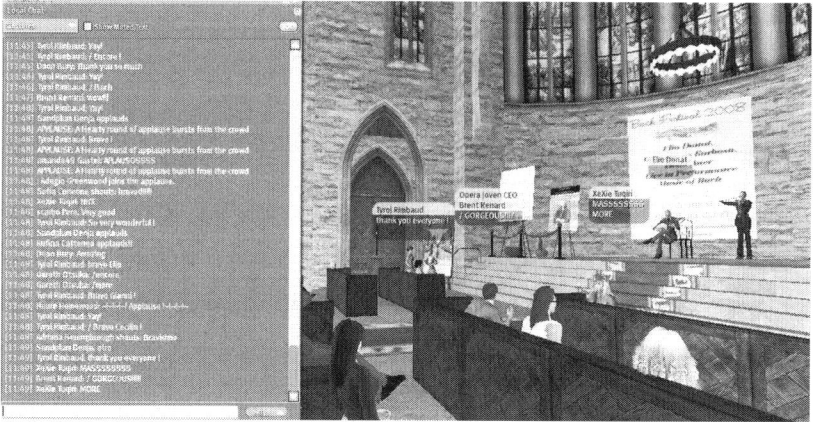

**Figure 10.2**  Concert at the Santa Maria del Pi Church, Second Life, 12 April 2008

said: though in real life they were scattered round the globe; there was a strong sense of listening together such as one might associate with a jazz club or tarab culture rather than with the classical concert. And when it stopped, they texted in their enthusiastic applause, though I couldn't help noticing that about half of it came from Rimbaud (Figure 10.2).

If the iPod creates a private space within the public space of an underground train, the nesting in Second Life works the other way round: a public space is embedded within the private, for while you play the game from the privacy of your own computer, you are interacting with other people in a public arena, though under a cloak of anonymity (unless, that is, you choose to disclose your first life identity in your avatar's profile, but most Second Lifers do not). The limitation, as far as music is concerned, lies in the nature of that interaction. In concerts such as the one in Santa Maria del Pi the music is live, in the sense that it is being streamed in real time, though often the accompaniments are all too obviously MIDI sequenced; indeed 19 July 2009 saw the first simulcast concert on Second Life, broadcast in several Second Life locations as well as in RL. (Again there were sound problems in the main SL venue, and after much anxious discussion the audience dispersed to other locations.) Yet it is hard to *experience* the music as live. There is no synchronisation between the music and the performer animations (which are simply repeating loops), and though the texting in of comments creates interaction, the time lag resulting both from the typing and its relay through the Second Life network means that there is no real correlate to the immediacy and fine-grained temporality of interaction in live, RL music. To this extent Second Life musical performance lacks the specifically musical 'sharing of the other's flux of experiences in inner time', the 'living through a vivid present in common', that Alfred Schutz (1971 (1964): 173) regarded as the model for 'the mutual tuning-in relationship, the experience of the "We", which is at the foundation of all possible communication'.

While Second Life concerts do have the community-building aspects described by their promoters, then, and while they represent an intriguing research resource for exploring responses to music on the neutral ground established by role-playing, the music itself is simply inserted into a virtual space constructed by other means: the music is not, as Second Lifers say, being made in-world. And to this extent, Second Life acts as a negative demonstration. The kind of inherently musical community that Schutz envisioned – a community brought into being by an entire range of musical activities from jazz or string quartet performances to therapeutic interventions – involves more than the panoramic landscapes and relationships of centre and periphery described by tonal theorists, which like virtually all established music theory are based on notational categories. The space within which Schutz's intersubjectivity is enacted is grounded in subnotational nuance, in those evanescent aspects of making music together that fall between the categories of musical writing and in consequence have generally been overlooked by musicology. It is grounded in the same exquisitely sensed entrainment between individuals that lies behind social dancing or the use of music to co-ordinate collective labour. It is, in short, a space irreducibly figured by time. The difference, then, is between music being inserted into a space created by other means and the creation of a specifically musical space for social interaction, and the contrast is underlined by comparison with a final, much touted example of music's community-forming potential: the West–Eastern Divan Orchestra, which was created in 1999 by Daniel Barenboim and Edward Said as both a symbol and a practical step towards reconciliation between Jews and Arabs. It is hard to miss the resonance between the Barenboim–Said project and the fleeting transcendence of racial divisions that was promised by chamber music in the Bösendorfer-Saal before the First World War or in European Jewish homes between the wars.

In terms of macro-space, the West–Eastern Divan Orchestra relocates young Israeli and Palestinian musicians to the neutral ground of Andalusia, where the Barenboim–Said Foundation is situated, creating a community that extends to a wide range of educational and cultural activities. But its core activity takes place in the micro-space of personal interaction: in Barenboim and Said's words, 'An orchestra requires musicians to listen to each other; none should attempt to play louder than the next, they must respect and know each other' (Barenboim and Said 2002). To make music is to make oneself uniquely vulnerable, for my knowledge of what I play is not privileged over yours, there is no space for dissimulation, and in this way the private and the public are enfolded together in what might be termed (to adapt Schutz) the inner space–time of performance. And in this way making music together constructs a reality that is virtual in the sense that it is not simply an epiphenomenon of the world beyond music, but rather embodies the actions of free individuals motivated by inherently musical concerns. By analogy with Second Life, one might think of the reconciliation prompted by the West–Eastern Divan Orchestra as created in-world, as in-musical; yet unlike Second Life, the musically mediated interactions between the musicians of the West–Eastern Divan Orchestra do not take place under the cover of anonymous role-playing. In other words the space of musical performance is both a virtual and a real one, and it is in the crossover from the one to the other – in the possibility that what is done in music will have consequences in RL – that hopes of the orchestra's efficacy as an agent of reconciliation must lie. There is no doubt that the West–Eastern Divan Orchestra presents an irresistible image of music's ability to transcend political divisions. How long the reconciliation can survive the transition from the evanescent world of musical performance to the abiding world of intractable histories, and whether the orchestra amounts to more than a diversion from the economic, political and religious realities of the Israeli–Palestinian conflict, are questions into which I shall not enter here.

Music, in conclusion, shapes space in a great diversity of ways, as I have indicated, and at the same time shapes the social interactions that take place within those spaces. Live music takes place in physical space; recorded music multiplies and links such spaces across the globe as well as through time. But my principal concern has been with what I called the inherently musical properties that music brings to space – properties that have given rise on the one hand to the spatialised cartographies of music theory, and on the other to any number of ways of articulating and figuring space as public or private. When music creates boundaries, when it distinguishes my space from yours, it draws principally on its extraordinary capacity for generic differentiation: the walls between people erected by the constantly evolving sub-genres of dance music are as solid as any architect's (or Phil Spector's). But when it forges or shapes community, music builds on real-time nuance, on the shared experience of Schutz's mutual tuning-in, resulting in what I termed inner space–time – in a world that can be seen as both virtual and real. The musical shaping of space, then, revolves around music's Janus-like nature: the tension between its tendency to autonomy and reification on the one hand, and the manner in which it flows into and penetrates the furthest reaches of our everyday life on the other. Music is an integral element of the political economy of the public and the private, even as it shows that such distinctions are not impermeable.

# 11 | Civil twilight: country music, alcohol and the spaces of Manitoban aboriginal sociability

BYRON DUECK

This chapter looks at music venues that serve a largely aboriginal clientele in the western Canadian city of Winnipeg, as well as the music that fills them and the stigma that weighs upon their patrons. These clubs, halls and rooms occupy what is here called 'civil twilight' in two respects. First, they accommodate distinct but intersecting kinds of sociability: they are oriented to social imaginaries, hailing publics of strangers, yet they are simultaneously sites of intimacy, places within which known and knowable persons interact.[1] The connection between imagining and intimacy is particularly evident in the collaborations that take place within these venues: attendees engage in face-to-face musical and social interactions, but these are informed and enabled by a familiarity with skills and knowledge that circulate in mass-mediated form (i.e. in imaginaries). So, for instance, musicians often perform together with people they have not met before, such collaborations being possible because all concerned have learned songs and conventions that circulate in broadcasts and recordings. Similarly, patrons meeting one another for the first time make conversation in part through reference to news and opinions disseminated in the national media, including concerned discussions of 'aboriginal drinking'.

This introduces the second sense of 'civil twilight'. Since the sale of alcohol to Status Indians was legalised in the 1950s, the Manitoban and national media have voiced concern regarding bars that cater to a primarily working-class aboriginal clientele. These venues have been perceived as sites of faulty civility (or 'counterpublicity': Warner 2002; Hirschkind 2006) and of intemperate drinking that hurts the bodies of aboriginal people and of their unborn children and leads to violence, abuse and neglect. Contemporary indigenous discourse reflects awareness of these discussions and of a long history of state intervention. Aboriginal public culture

---

[1] On the dialectic between intimacy and publicness, see Michael Warner 2002, Lauren Berlant 2000, 2008 and Elizabeth Povinelli 1998, 2002. Their work, which inspires arguments developed here, examines how intimacy forms the basis for both normative and subaltern forms of publicness. At the same time, as should become clearer below, this chapter privileges not the representations of intimacy that circulate in public culture, but rather actual face-to-face interactions between known and knowable persons (see also Goffman 1967, 1974).

thus stands in the shadow of national discourses and interpositions that have continually construed indigenous drinking as something troubled and troubling.

'Civil twilight' should therefore be understood in two distinct senses. On the one hand it refers to an in-betweenness: to the way public venues are simultaneously oriented to 'intimates' and 'social imaginaries'. On the other hand, it describes a peripherality: how aboriginal public culture stands on the outskirts of normalised national civility – and how members of the aboriginal public ruefully perceive their existence in terms of this relationship. The two aspects of civil twilight are particularly evident in the musical interactions that constitute the Manitoban aboriginal soundscape, especially those that involve country music. Country music and related styles are preferred genres in many of the public spaces of aboriginal sociability, and are in this way fundamentally implicated in the forms of intimate and imagining sociability enacted therein. They are also important insofar as they allow Native musicians to speak about their social peripherality. Song lyrics, musical gatherings and the discourses that surround them evidence a range of ethical and affective perspectives regarding the stigmatised social practice of drinking.

## Aboriginal public culture

The ethnographic accounts that follow explore musical performances and talk that animate aboriginal public assembly and circulate in recordings and broadcasts. They also describe the venues where such performances take place: on the one hand 'wet' drinking establishments where performers play country music, and on the other 'dry' events where attendees sing Christian songs. Such spaces have a complementary but oppositional relationship in Winnipeg's aboriginal public culture. Despite many dissimilarities, especially in the ethical conceptions of attendees, they are connected to one another musically: the country music heard in wet venues and the hymns and 'country gospel' songs performed in dry ones are similar enough that musicians can move between these genres and spaces with ease.

This chapter draws on fieldwork conducted primarily in the city of Winnipeg since 2002. My interactions have been for the most part with northern Algonquians: people who are members of Cree or Ojibwe First Nations and Métis people who share with them a similar heritage. The Cree and Ojibwe who live in neighbouring territories in Manitoba's forested northern Shield region share many linguistic and cultural commonalities (Hallowell 1955: 112–16; Brown and Brightman 1988). These similarities, as well as their close affiliations with some Métis, mean that it is possible to talk about an 'aboriginal' public culture that connects Cree, Ojibwe and some Métis Manitobans. And indeed, many of the people I interacted with used the term 'aboriginal' to describe themselves and their culture.

A designation such as 'aboriginal public culture' can have drawbacks. Unless it is used carefully, the term can obscure the centrality of northern Algonquian cultures to this group and suggest something generically 'indigenous'. It can also veil the existence of non-Algonquian groups in Manitoba, such as the Dakota or the Dene. Yet if the nuances and limitations of the term – as it signifies in context – are understood, it becomes a powerful emic designation of a broad structure of affiliation in Manitoba: a social imaginary or public in which northern Algonquian cultures, languages and expressive practices tend to be particularly important.

Traditional and neo-traditional expressive practices such as powwow are perhaps the most familiar objects of musical scholarship on North American indigenous community life and public culture (Browner 2002; Scales 2004; Ellis, Lassiter and Dunham 2005). But in recent years ostensibly 'Western' practices such as fiddling, hymnody and popular music have also been explored (Lederman 1988; McNally 2000; Diamond 2002; Samuels 2004). It is not only because indigenous performers and communities have a very real sense of connection to and ownership of these genres that they are worthy of investigation. It is because they also permit valuable insights into how indigenous communities and publics have navigated their colonial and postcolonial experiences, as this chapter will show.

## Partying at the Westbrook

During 2002 and 2003 I attended several performances by aboriginal country bands at the Westbrook Inn, a Winnipeg drinking establishment with a largely Native clientele and a reputation as a venue frequented by gang members. On Saturday afternoons radio station NCI FM broadcast live performances from the hotel to a network of First Nations and Métis communities stretched across an area approximately the size of Afghanistan. The radio host dedicated songs to various communities in the province, conveyed greetings from listeners (some in the live audience and others phoning from their homes) and invited people who lived close by to come on down. The event clearly addressed two, not entirely exclusive, audiences: 'the people here at the Westbrook and across the province', as the host put it (NCI broadcast of 7 September 2002). In short, it was oriented to intimates – those knowable persons who had gathered together within the bar – as well as to a social imaginary – the audience for NCI FM that afternoon.

The decor inside the bar was somewhat old, but not unusually so for a Winnipeg drinking establishment. The seating encircled the stage and dance floor, which were clearly the centre of attention (at least at weekends), while a small games table and a bank of video lottery terminals occupied the periphery. In contrast to other city venues, seating at the Westbrook was set up to facilitate large groups, including family outings. Serving staff came around regularly to take drink orders, and intoxication was not uncommon. In fact, for some attendees Saturdays were a kind of all-day party, with the music getting under way in the early afternoon and concluding well after midnight.

Typically, headlining acts performed their strongest material during the radio broadcast and then again at the end of the night. In between, they frequently fell into the role of 'backing band' for members of the audience who wanted to come up to sing. In short, Saturday performances often became jam sessions. In some cases the singers who came up chose songs that everyone knew; in other instances they picked ones that were less familiar. Yet, as I discovered at other jams I took part in as a performer, musical interactions could take place even when not all of the musicians knew the songs. This was because singers most often chose numbers with predictable stylistic characteristics: a straightforward three- or four-chord harmonic palette (often in the keys of G, C or D), a pronounced dominant–tonic opposition, antecedent–consequent phrasing and simple strophic forms. This made it easier for musicians to accompany, even when they did not remember a song well or had not played it before.

Such 'common-practice' tonal structures underlie a great deal of hymnody, fiddle music and gospel song – genres many aboriginal musicians I knew had a close acquaintance with. They are also characteristic of the country music that was popular in bars such as the Westbrook. Most of my subjects regarded these genres as aboriginal music, although there were some who considered drum song to be a more authentic manifestation of indigeneity. In fact, Manitoban aboriginal people have appropriated and adapted the structures of European common-practice music over the course of centuries: initially during the course of the fur trade, later under western Canadian high colonialism (roughly 1871 to 1956), and especially after the rise of radio and recordings.

The performers at the Westbrook drew upon not only a body of shared songs and stylistic conventions, but also a set of 'hard country' (Ching 2001) themes including drinking and heartache. On one visit to the Westbrook I heard singer and songwriter Cal Richard perform 'Family Tree'. Harmonically, his song would have been easy for a jam session band to accompany, even if the musicians had never heard it before. As in several well-known country songs, including Kitty Wells's 'It Wasn't God Who Made Honky Tonk Angels' and Hank Williams's 'Family Tradition' (the latter probably a touchstone lyrically), the verses cycled twice through the harmonic progression tonic–subdominant–dominant–tonic. The lyrics, meanwhile, addressed the well-established hard country subjects of drinking and good-timing. In the first verse of the recording Richard eventually made of the song (Richard n.d.), the narrator's mother enjoins him to get a job, save money and start a family. He replies that he already does have a job – partying with his friends; that they have a financial plan – pooling their money; and that he regards his fellow revellers as relatives. In short, he has already been adding branches to the family tree. While the narrator strikes a contrary pose in response to the exhortations to lead a responsible life, the song in fact affirms the social norms it defies. In the end its bluster is comical and dismissible: the claim that partying is a respectable occupation is clearly and playfully without merit.

More serious reflections upon drinking were also in evidence at the Westbrook. One Saturday, I got into a conversation with a Métis man of perhaps sixty years who appeared to have been drinking for a while. Although his mood initially seemed good, the conversation frequently turned melancholic. We discussed his family, music, politics and his unhappy relationship with his son; we also talked about aboriginal–white relations. He asked me several times whether I, as a white person, liked Natives, and whether my parents ever told me, 'Don't hang around with those Indians.' And he told me at least twice that he was 'ashamed' of aboriginal people. Later in the evening, after we had talked for a while, I went to the men's room, and when I came back he was drinking my bottle of beer, having finished the one he had asked me to buy him. The conversation ground to a halt a while later.

The foregoing account might easily be thought to be a banal example of a narrative genre familiar to middle-class western Canadian whites: vignettes of adventures in 'Indian bars' featuring abject aboriginal 'alcoholics'. Such stories risk reviving powerful stereotypes. In the Manitoban communities where I grew up in the 1970s and 1980s, drinking was seen as a Native problem – a perception that persists, including among aboriginal people. But in fact the situation is complex. Certainly drinking has been a cause of misery for many aboriginal people and has a long association with violence, crime, child neglect and foetal alcohol spectrum disorders. Yet indigenous Canadians are much more likely than non-indigenous ones to abstain completely from alcohol (Thatcher 2004: 23–5).

Why then tell a story such as the one just related here? One reason is to point to the cultural priming my drinking companion's remarks acknowledged: the way the tavern, its aboriginal patrons, the country music and the day-long drinking were understood as something to be ashamed of. Our encounter was from the start a 'genred' meeting between whiteness and indigeneity.

## Troubling alcohol consumption

My drinking companion's remarks and shame should be understood in the context of Canada's colonial and postcolonial history. In 1876, having recently begun the process of entering into treaties with western Canadian indigenous groups, the federal Government passed the Indian Act, a law that established the character of Canadian high colonialism. The act construed 'Indians' as uncivilised bands whose members aspired eventually to become full citizens; it also established the means by which such enfranchisement could take place (Canada 1876: sections 86–94). One distinction between Indians and citizens was the right to consume intoxicants: the Indian Act prohibited the sale, gift and barter of alcohol to Status Indians and made it illegal for them to be inebriated (Canada 1876: sections 79, 83).

These prohibitions remained in effect in Manitoba until 1956 (Manitoba 1956), when First Nations people began to be able to drink and visit bars. Non-aboriginal Manitobans soon began to express worry about the drinking behaviour of Natives and its implications for violent crime, child neglect and social and economic integration. Newspapers ran concerned articles (UMASC (2002)). Child welfare agencies responded to troubling drinking practices (alongside other perceived problems) by taking great numbers of Native children into care, placing them in foster homes or putting them up for adoption (Johnston 1983: 76–7). And thus, while racially discriminatory colonial laws were overturned in the post-war era, extensive state intervention in indigenous communities persisted, in part in response to what the national public perceived to be the intolerable comportment of indigenous people under the influence of alcohol (compare Povinelli 1998). In many respects the same situation persists today.

Lest it seem that only non-aboriginal people have been critical of aboriginal alcohol consumption, it should be emphasised that there is a long history of opposition to drink within indigenous communities themselves (MacAndrew and Edgerton 1969). Indeed, in the present day many First Nations communities are dry by member vote and it is illegal to buy, sell or possess alcohol within their boundaries. During fieldwork I came to know many people who were long-time teetotallers and who criticised the use of alcohol in no uncertain terms. Thus, indigenous drinking and the sentiments of embarrassment and shame that surround it arise from a complex history. In Canadian discourse, aboriginal drinking has been understood as troubled and troubling and as meriting intervention for nearly a century and a half. Complicating matters is that many aboriginal people regard alcohol as an evil, and many Native communities actively seek to restrict the consumption of it.

Understanding something of the social and political context for drinking helps to explain the shame of my companion at the Westbrook, and the sharpness the lyrics of party songs such as Cal Richard's can have for Native listeners. But it may also help to explain the popularity of country music among aboriginal people. Although its prominence probably has something to do with what Aaron Fox identifies as a surge in working-class pay and empowerment during the decades that followed the Second World War (Fox 2004), it is also tied up with a set of historical experiences particular to western Canada. Country music was, among other things, the soundscape and poetry of the working-class tavern during the decade when aboriginal drinkers were first allowed entrance to it.

## A drug- and alcohol-free gathering

The country bar is an important part of Winnipeg's contemporary aboriginal soundscape, but certainly not the only one. Other venues extend alternative modes of indigenous publicness, as 'dry' counterparts to the 'wet' spaces where alcohol is served, and are accordingly understood to manifest a more upright kind of sociability. There exists a morally freighted opposition between events and venues where alcohol is served and ones where it is avoided, then, and organisers communicate the legitimacy or seriousness of an event or undertaking in part by making it dry. This is particularly true of powwows,[2] but also of numerous events where music in a country style is performed.

---

[2] Full consideration of the powwow is outside the scope of this chapter, but there also tend to be prohibitions on drinking at these highly esteemed events, which celebrate dance and song traditions of indigenous origin (Browner 2002).

Although wet and dry spaces tend to stand in moral opposition, they are in many cases musically connected. While I conducted fieldwork, indigenous political organisations – reserve governments and the Manitoba Métis Federation, for instance – frequently hosted events that centred on country music, but were dry. These largely secular jamborees, talent shows and jam sessions featured performances very similar to those that could be heard in bars such as the Westbrook. (There were a few differences, of course: there tended to be less rock and roll and more 'classic country', for instance, and there were also fewer 'hard country' songs defiantly celebrating drinking and good-timing.)

But especially interesting for the purposes of this chapter were the frequent dry gatherings – coffee houses and jams – where sacred music was featured. At these events, typically organised by laypeople, musicians and listeners came together to enjoy hymns and gospel music. Notably, the music performed at these events had many characteristics in common with the 'classic' country performed at secular gatherings. Indeed, two of the events I regularly attended described themselves as 'country gospel' coffee houses. I was most closely involved with one held at the William Whyte elementary school in Winnipeg's North End. On Wednesday nights during the school year, singers and musicians gathered in the echoing gymnasium to play and sing. Chairs and tables were set up for attendees, and a loosely constituted 'house band' accompanied the singing. The instrumentation, consisting of acoustic guitar, electric guitar (playing lead parts) and electric bass, was well suited to country music. Occasionally a keyboardist or a violinist would sit in.

The William Whyte coffee house, like the others that ran in the North End, was explicitly promoted as a dry event and as an alternative to social contexts in which drugs and alcohol were used. These coffee houses, unlike the Westbrook, did not extend mass-mediated invitations to a public of strangers through radio advertisements. News of them tended to circulate by word of mouth and especially through the personal invitations that their organisers and promoters extended. Nevertheless, they were understood to be open to the public and, as will become evident below, interactions at them relied upon mass-mediated 'imagining' in crucial ways.

During the course of an evening, an event organiser carried around a clipboard and signed up people who wanted to sing; they were subsequently called up one by one. Anyone who wanted to perform could do so. Some singers were amateurs who only knew a few songs, but a good many were active musicians. Some were engaged in Christian ministry and led worship services, animated revival meetings or sang at traditional wakes.

Others also performed secular country music, sometimes on the bar circuit. Many of the latter were former drinkers who had become teetotallers, a change in lifestyle that was marked in part by an increased interest in sacred song. Interestingly, few of the male singers on the coffee house circuit had strong ties to any particular denomination or congregation. Many seemed uncomfortable with the idea of being identified as holy rollers, and two or three acknowledged that they were more drawn to traditional aboriginal practices than Christianity. Nevertheless, all of them found gospel music appealing.

The musicians included Cree, Ojibwe, Métis and (occasionally) non-aboriginal people. They performed songs in aboriginal languages, but perhaps four-fifths or more of the singing was in English. The music they chose belonged to a variety of genres, including protestant hymns such as 'Amazing Grace' ('Kihci kisewaatisiwin' in Cree) and 'I Would Not Be Denied', and 'choruses' associated with the charismatic worship movement, for instance 'Create in Me a Clean Heart' and 'Soon and Very Soon'. Perhaps the most widely popular songs, however, were those participants referred to as 'country gospel': pieces on sacred themes that were sung in a classic country style and had in many cases been popularised by well-known country artists. These included 'Where the Roses Never Fade', 'In the Sweet By and By' and 'I'll Fly Away'.

Many of the lyrics of the most popular and frequently sung songs were about heaven and the afterlife, a fact that probably reflected the most auspicious setting in which they were heard, namely the funerary wake. But it is the sound and musical structure of the repertory that is most salient to the argument here, since it demonstrates a unity that transcends social divisions in Manitoba's aboriginal soundscape. Almost all of the songs performed at coffee houses shared musical characteristics with the repertories performed in bars and at wet events. Country gospel songs – but also older hymns – made use of basic common-practice conventions: a limited harmonic palette whose tonic, subdominant and dominant harmonies stood in predictable relationships, straightforward pairings of strong and weak cadences and simple, familiar strophic forms. And songs were almost always sung in a country style: in a somewhat pinched voice, and decorated by expressive breaks and bends.

The overlap between sonic worlds was evident on a number of levels: aboriginal musicians such as Chris Beach, Stan Cook, Jack Meade, Ernest Monias and Stirling Ranville sang both country and country gospel music. Singers at the William Whyte coffee house – the most 'secular' of the three that ran while I was working in Winnipeg – often performed country songs. And there were even some gospel songs that were contrafacts (i.e. retextings) of popular country tunes. One entitled 'On My Way to Heaven' set new lyrics to Waylon Jennings's hard country classic, 'Good Hearted Woman'. In another, the words 'Jesus, I love you' were sung to the tune that Donna Fargo uses to sing 'Funny face, I love you'.[3]

Occasionally, the connections between country and gospel, and between the Westbrook Inn and the coffee house, were particularly dramatic. One spring night in 2003, the coffee house at William Whyte began as usual, with a prayer and gospel singing. But at a certain point singers began to perform secular music exclusively, and the evening concluded with love songs such as 'He Stopped Loving Her Today' and 'I'm Moving On'. Although there were one or two secular songs early on, it was probably the sixth performer, a well-known singer, who changed the course of the evening decisively. He played four love songs in a row, to the audience's audible appreciation. Given the somewhat competitive context of the coffee house, the following singer may have felt a need to deliver a performance that was equally appealing. Whatever the case, he launched into a long set of secular songs. Since he was a teetotaller and regarded by some as a holy roller, it was something of a surprise when, near the end of the set, he performed a version of Moe Bandy's 1976 'Here I Am Drunk Again' in Cree, his mother tongue. In it, the narrator describes drinking 'whiskey, beer and wine' because his love has cheated and their relationship is ending.

It was striking that an abstinent singer had performed a 'drinking song', and that the coffee house, explicitly conceived as a place of sacred song and a haven from intoxicant abuse, had momentarily become a space where such a piece could be performed and enjoyed. On the one hand, this shift revealed a kind of ambivalence about drinking that transgressed the normally strictly enforced divisions between wet and dry, teetotaller and partier, bar band and gospel band. This ambivalence was evident on many occasions in interactions with friends and consultants. Teetotallers rejected their old ways and condemned drinking – yet told stories that laid proud claim to their partying days. In other words people used song and narrative to assimilate behaviours and periods of their lives otherwise regarded as problematic. On the other hand, the shift from dry to wet points to the underlying musical similarities that connect some of the most popular Manitoban aboriginal vernacular genres. It was easy to move into country music because country gospel shared the same instrumentation and musical structures.

[3] Thanks to Chris Beach for pointing these contrafacts out.

## Musical intimacies and imaginaries

While doing fieldwork I visited a steady succession of talent shows, jam sessions and coffee houses and became a regular contributor at one of them. A number of things were striking about such events, musically speaking. First, they facilitated widespread and democratic participation: it was not only trained, professional or semi-professional musicians who contributed, but also amateurs who simply liked to sing country or gospel music or play the fiddle. Second, musicians seemed continually to find themselves in situations where they were putting together performances on the spur of the moment, without rehearsal. During any given night at the William Whyte coffee house, for instance, well over thirty different songs might be performed without the benefit of sheet music or even chord symbols. Certainly the members of the house band were familiar with a great many songs, but even they frequently had to look over at other musicians to confirm that they were getting the harmonic changes right. And while performances often involved long-time musical collaborators, on many other occasions they brought together musicians who had not previously met. Such encounters occurred time and time again.

One way to understand music-making at the Westbrook and the William Whyte coffee house is as a meeting between two distinct but intersecting modes of sociability. On the one hand musical encounters involved intimacy: real-time 'interaction rituals' (Goffman 1967, 1974) between known or knowable persons sharing the same space.[4] On the other hand these encounters involved, and were facilitated by, social imagining: the stranger-sociability that holds between the members of 'imagined communities' (Anderson 1991 (1983)) and publics (Warner 2002), and in particular the relationship that exists between people who understand themselves to have something in common with others through mass mediation.

To elaborate, the public spaces considered here were sites of intimacy, of interaction between known and knowable persons. Patrons at the Westbrook struck up conversations with one another, the audience at the coffee house gave immediate, audible feedback to performers, and musicians and dancers at various venues co-ordinated their musical and

---

[4] Intimacy as conceived here does not require *literal* temporal or spatial proximity, although these are emphasised given the focus here on venues. The broader distinction set up here is between various types of person-to-person interaction and the 'stranger sociability' that is in operation in acts of mass-mediated publication.

choreographic contributions. Yet at the same time these venues were oriented to social imaginaries, that is to audiences of strangers. Radio broadcasts advertised the Westbrook to an aboriginal public that stretched across
Manitoba. And even as the radio announcer engaged particular callers-in
and members of the live audience on a first-name basis, he also addressed
a 'radioland' of potential listeners. Admittedly, the coffee houses I attended
were not advertised through the radio, print or internet – and yet participants would have said that these gatherings were open to anyone who
wanted to come.

Intimacy and imagining intersect in particularly musical ways, and these
connections help to explain how musicians navigated the fledgling intimacies involved in, for instance, performing songs they did not know with
musicians they had not previously met. In such situations interaction was
enabled by a shared orientation to a social imaginary that pre-existed the
moment of encounter. Singers performed songs that they expected their
collaborators to be able to accompany, and accompanists performed in the
expectation that singers would follow certain genre-specific patterns.

All parties had prepared themselves for such encounters in advance in
part through a mutual orientation to a musical public. This involved learning a set of frequently performed songs and tunes, many of which circulated
in the form of recordings and broadcasts. It also meant attuning oneself to
musical patterns and stylistic conventions: the chords that tended to follow
one another in various keys, the accompanimental devices that were appropriate in country and country gospel, and the song structures that were
most frequently mobilised. In short, it involved disciplining mind and body
to replicate the same structures performed by imagined others constituting
a country music public.

Nelson Menow, a singer, songwriter and guitarist and the cornerstone
of the William Whyte house band, told me that during the 1940s, in the
northern community of Norway House, he and his father would listen to
Nashville programmes on a battery-powered radio. 'I used to listen to the
likes of Jimmie Rodgers and Hank Snow, Hank Williams, Roy Acuff, Kitty
Wells and … Minnie Pearl', he told me. 'The music that I was listening to
was very fantastical to me … I never played guitar before but I was listening
to them and gradually I started earning for a guitar. I wanted to play it so
badly like these country singers.' Menow thus engaged with broadcasts of
country musicians not only as a listener, but also as someone who hoped to
be able to make music in the same way they did. His desire to learn suggests
the energy many of my consultants had devoted to making country music

their own. Such efforts prepared them to interact with other members of a country music public. But additionally, they extended and expanded that public, increasing its strength through the competency of additional contributors.

Certainly not all learning of country music prioritised social imaginaries: in many cases, people learned songs from friends and acquaintances and were more concerned about their relationships to known musicians than a public of strangers. The bearing towards a public has probably changed quite a bit historically: while very limited in the nineteenth century, when indigenous people living in what is now Manitoba first encountered printed hymnals, in the current era it is much heightened. Equally importantly, *how* the 'aboriginal musical public' is construed has changed over time. New songs have become part of the repertory that singers and instrumentalists expect one another to know. Musicians are introducing more adventurous harmonies and structures at jam sessions and coffee houses. And singers at talent shows are increasingly performing rock and pop songs. Such changes occur in part because of the performative nature of public culture. A public is not a population; it is rather a social formation that comes together through acts of mutual orientation and through the mass-mediated circulation of performances and publications (Warner 2002). As these acts of mutual attentiveness, performances and publications change over time, so too does public culture – and the soundscapes of aboriginal public spaces.

## Alcohol, country music and twilight civility

As explained earlier, the national public has perceived aboriginal drinking as troubled and troubling, and as meriting intervention, from the colonial era to the present day. This surveillance and discipline has in turn had implications for aboriginal subjectivity. Drinking has become a site of what Michael Herzfeld (1997) calls 'cultural intimacy': a 'rueful recognition' among aboriginal people that the mainstream public perceives certain aspects of 'their' habitus as problematic. Moreover, and again as argued above, there are sharp and morally freighted divisions between wet and dry events and between drinkers and non-drinkers. I do not want to exclude the possibility that such oppositions have roots in older northern Algonquian cultural practices – nevertheless, it is hard to imagine that they have not been significantly impacted by colonial and postcolonial experiences.

In short, aboriginal drinking has often been regarded as a faulty mode of civility in the eyes of the national public. Moreover, there is among aboriginal people an awareness of this problematic status. And so it is not simply differing kinds of alcohol consumption that constitute civil twilight. It is additionally an awareness of how such behaviours are perceived by a more dominant public, and it is the critical, ironic, ludic and rueful reflections upon those behaviours that circulate in aboriginal song and discourse.

On the last day of 2002 I got into a car with two friends, long-time tee-totallers, and headed out of the city to an Ojibwe First Nation reserve on the eastern side of Lake Winnipeg. We were on our way to a dry square dance being held to celebrate the arrival of the new year. The dance offered an alternative to the drinking parties that would also be taking place in the community that night. We arrived at the reserve somewhat early, and so headed over to the house of a dancer my friends knew. He made some coffee and fed us moose meat and bannock. His family was busy getting ready for New Year's Eve – the younger members were washing, doing their hair and getting dressed up. Some of them were coming to the dance, while others had different plans. One of our host's sons asked me if I drank; I explained that I did, but not around my sober friends. At some point, the same young man began to strum a guitar and sing a sad country song. One of the friends I had driven up with heard it from the kitchen. 'Waiter', he responded, shouting and playfully affecting slurred speech, 'Bud Light!' He repeated his joke but nobody seemed to find it particularly funny. He was evoking a charged stereotype: the abject Native drinker, afloat in a sea of booze and country music.

The exchange between the young musician and my older friend resonated on a number of levels. First, my friend's playful evocation or 'keying' (Goffman 1974) of tear-in-my-beer country music pointed to a familiar figure, both comical and embarrassing: the stereotype of the 'drunken Native'. But additionally, coming as it did from an erstwhile drinker, it parodied the lifestyle of a drunken former self and juxtaposed it with a sober present-day one. It may also have pointed subtly to the spatial and moral division that we would soon be articulating alongside the rest of the community, with wet parties in some homes and a dry dance in the reserve hall. Additionally – and particularly significantly from the perspective of the argument advanced here – the exchange illustrated an everyday intersection between imagining and intimacy. My older friend and his younger interlocutor were able to engage with one another face-to-face insofar as their interactions made reference to a shared knowledge of aboriginal public culture and its soundscape.

Their exchange, in other words, pointed to an aboriginal imaginary. When my friend responded to the young man's singing, he encouraged the rest of us to hear it not 'in itself', but rather as part of the soundscape of a working-class 'Indian bar', and to associate it with the figure of a drunken patron. In doing so, he was presuming that his audience was familiar with particular aspects of aboriginal public culture: with certain drinking establishments and the people who frequented them, but also with the embarrassing or 'shameful' place such drinkers had in the national imagination and in aboriginal discourse. In other words, just as a singer at a Manitoban aboriginal jam session might launch into a classic country number in the reasonable expectation that her accompanists would be able to follow along, so too could a joker make a reference to an embarrassing stereotype in the expectation that his interlocutors would follow him. A seemingly simple exchange located its participants in relation to a broader national sphere in which aboriginal drinking was problematised.

A few additional points might be appropriate at this point regarding country music, whose sounds play such an important part in constructing aboriginal spaces of interaction. Although the exchange just described momentarily fixed country music as a kind of soundtrack to drunkenness, this was only one of its roles. Indeed, those of us who headed off to the dry dance heard the band there play a number of country songs. Again, the sounds of country music cross the moral and social boundaries separating bars from more reputable assemblies. Wet and dry sociability, strictly opposed in many ways, nevertheless share a similar soundscape, and a consistency in harmonic, melodic and formal language enables musicians and singers to move comfortably between the bar, the dry social, the gospel coffee house, the revival meeting and the wake. It is not unusual to find musicians who sing both country and gospel music, or who give up the barroom for drier performance contexts as they get older.

The close musical connections between country and country gospel music bring to mind a characteristic of traditional Ojibwe social life observed by anthropologist A. Irving Hallowell (1992: 81–2), who remarked: 'I soon discovered that any facile distinction between the secular and the sacred from the Ojibwa point of view was not so easy to draw. If I missed the first few minutes of what I thought might be a purely secular "dance", I also missed a smoke offering to "our grandfathers".[5] Hallowell's statement accorded with my own observations: it was difficult to draw strict lines between sacred and secular music and social gatherings.

---

[5] Hallowell conducted field research in the Berens River Ojibwe community in the 1930s.

Nevertheless, the closeness between country and country gospel music is not only evident in Manitoban aboriginal public culture. Many well-known country singers have recorded and performed gospel music in addition to secular songs, including the Carter Family, Hank Williams, Johnny Cash and George Jones. Their flexibility in this regard was well known to my consultants; indeed, at least two musicians remarked to me that they had appreciated the way the old Nashville radio programmes had concluded with gospel singing. As on the Manitoban scene, movement between sacred and secular styles was facilitated by musical similarities. The close relationship between genres attests to the use of musical materials that are ready to hand – to musical bricolage (Lévi-Strauss 1966). Secular songs draw upon the same common-practice building blocks used in older strophic hymns, while sacred songs are contrafacts of secular ones. The fluidity of motion perhaps also suggests that country and gospel belong to a body of working-class practices (Fox 2004) that do not rigorously or anxiously distinguish high from low and sacred from secular. Shared musical structures permit singers to be both sinners and saints, lyrically and indeed biographically – thus Hank Williams could sing both 'How Can You Refuse Him Now' and 'Tear in My Beer', as could Manitoban Cree singer Ernest Monias. The shared musical language and the migration of singers from one genre to another means that sounds, lyrics and public personas have multiple, mutually enriching sacred and secular associations.

Again, while the seemingly fluid movements between sacred and secular and country and gospel music may perpetuate a traditional northern Algonquian lifestyle in which sacred practice was thoroughly integrated with the everyday, a similar fluidity seems evident in non-aboriginal country music practices. What most clearly distinguishes the aboriginal soundscape from non-aboriginal country music practices, then, is probably not the sacred–secular continuum. It is rather the unique social and political context of aboriginal drinking: namely, how the state has invigilated and restricted indigenous drinking, how the national public has construed it as a faulty form of publicness and how this has impacted on aboriginal subjectivities. The racialised perception of problem drinking in Canada has heightened the stakes so far as intoxicant use is concerned. Perhaps for this reason contradictions and ambivalences regarding alcohol consumption seem dramatically heightened in Native community life, discourse and musical interactions. The accounts related in this chapter suggest that aboriginal people are burdened by the way 'their' drinking troubles the national public, but also that this burden provides the basis for rueful reflection, playful contemplation, artful construction and dramatic transgression. Moreover, the flexibility of country music facilitates such creative elaborations in wet and dry spaces alike.

## Conclusion

This chapter has explored music and sociability in venues that serve predominantly aboriginal audiences in Winnipeg. I have argued that the social interactions that occur in the wet venues of aboriginal public culture have been understood as a flawed form of civility in dominant Canadian discourses, and indeed by many indigenous Manitobans. This has at least two implications. First, indigenous song and conversation about drinking are characterised by a kind of embarrassed recognition of the problematic status that drinking has nationally. Second, aboriginal public culture makes a particularly acute social and moral distinction between wet and dry socialising. Notably, however, a number of musical continuities traverse these social and moral boundaries. Performers mobilise the sounds and structures of country music not only in the bar-room, but also in dry jamborees and at country gospel evenings. Love songs, good-timing music, fiddle tunes, hymns and gospel songs share harmonic, melodic and formal structures; and the spaces of sacred and secular expression overlap, sometimes in ways that might seem incongruous. Certainly, the complementary relationship between country and gospel is not unique to the soundscape considered here. But it seems to have particular potential in the Manitoban aboriginal context, where it enables the expression of widely varying moral and affective orientations to a practice that has been regarded as problematic by both insiders and outsiders.

A further argument is that the intimate social and musical interactions between patrons of these venues stand in complex relationships with wider social imaginaries. On the one hand, personal encounters are facilitated by the ways that participants have prepared themselves ahead of time to interact with imagined others. Jam sessions and other similar events work because musicians have learned the same publicly circulating songs and structures, thus orienting themselves to one another before they even meet. On the other hand, the intimate social and musical interactions that take place in public music venues play a role in constituting those wider imaginaries.

Finally, aboriginal socialising and music-making exist at the intersection of two social imaginaries. One is constituted by national media and normative discourses, which view and discuss aboriginal drinking with concern. The other consists in aboriginal public culture and its rueful and ambivalent, but also ludic and affectionate, collective self-reflections on moral susceptibility. Thus, aboriginal music venues are intensely interstitial zones: sites of intimate interaction articulated to social imaginaries, closely watched by the national public even as they address its other.

# PART IV

# Music and sound: torture, healing and love

## 12 | Music space as healing space: community music therapy and the negotiation of identity in a mental health centre

TIA DENORA

## Introduction

As a music sociologist, I have had a long-term interest in music's role as an active ingredient in social life. In collaboration with Dr Gary Ansdell, of the Nordoff Robbins Centre for Music Therapy, I have been examining this theme in the context of a longitudinal study of community music therapy in a centre for mental health. Our preliminary research has examined clients' creation and negotiation of shared musical–aesthetic space. In collaboration with music therapists and each other, and by drawing together musical performance and extra-musical acts, clients can be seen to shape this space and tap the opportunities for communicative action that the space affords by playing with musical culture. They can also be seen to assist each other in this process. Through these user- or client-led practices, music is a medium of well-being, a mode in which clients are able to exhibit and experience wellness, forge links between each other and develop transferable skills. Musically configured spaces may thus also provide spaces for healing. In this sense, they are places where clients may pass from (on the one hand and however fleeting or fluid) illness-identities, acute treatment facilities and social sequestering, to (on the other hand) health-identities, the wider community and social connection. These passages are mundane socio-cultural achievements, built from many types of resources and materials and accomplished through small but continuous steps.

## The place

The Borough (Centre for) Rehabilitation, Interaction, Group Activity, Hospitality and Training (BRIGHT)[1] supports people in recovery from

---

[1] This is a pseudonym. Names and places have been changed and some accounts have been fictionalised so as to protect participants' identities.

chronic mental illness. Located in the basement of a building directly across a courtyard from a major urban mental health centre, BRIGHT takes the form of a public café that is open 365 days a year. It offers career support, IT facilities and opportunities for employment through projects such as gardening, floristry and a packing/mailing service, and its service provision is expanding. A beacon in the realm of user-led service, BRIGHT also sponsors a range of social activities, from weekend and evening clubs to group holidays for up to forty people a year and – the subject of this chapter – a popular Tuesday afternoon music session.

A typical BRIGHT music session involves between twenty and thirty people. Some are hospital residents from open wards, others mental health clients who have returned to the community in different stages of 'recovery'. A few others are members of the public, either regulars or, occasionally, people who simply happen upon the scene, drawn in some cases by the sound of music-making spilling out to the street. BRIGHT's catchment area includes one of the city's poorest housing estates as well as some lavish mansions and apartments. Participants come from a diverse range of ages, ethnic, racial, economic and social statuses. For many of these participants the mental health experience takes the form of a chronic mixture of good and bad times. The challenge – for all participants, which include BRIGHT staff, hospital staff, music therapists and, not least, clients themselves – is to provide an environment conducive to recognising and building upon resources and thus to healing and development in the widest meaning of those terms.

## A BRIGHT musical session, ethnographic notes

Before a BRIGHT music session, we walk across to the hospital where the percussion instruments are kept. We pile maracas, tambourines, rhythm sticks, bells, rattles and bongo drums onto a trolley and carry a cymbal on a stand, a microphone, an electric guitar and colour-coded songbooks (red, blue, yellow) across and down the stairs to BRIGHT's café. The instruments are placed on a side table and participants choose one or two that they tend to use throughout a session. Other times, they are offered round at the same time as the songbooks (compilations of lyrics from group favourites, pop, folk and standard classics). Some people have become associated with 'their' instrument; Hermione, for example, always selects the tambourine, while Billy, a professional musician, routinely takes one of the electric guitars. There is tacit respect for these regularities: I remember being gently warned off the tambourine the first time I arrived, since that was 'Hermione's instrument'.

These mundane details of ordering highlight immediately that BRIGHT is a space in which norms govern a musically configured community and where there is mutual respect. BRIGHT's ethos and aesthetic code, moreover, eschews hierarchy, at least ostensibly in terms of how that ethos is performed and described by participants. There is no sense, for example, that playing the electric guitar is any 'better' or more 'advanced' than playing the tambourine, despite their obvious differences in cost, size or dynamic capacity. To the contrary, a gourd, a set of rhythm sticks, a triangle, castanets and an electric guitar seem of equal import as objects for playing, since to play is to participate, and to participate is to affirm. That said, participants nonetheless acknowledge and are quick to admire the skill involved in mastering the latter.

Since BRIGHT music sessions are held in the café, participants tend to cluster at tables, neatly arranged in rows, with the piano and microphone up front. Individuals tend to occupy particular segments of the physical room from week to week. Sessions are organised around a mix of group sing-along, individual and small group performances at the mic facing the audience, and instrumental–vocal improvisations by the group as instigated by Gary. These performances allow the group to perceive and display itself to itself from a variety of musical angles and socio-musical combinations. The talk that is linked to them, about the music, before and after, further highlights the self-reflective character of music at BRIGHT. Performance is, in other words, the medium through which the group becomes not only a group, but a socially textured group, both cohesive *and* differentiated individuals, linked through shared and negotiated practices, values and norms. Each session mixes group singing, group improvising and open-mic (solo or group performances), and follows a loose pattern. It begins with some solo piano playing from Gary. Sometimes it begins with a song, sometimes the music is improvised, sometimes upbeat, sometimes languid. What he chooses to do musically will depend upon how Gary himself is feeling, his soundings of the atmosphere and his knowledge of how things have gone over the past week. Typically, he will encourage the group to join in about two-thirds into this opening playing and then, taking cues from us and apparently seamlessly (using a combination of musical cues, gesture and talk), he will shift the group into an initial group song.

This first song is often one of the general favourites (The Beatles' 'Michelle' is one of these), one that lets us warm up our voices and hear them amassed. How this first song is chosen varies: sometimes Gary simply begins to play the introduction to a song, sometimes he will ask what we want to sing or someone will call out a request from the book. There is usually a bit of a scramble to find the right page – sometimes books are shared between two (a way of affording micro-cohesion) – and we're off. Gary will then normally ask for a solo performance at the mic. All the while, in a little office behind the piano, BRIGHT's administrator and director continue their work, usually with the Perspex door half open and often popping in and mingling. Mary, a former client, stands by at the tea counter, occasionally joining in with the musical activity and generally facilitating momentum, for example, echoing Gary's requests for individual performances from certain people ('Go on X – we love to hear you sing'). At BRIGHT the 'audience'/group may need to do little but applaud or they may be called upon to do everything, helping a trembling performer 'make it through' a solo with constant musical and verbal encouragement. What, then, is involved in performing a song, and in performing a song, temporarily holding the floor, controlling the musical space, projecting into that space in ways that help to shape it?

To put the answer to this question up front, I will suggest that musical activity at BRIGHT provides a case study in which it is possible to see individuals (mental health clients and others) creating little, temporary 'asylums'. By asylums, I mean situations, moments or environments that, albeit fleetingly, permit individuals to flourish, to have respite from a troubling world and to have space (Goffman (1968 (1961): 310) speaks here of creating 'elbow room') that can be appropriated for self-development. Simultaneously, I mean places in which individuals may forge connections to others. Musical activity, to the extent that it confronts individuals as a medium that stands outside of, but as a resource for, the self, offers a means for creating selves and collective identities. In this way it facilitates individuals' progression along what Goffman (1968 (1961): 125–71) terms 'moral careers': 'the regular sequence of changes that career entails in the person's self and in his framework of imagery for judging himself and others.'

## The double performance of song and self in socio-musical space

Solo-singing at BRIGHT is a double performance. It is the performance of a song and, via song, it is the performance of a self. That self is itself the outcome of repeated alliances between repertoire, performance and reception, and the habitus exhibited/constructed through this

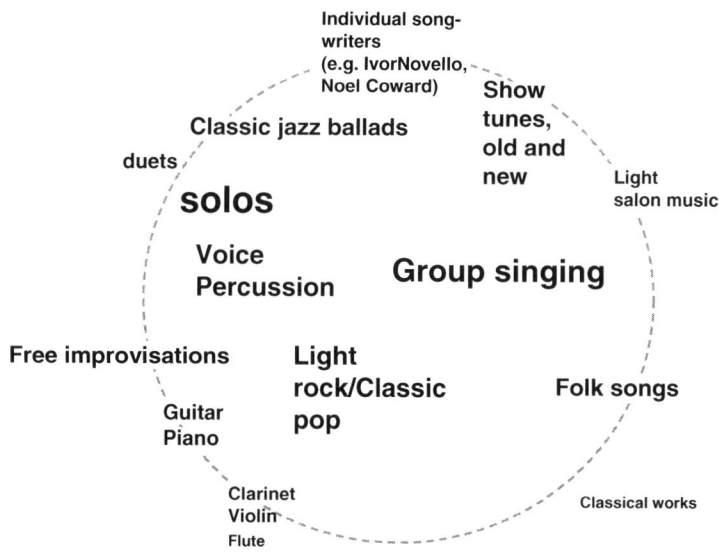

**Figure 12.1** BRIGHT musical space

performance is contextually produced (Lahire 2003); indeed, this is one of the reasons that music works so well as a medium of psycho-social change, as I will discuss below. The performing self is, in other words, the outcome of a negotiation of (what comes to count as) 'successful' performance. All solo performers at BRIGHT are at least implicitly affiliated with song repertoires, though the scope of their individual repertoires varies. (Some participants perform the same song from week to week.) Taken collectively, these musical repertoires mediate social repertoires of affect and agency – the psycho-cultural and symbolic space of available ways of being within BRIGHT's socio-musical compass. It is from within this compass that the double performance of song and self occurs. BRIGHT's musical space can be understood as a topology, in Bourdieu's (1985) sense. Some musical modes (genre, song style, performance format (solo, group, duet), instruments, song title) are prominent, some as 'specialist corners', and their presence correlates with the scheduling of a BRIGHT afternoon. In Figure 12.1, this space is represented circa 2006, with font size indicating degree of frequency of performance (how often a genre is performed).

Music within a BRIGHT event may be combined and spaced loosely, with a few regularities that I describe below. For example, a classical work or light salon song may precede and follow a light rock or pop number or improvised work.

At a basic level, performing a song is about managing to get through from start to finish, and about being associated with song repertoires. At a more complex level, it includes musical delivery styles – timbres, rhythmic tendencies, embodied stance and gesture. Some of these stylistic patterns are unintended, for example, Tom's gravelly bass is highly distinctive and routinely causes comment. Others are para-musical, for example, Jane, who takes time to set herself up for a solo performance (arranging the sheet music, discussing interpretation). Indeed a number of other participants also stretch their performances with an additional layer of para-musical work, through talk about the music they perform. For example, Robbie mentions in an offhand way as he prepares to sing a well-known ballad that he *is* Billie Holiday ('I am Billie Holiday'). (His song style when performing jazz ballads is indeed redolent of Holiday's subtle rhythmic nuance and its associated detached cool.) Others take care to explain the background of their chosen songs in music–historical contexts. At another, more explicitly 'therapeutic' level, music performance at BRIGHT provides a way of inhabiting the musical space, a means of projecting self into music and music into self ('I am Billie Holiday'). This projection is promissory of what we might expect from the person in future – Holiday here serves as an exemplar perhaps for extra-musical style and conduct forms, that is for the development and deployment of a mode of sensibility and thus action in the world. That promissory quality is simultaneously tactical: it involves a musical–spatial location, a 'this is where you will find me here' proclamation. The elements of performance style, in other words, become proxies for identity, signs of embodied and tacit dispositions that shoot through and structure social action. It is not, perhaps, surprising that the question of how a song is to be rendered is potentially contentious (see Hennion 2007) since, as Cook (2003) and McCormick (2009) describe, performance instantiates social relations. In this sense musical activity can be understood to be an active ingredient of community formation; as McCormick (2009: 7) puts it, 'the context of musical performance is itself the result of an ongoing process of cultural construction.'

On one occasion at BRIGHT, for example, there was an overt struggle over how to render a standard jazz ballad. This struggle took the form of a musical–stylistic tug-of-war, with Gary (the music therapist/accompanist) functioning as the rope and we (the 'audience') being enlisted as further 'musical muscle' by each of the vying parties. On the one hand, the participant who had initiated the performance began to sing it as a lyrical ballad, and Gary's musical introduction announced it in this way. On hearing the opening notes, another participant went up to the mic to join the first singer because, as she put it, 'this is my song, I've got to sing this song'. Her rendition was musically different, however – it was a swing version. A musical 'debate' then ensued, with each participant pulling the music in stylistically different directions. Musical styles, in other words, not only offer, as Schutz has described (1971 (1964)) in his work on musical attunement, their proponents a mode of being-in-time (and thus personas over time), they also furnish or aesthetically inflect the spaces into which they are projected. They provide, as it were, statements and exemplars of 'how to be' and of preferred versions of practice, aesthetic and social.

## Projecting self in space and time

For its existence, as Erving Goffman (1968 (1961): 168) taught us, the self (and its perceived manifestation as self-identity, and even if that self is multiple, stranded or fragmentary and variously known to different observers) has to be registered if it is to be known to self and/or others. That registration takes shape through presentational and behavioural styles, devices, gambits and stances. Through how I hold my body and facial posture, through what I 'choose' to say and how I say it (volume, pitch, accent), through what I can mobilise (humour, knowledge, experience, others), I come to be known as a type of person – quiet or aggressive, shy or shrill, halting or brisk (note the musical features here), stylish or dowdy, competent in some realm(s), incompetent in others. The self in these examples is thus a 'pro-ject': it involves a projection through various media in two directions that reciprocally affect each other: from self to other(s) (who include one's own self, looking at self) and back from other(s) to self in the form of attributions and orientations. This process of projection and introjection, and the identification work that it achieves, is, moreover, not only creating the individual self, but its performance simultaneously creates the environment and resources for self-formation. It highlights some of the links between ethnography and psychoanalysis (Bondi 2003).

This 'pro-jection' of self is especially interesting, sociologically, when it involves conscious or desired identity-transformation. For example, as an 'inmate' of some sphere of my everyday life, I might wish to be 'taken more seriously' or to improve my standing with some social group, thought to be 'normal' and so on. Or you, as my friend, teacher or therapist, might think that I would benefit from this improvement. In either of these cases, if I or we take steps to facilitate this movement, I will need to find *a way of moving* from A to B, and that way of moving can be understood, both prospectively and retrospectively, to consist of path-making activity.

It is the study of these ways of moving that my colleagues at BRIGHT and I are investigating, in particular how music provides resources for the forging of these pathways. So, for example, when Robbie performs himself musically, in the persona of Billie Holiday, and when, after the performance ends, he remains half in role, employing verbally an echo of Holiday's musical manner, he has found a modus operandi that transfers from making music to performing self through the medium of spoken interaction. He has found a social vehicle for getting into and through a situation. Or when two or more participants co-ordinate their musical activities, they are entering into a shared temporal and spatial world and simultaneously developing skills that can be applied to extra-musical settings. Indeed, the very point of BRIGHT music is to provide yet another medium within which self may be projected and – outside of BRIGHT – converted into extra-musical resources with which to build bridges to the worlds and identities that lie outside BRIGHT's walls. So, for example, if I can acquire the knack of presenting myself musically, perhaps even forging a musical identity indexed by some regularity of style, repertoire and persona, I have developed my more general skill of sustaining a self[2] through the mastery of competences in one form of medium. At the very least, as we have seen repeatedly at BRIGHT, this musical success will boost my confidence, which itself will serve as a resource for the way of moving I might be seeking to achieve somewhere else.

So musical performance is a means for resource generation, a way of generating materials for the sustenance and development of self. Thus, when I go to another social gathering tomorrow, I can talk about my musical hobby or interest and, if only to myself, recall that I did well there yesterday. In doing this, I am converting my musical activity into something extra-musical – a topic of conversation. By doing so, I have just pro-jected or 'spread' my self or presence across two days and two spaces. I have expanded my self by tapping the resource that I created for myself via my musical projection of self. Thus, like laying down pavement, in collaboration with others I can pave

---

[2] There may be many kinds of self at stake here. It is also important to note that self-sustenance is not synonymous with 'quality of performance'. For example, it matters less that I am able to do a good 'imitation' of, say, Billie Holiday, than that I am able to convert my performance into my 'own' repertoire of self-presentation, to appropriate some of her signature skills for new purposes. Key here is the degree of transferability and adaptation – the product to be crafted is not music, but person.

the way to expanded and changed identities and associated health-states, paving block by paving block, as it were.

## The ethics of identity – taking a stand

As Goffman suggested, it is through various cultural media that the self is registered as an 'object' for and in relation to others. For Goffman (1968 (1961): 168), the 'moral career of the mental patient' involved, as he put it, 'a standard sequence of changes in his way of conceiving of selves, including, importantly, his own'. Goffman continues in this vein by suggesting that this process consists of 'half buried lines of development [that] can be followed by studying … happenings which mark a turning point in the way in which the person views the world' (1968 (1961): 168). The methodology Goffman implicitly advocates for illuminating these processes consists of a focus on the *stands* that individuals take 'before specifiable others, whatever the hidden and variable nature of his inward attachment to these presentations' (1968 (1961): 168). By noting these 'stands', Goffman suggests, it is possible to 'obtain a relatively objective tracing of relatively subjective matters' (1968 (1961): 168).

Within BRIGHT such 'stands' are taken by mobilising publicly available musical resources (repertoires, performance styles) in ways that illuminate the external materials through which apparently 'subjective' or 'inner' psychic space is constituted. Indeed, the expectation of stand-taking is part of BRIGHT's tacit ethic. The 'solo slot' in BRIGHT's structure can be understood as a 'non-therapeutic therapy'. A requirement for action (solo-singing with Gary's tacit support) allows clients to put *themselves* in situations where they 'pull themselves together' in a public situation (similar to a karaoke or amateur music association concert) while being able to stand outside the trappings of the therapeutic encounter, the 'sick role' and the client–therapist relationship. The key issue here is that these 'community music therapy' practices, and the client–therapist roles they configure (deconstructing those roles in fact), highlight what all of us in the setting have in common: 'we are making music here today and will do next week', for example.

Gary knows who he can rely upon to get the ball rolling at the start of BRIGHT events for, in the conventional sense of musical skill (singing in tune, in rhythm with a penetrating voice – these values are, of course, always open to contestation at BRIGHT and elsewhere), there is a wealth of talent at BRIGHT: for example, Trevor, who strides in from the basement garden like the star he is, shouldering his way, as it were, to the stage. Trevor sings one of what Gary calls 'the diva songs' (e.g. Elton John's 'Candle in the Wind') or an old group favourite (e.g. The Beatles' song 'Hey Jude'). The custom is to applaud after each solo. While we do so, Trevor heads back to the garden, as if he is already late for another important engagement. We are still clapping after he has, as it were, left the arena.

Other members, such as Lawrence, tend to be called upon once the session is in full swing, and provide a kind of artistic 'peak' in this socio-musical topology. A trim and neatly dressed pensioner, Lawrence offers one or two new songs that he has practised for this occasion. He hands Gary the chosen sheet music (mostly light salon classics or classic ballads and folk tunes – 'A Nightingale Sang in Berkeley Square', or 'Old Man River'). Lawrence's performances are quasi-choreographed, hand and arm gestures reminiscent of the recital stage, lieder performance and opera. His classical music voice is always greeted with enthusiastic applause.

Not everyone offers solo song performances: Hermione, for example, whom I have mentioned already, me (and not merely because I am a 'researcher' but also because I am an unskilled singer and uncomfortable singing in front of a mic!) and, at age 87, gamine Maggie, a member of the public and friend of one of the clients who comes because she enjoys these afternoons. Though we would be unlikely to sing solo, each of us contributes in our way and in ways that are 'meaningful' to us, however small or infrequent our acts. In my own case, I feel I 'perform' through a quiet and (I like to think!) judicious use of the rhythm sticks (I happen to like their 'woody sound' – a topic that could of course be explored), and through my attempts to be helpful and chatty (or a good listener) at teatime (which is by no means to say I am perceived this way by others). Hermione also has a role (as tambourinist, described above) and Maggie is a true sport: although she does not sing, she can be counted on to keep energy and motivation levels up – even dancing in the aisles on one occasion (to our collective cheers).

Then there are those new or less secure performers (of which I would no doubt be one, if I were ever to venture forth onto solo territory myself) whose musical activity needs considerable support. Here is where we see the 'therapy of non-therapy'. On these occasions, the concept of musical 'accompaniment' is brought to the fore and it is possible to see Gary's considerable craft – both as a musician and music therapist. That craft enables him to move adroitly from musical foreground to background, to lend musical and social support when it is called for, and to preserve all the while an aura of a non-therapeutic situation, a time in which 'nothing' is happening except that people are making music and having fun. This juggling act is complex, virtuosic and self-effacing – as, to a much lesser extent, is our own as participant members of 'the audience', clapping, commenting, cheering, encouraging, with the promise of musical support (the chorus) always on tap.

Take Andrew, for example: an elderly man, he has to be gently coaxed up to sing and when he does, he almost always chooses the same song. His voice wavers and sometimes cracks in the upper register. Gary does what he can to help, singing along, playing the melodic line emphatically to keep Andrew on track when he falters, cueing the rest of us to join in, and when he excels, cueing the rest of us to drop out (so as to highlight Andrew's 'best practice'). In addition, Gary modulates, if required to follow a singer's pitch shifts, makes use of shifts in tempo or dynamics, ornaments or rhythmic figures, and does many other things as required in order to shepherd a singer, musically, from the start to the ('successful') end of a complete performance. After Andrew finishes, we clap. I say to him, as he sits down next to me, that I enjoyed his performance (to me, and for whatever reasons, personal or professional, his voice is poignantly beautiful) and he flushes with obvious pleasure and smiles warmly.

In the next phase of our work at BRIGHT, we will follow individuals as they sculpt and navigate this musical space; how their pathways through and away from it alter over time is a topic of ongoing research. We are also considering how traversals of musical space in turn provide resources for ventures outside the musical space, ventures that perhaps drag new things back into the musical space (and thus provide highly grounded case studies in creative cultural innovation). In this way, musical repertoires and skills provide resources for extra-musical ones, and vice versa. To be able to function in numerous parts of this space, I suggest, is to be in possession of a wide cultural repertoire. And a repertoire in turn affords opportunities for experience in common, for community. These opportunities are, simultaneously, the means for social mobility, understood here as the ability to traverse varied socio-musical terrain. There are transferable skills involved in this process, namely learning the knack of deploying a flexible self. For this informal learning, music is both a practice medium and the message, a way of opening the self out and into participatory action with others.

## The 'triple time' (and multiple spaces) of a musical event

To be able to explore this question from, as it were, the 'inside' of interaction over time, I have been using the concept of the musical event, developed in previous work (Figure 12.2).

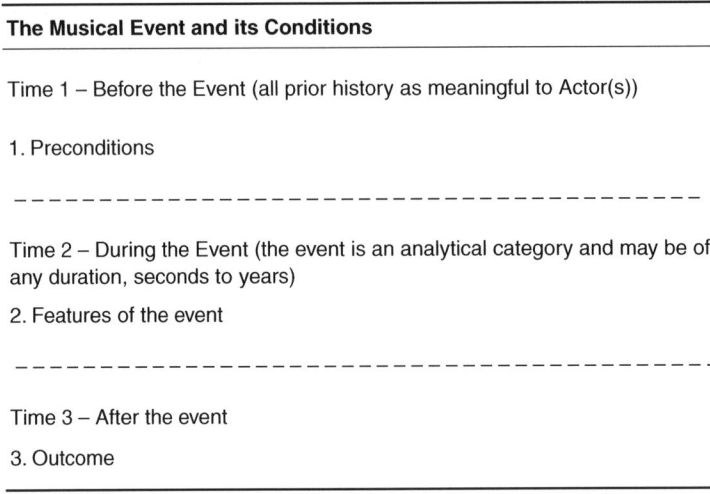

Figure 12.2  The musical event (from DeNora 2003)

The musical event provides a schema for following how 'doing things with music' draws together three time phases. The first of these (Time 1) is *the past*. Things past include everything/anything associated by an individual with music prior to the present moment. This set of associations includes personal associations and memories, tastes and past musical practices. For example, at BRIGHT it includes prior involvement in one-on-one music therapy sessions. The past also includes impersonal, generic and conventional associations between music, action and reception, such as the set of musical forms, genres and styles (as understood by actors) and the prior collective, organisational or institutional histories of the use of these forms, genres and styles.

The second time phase (Time 2) is *the present*, when people are performing, talking about, listening to or writing about music. What is paired with music and how, when and where is this pairing done and with reference to what other things? So, for example, as described above, how might a song be paired with a particular stylistic rendering and/or how might it also be paired with talk about that rendering or talk about the song?

Finally, the third time phase (Time 3) is *the future*. At some later time (for example, in talk about a BRIGHT performance after a session, a follow-on performance or some situation outside of BRIGHT entirely) something happens that can be shown to be linked in some way to the musicking. To take a simple example, one hears a snippet of music in a shop, it evokes memories, one goes home and looks through an old photograph album, which in turn leads one to write a letter to a distant relative.

Here, the musical event schema may be of service in tracing the ways in which the musical 'stands' taken by individuals do or do not result in transformations of the musical space, relations within that space and/or individuals' capacities for traversing space and converting musical into extra-musical resources. To illustrate these themes, consider the following fictionalised BRIGHT member, Peter, within this schema:

**Time One ('before'):** Peter has earlier spoken to Rob (the research assistant on the pilot for this research project) of his love for Scottish folk music, which, when growing up in Scotland, his grandmother used to sing to him. He values BRIGHT, he says, because it provides a place where these songs can be shared.

**Time Two ('during'):** Peter is up at the mic, describing a song, 'The Bonny Earl of Murray'. He shows a tartan-covered booklet of songs, brought from home. His performance is a bit of a struggle and Gary's role as musical shepherd is now fully apparent (though not obtrusive). Peter finishes his performance and we duly applaud.

**Time Three ('after'):** Peter has already told Rob in interview that he feels 'pleased with [him]self' after he performs. Some weeks later Barbara comes up to the mic. She announces her song (which Peter has often offered us), 'The Flowers of Edinburgh'. Peter's face lights up. He gets up, joins Barbara at the mic, which she unhooks from the stand so it can be held between them, and she asks if he would sing it with her. They sing together, sharing mic and sheet music. It appears very companionable. The music has visibly – if only for this one occasion – drawn them together. They have 'performed' their bond through the medium of their duet and the musical affiliation that it signified. The small corner of musical space devoted to Scottish folk music has just been ever-so-slightly expanded, now big enough for at least the two of them to stand shoulder to shoulder as new musical allies.

Thus, Peter's persistence in his desire to 'air' the songs he loves has paid off, albeit in a small way. His music is now a small part of shared BRIGHT musical space and, by association, he is therefore more deeply integrated into the space that, reflexively, he has helped to make through his musical performance. The space has become, in other words, more hospitable to Peter's future performances, and thus to Peter. Meanwhile, Barbara has expanded her musical competences and added to her repertoire this new Scottish song, 'The Flowers of Edinburgh'. A musical competence provides a pathway to a social link, and the social link consolidates the musical con-nection between Peter and Barbara: what they have in common, musically speaking. Through these connections, forged in real musical/social time through performance, their musical trails converge and the space allocated to folk music at BRIGHT grows a little.

The schema of the musical event, albeit heuristic (since exactly where does one event end and another begin, and where is the boundary between present moment and past?), is helpful nonetheless in highlighting the mechanisms by which places (physical and social spaces and their personnel) and/or psycho-cultural spaces (the internal geography of reminiscence, mood, reverie) may be understood as health-promoting (or health-demoting) through what they afford. The schema of the event also highlights BRIGHT as a collaboratively produced, collaboratively supported musical workspace (DeNora 1986) in which, to paraphrase John Austin (1962), things can be done with music.

## Conclusion

BRIGHT's health-promotional ambience is achieved and constantly renewed through what it can be made to afford. There would appear, at BRIGHT, to be no automatic connection between music, agency and affordance. Rather, affordances must be found and made manifest within a space. This activity is creative and collaborative. It is put together by BRIGHT's actors using BRIGHT's musical resources and supported by the music therapeutic team working as musical mentors. BRIGHT is, in other words, a space in which its participants can be seen to be engaged in paving pathways to and extending selves through a series of often-minute 'happenings which mark a turning point', in Goffman's (1968 (1961): 168) phrase. These 'happenings' at BRIGHT in the form of musical 'stands' – that is, the display of musical personas and musical affiliations – provide the building materials for 'moral careers'.

The musical stands taken at BRIGHT are, as I described above, the traceable outward manifestations of an otherwise inaccessible process (though one that is by no means simply 'internal' to the individual). They show us identification work: the ways in which selves are achieved (performed) through the couplings of individuals and materials – in this case, music (DeNora 1999; Hennion 2007). How these stands come to be remembered or, perhaps more accurately, how they provide fragments or remnants of self, building materials that prompt and draw out stances and dispositions – embodied (as they develop into *habitus* or mobile bodily dispositions (DeNora 2000; Delamont and Stephens 2008)) and conceptual (DeNora 2011) – is how agency and culture are co-performed. The former taps the resources of the latter, and in so doing, the latter comes to be constituted as the field or matrix for agency and self *in situ.*

For example, a musical persona, cultivated over time through solo musical display, may provide a modus operandi for embodied conduct and for the prosodic and paralinguistic features of spoken communication (as when, for example, one speaks in a style commensurate with a musical persona (e.g. Billie Holiday)) and for the production of continuous self-identity (as, for example, when one moves from setting to setting by thinking about how one 'is' or rather 'is like' Billie Holiday in manner). Or a musical structure may provide a template against which imagery or conceptual recognition occurs, when extra-musical matters are mapped on to (or led by) music's parameters in time and space, perhaps best exemplified in the Bonny Method of Guided Imagery and Music (GIM), a therapeutic technique where a client listens to music and, with support from a therapist, imagines visual imagery in ways that map on to the music's structures and materials (DeNora 2000, 2003, 2011).

In offering health-situations, BRIGHT also offers object lessons, as described at the outset of this chapter, in the concept of musical community and musical democracy, pragmatically conceived. BRIGHT musicking offers a flexible socio-musical space, one that is not dedicated to any single 'adequate mode of listening' (or performing) (Stockfelt 1997), while still managing to sustain a sense of an overall BRIGHT attitude or umbrella aesthetic of musical value and musical production/reception conventions. The range of appropriate or 'adequate' modes is wide, and that width is an important feature of BRIGHT's aesthetic culture.

From another perspective, BRIGHT is a space in the sense that Bourdieu (1985) has described, one in which individual and group habitus is asserted and developed. It is certainly not, however, the zero-sum-game-based, hierarchical and economic vision of space typically associated with Bourdieu (1985), in which spatial properties confer 'strength' on their holders in relation to others in a social economy. Rather, and in contrast to Bourdieu's vision, BRIGHT's space is encomiastic not economic; it is a place where many varied – indeed, in other contexts, possibly contradictory – musical 'goods' may be valued and respected, a place where aesthetic worth can be compounded rather than distributed according to some zero-sum-game-based scheme. Honour, praise and applause, indeed the very concept of what is 'good', are all constantly under revision and configured with reference to their contexts and histories of production such that even the shakiest of renditions can and is often beheld as a moment of beauty. There is no aesthetic waste: within BRIGHT's musical shelter (and beyond, to the extent that it is beheld) this is 'good music'. There is pleasure in observing each other succeed at the mic, and pleasure, too, in being able to describe how BRIGHT performed on stage at a different location and as part of a 'proper' concert.

Finally, BRIGHT is also a space in which a fragile power (music) is powerful *because* of its fragility, its dependence upon local generation and maintenance. This local production is also the feature that distinguishes BRIGHT as not merely a socio-musical space but a socio-musical *community*, one in which everyone feels obliged to take a 'turn at the pump' – albeit 'each according to his [or her] ability', and one in which 'the pump' is aesthetically flexible. To behold BRIGHT's sustainable, indeed resourceful generation and allocation of aesthetic media, and its culture of music appreciation, is to locate a perspective in which the sociological study of identity and well-being, the therapeutic crafting of self through music and the ordinary decencies of mutual respect, care and kindness are aligned with seemingly mundane forms of pleasure and joy.

# 13 | Towards an acoustemology of detention in the 'global war on terror'

SUZANNE G. CUSICK

It is now a well-established fact that 'loud music' has been systematically used as an element of detention and 'harsh interrogation' in the archipelago of prisons that United States authorities have operated in the so-called 'global war on terror'. Jocular or bemused press accounts and creepy parlour games (online and off) about compiling ideal 'torture playlists' have given way to increasingly nuanced accounts based on the statements of released prisoners, their interrogators and their guards.[1] Along with declassified documents from the United States' Department of Defense and Central Intelligence Agency, these statements allow us to begin piecing together a narrative of how 'loud music' and other manipulations of the acoustical environment have been used in specific locations, as well as a narrative of the effects that prison authorities understood such manipulations to have. We now know that 'loud music' and other sounds were to produce officially sanctioned if debilitating effects on prisoners believed to have high-value intelligence. 'Loud music' was, for example, one of several means to produce sleep deprivation. Like 'gender manipulation' and often in tandem with it, 'loud music' was sanctioned as part of a 'futility approach' to interrogation, meant to persuade prisoners of their interrogators' omnipotence. Whether as part of a prison's soundscape or as part of a particular prisoner's individualised interrogation plan, loud Western music could be a medium for delivering cultural and religious affront. Thanks to the meticulous research of Alfred McCoy, Jane Mayer, Michael Otterman and others, we believe that all these uses of 'loud music' are part of a larger congeries of interrogation techniques developed from psychological research on sensory manipulation sponsored by Anglophone security services in the 1950s and codified in the early 1960s in a now-declassified interrogation manual for CIA operatives, known as Kubark.[2] We further believe that these techniques, long officially repudiated, crept into the standard operating procedures for prisons in the current 'war on terror' because the United States

---

[1] Not all early press accounts were jocular. For serious press accounts, see especially Bayoumi 2005, Peisner 2006, 2009 and Sharrock 2008. For a preliminary account of jocular responses in the blogosphere, see Cusick 2006.

[2] See McCoy 2006, Mayer 2008, Otterman 2007, Worthington 2007 and Cusick 2008: 1–26.

had continued to train some military personnel to resist them, in a training programme known as SERE.[3]

Indeed, we know so much about the use of 'loud music' as a form of what some writers call 'torture lite' that we can easily think we know it all. Yet there are at least three things about this practice that, I think, we do not yet understand. We do not understand how, exactly, manipulations of the acoustical environment might actually achieve the explicit goal of 'harsh interrogation' as advocated by its authors in the Kubark manual – the destruction of prisoners' subjectivities. We do not know how the sheer power of loud music's acoustical energy, forcing prisoners' very bodies to vibrate sympathetically with their enemies' tunes, might contribute to that destruction. Nor do we yet appreciate the relationship between the targeted use of acoustical violence against prisoners believed to have high-value intelligence and the evidence that ubiquitous audio surveillance was an equally important part of these prisons' soundscapes. As a result, we are not yet able to think well about how prison authorities have manipulated the acoustic as a force field of power.

This chapter will begin to address these gaps. Drawing on the first-person accounts of former prisoners, I show how manipulations of the acoustic disrupted prisoners' use of hearing and vocalisation both to locate themselves in intelligible worlds and to create relationships with those worlds. It is this disruption of ordinary relationality that produces the desired destruction of subjectivity. Further, I show that a focus on hearing, vocalisation and psychological trauma is insufficient to explain the violence of what one former prisoner called 'the music programme'. The destruction of prisoners' subjectivities partly depends on the acoustically and philosophically salient fact that manipulations of the acoustical environment always produce the somatic effect of sympathetic vibration. Always compelled by the physical properties of sound to vibrate in their very bones with those sounds, the prisoners subjected to the music programme have no choice but to become, themselves, the characteristic sounds of their captors. This is, I argue, an ultimate violence that batters prisoners' bodies, shatters (however temporarily) the capacity to control the acoustical relationality that is the foundation of subjectivity and blasts away all sense of privacy, leaving in its place a feeling of paradoxically unprivate isolation.

The first-person accounts on which I will draw are those of four men who were imprisoned by the United States authorities for periods ranging from

---

[3] SERE is an acronym that stands for 'Survive–Evade–Resist–Escape'. See Mayer 2008 for more on the relationship of SERE training to detention conditions at Guantanamo.

ninety-seven days to six years.[4] Ranging in age from their late twenties to their late forties, all have spent most of their lives in the West; although they come from widely disparate class backgrounds, all have been to university. All have spoken English most of their lives, and all now describe themselves as religious, although not all of them were at the time of their capture. All have been released without charges, although also without explicit exoneration, and all now spend some of their time protesting against the conditions of detention and interrogation that they experienced. I contacted each of them initially through the individual, firm or agency that represents their legal interests. Our wide-ranging conversations took place in person, on the phone and via e-mail. Each man agreed that I could use the substance of those conversations in my published scholarly work. To preserve their privacy, I have not used these men's names here, nor have I included details of their imprisonment that would make it easy to identify them. With the same intention to preserve their privacy, I have tried to minimise direct quotations. Although it might have been more efficient to organise my argument around the common themes shared by these men's narratives of imprisonment, I have chosen to present each man's story separately, in a rhetorical effort to respect the right each has to subjectivity.

In the time that has elapsed since my conversations with these men, I have tried to hear their memories of their imprisonment's soundscape through two frameworks for thinking about human acoustical experience that circulate in contemporary common sense. Although these frameworks have equally distinguished intellectual pedigrees (in psychology, philosophy and acoustemology), they are seldom combined in musicological thought. Yet the accounts of my four interlocutors suggest that both are necessary to understanding the acoustical practices of detention in the 'war on terror'.

The first of these is the now classical notion that human subjectivity is produced through the interaction of sensory reception and sensorily perceptible response. In terms of the acoustic, people who hear perceive our senses' reception of some vibrations around us as sounds. We process those sounds as information about our own and other entities' location in space, coming to associate some sounds with danger, others with sources of food

---

[4] It needs to be said that in some ways acoustical manipulations might seem to have been the least of these men's troubles in detention. Horrible things happened to them during their captivity, including direct physical brutality that left permanent organ damage and a wide range of psychologically damaging humiliations. They themselves, however, argue that the psychological harm accomplished by 'torture lite' ought to be considered, if anything, more horrible than physical harm. As one man said to me, 'if what is happening to you is making you lose your self, lose your senses, lose your thought process, then that's it. After that, you're gone. You're *gone*.'

and nurture. Thus do we turn space into place, and place into intelligible, navigable worlds. Eventually, we make sounds ourselves, in response to the sounds we hear and in an effort to act on and in the worlds our hearing has helped us to map. Through the interaction of our vocalised sound-making with the sounds we hear other entities make, we are interpellated in a symbolic order, into language and into social relations with the other hearing entities who make sound. The ability to control our interventions in our acoustic environment, as a way of creating and controlling the relationship of our selves to all manner of others, is fundamental to subjectivity as it is commonly construed. Moreover, that same ability is the premise for liberal claims both to the privacy of our individual thoughts (our right to remain silent) and to the universal right to share those thoughts freely in a public sphere.

Dense with explanatory power though it is, this framework is marred by both anthropocentricity and what Teresa Brennan (2004: 14) called a foundational fantasy of self-containment. It so foregrounds human hearing and vocalisation as nearly to erase the acoustical fact on which it is based, namely that all human beings, whether hearing or not, are immersed in a vibrating world. Vibrations that human ears cannot perceive, nor human brains process, nonetheless affect our bodies.[5] We vibrate sympathetically with other entities in our environments, as they do with us. It is our own sympathetic vibrations (mostly in the small bones of our heads) that we describe as sound. Thus, we are never quite as separate from other vibrating entities as the narrative of the first framework implies. Instead, we exist in something like a continuous feedback loop of vibrations, an environment dense with what philosopher Jean-Luc Nancy (2007) calls the 're-soundings' *by* all the vibrating entities in a space *of* all the vibrating entities in that space.[6]

How might we imagine that this notion of our immersion in an always already mutually vibrating world could interact with an anthropocentric notion of subjectivity to produce a second, vibration-centred framework? In a vibration-centred understanding of the acoustic, both privacy and isolation are necessarily illusions, because we are all always literally in touch with each other through our shared vibrations. Further, in this understanding

---

[5] One need only think about the barely audible, high-frequency sounds used to discourage adolescents from loitering at shopping malls, or about the life-threatening effects of infrasound on internal organs. One excellent survey of the literature on music as sound that discusses both examples is Johnson and Cloonan 2009: 13–30.

[6] Enrica Lisicani Petrini's introduction to *All'ascolto* (Nancy 2004), the Italian edition of Nancy's *Listening* (2007), gives a helpful synopsis of the relationship of Nancy's acoustemological ideas to his broader philosophical concern with the relationship of individuals in the community.

the call-and-response dynamic that characterises the anthropocentric theory of subject formation must be understood as always enacted in counterpoint to a ground of ongoing, mutually sympathetic vibrations. In effect,
the call-and-response drama of subject formation and interpellation would
have to be understood as always a shaping of the intensity and degree of
reciprocity with which the entities in a given space touch and retouch each
other. The dynamic created by the shifting intensities of these touchings
constitutes the field of power in which differentiated degrees of agency,
autonomy, presence and relationality are produced. When condensed into
mutually intelligible gestures that humans can combine, recombine, recognise and repeat, and then systematised, these differentiations constitute
the mostly audible symbolic systems that we use to create the apparently
necessary illusion that we are subjects with a modicum of control over the
content and direction of our private (inaudible) thoughts, over the audible
sounds we make to define boundaries between ourselves and other vibrating entities, and over the relationships (audible and not) we have with each
other.

Nearly all the released prisoners who have written or spoken about the
role of music in their detention have reached a point where their powers of
narration cannot articulate the music's effects. They can say only something
like 'I don't have the words to describe it', or 'It makes you feel as if you're
going mad.' The vividly remembered moment before which their effort at
language fails seems to me very like the moment of ruptured subjectivity
described in the erstwhile CIA interrogation manual known as Kubark:

> There is an interval – which may be extremely brief – of suspended animation, of
> psychological shock or paralysis. It is caused by a traumatic or subtraumatic experi-
> ence which explodes, as it were, the world that is familiar to the subject as well as
> his image of himself within that world.[7]

I try below to use both the anthropocentric and the vibration-centred
frameworks to interpret these unspeakable moments in my interlocutors'
accounts. That effort has led me to notice that each account includes evidence that the use of sound in the harassment, interrogation or punishment
of prisoners in United States' custody always took place under conditions
in which the usual distinction between private and public was elided. This
elision complemented the disruption of patterned acoustical behaviours by

---

[7] Central Intelligence Agency 1962: 65. The declassified parts of the manual can be consulted
or downloaded at the online National Security Archive maintained by George Washington
University.

which hearing, vocalising human beings could be expected to establish and maintain the relationship with the world that we call subjectivity.

## 'It's devastating': acoustical harassment at Camp Cropper

In one way, Z's account of four months at Baghdad's Camp Cropper[8] would seem most susceptible to analysis from a vibration-centred approach. For Z's experience there of what he calls 'the music programme' was shared by all the prisoners in the section of Camp Cropper's prison reserved for people believed to have high-value intelligence. Large speakers at the entryways to the prison's high-value section ensured that both sides of the building would hear the same music.[9] Thus, prison authorities ensured that every body in that space would vibrate sympathetically, every day, to sounds that produced power's presence as a palpable, physical force. However isolated each prisoner was in his individual cell, each was denied by the ubiquitous, shared music any illusion that enforced solitude could grant him privacy. The music obviated any effort to distinguish between public and private space in the block. More, it wreaked havoc with prisoners' efforts to sustain the mutuality of acoustical agency that characterises the permeable boundary of a healthy subjectivity.

The ubiquitous, shared music also disrupted prisoners' ability to use the acoustical behaviours of hearing and vocalisation to maintain relationships with their environments in which they could feel a modicum of control. Z remembers that he spent hours on his knees, pressing his ears to the door of his cell to capture what he called 'outside' sounds. He remembers both what he heard and what his mind made of it. Voices, sometimes conversations, sometimes guards calling out the number of a prisoner who was to be taken to interrogation, the squeak of the cart that brought meals at irregular intervals by which he tried to tell the time of day. The loud ticking or popping sound, 'like a BB gun', that told him the guards were practising with their Taser guns on a plastic dummy in the hall. The hollow steel doors of other men's cells slamming shut, 'doof, doof', when they were taken to or

---

[8]  Camp Cropper is one of several facilities operated by the United States Department of Defense at Baghdad International Airport. From 2003 to 2007 it functioned as the US Army's central booking facility for the city, and included at least one block dedicated to 'high-value detainees (HVDs)'. Z was held in the HVD block for four months before being released without charges.

[9]  My conversations with Z took place by email and by telephone in late 2006 and 2007. All quotations are from the emails, or from my transcriptions of our phone conversations, and are used with permission.

returned from interrogation, a sound that to Z seemed to repeat what he already knew to be true: 'We control the door, you're not going anywhere.' The daily calls to prayer, continuing in spite of the music and in spite of the guards' verbal heckling of prisoners as they prayed. Z self-consciously used these sounds to create a mental image of the environment beyond his cell – a mental image, that is, that would transform unknowable space into an imaginable world.

Mostly, though, Z remembers the music, blaring down the corridor all day, every day, for twelve or fifteen hours at a time, so loud that the guards posted at either end could not communicate with each other. When the music was on, he could not hear the environmental cues that allowed his imagination to turn space into place and place into a world where he could map his own location. He could not hear other prisoners' talk. Indeed, sometimes he could not hear the sound of his own voice. Thus for Z, as for all the other prisoners in the high-value section, the long, daily blasts of music frustrated one of the fundamental acoustical practices by which sub-jectivity is sustained. Z and everyone else in his section were daily forced to reconstitute the imaginary map that attentive hearing of ambient sounds could allow them to form of the environment outside their cells. That is, they were daily forced to use the time when the music was silent to recon-stitute one element of subjectivity as classically conceived.

At first, Z found the music 'just annoying; then it became something else. I realised it was a war of wills, a personal attack against me, they were trying to harm me.' He had heard that the way to resist what he called 'the music programme' was to talk to yourself; so he did. All day, every day, for as long as the music played, often with his fingers in his ears so that he could hear himself, Z would tell himself stories, tell himself jokes to which he already knew the punchline, anything to keep control of his acoustical agency, his speech, his thoughts. When he exercised in the recreation yard with a friend from his country who was also held in the high-value block, Z talked to him and to the guards that watched them. 'I would talk about anything with the guards', Z remembers, even though he knew that any-thing he said would be shared with his interrogators. Such resistance was hard work, because the kind of music being played 'jumped' unpredictably among hard rock, country and rap.[10] It was especially hard when he heard

---

[10] Z noted that, in Baghdad, Armed Forces Radio quite predictably played hard rock in the mornings, country music in the afternoons and rap in the evenings. I conjecture, therefore, that the stylistic jumping may have been intended quite straightforwardly to confuse prisoners' temporality, as well as any kind of entrainment that would have allowed them to 'groove' to the ambient music.

a song he had known outside, before his capture, because then Z could find himself singing along, and that, he said, 'just once again began destroying me'. Fatigue and hunger could distract him from the work of vocalised resistance, too. Z described how it felt when his attention to the work of resistance through speech would flag thus: 'Boom, it hits you.' Asked to elaborate, he said simply, 'It's devastating', but he was hard pressed to say what had been devastated.

Z's recourse to constant vocalising in the presence of the music would seem to have been an assertion of subjectivity in the face of an acoustically overwhelming environment. In a way, his talk replicated the vocalising action of an emerging subject who sought to establish both a boundary to the self and relationality with the other based on controlled, mutually responsive interventions in the acoustical environment. But this fundamental pattern of subject formation was distorted. The sheer loudness, ubiquity and mechanised unpredictability of what Z called 'the goddamn blaring music' forced him to try not to hear it and to turn instead ever more desperately into himself, mining his memories for the content of a talking intended only to produce self-preservation, not the call-and-response relationship with the world that characterises well-formed subjectivity. Thus, even when Z's recourse to constant talk seemed successful to him, as resistance, he was daily rehearsing a drama of damaged subject formation and daily unlearning the pattern of healthy subject formation. When Z's efforts to sustain his talk and thus sustain that damaged subjectivity failed, there was nothing left. Devastated, the former subject known as Z had to gather the fragments of his shattered self and try to enact the fundamental drama of subject formation again, and again, and again. Even as the very bones of his and every other body in the high-value block vibrated with the implacable music that elided any difference between the block's public and private space, the music intended to shatter their subjectivities and leave them helpless, in shared isolation.

## 'It makes you feel like you're going mad': the interrogation of X at Guantanamo

X is the only person with whom I have spoken who experienced loud music in direct connection with his interrogation.[11] His is therefore an account of

---

[11] My conversation with X took place in 2009; all quotations are either from the recording of that conversation that he allowed me to make, or from a video interview that circulated online in 2008. All are used with permission.

a highly individualised, targeted experience not shared by all prisoners of a certain type; it is also the account that most easily seems like a narrative of 'interrogational torture'.[12]

Although he was held at Guantanamo for about two years, X's experience of 'loud music' at Guantanamo was limited to the five or six months when he was suspected of having participated in the planning of the 9/11 attacks, or at least of knowing details of Al Qaeda planning norms that could have had very high intelligence value. During this period, X was kept in isolation and was subject to harsh interrogation. In his case, that meant he endured in alternation sessions of questioning and sessions in which stress positions, strobe lights and loud music were imposed on him because his claims of utter ignorance and innocence failed to satisfy his interrogators. Once authorities ascertained that he was, in fact, innocent of these particular charges, his harsh interrogation ended.

X was questioned in a small room furnished with a table and two chairs. When his answers failed to satisfy, the table and chairs would be removed, a strobe light and a music player would be moved in and he would be shackled to an iron ring in the floor in a stress position. The position imposed on him required him to squat with his weight on the tips of his toes, his arms beneath and behind his knees, and his wrists short-shackled to the floor behind his ankles so that he could not fall backward or to the side for relief or get his weight back off his toes. Once X was in place, the room's lights were turned out and the music – almost always hard rock or metal – would be turned on. His interrogators would leave him alone like that for intervals that ranged from about five minutes to, he thinks, three days – alone except for the sound, the lights and, if he were left there for a long time, the muscle cramps in his legs and the back pain that one would expect such a position to produce. In a videotaped interview after his release that circulated for a while on the internet, X explained that the main effect of the music was to prevent him from focusing his mind away from the physical pain, making that pain more vivid. X said of his inability to distract himself with his own thoughts, 'It makes you feel like you're going mad.' When X's interrogators decided that his session of music-accompanied pain was over, they returned, uncuffed him, turned the music and strobe off and the room

---

[12] I take the term from Gross 2010: 123. There, Gross distinguishes between 'interrogational torture', which is intended to elicit information and is therefore, in his view, sometimes justifiable, and 'terroristic torture', which is intended to brutalise or intimidate and is therefore never justifiable. Gross does not unambivalently address the moral dilemma of using interrogational torture on a person with no information to give, as was the case with X.

lights back on, then cuffed him again and marched him back to his isolation cell. Exhausted, he would fall asleep, only to awaken feeling

like crap … like you're not yourself … depressed … You think, hmm, hope it isn't going to happen again, but you know that it is going to happen again, and you're dreading for that time to come.

X's account makes it quite clear that he understood the addition of the music to the pain to have been what put his subjectivity under repeated, at least partially successful attack during these sessions. It was the music overwhelming the content of his consciousness that prevented him from turning inward to retrieve memories either for his own solace or for his next intervocal exchange with his interrogators. Thus the music disrupted X's effort to maintain the relationality on which subjectivity depends in a way somewhat different from the way it functioned for Z. Z's effort to resist sound with sound, however intermittently successful, forced him to turn in on himself for hours every day, and thus to learn a dysfunctional pattern for maintaining subjectivity that primed his sense of self for implosion when his concentration failed. X, by contrast, responded to his situation with one very common human response to pain: rather than resist sound with sound, he tried to resist pain with thought. Thought promised to move him out of himself, to a mental place where his self could transcend his body's experience of the pain. But when he tried to move outside of himself, into the mental space of transcendence, he encountered a space already so filled with music as to force his thoughts back to the pain, whence his thoughts would seek to escape again, only to be forced back to the pain again, over and over in a cycle of futility. His thoroughly dysfunctional alternation between mismatched registers of sensory experience – between what might have seemed like body and mind, sensation and thought – became an irreconcilable conflict between somatic and acoustic distress. The irreconcilability alone would have been more than enough to render X temporarily incapable of sustaining thought, or of sustaining in any register the several reciprocal relationships on which a healthy subjectivity usually depends.

The acoustically assisted jamming of X's access to his own thoughts was not the only disruption of the actions by which he might have sustained a sense of self. During the period of his harsh interrogation, he moved between a soundproofed interrogation room filled with music and a soundproofed isolation cell. Both environments prevented him from using cues from the acoustical environment to create a sense of place, and thus to locate himself in the world. Indeed, he said as much in his description of how he felt after a session: 'You feel like a zombie, you feel not in this world, you feel out of place.' But although his experience may have made him feel as though he were not in *this* world, he was definitely in *a* world. It was a world divided acoustically between the aggressively noisy and the silent, an acoustic dystopia over which he had no control and in which he could not even find solace in the privacy of his own thoughts. Moreover, it was a dystopia that he was forced to endure alone.

X was never really alone, of course, and the exaggeratedly vibrating presence of the music that his interrogators left in the room as their surrogate ensured that he would know it in spite of the absence of visible companions. The presence produced by the music produced, as well, a situation in which X could feel as though he were isolated, even abandoned during the session, while he could simultaneously feel in the acoustical pressure on his skin and the vibration of his bones the certainty that he was not alone. Indeed, although he did not understand it at first, he was both watched and videotaped during the stress-strobe-and-music sessions from behind a one-way mirror. Thus, the destruction of X's sense of interiority and relationality occurred in an environment that paradoxically combined elements of isolation and elements of public spectacle. His treatment was like a set of Chinese boxes of violation: the violation of interiority (his ability to concentrate on thoughts of his own choosing disrupted by sound) sat inside a violation of individuation (his body's inevitable sympathetic vibration to music he despised), which sat inside a violation of his privacy (his suffering's videotaped documentation), all of it to be endured alone, in an acoustical environment that made his own voice inaudible, and all of it a spectacle for the eyes of people not violated by the music. It is little wonder that such extreme violence against the components of subjectivity would have disrupted X's sense of himself as a self, as a subject who could engage in relations of reciprocity with his world. That was the point. Or perhaps the point was to interpellate him into an alternative symbolic order, one in which non-individuated persons without privacy would nonetheless feel not connected to others but isolated, even though they were palpably in the presence of an invisible other with the power to deny them access to their own thoughts.

## From the CIA's 'dark prison' to Guantanamo: the acoustical punishments of Y

As at Camp Cropper the presence of irresistibly vibrating music defined the space of the CIA's so-called 'dark prison'[13] near Kabul, eliding the distinction

---

[13] For the most recent published account of conditions at the dark prison, see Worthington 2009. My conversation with Y took place in 2009; all quotations are from the recording he allowed me to make, and are used with permission.

between public and private space to produce an experience of shared isolation that complemented the authorities' intended attack on each and every prisoner's subjectivity. But in the 'dark prison' conditions were far more extreme. Or so Y remembers it.

Y spent about a month in the 'dark prison' in 2002 without ever being interrogated.[14] According to him, prisoners there were kept in individual cells where the darkness was nearly absolute, where ambient temperatures were kept so low that prisoners huddled shivering in the corners of their cells and where very skimpy rations of food and water arrived at unpredictable intervals. Apart from the cold, the one consistent sensory stimulation for prisoners was the 'music', which Y described as 'not *music* music' but a set of 'very aggressive, intrusive, annoying sounds'. He heard these sounds over and over again, played as if in a continuous loop from speakers that seemed to him as if they were mounted near the ceiling of his cell and the ceiling of every other cell nearby. Eventually, Y began to repeat the sounds, even when, like Z at Camp Cropper, he had his fingers in his ears: 'they're not like proper words, but … you start repeating it yourself, you start talking with yourself like you've almost gone mad … repeating those sounds'. Not knowing, as Z had, that he could try to resist the ambient sound with talk of his own devising, and not having any other source for sensory stimulation, Y became, in effect, all ears. His subjectivity was overwhelmed by the music, absorbed into it. Or, to think about his experience in a vibration-centred way, Y's psychological resistance to his situation had collapsed, betrayed by his own body's constantly repeated re-sounding of the acoustical energy that filled his space.

Y came to believe that the 'music' came from something like a tape that needed to be turned over or otherwise restarted periodically. Every so often there would be a few seconds of silence, during which prisoners would call out to each other in the dark, hoping to receive an answering call that would let them know who else shared their condition. But the silence never lasted long enough for many calls to receive responses. The 'tape' would start up again, 'exactly the same sounds … loud enough that you literally can't hear yourself and you can't hear anybody else'. Unable to use his hearing to know or to construct a notion of the world around him; unable to hear his own or other's voices except in those brief, frustrating moments of unanswered cries; unable to resist the temptation to vocalise the sounds of his captors

---

[14] According to Gross's taxonomy of torture, cited in note 12, Y's treatment both at the 'dark prison' and at Guantanamo constituted instances of terroristic torture, intended not to elicit information but to brutalise.

that came from his own participation as a vibrating object in the acoustical world, Y was denied by the 'music' of the dark prison all ability to engage in a reciprocal relationship with his acoustical environment. Thus one of the most important means by which human subjectivity is constructed in the acoustic – the voluntary intervocal exchange of self with an other that leads to language and speech – was blocked for the duration of his stay. So, apparently, was his ability to think.

Nothing focused, in terms of, like, let me think now of, for example, a topic or a story. Nothing comes to your head; it's just that the experience you're going through is so intense … that it takes you away from everything else, everything else besides it.

After his month at the dark prison and a few more at the famously silent prison in Bagram, Y spent several years at Guantanamo, where he says he was interrogated hundreds of times.[15] He remembers that it was either when his interrogators wanted to punish him or when he tried publicly to object to elements of the prison's regime that he would be sent to the Romeo block of Guantanamo's Camp Delta, where he would be subjected to acoustical punishment.[16] His memories emphasise the physical effects of music there more than the psychological ones.

In Y's experience, speakers 'like you would see in a disco' or, in recent years, special cone-shaped speakers with a high degree of directionality would be placed directly outside a prisoner's cell, at a distance that could range from 'a few feet' to fifteen feet.[17] Y described the sound these speakers produced as 'very, very much louder, maybe ten-fold louder' than the sound that had filled the dark prison. When the sound in Romeo block would stop, Y would be unable to concentrate, focus or read. He described his mental disorientation by saying that he felt like a cat 'just turning in a spot, saying "What's going on? What's going on?"'

---

[15] The prison at Bagram Air Force Base near Kabul was not literally silent, of course; it was simply a place where prisoners were absolutely forbidden to speak or vocalise except during questioning and prayer. See Begg 2006: 137–9.

[16] The Romeo and Tango blocks consisted of isolation cells reserved for high-value or troublemaking prisoners. Online accounts of conditions in the Romeo block include the common report that all prisoners were stripped naked on arrival, then forced to wear only short pants that did not cover their knees. Because observant Muslim men are required to cover their knees during prayer, these prisoners were forced to lower their pants and expose their genitals as they prayed; it was a trick that neatly combined religious and sexual harassment. Romeo was the usual site for 'harsh interrogation'.

[17] Y also remembered that sometimes the acoustical intervention would be as simple as leaving a vacuum cleaner running outside someone's cell for hours on end.

Though less stark than Z's understated 'It's devastating' and less dramatic than X's 'You feel like you're going mad', Y's description of the music programme's psychological effect clearly points to a similar experience of what X matter-of-factly called psychological torture – that is, an experience clearly intended to disrupt human beings' reflexive ways of using acoustical behaviours to construct and sustain subjectivity. Y emphasised that the music programme as he experienced it at Guantanamo was physically as well as psychologically violent:

You feel like your body is being bombarded with something … Really, literally, so it was much more harmful [than the dark prison], physically, mentally, and intrusively … in Guantanamo the music affects your mind, your body, your senses … It's like you're being hit with a hammer, *din din din din*. When it stops, it's like a beating has stopped.

Y's words confirm something that most of us have known about the music programme all along. When music or other sounds are played loudly enough, on suitably designed and directed speakers, its sheer acoustical energy becomes a physical force in the world. It is no longer a metaphor for power, no longer only a medium by which prison authorities can reconfigure their wards' experiences of space and place so as to obviate any illusion of privacy, nor only a medium by which to distort their efforts to sustain subjectivity. Music becomes not a metaphor for power, but power itself, literally – a vibrating presence of power that can deliver a miraculously ubiquitous battering to the sympathetically vibrating bones and skin of a man, beating him from within and without, while leaving no marks. This, too, is a way of destroying a person's subjectivity, his sense of interior and exterior, private and public, a way of trying to reduce him to a vibrating object with its fingers in its ears.

## Acoustical monopoly

Whether ubiquitously battering individual prisoners from within and without, eliciting patterns of acoustical behaviour so aporetic or misdirected as to cause prisoners' subjectivities to implode, or jamming prisoners' efforts to hear their way into an understanding of space and place that could constitute a world, the sound effects directed at them by their captors stripped these prisoners of acoustical agency. But the production of intentionally harmful sound was not the only way that prison authorities established as absolute a monopoly on acoustical agency as they had on the right to food, water, temperature, sleep, access to personal hygiene, genital privacy or prayer. As Z was well aware, and as prisoners at Guantanamo only gradually came to realise, every sound a prisoner might produce was subject to acoustical surveillance. To put this another way, power in these prisons is not only a battering, disrupting, jamming voice. Power in these prisons is also an ear that, implacable, silences by the way that it hears.

A fourth former prisoner, W, remembers his shock at discovering that even conversations between prisoners and their lawyers at Guantanamo were overheard by prison officials.[18] Like Z, X and Y, W has spoken and read English most of his life, and as a result he often helped fellow prisoners read documents relevant to their cases. At some point, an American lawyer left a contraband document with his client: it was the document all lawyers there were required to sign, agreeing to this acoustical surveillance as a condition of their admission to the prison. Shocked that lawyers were, in effect, being required to do the work of interrogators, W suddenly understood why his fellow prisoners' confidences to their lawyers about their vulnerabilities would be followed so quickly by the exploitation of those very vulnerabilities. He understood, too, as Z had at Camp Cropper, that everything a prisoner might say in the recreation yard was overheard, either by guards or by listening devices. Thus everything a prisoner might think he had said in private was not private but public. Every vocal intervention in the acoustical environment that a prisoner might make could become a weapon against him.

The silencing effect of power's ubiquitous ear perfectly complements and completes the effects of power's voice in these prisons. Prison authorities' monopoly over the acoustic produces the presence of a ubiquitous but invisible power with which there can be no negotiating a mutuality of acoustical agency. Thus, even in the recreation yard, an apparently public and communal space where compliant prisoners were sure to be free of the 'music', the acoustic ecology created at Guantanamo ensured they would not have access to subjectivity as it is conceived in the anthropocentric model from which liberal Western notions of the politically private and public spheres derive. One might almost conclude that the acoustic ecology authorities have created at Guantanamo and elsewhere in the war on terror's prisons is designed to deny inmates access to *Western*, classically *liberal* forms of subjectivity and to encourage them to substitute for it patterns of subjectivity more in line with Western fantasies of an illiberal non-West.

---

[18] I spoke with W in 2009.

Such a conclusion, however, might also be both a bit too neat and a bit too narrow in its focus on acoustical practices that could be understood as mere exigencies of war. While they can be understood that way, I believe that the acoustical practices by which United States personnel have tried, in a time of war, to manipulate and manage prisoners' experiences of subjectivity must surely constitute evidence about contemporary belief. Moreover, I believe attention both to the practices and to the apparent beliefs behind them may have some predictive value. Many technologies of war, both mechanical and human, become civilian commonplaces in the subsequent peace. What, then, might we infer from the acoustical practices of detention in the war on terror about contemporary beliefs or emerging technologies of subjectivity?

It would seem that United States authorities believe that the acoustic is an extremely important register for the construction and sustaining of subjectivity, otherwise these authorities would not have concentrated their manipulations of detention's acoustic ecology on prisoners believed to have high intelligence value. Furthermore, and interestingly, it seems that these authorities' beliefs about the interaction of acoustical experience and subjectivity hover between the anthropocentric and the vibration-centred models, for these men's accounts suggest that each has been exploited successfully to inflict psychological harm (partly through physical means). Indeed, the acoustical policies of detention seem to depend more on the vibration-centred model than on the anthropocentric one.

Jean-Luc Nancy (2000) has tried to use the central fact of the vibration-centred model – that we live immersed in a vibrating world that keeps us all always already in constantly re-sounding touch with every other vibrating entity (human and not) – as the basis for imagining a post-liberal notion of human sociality. The dynamic of 'being singular plural' that he posits promises an appealing, even utopian alternative to the political formulations based on Enlightenment ideas such as 'individualism' and 'community' that wrought such havoc in the twentieth century's wars. Yet the acoustical practices of detention in the war on terror show that decidedly dystopian political possibilities are implicit in the vibration-centred model, as well. Whatever prison authorities may consciously believe, their practices produce prison populations that amount to a conglomeration of hearing, speaking people who do not hear, vocalise and co-create with each other an acoustical environment characterised by relationships of reciprocity between self and other, individual and collective, private and public. Isolated without ever being alone, palpably in the presence of an invisible presence with the power to reduce them to 'all ears' (like Y in the dark prison) or to vibrating objects (like Y in Guantanamo), denied both the privacy-based right to silence and the public right to free speech, these prisoners have experienced a preview of one very dark symbolic order that could logically follow from the possibility for stark differentiations of acoustical agency in the vibration-centred model. It is a symbolic order we would be wise to avoid.

## 14 | Faith, hope, and the hope of love: on the fidelity of the phonographic voice

RICHARD MIDDLETON

### Rufus, Judy and the politics of fidelity

The voice swoops and soars, traversing a space that conjoins tenor and alto registers, moving with a silky smoothness given a hint of gritty reality by a torch singer's throaty rasp (chest, throat and nose working throughout the range, apart from the occasional floated headnote). Constantly reaching for, gliding up to the pitch, working hard at the blue notes, suffusing the line with a wide, tremulous vibrato, this voice signals – or better, performs for us – an experience of intense feeling (the song concerns the discovery of love, its kisses, thrills and ecstasies). Moving from murmured beginnings, through a thrilling climax, to a dying close, it mimics the contours of the sexual encounter itself.

Hard to place, this voice, at least in terms of race and gender; but not in terms of musical genre. I'm listening to the extraordinary Rufus Wainwright (2007) singing the equally wonderful bluesy ballad by George and Ira Gershwin, 'How Long Has This Been Going On?' As an example of the ballad genre, there's nothing too out of the way about this one – other than the captivating quality of song and performance. Typically, we hear a man – it might just as easily have been a woman, as my description of the voice perhaps suggested; indeed, Wainwright's performance is a tribute to Judy Garland, and the concert from which his recording comes was an attempt to recreate Garland's celebrated Carnegie Hall concert of 1961 – typically, we hear a man singing about his feelings for a lover, or more exactly perhaps, the feelings stirred up in him by the love-event. In the world of popular song, we could hardly be more used to this. A little further reflection, though, might suggest how extraordinary this actually is. Here is someone, shaken to the marrow by the most personal, intimate emotion, choosing to shout about it in public – indeed, through the mediation of the phonographic form, to bare his soul to anyone who might hear the record. Of course, the idea that a love-song might be sung in public is hardly unique. But what is unusual, I think, is that in the popular ballad we identify the singer with the song, with a protagonist in the song, and we must believe that he is singing about himself, about real feelings; the success of the performance stands or falls on his sincerity; 'authenticity' – which we might also name as 'fidelity' – is the key trope that organises the discourse within which the music is understood.

Richard Sennett, in *The Fall of Public Man* (2002 (1977)), has given us the basic tools to explain this phenomenon historically. For Sennett, with Marx and Weber behind him, the culture of the public sphere in the nineteenth and especially the twentieth centuries becomes empty, formulaic, alienated, as the mechanisms previously governing behaviour atrophy; at the same time, in response to this tendency, privatisation of the psyche produces cults of narcissism, of commodified 'personality' and of 'authenticity' conceived as direct (rather than codified) expression of emotion. Because of the decay of discrete codes of public behaviour, a gap opens which is filled by the projection of the private mechanisms on to public activities, objects and individuals, and these are increasingly treated in psychological terms: personality, charisma, star quality. Sennett (2002 (1977): 157) points to the religious roots of this process – the Protestant soul as self-regarding centre of experience – emphasising its fetishistic quality: 'Personality is everywhere present in social relations but is mystifying'; and one manifestation of this is the way in which the larger-than-life persona of the star ballad singer, directed outwards to his or her adoring audience, gets reflected back on to the singer, constructed now as a gigantic image of universal emotion. Here it is not difficult to see the force of Simon Frith's (2001: 107) suggestion that the roots of the modern ballad lie in the eighteenth-century Protestant hymn and its nineteenth-century evangelical successors; nor that of Dave Laing's (1969: 57–60) argument that the source lies even earlier, in secular derivations from the cult of Mary. In the march of modernity, the historical sequence running from medieval Mariolatry through the Protestant's individualised relationship with a personal God to the ballad's secularising adaptation of this relationship locates the Protestant phase in the role of what Jameson (1988) and Žižek (2002: 179–97) have called a 'vanishing mediator': it has done its mediating work and retreats into invisibility, disavowed or repressed. The reduction of the key lineaments of the social body – the structures of kinship – to the dynamics of a purely private sphere, which at the same time are generalised as the only available building bricks of mass society, produces the crisis point in this narrative. This process – the privatisation of patriarchy, as Juliet Mitchell (2003: 18) calls it – projects kinship relations on to the theatrical space of the Freudian 'family romance', as well as that of its musical analogue, the popular ballad. And in both spheres the symptoms of this move – private desires and traumas performed out in public – take on many of the qualities of the psychoanalytic condition of *hysteria*. I will come back to this point – though it would be worth noting here that the history of this condition intertwines with the broader history of capitalism itself, from that sixteenth-century moment when the symptoms of 'possession' are de-demonised and the link first made with the term 'hysteria', to that later *fin de siècle* when new neuro-psychiatric discourses burst out of the Paris and Vienna clinics, accompanied by the contemporaneous explosions of modernism, of monopolistic economic structures and mass social movements – and, of course, of phonography.

What Sennett describes is the resculpting of a space that has become familiar to critical theory. It is that space where, at the centre of tightly imbricated understandings of voice, body and self, the liberal bourgeois subject has its home – a space necessarily, then, divided up (albeit in shifting ways) into 'private' and 'public' spheres. The early twentieth-century popular ballad inhabits a particularly fraught moment in this resculpting process. Sennett has little to say about the phonographic dimension of the shift he describes. As with ballad, 'fidelity' is a central trope here too: faithful reproduction is the guarantee. Here, too, we are invited into a sphere of private feeling: voice and message, signifier and emotion, coincide in a single moment, and this presence is available anytime – it's eternalised. And yet here, too, this presentation of 'life' is secured only at the cost of a certain 'death': the moment of origin is definitively lost – indeed, in the modern studio recording regime, it may never have existed – and the record is both a memorial and, potentially, a deconstruction. Despite the signs of live performance embedded within Wainwright's CD, these are symptoms of disavowal: we aren't there, we never were, and we don't even hear Wainwright; we hear the ghostly simulacrum offered by a machine. In this sense phonography replays the Christian narrative in a form tailored to post-Nietzschean modernity: the ghost in the machine, the *deus ex machina*, has become human, all too human – His Master's Voice – but the price of such narcissistic *hubris* is death, self-loss, as recorded voice refuses the boundaries of any given body. It is in this uncertain universe that recorded ballad subsists.

Seen in this way, the phonographic moment begins to take on the dimensions of what Barbara Engh (1999: 54) has called 'an anthropological revolution in human history – not just another in a series of technological innovations … The phonograph dissociated the voice and embodied consciousness, which formerly had been thought to be so coterminous as to virtually define each other.' I agree with her about the significance of this, but I would take a more Derridean-cum-Lacanian line: the dissociation of voice and 'its' body was always (potentially, incipiently, hauntingly) in play, albeit typically disavowed, and the revolution was in degree and scope on the one hand, in self-awareness on the other: phonographic technology as (no doubt traumatising) deconstruction. In this sense, the phonograph was certainly a midwife, to the extent that we may want to claim for its moment the status of what Alain Badiou, searching for a political ethics appropriate to a post-foundational episteme, terms an 'event'. For Badiou (2005 (1988): 29, 507), event is what he calls an 'ultra-one'. It happens, if it happens at all, at an 'evental site' – that is, a situation containing a singularity, some content not recognised in the situation's own self-understanding. It, event, belongs to itself, 'interposes itself between the void and itself'. It appears when named, by an act of 'interpretative intervention', and then survives through operations of 'fidelity' that assemble a 'generic' (that is, autochthonous) net-work of 'truths'.[1] In the advent of recorded voice, a multifarious exercise of naming struggled to identify the significance of this technical miracle: neologisms (phonograph, gramophone) went along with reworked topoi (notably that of *fidelity* – His Master's Voice) and with hysterical supernat-ural imagery (for the dead could now speak and the machine was inhab-ited by spirits). Fidelity – or 'authenticity', a core trope for popular song throughout the twentieth century – would, in a neat historical circularity, become the key organising thread for the operation of fidelity to this event. It is worth pointing out that this event pretty well coincides with the defini-tive murder of God, by Nietzsche – as if 'fidelity', faith, transfers from one object to another. It also coincides, more or less, with Freud's theorisation of the part–object, object–cause of desire or *objet a* in Lacan's formulation; including object–voice, that object always already outside as well as inside, always split, but now put even more powerfully at issue by the disembodying technology of recording: a voice belonging, then, to a body that is *dis-eased*, *dis-located*, transposed into an anatomy calling for constant reimagination and beyond any simple distinction between private and public.

As far as I know, Badiou himself doesn't classify phonography as an 'event'. It is unlikely that he would. He restricts evental sites to four ter-ritories: science, art, politics and – love. Upheavals in the mode of pro-duction don't seem to count, an odd omission in the work of an avowedly Marxist philosopher. If he wanted to say that the love-event can *stand in* for events working elsewhere, I would agree with him; I take romantic love to do metonymic work. But Badiou's omission has the air of a denial, of a disavowal of a structure of fidelity at a deeper level. For the phono-graphic event, if conceived broadly enough, provides for Badiou's theory

---

[1] For a more detailed account of my extrapolation from Badiou, see Middleton 2009e.

the historical condition of possibility that, he himself argues, any philosophy requires; the antinomy between the longing for 'authenticity' and its
Derridean deferral structures modern thought as a whole. The parallel then
becomes telling between Badiou's tendency to fetishise the condition of
fidelity – as if the absolute need to keep faith is itself a matter of faith – and
the valorisation of high fidelity in recorded music, which struggles to disguise the contradictions inherent in the technology: the way, for instance,
that hi-fi can never be 'hi' enough, and the higher it gets, the more we notice
the remaining 'flaws'; while if the flaws are 'touched up', if the technology is
used to enhance the intimacy, the resonance, the close-up, the result is an
impossibility, is un-real or super-real, that is, an infidelity.

A similar parallel can be drawn with the vicissitudes of fidelity in the
love-song, where public anonymity of reception constantly belies the performance of intimacy, the address to 'you alone'. In all three cases – Badiou,
recording technology, ballad – the spiralling groove of reproduction
depends upon, but undermines, an originary event: 'Repetition *and* first
time', as Derrida (2006 (1993): 10) has it: 'this is perhaps the question of the
event as question of the ghost … Repetition *and* first time, but also repetition *and* last time, since the singularity of any *first time* makes of it also
a *last time*.' Fidelity here can be at best a hope, a utopian 'as if', a construction that, evidently, deconstructs itself as soon as it is thought. I would go
even further. If the principal lesson of phonography is the revelation that
embodiment is mutable and mobile, fidelity to this truth would have to be
not only a *critical* fidelity, as Derrida proposes; it would have to recognise
that, in offering us the tools to 'operate' processes of territorialisation and
deterritorialisation, phonographic fidelity produces an irreducible ethical
*undecidability*. Faith, we could say, might *require* betrayal; fidelity implies
infidelity. True fidelity – to use theological language – is not to the letter
but to the spirit, the eternal core that, in a Nietzschean or Deleuzian repetition, can *only* show itself as difference. The demand made, apparently, by
recorded voice, its source invisible, undecidable, spectral, can thus never be
met – a condition nowhere more starkly obvious than in the ballad, where
'the abyss at the heart of love', as George Steiner (2008: 200) puts it, post-
pones fulfilment indefinitely. This gap, or deferral, is crystallised in the performativity of Wainwright's vocal persona, especially as it 'quotes' Garland
(so close yet so distant;[2] and a Garland who herself is quoting … whom?),
pointing to that emptiness not only of the other but of the self which is
the true mark of the modern. Fidelity, we can now see, in love as in the

---

[2] See Garland 2001 (1961).

recording technologies devoted so obsessively to love's expression, is always structured *en abîme*.[3]

As I said, for Badiou, *naming* is vital. Event – the French Revolution, theory of relativity, serial technique in music, a love-relationship – exists qua 'event' only once it's recognised as such and named. Wainwright and Garland circle round an absence here, struggling to name what is happening and with whom. This is common in ballads, where a pronominal emphasis – the I, the You – exploits the structure of deferral I just mentioned, leaving identification open, a situation intensified as well, as I also suggested, by the structure of phonographic production. At the same time, though, we know – don't we? – that this is Rufus, this is Judy, this is a *star*, a fetish attracting desire and adoration. His Master's Voice, which is what we hear, is the voice that stands in for, hence so to speak *names*, the star. But these practices of naming stand in relation to a rich and long-elaborated discursive territory. In Lacanian psychoanalysis, for example, the Name-of-the-Father refers to the paternal metaphor that gives the Symbolic order its authority; standing in for a missing God, it's the master-signifier that ties the structure together. Drawing on this imagery, on Hegel and on Kripke, Slavoj Žižek (1989: 89–92) has developed an anti-descriptivist theory of naming according to which names don't acquire meaning through reference to given properties but through a 'primal baptism' followed up in a 'chain of tradition'. The similarity to Badiou is striking. But for Žižek there's a corollary, namely the Lacanian 'non-all set', a figure registering the idea that the universalising, quasi-magical effects of all such totalising names are actually founded on boundary-forming exceptions. Most provocatively, this gives rise to the notorious Lacanian aphorism, 'Woman does not exist' (so that Man can). Similarly, in an extrapolation I have made elsewhere, 'Popular music does not exist' (so that Music can).[4] And, in the context of their records, the same would be true of 'Rufus' or 'Judy', whose voices can never quite coincide with the territory the names delineate.

I am reminded here of Walter Benjamin's theory of language.[5] For Benjamin, God created and named in one movement. His gift to men was then a similar faculty, names proper to objects bestowed without intention or cognitive function conceived as a utopian unity of thing and symbol; a unity then fractured by a Fall bringing sign systems, Saussurean difference

---

[3] A text or process structured *en abîme* embeds within the whole a smaller image that reflects it; as with the example of parallel mirrors, the reflexive 'descent' is potentially endless.

[4] For both Žižek's theory and mine, see Middleton 2006: 32–5.

[5] See e.g. Benjamin 1979 (1916).

and the babel of multiple languages. It is this mystical theory that Adorno (2002b, 2002c) seems to have in mind in his early writings on the phonograph when he celebrates its ability, apparently, to bypass the mediations of notation and inscribe a mimetic groove – a sort of pre-lapsarian language-as-such – directly. This writing, he suggests, 'delicately scribbled, utterly illegible … committed to the sound that inhabits this and no other acoustic groove', suggests a pre-representational 'hieroglyphics' that point towards music's utopian mission – 'the idea of music is the form of the divine name', and music's task is to 'name the name itself' in a form of 'demythologised prayer' – at the same time as they present the record form in the shape of 'missives' in the 'traffic with technology', 'whose formulations capture the sounds of creation, the first and last sounds, judgement upon life and message about that which may come thereafter' (Adorno 2002c: 277; Adorno quoted in Levin 1990: 41; Adorno 2002c: 280).

We might want to seize and hold on to this utopian moment – it's an 'as if' worth protecting – even if, needless to say, it speaks of a fullness always already lost; just as Badiou's event, the singularity that comes into being when given its proper name, falls victim to the critique of totality mounted by Lacan and Žižek (not to mention, in dialectical movement, by Adorno himself). Naming is also an act of territorialisation. Naming an event – a moment of love, let's say – is dangerous because it 'proper-ties' it, that is, turns it into object, into possession – plays god. Records, in their guise as commodities and star-vehicles, are complicit in this move at the same time as, breaking the fixity of body, origin and presence, they undercut it. (If property is the original sin, initiated in the 'gift' of proper names – to each owner, his own – this originates, in the Judaeo-Christian tradition, with God himself, as Benjamin recognised. Yet God's name, 'Yahweh' in its most common transliteration, references *being* more than *having* – 'I AM THAT I AM' (Exodus 3:14) – and its vocalisation is often proscribed; the One God is at the same time the ineffable mover and shaker, an actor-creator veiled from view – a 'No-One', a No-body. This, I guess, is the sense of 'naming the name' that Adorno had in mind for music's utopian task.)

For, returning to Wainwright's performance, in what sense can we say who – or what – is vocalising here? Who, or what, is addressed, and what is the love-object? 'Tell me now, how long has this been going on?' – a variation of the Lacanian question-of-questions to the other, '*che vuoi?*', what do you want of me? The detachment of voice from body, of master's voice from the Name-of-the-Father, gives to the voice here a sense that it's addressing its own self as much as an external protagonist, expressing an incredulity at the foreign force invading its space: '*Mensch, es spukt in deinem Kopfe!*' (Man, it spooks in your head), in the discursive tradition of Marx and Freud. (Marx takes this quotation from the young-Hegelian philosopher Max Stirner, whom he critiques in *The German Ideology* – critiqued in turn by Derrida in *Spectres of Marx* – but its gist resurfaces too in Freud's concept of the uncanny.)[6] But Wainwright's spook *is* external (as well as internal); it's *love* that takes the position of object, of addressee, made up of a conjunction of 'spirit' and carnality that for Derrida, following both Marx and Freud, defines *spectre*, and which is thrillingly encapsulated here in the heavenly but definitely sensual kisses that Wainwright conjures.

The body that Wainwright summons here is what Steven Connor (2000b: 35) has christened a 'vocalic body' – 'the idea of a surrogate or secondary body, a projection of a new way of having or being a body, formed and sustained out of the autonomous operations of the voice' – except that, under the phonographic regime voice is no longer autonomous in the same way. This body is traversed by what I have called elsewhere the 'vocalimentary canal' (Middleton 2006: 93), joining up mouth, lungs, digestive tract, genitalia in an imaginary anatomy which, intriguingly, maps the configuration of the Freudian part-objects in an economy the rhythms of which – ingestion and ejaculation constantly producing each other – enter a permanent query against any simple boundaries between inside and outside, private and public (not to mention tracing the contours of the territory characteristically inhabited by the hysterical symptoms). In particular, the rupture in everyday bodily territorialisations of voice brought about by phonography puts at issue, potentially, the conventional vocal markers of gender, race, sexuality – *all* social markers. When Wainwright – a flamboyantly gay man who sometimes performs cross-dressed, his voice crossing registers confusingly – cites Garland – innocent turned raddled star-commodity but also gay icon, her singing influenced by contemporary black as well as white singers, not to mention the blackfaced Al Jolson – performing a song composed by a Jewish American who defined himself in large part through his appropriations of African-American music – when we hold these intertextual slippages in view, the bodily territory that is invoked, shifting, ill-defined and even contested though it is, is social and political as much as personal.

The potential offered by this moment may prompt utopian readings – cyborgian meta-bodies and posthuman futures – or, just as easily, gloomy dystopian ones: evacuation of 'the human' in favour of pure 'information', excision of awkward bodies in favour of processions of simulacra. Too

---

[6] For Derrida's take on this genealogy, see Derrida 2006 (1993): 156–221 (216 for the quote from Stirner).

much (simple-minded) fidelity here! More adequate to the demands of ethical undecidability – that is, of active critical work – is the concept of a 'zone of indeterminacy' where Giorgio Agamben (2004) locates the space of decision between 'man' and 'animal', or more broadly 'humanity' and 'nature'; and, by extrapolation, between 'man' and 'machine', and between genders, races, sexualities and other 'species'; between – to use an older language – body and soul; between – to use a newer one – the Deleuzian 'body-without-organs' and its Žižekian counter, the 'organ – such as voice – without-a-body'.[7] This is also the zone of love, of the abyss of love. That such indeterminacy is of our nature, and that therefore such decisions have to be worked for, is what phonography has to tell us. Right across this terrain, the phonographic rupture puts at issue settled master-and-slave structures: does, for example, the machine provide 'anthropophorous' support, as Agamben calls it, 'human-carrying' support for the master's voice? Or is it the other way round? Or is the relationship, precisely, inde-terminate, at the mercy of the pressures of (in)fidelity? Indeterminacy here means: *no guarantees* (as the grotesques and monsters summoned up by some popular phonographic vocalic bodies remind us). Here, then, *posses-sion* – commodification, territory, ventriloquial voice – is *undecidable*, and the question becomes: who speaks, to whom, from what bodily location and with what authority?

## Phonographic families

This territory – the territory of possession – is structured by what, follow-ing Lacan, I have called an economy of having-and-being, an economy that moulds not only the dynamics of 'family romance' (as Lacan details) but also (looking inwards) the ideological processes of subjectivation and its ven-triloquial vocal machinery, and (looking outwards) the master-and-slave configurations of social relations, manifested especially in the intersection of capital and labour in the fetishistic form of the commodity.[8] If we pursue the idea – continually elaborated across the range of historically located dis-courses – that this economy may be pictured as a multilevelled *body* (per-sonal, social, political), it becomes clear that this body falls into crisis, on all levels, at the turn of the nineteenth century. I want to explore the suggestion

---

[7] For my take on this dialectic, and the background in Deleuze and Žižek, see Middleton 2009b: 226–8.

[8] See Middleton 2006: 29–30 and *passim*.

that this crisis, which I have already hinted may be thought under the sign of hysteria, is exposed to us in distinct but interlinked ways by the twin technologies of psychoanalysis (which probes its 'secrets and lies' in a private setting) and phonography (which blows them up on a public screen), both technologies being themselves configured as intrinsically hysterical economies of (in)fidelity.

What does it mean to claim that phonography is intrinsically hysterical? The hysteric's question is at bottom the existential question: who am I? Am I alive or dead? – often mediated by social category, usually gender (am I a woman? What is it to be a woman, what a man?), sometimes race (what is it to be black?), questions that are themselves often further specified by the problematic of procreation: can/might I reproduce (and what kind of creature – master or slave – would be brought forth)?[9] Cast adrift by her refusal of normative identity, the hysteric acts out a fantasy-theatre, enunciated in the name of her object of desire, addressed – usually deviously, indirectly or unknowingly – to a new but absent master. Recorded voice – at least tendentially – *is* such an object. Far from the virtual information flow described in some theories of the posthuman, this spectral presence, this 'bit of body', acting as both mirror and screen, mediates between the singer's and the listener's desire, channelling the hysterical question – what do you want me to be? – to a master who is always under erasure. To put this another way, under the phonographic regime, the gap between what Lacan calls ego-ideal and ideal ego, that is, between the 'vocal image' we desire for ourselves and the location in the field of the gaze of the Other from where we imagine ourselves to be heard, *is structurally always already in place*. The hysteric *wants* to be possessed – but by whom? His or her address thus acts out a lie – the master's voice always misrepresents, it's never *there* where it's supposed to be, its name cannot substantiate itself – but at the same time represents a truth, marking out a loss that is irreducible and, like screen-memory, maintaining this mark through an eternal reproductive rhythm as the records spin. This antinomy delineates the structure of *fidelity* – that is, of *in*fidelity – which the phonographic apparatus lays out. (It might be worth making the obvious point that it also delineates the structure of fidelity associated with the mechanisms of the psychoanalytic transference: as Edison said, 'The phonograph knows more about us than we know ourselves.'[10]) The machinery of ego – and with it that of the economy of possessive individualism, hence of the kinship relations, the social

---

[9]  See Lacan 1993: 168–79.
[10]  Quoted in Milner 2009: 34.

body, that it subtends – is put at risk, for there's a suspicion that the master is actually a slave, his voice is owned elsewhere, is that of a ventriloquist's dummy – or is even a function (a *Doppelgänger*) of the self. As Derrida (2006 (1993): 166) puts it, 'Ego equals ghost. Therefore "I am" would mean "I am haunted": I am haunted by myself who am (haunted by myself who am … and so forth). Wherever there is Ego, *es spukt*, "it spooks" … The essential mode of self-presence of the *cogito* would be the haunting obsession of this "es spukt". And the spook is *noisy* – all the more so in a phonographically oriented world. The circulation, the endless regression, is one populated by *ventriloquial voices* – spirits possessing subjects, subjects essaying control of the dummies they so desire to possess.

If the phonographic event is a conduit and catalyst of a certain reconfiguration, this does not mean, however, that its effects have been uniform or historically stable. Much is at issue here, not least in relation to the manifold ways in which currents in the technology have intersected with varying manifestations of recorded voice and of the spaces they're heard as inhabiting. But, given the limits of a single chapter, I want to focus on the distinction and shift (it is both but in a complex way) that is most pregnant for my purposes, that between analogue and digital technologies.

The basic difference seems clear-cut. Analogue and digital have different modes of fidelity, in the one case 'natural', in the other via convention; referencing a precise, unique historical moment on the one hand, a universal, ahistorical code on the other. The contrast is between tree and rhizome; between mimetic gesture – which always fails but which will claim to preserve the essence through a process of lineal descent – and discontinuous sample within a prescribed margin of error, the sequences of simulacra fanning out serially across, potentially, all formats; between 'approximating perfection' and 'perfecting approximation' (Milner 2009: 194).[11] One *reproduces* – the tropes are genealogical – while the other *replicates* – the tropes are cyborgian. One can identify the outline of a developmental process: to the extent that analogue phonography holds on to certain features of older, speech- and writing-based paradigms, notably the quest for unique origin, it gives way to more explicit forms of simulation, most clearly in many contemporary modes of studio practice. At the same time, however, such 'infidelity' is already implicit in analogue technology, which from the start, and then more obviously in hi-fi ideology, was wont to present the recording as *more* faithful to 'the music' than live performance could ever be. In this

---

[11] See also Rothenbuler and Peters 1997; Chang 2009.

sense, analogue can be located as a 'vanishing mediator'. This story and its implications for cultural practice and human self-understanding, both at a general level – McLuhan's (1964) 'global village'; Teilhard de Chardin's (1959) step-change in the structure of the 'noosphere'[12] – and in terms of specific effects of phonography, including those of digitisation,[13] have been thoroughly explored. Less familiar are what I will call the psycho-technics that may be associated with the analogue/digital nexus.

Analogue logic is triangular, its parent-and-child ontology, along with its sympathy for original-and-cover kinship, analogous (sic) to the Oedipal logic of the 'family romance'. Digital logic is multilateral, extending sideways a squaring of the triangle that follows from the incursion of a fourth term; this term, we may say – extrapolating from Juliet Mitchell – occupies the position of *siblinghood*. Identifying 'a decline of the importance of descent and a rise of the importance of alliance' (Mitchell 2003: 4), Mitchell wants to rewrite the Freudian family romance, structured round the Law of the Father, by means of a sibling supplement. The sibling's existential question is that of (as we may phrase it) the sample: the 'self-same other [that] is both the same as the self ... while simultaneously other than oneself – likeness in unlikeness, unlikeness in likeness' (Mitchell 2003: 125); and her law is not that of the Symbolic but that of seriality, of counting: siblings 'are "equilateral"', in other words, 'they are not defined by what is missing [the murdered Father, the Master's voice]. [They] ... explore what is *there*, not what is not' (Mitchell 2003: 128).

The sibling supplement turns the Oedipal structure regarded by psychoanalysis as normative from a triangular into what we might call a quadrilateral logic; and this logic summons the discourse of hysteria, for the incursive position disrupts the normative structure.[14] But this disruption is exacerbated when 'ballad logic' is ranged against the sibling logic of dancing samples and peer-to-peer relations, for the whole basis of mimesis – of possession, reproduction, identity – is put at issue. To analogue nostalgists,

---

[12] '[T]hanks to the prodigious biological event represented by the discovery of electro-magnetic waves, each individual finds himself henceforth (actively and passively) simultaneously present, over land and sea, in every corner of the earth': de Chardin 1959: 240.

[13] From Schafer 1994 (1977) through Kittler 1999 to Sterne 2003, Milner 2009 and many others.

[14] Note, however, that for Lacan, the Oedipal structure always had a fourth point, the supplement being the phallus as such, conceived as the *objet petit a* that stands for the fantasmatic impossibility of totality. Might this impossible fantasy, typically occluded, offer a pointer to the source of analogue hysteria? At the same time, perhaps it reveals a certain disavowal in Lacan: what if the phallus as *objet petit a*, in this context, stands in for a force that his theory doesn't recognise, namely, the disruptive force of the sibling relation? After all, it's when siblings squabble over the phallus that patriarchal authority is put at issue. In this event, the phallic regime of family begins to look like an 'analogue fantasy'.

confronted with the vocodered and auto-tuned voices of a digitised world, the sibling question takes on the form: Am I a *clone*? Meanwhile, digiphile utopianists, thinking to have escaped any originary Master, are inevitably brought up against authority, against the Author, most concretely in the shape of intellectual property law. Cain's fratricide supplements (rather than supersedes) the Oedipal patricide; and then, in the post-Christian West at least, the legacy of a third and ultimate crime – the murder of God himself, self-abandoned and human, all too human – twists the traumatic knot still tighter, transplanting the hysterical *mise-en-scène* into the multivalent spaces, an indeterminately configured *oikos*, of a secularised mediascape.

As this suggests, analogue and digital regimes, far from being distinct categories, constantly interpenetrate, incarnate each other. Digital samples, before their replicant processing begins, are commonly sourced from 'homely' vinyl originals, the relationships construed as valued genealogies; conversely, analogue production almost from its beginnings 'lied' about fidelity, cultivating sounds impossible to produce outside a studio. (Examples could be multiplied. For instance, the Rufus Wainwright CD from which this discussion started presents or mimics – at any rate, offers an analogue of – a singular event (which in turn is an analogue – of Garland's concert – itself an analogue (of the 'original' compositions)), but offers it to us via a digitally coded engineering process whose glossy, homogeneous sound comes courtesy of 'the Pro Tooling of the world' (Milner 2009: 301).[15]) Two (impossible) utopias – 'organic' versus 'cyber', patriarchal versus fraternal – argue it out; each, always falling short, produces the other at the same time as it negates it. It is a *family* dispute. Interestingly, recent years have seen the rise of a distinct discourse of fraternity – Blanchot (1988), Nancy (1991) and Esposito (2008, 2009) on 'community', Derrida (1997, 2006 (1993)) on a 'New International' and the politics of friendship, the neo-Spinozist thinkers around Negri on 'multitude' (Hardt and Negri 2000, 2004) – which, while undoubtedly significant, must also be carefully circumscribed: as Mitchell is quick to insist, 'castration', hence originary authority, is not so easily disavowed and the force of lineage, boundary, mastery is unlikely to disappear. Similarly, the Deleuzian critique of psychoanalysis – which might encourage us to query the quality that an Oedipally anxious Murray Schafer identified in phonographic culture as 'schizophonia' and reinterpret it as a joyfully schizoid rhizomatic machinery of 'desiring sound' – has meaning only when located in the embrace of its neo-Freudian parentage; Deleuze's quasi-digital, 'equilateral' Body-without-Organs cannot escape

---

[15]  Pro Tools software is credited in the liner notes.

the pull of its Žižekian obverse, the Organ-without-a-Body, with its impossible (analogue) fantasy of closure. If these various frameworks have the look of dialectical tensions, we shall search in vain for the *Aufhebung* (the synthesis or sublation) that Hegel would have expected. Rather, we should 'tarry with the negative', as Žižek often puts it: the dialectical moment of antithesis insists, persists, reverses, splits; its direction of travel is, moreover, indeterminate, with a temporality structured always by that hermeneutic reciprocity between the moments of originary event and its psychic effects, which, in the Freudian tradition, goes by the name of *Nachträglichkeit*.[16]

'The first thing the universe did was cut a record' (Milner 2009: 3). And in the spirit of this *nachträglich* 'it will have been', I want to conclude with a return: to music of pre-phonographic provenance, which is full, however, of proto-phonographic pointers, referencing most importantly the two key vectors of kinship already explored: *genealogy* (as encapsulated in the Oedipal world of ballad) and *siblinghood* (as captured in the racial politics of ballad's Other: blues). Rufus Wainwright's bluesy ballad finds here a point of departure – one that might also outline the hope of a future.

## Who's there? Nobody?

The proto-phonographic qualities of African-American music have been noted before.[17] Among them, the most significant for my purpose is the blackface mask, with its enduring legacy and culturally pervasive import. Denaturalising the performance act, it dramatically – hysterically – splits voice from its apparent bodily source, ear from eye, planting a ventriloquistic query. But this merely uncovers what is more often disavowed. The sensorial economy of voice and gaze, where subjectivity is produced together with a (sense of a) body, encompasses an uncanny theatre where, according to Lacanian theory, each sense, at the level of an *objet petit a*, acts as supplement to, covers over the inevitable gap in the field of, the other, stitching together a (fantasmatic) coherence.[18] Lacan (1979: 82–5), in his classic exposition of this, notes the analogy of the mask. The phonograph would take up and amplify the same function (as we see when radio listeners to the young Elvis Presley's first hit record could identify the voice as 'black'). In this sense, the phonographic disembodiment highlighted by Barbara Engh

---

[16] *Nachträglichkeit*: in this context, something like 'afterwardness'. For elaboration of the sort of 'negative dialectics' sketched here, see Middleton 2009d.

[17] E.g. Weheliye 2002; Biers 2006.

[18] See Žižek 1996.

(see above, p. 294) was already there in embryo in the nineteenth-century minstrel show.

There's an intriguing historical dimension to this relationship. If, as Richard Sennett argues, the developmental trajectory of modernity, at least for the dominant (white) social groups, encompassed an increasing tendency to inscribe the mechanisms of the private sphere on to public space, this process was arguably shadowed, in inversion, in the blackface economy, where the racial dynamics animating the larger social body were focused down on to the faces and voices of individual performers (white and black). Here, in this structure of displacement, Paul Gilroy's (1993) picture of the 'Black Atlantic' as a 'counterculture of modernity' attains its full power as the disavowed underside that alone makes dominant modernity possible. Under the conditions of phonographic culture, this aporetic tension is then generalised, ambivalent figures of mastery and slavery permeating everywhere and putting the topography of 'private' and 'public' itself at issue.

Bert Williams was a leading African-American comedian, composer and singer in the 1890s and early 1900s; typically for the period, he performed in blackface. His song 'Nobody', after the success of his 1906 recording (Williams 2004), became his signature tune, naming him, as it were, *in absentia* (like the children's game: 'Who's there? Mr Nobody'; recalling too Homer's Odysseus, tricking Polyphemus by playing punningly on his own name, on the proper name, the properties of name, as 'Nobody' – an episode picked up by the Coen Brothers in their filmed reworking of *The Odyssey*, *O Brother Where Art Thou?*, a blues-inflected exploration of fraternity). The verses, in a gloomy parlando, pile up an endless sequence of scenarios describing Williams's need for help, a friend, love, all unanswered. The chorus tries repetitively to take lyrical flight but its blues-inflected phrases always sink back in a sort of defiant resignation (see Music Example 14.1).

The song is neither a ballad nor a blues, but in its dark comedy we can hear a quality that connects to the emptiness identified in Wainwright's 'How Long', an emptiness that here prefigures the failures of both genres to fulfil their claims – to love and romance on the one hand, to sexual autonomy, fraternal swagger and carnivalesque good times on the other – and at the same time undercuts these failures by confronting them head-on. What does Williams want? Clearly, the object that Wainwright conjures up, however spectrally: a bodily encounter, which, however, Willams's narrative excludes. More deeply: to the extent that the song is generically a 'not-ballad' – its mock pathos parodies ballad expressivity – it 'wants to

**Music example 14.1** Chorus of 'Nobody' (1905) by Alex Rogers and Bert Williams (transcribed from the Archeophone reissue of the 1906 recording by the author)

be a ballad'; it yearns for love, even at the price of love's failure. At the same time, its blues elements – the chorus could almost be a W. C. Handy tune – point towards ballad's great Other, to blues' dystopian treatment of love, which, however, always stands metonymically for (and simultaneously masks) the trope of *fraternity*, indeed at the ultimate, of *fratricide*; for if all African-American music since slavery asks implicitly the (racially inflected) question, 'Who is my brother (or sister)?', blues pushes this question to a hysterical extreme. Ballad worries at the problematic of romance, and hence at the Oedipal structures of society, blues at the problematic of the orphan, the nomadic sexual encounter, as (in part) a metonym for kinship, and hence the structures of siblinghood. In mythopoeic terms, the Marian legacy of 'courtly love', together with its patriarchal assumptions, its extensions, perversions and reversals, comes up against an outlaw band of rebellious slaves, raisers of Cain and purveyors of devil music. The miscegenating progeny of this encounter – musical genres such as jazz, R&B and rock, along with the bodies they voice into being – muddy both Oedipal and sibling norms, a process subsequently amplified by the circuitous passages of the analogue/digital dialectic. It is in this prescient, and pre-active, place that 'Nobody' is located. Williams – Williams's recorded voice, doubly masked – wants *somebody* – *anybody*; but there is nobody: *no body*.[19]

Except for his own; which, however, has a distinctly spectral air. Derrida (2006 (1993): 123ff) has pointed out that spectres typically appear to us faceless – helmeted, masked. In *Spectres of Marx*, Derrida is overwhelmed by the precessions and processions of spectres that teem forth from Marx's texts. This is where the 'present-ness' of records – the sense that once we can hear *anything*, in the moment, now, history stops – finds its historical rendezvous: 'the grammatical present of the verb to be', says Derrida (2006 (1993): 61), 'seems to offer a predestined hospitality to the return of any and all spirits'; in the 'hauntology' produced by today's 'techno-tele-discursivity', as Derrida calls it, the missives of such spectres pile up around the feet of the phonographic apparatus, in a Benjaminian masquerade of progress. We must talk to the ghosts, says Derrida (2006 (1993): 221); we must engage with the spectral possibilities of recorded voice: such is the condition of true fidelity. As we listen to Bert Williams – more especially, if we listen against a context formed by ballad and blues, the two genres that in themselves and through their varied progeny have dominated popular song, in the Anglophone area at least, during the phonographic era – the question for us should be: what will we *do* with this gift that phonography bestows, this 'no body', 'no time'? In this case, a clue – and perhaps Williams's reply to my question – might be: 'follow the trombone'.

At the start of each chorus phrase, Williams's entry is pre-empted by an extravagant bluesy trombone smear; he's caught out, caught short, taken by surprise, by this voice that seems to come from behind his back (as the sheet music image – Figure 14.1 – indicates). What, we could ask, is the source of this voice, which, in the words of a contemporary observer, provokes Williams's 'apparently desperate efforts to catch up with it' (Rowland 1969 (1923): 67)? How would we construe its body? Is it an alter ego? A nobody? A *some*body – whose identity, however, is indeterminate; a ghost perhaps? A ventriloquial voice – the ego's spook? At the same time, might we identify it with the 'two souls … two warring ideals' that the African-American philosopher, historian and activist W. E. B. Du Bois (1999 (1903): 11) located as the core of the black American identity as such – a doubling exacerbated by the contortions of blackface performance? If so, how uncanny that it should also anticipate, like a historical as well as performative pre-echo, the techniques of double-tracking!

---

[19]  On blues and fraternity, see Middleton 2009c (which appears, in a different version, in Middleton 2006: 37–63).

**Figure 14.1** 'Nobody' by Bert Williams, original sheet music cover, 1905

Williams turns, looking for the gaze behind his back, the gaze of the (white) (br)other (or sister), without which the blackface mask makes no sense, the gaze that would *give him a body* – but finds (hears) only the trombone, a voice indeterminate in race and gender, located elsewhere and everywhere; speaking from behind the loudspeaker, this voice offers a secular echo of a message of universal kinship: take, hear (and eat – the vocalimentary canal doing its work), this is my body … your body … ours …

Perhaps. In this 'no time', the dis-possessive work of phonographic voice might seem to offer lessons in how – provided we have faith – 'no-body' might turn towards a *new* body, in Bataille's words, the body of a 'community of those without a community'.[20] This idea, of a *cum*, a 'with', that bypasses, overreaches, cuts across all self-contained inclusivities (whether 'I' or 'we') presses on us now from many, sometimes philosophically contradictory directions, ranging from phenomenology (for example, Nancy's

---

[20] George Bataille, quoted in Derrida 1997 : 37.

(2000) argument that the condition of 'being-with', in which singularity and plurality always imply each other, is the originary state of Being as such) to evolutionary economics (for instance, Paul Seabright's (2004) exploration of the biocultural role of *trust*, that human quality which in effect turns 'strangers' – unrelated individuals we may never even meet – into 'neighbours'). Would this 'with' be the mark of true love? Again, perhaps. Given the 'world community' we actually have, the qualification is important (and we might note Nancy's definition of 'compassion', of 'feeling-with': 'the disturbance of violent relatedness' (Nancy 2000: xiii), which surely would describe the dynamics of many phonographic encounters). For the (in)fidelity that has provided the thread of my argument here is surely also the *peut-être* that runs constantly through Derrida's *Politics of Friendship* (1997): an aporia that locates love beyond 'equivalence', beyond 'appropriation', 'thereby exceeding all reappropriation of the proper', of 'property', its genealogy aptly inscribed by the philosopher in the figure of – *justice*.

Justice – which, following Derrida, I will gloss as an unconditional openness to the unappropriated other, that is, an other conceived in a way opened to thought by Hegel's idea of 'singular, or concrete, universal' – supervenes on the territory sculpted by the historically configured demarcations of 'public' and 'private'.[21] Eric Lott (1993), in his book on blackface performance, describes the racial dynamics – the family dynamics, one might say – of this territory in terms of 'love and theft'; justice, then, would invoke a quality of what I have called 'love without theft' – or, to put this in older terms, of *agapē*, the revolutionary love informing Pauline universalism, a fragile absolute whose legacy is worth defending, as Žižek (2000) has observed (Middleton 2009a: xxi–xxiii). Of course, *agapē* and *eros*, where ballad has its home, would traditionally be regarded as incompatible. But what if 'romance' and 'fraternity' could constitute themselves not as contradiction, still less as sublating dialectic, but as (productive) aporia? What if 'family', via the sibling incursion and its potentially infinite expansion, were capable of triggering moments pointing towards an ecology (an *oikos* or household) of global kinship? – as if the phonographic body, imagining itself as a figure of universal 'excursion' uncannily resembling that society of stranger-neighbours on which radical Christianity would build itself, really were theophorous; as if its voice – human, all too human (which is to say, at

---

[21] Derrida 1997: 61–5. Or, in Nancy's post-Hegelian, indeed post-Heideggerian words: 'being-with designates the other that never comes back to the same, the plurality of origins. The just measure of the with or, more exactly, the with or being-with as just measure, as justness and justice, is the measure of dis-position as such: the measure of the distance from one origin to another' (Nancy 2000: 81).

the same time both less than and more than 'human') – promised to sound for us every origin … How long has this been going on? Long enough, perhaps, to prompt utopian thoughts of 'the final explosive liberation of the Christian Thing: a liberation operating neither high-above nor deep-within, but in a transformed *world* of total friendship: a world of Home' (Bloch 2009 (1972): 247).

# Bibliography

Aarne, A. 1961 *The Types of the Folktale: A Classification and Bibliography*, S. Thompson (trans.), 2nd revision, Helsinki: Academia Scientarum Fennica

Abu-Lughod, J. L. 1987 'The Islamic city – historic myth, Islamic essence, and contemporary relevance', *International Journal of Middle East Studies*, 19, 155–76

Adkins, M. and Isaacs, B. (eds.) 2011 *Proceedings of the International Computer Music Conference 2011*, Centre for Research on New Music, University of Huddersfield

Adorno, T. W. 2002a (1928) *Essays on Music*, R. Leppert (ed. and various trans.), Berkeley: University of California Press

2002b (1928) 'The curves of the needle', T. Y. Levin (trans.), in R. Leppert (ed.), *Essays on Music*, Berkeley: University of California Press, pp. 271–6

2002c (1928) 'The form of the phonograph record', T. Y. Levin (trans.), in R. Leppert (ed.), *Essays on Music*, Berkeley: University of California Press, pp. 277–82

Agamben, G. 2004 *The Open: Man and Animal*, K. Attell (trans.), Stanford University Press

2005 *State of Exception*, K. Attell (trans.), University of Chicago Press

2009 *'What is an Apparatus?' and Other Essays*, D. Kishik and S. Pedatella (trans.), Stanford University Press

Ahmed, M. and Burgess, K. 2009 'Young music fans deaf to iPod's limitations', *The Times*, 5 May

Ahmed, S. 2006 *Queer Phenomenology: Orientations, Objects, Others*, Durham, NC: Duke University Press

Al-Bukhari, M. I. I. 1997 *Sahih Al-Bukhari (Arabic–English)*, vol. II, M. Muhsin Khan (trans.), Riyadh: Darussalam

Allen, J. de V. 1979 'The Swahili house: Cultural and ritual concepts underlying its plan and structure', *Art and Archaeology Research Papers*, 9, 1–32

Altermatt, U., Delgado, M. and Vergauwen, G. (eds.) 2006 *Der Islam in Europa: Zwischen Weltpolitik und Alltag*, Stuttgart: W. Kohlhammer

Altman, R. 1992a 'The material heterogeneity of recorded sound', in R. Altman, (ed.), *Sound Theory/Sound Practice*, New York: Routledge, pp. 15–31

(ed.) 1992b *Sound Theory/Sound Practice*, New York: Routledge

Amin, A. and Thrift, N. 2002 *Cities: Reimagining the Urban*, Cambridge: Polity

Ammann, L. 2006 *Private and Public in Muslim Civilization*, Istanbul: Bilgi University Press

Anderson, B. 1991 (1983) *Imagined Communities: Reflections on the Origin and Spread of Nationalism*, London: Verso

Anderson, B. and Harrison, P. 2010 *Taking-Place: Non-Representational Theories and Geography*, Farnham: Ashgate

Anderson, N. 2009 'Pirate Bay moves to decentralized DHT protocol, kills tracker', *Ars Technica*, 17 November, http://arstechnica.com/tech-policy/news/2009/11/pirate-bay-kills-its-own-bittorrent-tracker.ars (last accessed 18 August 2012)

Angwin, J. 2010 'The web's new gold mine: Your secrets', *Wall Street Journal*, 20 July, http://online.wsj.com/article/SB10001424052748703940090457539507351298 9404.html (last accessed 18 August 2012)

Arendt, H. 1989 (1958) *The Human Condition*, University of Chicago Press

Attali, J. 1985 *Noise: The Political Economy of Music*, B. Massumi (trans.), Manchester University Press

Aubert, L. 2007 *The Music of the Other: New Challenges for Ethnomusicology in a Global Age*, C. Ribeiro (trans.), Aldershot: Ashgate

Augaitis, D. and Lander, D. (eds.) 1994 *Radio Rethink: Art, Sound and Transmission*, Banff: Walter Philips Gallery

Augé, M. 1995 *Non-Places: Introduction to an Anthropology of Supermodernity*, London: Verso

Auslander, P. 1999 *Liveness: Performance in a Mediatized Culture*, London: Routledge

Austin, J. 1962 *How to Do Things with Words: The William James Lectures Delivered at Harvard University in 1955*, Oxford: Clarendon

Back, L. 2007 *The Art of Listening*, Oxford: Berg

Badiou, A. 2005 (1988) *Being and Event*, O. Feltham (trans.), London: Continuum

Bakari, M. b. M. 1981 *The Customs of the Swahili People: The Desturi Za Waswahili of Mtoro Bin Mwinyi Bakari and Other Swahili Persons*, J. W. T. Allen (ed. and trans.), Berkeley: University of California Press

Baldry, C. 1997 'The social construction of office space', *International Labour Review*, 136, 365–78

Barber, K. 1997 'Preliminary notes on audiences in Africa', *Africa*, 67, 347–62

  2007 *The Anthropology of Texts, Persons and Publics: Oral and Written Culture in Africa and Beyond*, Cambridge University Press

  (ed.) 2006 *Africa's Hidden Histories: Everyday Literacy and Making the Self*, Bloomington, IN: Indiana University Press

Barenboim, D. and Said, E. 2002 'Daniel Barenboim and Edward Said upon receiving the "Principe de Asturias" Prize', October, www.danielbarenboim.com/index.php?id=44 (last accessed 18 August 2012)

Barrass, S., Whitelaw, M. and Bailes, F. 2006 'Listening to the mind listening: An analysis of sonification reviews, designs and correspondences', *Leonardo Music Journal*, 16, 13–19

Barry, A. and Thrift, N. 2007 'Gabriel Tarde: Imitation, invention and economy', *Economy and Society*, 36, 509–25

Barthes, R. 1985 'The grain of the voice', R. Howard (trans.) in *The Responsibility of Forms: Critical Essays on Music, Art and Representation*, New York: Hill and Wang, pp. 267–77

Baxter, V. and Kroll-Smith, S. 2005 'Normalizing the workplace nap: Blurring the boundaries between public and private space and time', *Current Sociology*, 53, 33–55

Bayoumi, M. 2005 'Disco inferno', *The Nation*, 26 December, www.thenation.com/article/disco-inferno (last accessed 18 August 2012)

Bech, S. 1992 'Selection and training of subjects for listening tests on sound-reproducing equipment', *Journal of the Audio Engineering Society*, 40, 590–610

Bech, S. and Zacharov, N. 2006 *Perceptual Audio Evaluation: Theory, Method and Application*, Hoboken, NJ: Wiley and Sons

Beck, U. and Beck-Gernsheim, E. (eds.) 2002 *Individualization: Institutionalized Individualism and its Social and Political Consequences*, London: Sage

Beckles Willson, R. 2009 'Whose utopia?: Perspectives on the West–Eastern Divan Orchestra', *Music and Politics*, 3, 1–21

Beer, D. 2007 'Tune out: Music, soundscapes and the urban *mise-en-scène*', *Information, Communication and Society*, 10, 846–66

Begg, M. 2006 *Enemy Combatant: My Imprisonment at Guantanamo, Bagram and Kandahar*, New York: New Press

Beinhauer-Köhler, B. and Leggewie, C. 2009 *Moscheen in Deutschland: Religiöse Heimat und gesellschaftliche Herausforderung*, Munich: C. H. Beck

bellalou. 2010 'Re: What's your favourite PowerSong/', 4 October, forums.nike.com/thread.jspa?threadID=30551&start=90&tstart=0 (last accessed 17 December 2010 – content no longer accessible as of 23 May 2012)

Belmore, R. 1991 *Ayumee-aawach Oomama-mowan: Speaking to Their Mother*, www.rebeccabelmore.com/exhibit/Speaking-to-Their-Mother.html (last accessed 18 August 2012)

Benjamin, W. 1979 (1916) 'On language as such and on the language of man', in E. Jephcott and K. Shorter (eds.), *One-Way Street and Other Writings*, London: New Left Books, pp. 107–23

Bennett, T. and Joyce, P. 2010 *Material Powers: Cultural Studies, History and the Material Turn*, London: Routledge

Bergeron, K. 1992 'Prologue: Disciplining music', in K. Bergeron and P. V. Bohlman (eds.), *Disciplining Music: Musicology and its Canons*, University of Chicago Press, pp. 1–9

Bergman, S., Grewin, C. *et al.* 1990 *MPEG/Audio Subjective Assessments Test Report*, Stockholm, International Organization for Standardization, ISO/IEC JTC1/SC2/WG8

1991 *The SR Report on the MPEG/Audio Subjective Listening Test*, Stockholm, International Organization for Standardization, April/May, ISO/IEC JTC1/SC2/WG11

Berland, J. 1998 'Locating listening: Technological space, popular music, and Canadian mediations', in A. Leyshon, D. Matless and G. Revill (eds.), *The Place of Music*, New York: Guilford, pp. 129–50

2009 *North of Empire: Essays on the Cultural Technologies of Space*, Durham, NC: Duke University Press

Berlant, L. 2008 *The Female Complaint: The Unfinished Business of Sentimentality in American Culture*, Durham, NC: Duke University Press

(ed.) 2000 *Intimacy: A Special Issue* (republication of *Critical Inquiry*, 24/2), University of Chicago Press

Berlant, L. and Warner, M. 1998 'Sex in public', *Critical Inquiry*, 24, 547–66

Beuys, J. 1990 *Energy Plan for the Western Man: Writings by and Interviews with the Artist*, New York: Four Walls Eight Windows

Bharathan, T., Glodan, D., Ramesh, A., Vardhini, B., Baccash, E., Kiselev, P. and Goldenberg, G. 2007 'What do patterns of noise in a teaching hospital and nursing home suggest?', *Noise Health*, 9, 31–4

Biers, K. 2006 'Syncope fever: James Weldon Johnson and the black phonographic voice', *Representations*, 96, 99–125

Biersdorfer, J. D. and Pogue, D. 2009 *iPod: The Missing Manual*, Sebastopol, CA: O'Reilly Media

Bijsterveld, K. 2008 *Mechanical Sound: Technology, Culture, and Public Problems of Noise in the Twentieth Century*, Cambridge, MA: MIT Press

Bingham, N. and Thrift, N. 2000 'Some new instructions for travellers: The geography of Bruno Latour and Michel Serres', in M. Crang and N. Thrift (eds.), *Thinking Space*, London: Routledge, pp. 281–301

Birnholtz, J. P., Gutwin, C. and Hawkey, K. 2007 'Privacy in the open: How attention mediates awareness and privacy in open-plan offices', *Proceedings of the 2007 International ACM Conference on Supporting Group Work*, Sanibel Island, 4–7 November, pp. 51–60

Bishop, C. 2004 'Antagonism and relational aesthetics', *October*, 110, 51–79

Blackman, L. 2007 'Reinventing psychological matters: The importance of the suggestive realm of Tarde's ontology', *Economy and Society*, 36, 574–96

2008 'Affect, relationality and the problem of personality', *Theory, Culture & Society*, 25, 27–51

Blanchot, M. 1988 *The Unavowable Community*, P. Joris (trans.), Tarrytown, NY: Station Hill Press.

Bloch, E. 2009 (1972) *Atheism in Christianity: The Religion of the Exodus and the Kingdom*, J. T. Swan (trans.), London: Verso

Boal, A. 2000 *Theatre of the Oppressed*, C. A. Leal-McBridge, M.-O. Leal-McBridge and E. Fryer (trans.), London: Pluto

Bohlman, P. V. 1991 'Of Yekkes and chamber music in Israel', in S. Blum, P. Bohlman and D. Neuman (eds.), *Ethnomusicology and Modern Music History*, Urbana: University of Illinois Press, pp. 254–67

1993 'Musicology as a political act', *Journal of Musicology*, 11, 411–36

2007 'On colonialism and its aftermaths', *SEM Newsletter*, 41, 4–5

2009 '*Ex oriente lux*: Islam and the Eurovision Song Contest', in P. V. Bohlman, M. Sorce Keller and L. Azzaroni (eds.), *Antropologia della Musica nelle Culture Mediterranee: Interpretazione, Performance, Identità*, Bologna: CLUEB, pp. 171–80

Bondi, L. 2003 'Empathy and identification: Conceptual resources for feminist fieldwork', *ACME*, 2, 64–76

Borch, C. 2007 'Crowds and economic life: Bringing an old figure back in', *Economy and Society*, 36, 549–73

Borgo, D. 2005 *Sync or Swarm: Improvising Music in a Complex Age*, London: Continuum

forthcoming 'Beyond performance: Transmusicking in cyberspace', in N. Cook and R. Pettengill (eds.), *Taking it to the Bridge: Music as Performance*, Ann Arbor, MI: Michigan University Press

Born, G. 1991 'Music, modernism and signification', in A. Benjamin and P. Osborne (eds.), *Thinking Art: Beyond Traditional Aesthetics*, London: Institute of Contemporary Arts, pp. 157–78

1993 'Afterword: Music policy, aesthetic and social difference', in S. Frith, T. Bennett, L. Grossberg, J. Shepherd and G. Turner (eds.), *Rock and Popular Music: Politics, Policies, Institutions*, London: Routledge, pp. 266–93

1995 *Rationalizing Culture: IRCAM, Boulez, and the Institutionalization of the Musical Avant-Garde*, Berkeley: University of California Press

2000 'Music and the representation/articulation of sociocultural identities', in G. Born and D. Hesmondhalgh (eds.), *Western Music and Its Others: Difference, Representation, and Appropriation in Music*, Berkeley: University of California Press, pp. 31–7

2005 'On musical mediation: Ontology, technology and creativity', *Twentieth-Century Music*, 2, 7–36

2007 'Future-making: Corporate performativity and the temporal politics of markets', in D. Held and H. Moore (eds.), *Cultural Politics in a Global Age: Uncertainty, Solidarity and Innovation*, London: Oneworld, pp. 288–96

2009a 'Afterword: Recording: From reproduction to representation to remediation', in N. Cook, D. Leech-Wilkinson, E. Clarke and J. Rink (eds.), *The Cambridge Companion to Recorded Music*, Cambridge University Press, pp. 286–304

2009b 'Listening, mediation, event: Anthropological and sociological perspectives', *Journal of the Royal Musical Association*, 134, 79–89

2010a 'The social and the aesthetic: For a post-Bourdieuian theory of cultural production', *Cultural Sociology*, 4, 171–208

2010b 'For a relational musicology: Interdisciplinarity and music, beyond the practice turn', *Journal of the Royal Musical Association*, 135, 205–43

2011 'Music and the materialization of identities', *Journal of Material Culture*, 16, 376–88

2012 'Music and the social', in M. Clayton, T. Herbert and R. Middleton (eds.), *The Cultural Study of Music: A Critical Introduction*, 2nd Edition, London: Routledge, pp. 261–74

forthcoming 'Music: Ontology, agency, creativity', in L. Chua and M. Elliott (eds.), *Distributed Objects: Meaning and Mattering after Alfred Gell*, Oxford: Berghahn

Born, G. and Barry, A. 2010 'Art–science: From public understanding to public experiment', *Journal of Cultural Economy*, 3, 103–19

Born, G. and Hesmondhalgh, D. (eds.) 2000 *Western Music and Its Others: Difference, Representation, and Appropriation in Music*, Berkeley: University of California Press

Botstein, L. 1985 *Music and Its Public: Habits of Listening and the Crisis of Musical Modernism in Vienna, 1870–1914*, Ph.D. dissertation, Harvard University

1992 'Listening through reading: Musical literacy and the concert audience', *19th-Century Music*, 16, 129–45

Boudreault-Fournier, A. 2011 *Music, Digitization, Mediation: Consumption Study, October 2011 Fieldwork Report*, unpublished ms., University of Oxford

Boulez, P. 1971 *Boulez on Music Today*, S. Bradshaw and R. Rodney Bennett (trans.), London: Faber and Faber

Bourdieu, P. 1979 *Algeria 1960: Essays*, Cambridge University Press

1980 *The Logic of Practice*, R. Nice (trans.), Stanford University Press

1985 'The social space and the genesis of groups', *Theory and Society*, 14, 723–44

1989 'Social space and symbolic power', *Sociological Theory*, 7, 14–25

1990 *In Other Words: Essays Towards a Reflexive Sociology*, Cambridge: Polity

Bourriaud, N. 2002 *Relational Aesthetics*, S. Pleasance and F. Woods (trans.), Dijon: Les Presses du Réel

Bowen, J. R. 2010 *Can Islam Be French? Pluralism and Pragmatism in a Secularist State*, Princeton University Press

Brandenburg, K. 1999 'MP3 and AAC explained', *AES 17th International Conference on High Quality Audio Encoding*, Florence, Italy, September

Brant, H. 1967 'Space as an essential aspect of musical composition', in E. Schwartz and B. Childs (eds.), *Contemporary Composers on Contemporary Music*, New York: Holt, Rinehart and Winston, pp. 221–42

Bråten, S. (ed.) 2007 *On Being Moved: From Mirror Neurons to Empathy*, Amsterdam: John Benjamins

Bregman, A. S. 1994 (1990) *Auditory Scene Analysis: The Perceptual Organization of Sound*, Cambridge, MA: MIT Press

Bregman, A. S., Ahad, P. A., Crum, P. A. C. and O'Reilly, J. 2000 'Effects of time intervals and tone durations on auditory stream segregation', *Attention, Perception, & Psychophysics*, 62, 626–36

Brennan, J. R. 2008 'Lowering the sultan's flag: Sovereignty and decolonization in coastal Kenya', *Comparative Studies in Society and History*, 50, 831–61

Brennan, T. 2004 *The Transmission of Affect*, Ithaca, NY: Cornell University Press

Brill, M. 1985 *Using Office Design to Increase Productivity*, New York: Workplace Design and Productivity Inc.

Brown, G., Lawrence, T. B. and Robinson, S. L. 2005 'Territoriality in organisations', *Academy of Management Review*, 30, 577–94

Brown, J. S. H. and Brightman, R. 1988 *'The Orders of the Dreamed': George Nelson on Cree and Northern Ojibwa Religion and Myth, 1823*, Winnipeg: University of Manitoba Press

Browner, T. 2002 *Heartbeat of the People: Music and Dance of the Northern Pow-wow*, Urbana: University of Illinois Press

Bull, M. 2000 *Sounding Out the City: Personal Stereos and the Management of Everyday Life*, Oxford: Berg

    2007 *Sound Moves: iPod Culture and Urban Experience*, London: Routledge

Bull, M. and Back, L. (eds.) 2003 *The Auditory Culture Reader*, Oxford: Berg

Bunzl, M. 2007 *Anti-Semitism and Islamophobia: Hatreds Old and New in Europe*, Chicago, IL: Prickly Paradigm Press

Burkart, P. and McCourt, T. 2006 *Digital Music Wars*, Lanham, MD: Rowman and Littlefield

Burke, E. 1998 *Precision Heart Rate Training*, Champaign, IL: Human Kinetics Publishers

Burnham, S. 1995 *Beethoven Hero*, Princeton University Press

Cabrera, D. 1994 *Sound Space and Edgard Varèse's* Poème électronique, MA thesis, University of Technology, Sydney

Cage, J. 1961 *Silence*, Middletown, CT: Wesleyan University Press

Caldwell, C. 2009 *Reflections on the Revolution in Europe: Immigration, Islam, and the West*, New York: Doubleday

Callon, M. 2007 'What does it mean to say that economics is performative?', in D. MacKenzie, F. Muniesa and L. Siu (eds.), *Do Economists Make Markets?: On the Performativity of Economics*, Princeton University Press, pp. 311–57

Campbell, E. 2010 *Boulez, Music and Philosophy*, Cambridge University Press

Canada, 1876 'An act to amend and consolidate the laws respecting Indians [The Indian Act]', 12 April, on the *National Aboriginal Document Database*, epe. lac-bac.gc.ca/100/205/301/ic/cdc/aboriginaldocs/m-stat.htm (last accessed 18 August 2012)

Candea, M. 2010 'Introduction: Revisiting Tarde's house', in M. Candea (ed.), *The Social after Gabriel Tarde: Debates and Assessments*, London: Routledge, pp. 1–24

Carpenter, E. 1960 'Acoustic space', in E. Carpenter and M. McLuhan (eds.), *Explorations in Communication*, Boston, MA: Beacon Press, pp. 65–70

Casey, E. S. 1996 'How to get from space to place in a fairly short stretch of time: Phenomenological prolegomena', in S. Feld and K. H. Basso (eds.), *Senses of Place*, Santa Fe, NM: School of American Research Press, pp. 13–52

Central Intelligence Agency. 1963 *KUBARK Counterintelligence Interrogation*, July, www. gwu.edu/~nsarchiv/NSAEBB/NSAEBB122/index.htm#kubark (last accessed 18 August 2012)

Chakrabarty, D. 1992 'Postcoloniality and the artifice of history: Who speaks for "Indian" pasts?', *Representations*, 37, 1–26

Chanan, M. 1995 *Repeated Takes: A Short History of Recording and its Effects on Music*, London: Verso

Chang, V. 2009 'Records that play: The present past in sampling practice', *Popular Music*, 28, 143–59

Chiariglione, L. 2003 'Riding the media bits', http://ride.chiariglione.org/ (last accessed 18 August 2012)

Ching, B. 2001 *Wrong's What I Do Best: Hard Country Music and Contemporary Culture*, Oxford University Press

Chion, M. 1994 *Audio-Vision: Sound on Screen*, C. Gorbman (trans.), New York: Columbia University Press

Chowning, J. M. 1977 'The simulation of moving sound sources', *Computer Music Journal*, 1, 48–52

Christensen, T. 2008 'Tonalité before and after', *Paper Presented at the Tonality in Perspective Conference*, King's College, London, 27–9 March

Clark, C. 1997 'Forging identity: Beethoven's "Ode" as European anthem', *Critical Inquiry*, 23, 789–807

Clarke, E. F. 1999 'Subject-position and the specification of invariants in music by Frank Zappa and P. J. Harvey', *Music Analysis*, 18, 347–74

   2003 'Music and psychology', in M. Clayton, T. Herbert and R. Middleton (eds.), *The Cultural Study of Music: A Critical Introduction*, London: Routledge, pp. 113–23

   2005 *Ways of Listening: An Ecological Approach to the Perception of Musical Meaning*, Oxford University Press.

Clarke, D. and Clarke, E. F. (eds.) 2011 *Music and Consciousness: Philosophical, Psychological and Cultural Perspectives*, Oxford University Press

Clarke, E., Dibben, N. and Pitts, S. 2010 *Music and Mind in Everyday Life*, Oxford University Press

Clayton, M., Sager, R. and Will, U. 2004 'In time with the music: The concept of entrainment and its significance for ethnomusicology', *European Seminar in Ethnomusicology Counterpoint*, 1, www.open.ac.uk/Arts/experience/ InTimeWithTheMusic.pdf (last accessed 18 August 2012)

Cloonan, M. and Johnson, B. 2002 'Killing me softly with his song: An initial investigation into the use of popular music as a tool of oppression', *Popular Music*, 21, 27–39

Cobb, N. 1982 'A singles' club in disguise', *Boston Globe*, Boston, 27 June, 1

Connell, J. and Gibson, C. 2003 *Sound Tracks: Popular Music, Identity and Place*, London: Routledge

Connolly, W. E. 2011 *A World of Becoming*, Durham, NC: Duke University Press

Connor, S. 1997 'The modern auditory I', in R. Porter (ed.), *Rewriting the Self: Histories from the Renaissance to the Present*, London: Routledge, pp. 203–23

1999 'CP: Or, a few don'ts by a cultural phenomenologist', *Parallax*, 5, 17–31

2000a 'Making an issue of cultural phenomenology', *Critical Quarterly*, 42, 2–6

2000b *Dumbstruck: A Cultural History of Ventriloquism*, Oxford University Press

Cook, N. 2003 'Music as performance', in M. Clayton, T. Herbert and R. Middleton (eds.), *The Cultural Study of Music: A Critical Introduction*, London: Routledge, pp. 204–14

2007 *The Schenker Project: Culture, Race, and Music Theory in Fin-de-siècle Vienna*, Oxford University Press

2008 'We are all (ethno) musicologists now', in H. Stobart (ed.), *The New (Ethno-) Musicologies*, Lanham, MD: Scarecrow, pp. 48–70

Coombe, R. J. 1998 *The Cultural Life of Intellectual Properties: Authorship, Appropriation, and the Law*, Durham, NC: Duke University Press

Corbin, A. 1998 *Village Bells: Sound and Meaning in the Nineteenth-Century French Countryside*, New York: Columbia University Press.

Corbin, J. M. and Strauss, A. L. 2008 *Basics of Qualitative Research: Techniques and Procedures for Developing Grounded Theory*, 3rd edition, London: Sage

Crang, M. and Thrift, N. 2000 'Introduction: Thinking space', in M. Crang and N. Thrift (eds.), *Thinking Space*, London: Routledge, pp. 1–30

Csordas, T. J. 1997 *The Sacred Self: A Cultural Phenomenology of Charismatic Healing*, Berkeley: University of California Press

Cumming-Bruce, N. and Erlanger, S. 2009 'In bastion of tolerance, Swiss reject construction of minarets on mosques', *New York Times*, 30 November, pp. A6 and A12

Cun, K. 2007 'I heart Nike plus', 19 October, accessed on 15 December 2010, www.kimberlycun.com/2007/10/19/i/ (last accessed 18 August 2012)

Cusick, S. 2006 'Music as torture/music as weapon', *TRANS – Revista Transcultural de Musica*, 10, www.sibetrans.com/trans/a152/music-as-torture-music-as-weapon (last accessed 18 August 2012)

2008 '"You are in a place that is out of the world ...": Music in the detention camps of the global war on terror', *Journal of the Society of American Music*, 2, 1–26

Dalziel, K. 2008 'A patient's perspective', in V. Hume (ed.), *Transplant*, London: RB&H Arts

Dammann, G. 2007 'Classical music's new lease of Second Life', *guardian.co.uk Music Blog*, 15 August, www.guardian.co.uk/music/musicblog/2007/aug/15/classicalmusicsnewleaseof (last accessed 18 August 2012)

Davis, M. 1965 *The Undecidable: Basic Papers on Undecidable Propositions, Unsolvable Problems and Computable Functions*, New York: Raven Press

De Blij, H. J. 1968 *Mombasa: An African City*, Evanston, IL: Northwestern University Press

Debord, G. 2009 *Correspondence: The Foundation of the Situationist International (June 1957–August 1960)*, Los Angeles, CA: Semiotext(e)

de Chardin, T. 1959 *The Phenomenon of Man*, B. Wall (trans.), London: Collins

Delamont, S. and Stephens, N. 2008 'Up on the roof: The embodied habitus of diasporic capoeira', *Cultural Sociology*, 2, 57–74

de la Motte-Haber, H. 1998 'Ton–Raüme–Felder–Objekte/Sound–spaces–fields–objects', in B. Leitner (ed.), *Ton, Raum = Sound, Space*, Ostfildern-Ruit: Cantz, www.bernhardleitner.com/texts (last accessed 18 August 2012)

    1999 'Space–environment–shared world: Robin Minard's sound installations', in B. Schulz (ed.), *Robin Minard: Silent Music/Between Sound Art and Acoustic Design*, Heidelberg: Kehrer, pp. 34–56

Deleuze, G. and Guattari, F. 1987 *A Thousand Plateaus: Capitalism and Schizophrenia*, Minneapolis: University of Minnesota Press

Demers, J. T. 2010 *Listening Through the Noise: The Aesthetics of Experimental Electronic Music*, New York: Oxford University Press

DeNora, T. 1986 'How is extra-musical meaning possible? Music as a place and space for "work"', *Sociological Theory*, 4, 84–94

    1999 'Music as a technology of the self', *Poetics*, 7, 31–56

    2000 *Music in Everyday Life*, Cambridge University Press

    2003 *After Adorno: Rethinking Music Sociology*, Cambridge University Press

    2011 'Practical consciousness and social relation in *musecological* perspective', in D. Clarke and E. F. Clarke (eds.), *Music and Consciousness*, Oxford University Press

Derrida, J. 1997 *Politics of Friendship*, G. Collins (trans.), London: Verso

    2006 (1993) *Spectres of Marx: The State of the Debt, the Work of Mourning and the New International*, P. Kamuf (trans.), London: Routledge

des Jardins, G. (ed.) 1994 *Max Neuhaus, Sound Works, Volume 1: Inscription*, Ostfildern-Stuttgart: Catz

Diamond, B. 2002 'Native American contemporary music: The women', *The World of Music*, 44, 11–39

    2008 *Native American Music in Eastern North America: Experiencing Music, Expressing Culture*, Oxford University Press

Dibben, N. 2009 *Björk*, London: Equinox

Dibben, N. and Williamson, V. 2007 'An exploratory survey of in-vehicle music listening', *Psychology of Music*, 35, 571–89

Dickson, N. 2008 'iPods are antisocial', *Coals [2] Newcastle Blog*, 30 January, http://blog.coals2newcastle.com/2008/01/ipods-are-antisocial.html (last accessed 18 August 2012)

Ding, S. 2008 'Users privacy preferences in open plan offices', *Facilities*, 26, 401–17

Donley, L. W. 1982 'House power: Swahili space and symbolic markers', in I. Hodder (ed.), *Symbolic and Structural Archaeology*, Cambridge University Press, pp. 63–73

Doyle, P. 2005 *Echo and Reverb: Fabricating Space in Popular Music, 1900–1960*, Middletown, CT: Wesleyan University Press

Dozza, M., Horak, F. B. and Chiari, L. 2007 'Auditory biofeedback substitutes for loss of sensory information in maintaining stance', *Experimental Brain Research*, 178, 37–48

Drever, J. L. 1999 'The exploitation of "tangible ghosts": Conjectures on soundscape recording and its reappropriation in sound art', *Organised Sound*, 4, 25–9

Dr_Evil_MD. 2010 'Re: What's your favourite PowerSong/', 28 October, www.for-ums.nike.com/thread.jspa?threadID=30551&start=90&tstart=0 (last accessed 17 December 2010 – content no longer available as of 23 May 2012)

Drobnick, J. (ed.) 2004 *Aural Cultures*, Toronto: YYZ Books

Du Bois, W. E. B. 1999 (1903) *The Souls of Black Folk: Authoritative Text, Contexts, Criticism*, H. L. Gates Jr and T. H. Oliver (eds.), New York: Norton

Dueck, B. 2007 'Public and intimate sociability in First Nations and Métis fiddling', *Ethnomusicology*, 51, 30–63

   Forthcoming *Musical Intimacies and Indigenous Imaginaries: Aboriginal Music and Dance in Public Performance in Manitoba*, Oxford University Press

Du Gay, P., Hall, S., Janes, L., Mackay, H. and Negus, K. (eds.) 1997 *Doing Cultural Studies: The Story of the Sony Walkman*, London: Sage

Eade, J. 1996 'Nationalism, community, and the Islamization of space in London', in B. D. Metcalf (ed.), *Making Muslim Space in North America and Europe*, Berkeley: University of California Press, pp. 271–33

Elden, S. 2004 *Understanding Henri Lefebvre: Theory and the Possible*, London: Continuum

   2009 *Terror and Territory: The Spatial Extent of Sovereignty*, Minneapolis: University of Minnesota Press

El Guindi, F. 1999 *Veil: Modesty, Privacy, and Resistance*, New York: Berg

   2008 *By Noon Prayer: The Rhythm of Islam*, Oxford: Berg

Elias, N. 2000 *The Civilizing Process: Sociogenetic and Psychogenetic Investigations*, Oxford: Blackwell

Ellis, C., Lassiter, L. E. and Dunham, G. H. 2005 *Powwow*, Lincoln, NE: University of Nebraska Press

Ellman, M. 1993 *The Hunger Artists: Starving, Writing and Imprisonment*, London: Virago

el-Zein, A. H. M. 1974 *The Sacred Meadows: A Structural Analysis of Religious Symbolism in an East African Town*, Evanston, IL: Northwestern University Press

Emmerson, S. 1998 'Aural landscape: musical space', *Organised Sound*, 135–40

   (ed.) 1986 *The Language of Electroacoustic Music*, London: Macmillan

Engh, B. 1999 'After "His Master's Voice"', *New Formations*, 38, 54–63

Erlmann, V. (ed.) 2004 *Hearing Cultures: Essays on Sound, Listening and Modernity*, Oxford: Berg

Esposito, R. 2008 *Bíos: Biopolitics and Philosophy*, T. Campbell (trans.), Minneapolis: University of Minnesota Press

2009 *Communitas: The Origin and Destiny of Community*, T. Campbell (trans.), Stanford University Press

Etherington, B. 2007 'Instrumentalising musical ethics: Edward Said and the West–Eastern Divan Orchestra', *Australasian Music Research*, 9, 121–9

Farneth, D. 1996 'La Monte Young – Marian Zazeela: Ultra modern minimalists', *Metrobeat*, April, http://melafoundation.org/farneth.htm (last accessed 18 August 2012)

Fast, H. 2006 Invitation to *A Nightsong Action*, unpublished
2007 Artist Statement, unpublished

Featherstone, L. and United Students Against Sweatshops 2002 *Students Against Sweatshops: The Making of a Movement*, London: Verso

Federhofer, H. (ed.) 1990 *Heinrich Schenker als Essayist und Kritiker: Gesammelte Aufsätze, Rezensionen und kleinere Berichte aus den Jahren 1891–1901*, Hildesheim: Georg Olms Verlag

Feld, S. 1982 *Sound and Sentiment: Birds, Weeping, Poetics, and Song in Kaluli Expression*, Philadelphia: University of Pennsylvania Press
1994 'From ethnomusicology to echo-muse-ecology: Reading R. Murray Schafer in the Papua New Guinea rainforest', *The Soundscape Newsletter*, 8, www.acousticecology.org/writings/echomuseecology.html (last accessed 18 August 2012)
1996 'Waterfalls of song: An acoustemology of place resounding in Bosavi, Papua New Guinea', in S. Feld and K. H. Basso (eds.), *Senses of Place*, Santa Fe, NM: School of American Research Press, pp. 91–135

Feld, S. and Basso, K. H. (eds.) 1996 *Senses of Place*, Santa Fe, NM: School of American Research Press

Feld, S. and Brenneis, D. 2004 'Doing anthropology in sound', *American Ethnologist*, 31, 461–74

Fennes, N. 2010 *Muezzin Trifft Pummerin: Materielle Und Praktische Aspekte Des Islamischen Gebetsrufs in Wien*, MPhil dissertation, University of Vienna

Fisher, C. 1993 'Boredom at work: A neglected concept', *Human Relations*, 46, 395–417

Fisher, M. 2009 *Capitalist Realism: Is There No Alternative?* Winchester: Zero Books

Fishman-Johnson, E. 1993–4 'The movement of sound in space: An update', *Proceedings of the Bowling Green State University New Music and Art Festivals, 14 and 15 Paper Sessions, Contemporary Music Forum*, 5–6, 15–21

Fletcher, H. 1929 *Speech and Hearing, With an Introduction by H. D. Arnold*, New York: Van Nostrand

Foblets, M.-C. (ed.) 2008 *Islam and Europe: Challenges and Opportunities*, Leuven University Press

Foley, S. 1981 *Space, Time, Sound: Conceptual Art in the San Francisco Bay Area, the 1970s*, San Francisco Museum of Modern Art

Foucault, M. 1977 *Discipline and Punish: The Birth of the Prison*, A. Sheridan (trans.), New York: Vintage

    2003 '*Society Must Be Defended*': *Lectures at the Collège de France, 1975–76*, D. Macey (trans.), M. Bertani and A. Fontana (eds.), New York: Picador

Fox, A. A. 2004 *Real Country: Music and Language in Working-Class Culture*, Durham, NC: Duke University Press

Fox, T. 1972 Programme notes to *Action for a Tower Room*, unpublished

    1982 *Metaphorical Instruments*, Berlin: DAAD Galerie

Friedman, A. 1977 'Responsible autonomy versus direct control over the labour process', *Capital and Class*, 1, 43–57

Friedman, K. (ed.) 1998 *Fluxus Reader*, New York: Academy Editions

    (ed.) 1990 *Fluxus Performance Workbook*, Trondheim: G. Nordo

Friesen, G. 1987 *The Canadian Prairies: A History*, University of Toronto Press

Frith, S. 2001 'Pop music', in S. Frith, W. Straw and J. Street (eds.), *The Cambridge Companion to Pop and Rock*, Cambridge University Press, pp. 93–108

    2002 'Music and everyday life', *Critical Quarterly*, 44, 35–48

Fuchs, H. 1991 *Report on the MPEG/Audio Subjective Listening Test in Hannover (Draft)*, Hannover, Germany, International Organization for Standardization, ISO/IEC JTC1/SC2/WG11

Fuller, M. 2005 *Media Ecologies: Materialist Energies in Art and Technoculture*, Cambridge, MA: MIT Press

Gal, S. 2002 'A semiotics of the public/private distinction', *Differences*, 13, 77–95

Galloway, A. R. 2004 *Protocol: How Control Exists After Decentralization*, Cambridge, MA: MIT Press

Gatens, M. and Lloyd, G. 1999 *Collective Imaginings: Spinoza, Past and Present*, London: Routledge

Gaver, W. W. 1993a 'What in the world do we hear?: An ecological approach to auditory event perception', *Ecological Psychology*, 5, 1–29

    1993b 'How do we hear in the world?: Explorations in ecological acoustics', *Ecological Psychology*, 5, 285–313

Gerlach, J. 2006 *Zwischen Pop und Dschihad: Muslime Jugendliche in Deutschland*, Berlin: Ch. Links

Gernsback, H. 1958 '400 loudspeakers', *Radio-Electronics*, October, 47

Ghaidan, U. 1975 *Lamu: A Study of the Swahili Town*, Nairobi: Kenya Literature Bureau

Gilroy, P. 1993 *The Black Atlantic: Modernity and Double Consciousness*, London: Verso

Goehr, A. 1998 *Finding the Key: Selected Writings of Alexander Goehr*, D. Puffet (ed.), London: Faber and Faber

Goethe, J. W. von 1850 *Conversations of Goethe with Eckermann and Soret*, Vol. II, J. Oxenford (trans.), London: Smith, Elder and Co.

Goffman, E. 1967 *Interaction Ritual: Essays on Face-to-Face Behavior*, Chicago, IL: Aldine

1968 (1961) *Asylums: Essays on the Social Situation of Mental Patients and Other Inmates*, Harmondsworth: Penguin

1971 *The Presentation of the Self in Everyday Life*, Harmondsworth: Penguin

1974 *Frame Analysis: An Essay on the Organization of Experience*, New York: Harper & Row

Goldsmith, P. 2011 'The Mombasa Republican Council conflict assessment: Threats and opportunities for engagement', Kenya Civil Society Strengthening Programme, USAID-Kenya, unpublished report

Göle, N. 2002 'Islam in public: New visibilities and new imaginaries', *Public Culture*, 14, 173–90

2009 'Turkish delight in Vienna: Art, Islam, and European public culture', *Cultural Politics*, 5, 277–98

Göle, N. and Ammann, L. (eds.) 2006 *Islam in Public: Turkey, Iran and Europe*, Istanbul: Bilgi University Press

Goodman, S. 2009 *Sonic Warfare: Sound, Affect, and the Ecology of Fear*, Cambridge, MA: MIT Press

Graham, W. A. and Kermani, N. 2006 'Recitation and aesthetic reception', in J. D. McAuliffe (ed.), *The Cambridge Companion to the Qur'ān*, Cambridge University Press, pp. 115–44

Grewin, C. and Rydén, T. 1991 *Subjective Assessment of Low Bit-Rate Audio Codecs*, 10th International Conference of the Audio Engineering Society: Images of Audio, London

Gross, M. 2010 *Moral Dilemmas of Modern War: Torture, Assassination and Blackmail in an Age of Asymmetric Conflict*, Cambridge University Press

Grumet, G. W. 1993 'Pandemonium in the modern hospital', *New England Journal of Medicine*, 328, 433–7

Guilbault, J. 2010 'Music, politics, and pleasure: Live Soca in Trinidad', *Small Axe*, 14, 16–29

Gunaratnam, Y. 2009 'Auditory space, ethics and hospitality: "Noise", alterity and care at the end of life', *Body and Society*, 15, 1–19

Haake, A. B. 2010 *Music Listening in UK Offices: Balancing Internal Needs and External Considerations*, Ph.D. dissertation, University of Sheffield

2011 'Individual music listening in workplace settings: An exploratory survey of offices in the UK', *Musicae Scientiae*, 15, 107–29

Habermas, J. 1989 (1962) *The Structural Transformation of the Public Sphere: An Inquiry into a Category of Bourgeois Society*, T. Burger and F. Lawrence (trans.), Cambridge: Polity

Hall, E. T. 1969 *The Hidden Dimension: Man's Use of Space in Public and Private*, London: Bodley Head

1974 *Handbook for Proxemic Research*, Washington, DC: American Anthropological Association

Hallowell, A. I. 1955 *Culture and Experience*, Philadelphia: Pennsylvania University Press

1992 *The Ojibwa of Berens River: Ethnography into History*, Fort Worth, TX: Harcourt Bruce Jovanovich College Publishers

Hardt, M. and Negri, A. 2000 *Empire*, Cambridge, MA: Harvard University Press

2004 *Multitude: War and Democracy in the Age of Empire*, London: Hamish Hamilton

Harley, M. A. 1998 'Spatiality of sound and stream segregation in twentieth-century instrumental music', *Organised Sound*, 3, 147–66

Hayden, C. 2010 'The proper copy', *Journal of Cultural Economy*, 3, 85–102

Hecht, D. and Simone, M. A. 1994 *Invisible Governance: The Art of African Micro-Politics*, New York: Autonomedia

Heidegger, M. 1962 *Being and Time*, New York: Harper and Row

Hennion, A. 1993 *La Passion Musicale: Une Sociologie de la Médiation*, Paris: Métailié

2003 'Music and mediation: Toward a new sociology of music', in M. Clayton, T. Herbert and R. Middleton (eds.), *The Cultural Study of Music: A Critical Introduction*, London: Routledge, pp. 80–91

2007 'Those things that hold us together: Taste and sociology', *Cultural Sociology*, 1, 97–114

Herder, J. G. 1778–9 *Stimmen der Völker in Liedern: Volkslieder*, 2 vols., Leipzig: Weygandische Buchhandlung

1998 *Kalligone: Vom Angenehmen und Schönen*, in *Johann Gottfried Herder Werke*, vol. VIII, Frankfurt am Main: Deutscher Klassiker Verlag, pp. 641–964

Herzfeld, M. 1997 *Cultural Intimacy: Social Poetics in the Nation-State*, London: Routledge

Hesmondhalgh, D. 2002 *The Cultural Industries*, London: Sage

2009 'The digitalisation of music', in A. Pratt and P. Jeffcutt (eds.), *Creativity, Innovation and the Cultural Economy*, London: Routledge, pp. 57–72

Higgins, C. 2007 'Website sets out its stall for first online symphonic concert', *Guardian*, 14 August, www.guardian.co.uk/uk/2007/aug/14/musicnews.digitalmedia (last accessed 18 August 2012)

Higgins, H. 2002 *Fluxus Experience*, Berkeley: University of California Press

Hilmes, M. 2005 'Is there a field called Sound Culture Studies? And does it matter?', *American Quarterly*, 57, 249–59

Hinchliffe, S. 2010 'Working with multiples: A non-representational approach to environmental issues', in B. Anderson and P. Harrison (eds.), *Taking-Place: Non-Representational Theories and Geography*, London: Ashgate, pp. 303–20

Hirschkind, C. 2001a 'Civic virtue and religious reason: An Islamic counterpublic', *Cultural Anthropology*, 16, 3–34

2001b 'The ethics of listening: Cassette-sermon audition in contemporary Egypt', *American Ethnologist*, 28, 623–49

2004 'Hearing modernity: Egypt, Islam, and the pious ear', in V. Erlmann (ed.), *Hearing Cultures: Essays on Sound, Listening and Modernity*, Oxford: Berg, pp. 131–52

2006 *The Ethical Soundscape: Cassette Sermons and Islamic Counterpublics*, New York: Columbia University Press

Hochschild, A. 1997 *The Time Bind: When Work Becomes Home and Home Becomes Work*, New York: Metropolitan Books

Holt, F. 2007 *Genre in Popular Music*, University of Chicago Press

Hosokawa, S. 1984 'The Walkman effect', *Popular Music*, 4, 165–80

Howes, D. 1991 *The Varieties of Sensory Experience: A Sourcebook in the Anthropology of the Senses*, University of Toronto Press

Ihde, D. 1976 *Listening and Voice: A Phenomonology of Sound*, Athens, OH: University of Ohio Press

Ingham, A. 1985 'From public issue to personal trouble: Well-being and the fiscal crisis of the state', *Sociology of Sport Journal*, 2, 43–55

Ingold, T. 2000a. 'Culture, perception and cognition', in *The Perception of the Environment: Essays on Livelihood, Dwelling and Skill*, London: Routledge, pp. 157–71

    2000b. 'Stop, look and listen! Vision, hearing and human movement', in *The Perception of the Environment: Essays on Livelihood, Dwelling and Skill*, London: Routledge, pp. 243–87

Jakobs, K. 2003 'Information technology standards, standards setting and standards research', *Cotwolds Conference on Technology Standards and the Public Interest*, Cotswolds

James, D. 1997 '"Music of origin": Class, social category and the performers and audience of "Kiba", a South African migrant genre', *Africa*, 67, 454–75

Jameson, F. 1988 'The vanishing mediator; Or, Max Weber as storyteller', in *The Ideologies of Theory II*, Minneapolis: University of Minnesota Press

Jankélévitch, V. 2003 *Music and the Ineffable*, C. Abbate (trans.), Princeton University Press

Johnson, B. and Cloonan, M. 2009 *Dark Side of the Tune: Popular Music and Violence*, Burlington: Ashgate

Johnson, J. H. 1995 *Listening in Paris: A Cultural History*, Berkeley: University of California Press

Johnson, M. 1987 *The Body in the Mind: The Bodily Basis of Meaning, Imagination, and Reason*, Chicago University Press

Johnson, M. and Larson, S. 2003 '"Something in the way she moves" – Metaphors of musical motion', *Metaphor and Symbol*, 18, 63–84

Johnston, J. D. 1988 'Transform coding of audio signals using perceptual noise criteria', *IEEE Journal on Selected Areas in Communications*, 6, 314–23

Johnston, P. 1983 *Native Children and the Child Welfare System*, Toronto: Canadian Council on Social Development in association with James Lorimer and Company

Jones, S. and Schumacher, T. 1992 'Muzak: On functional music and power', *Critical Studies in Mass Communication*, 9, 156–69

Kahn, D. 1999 *Noise, Water, Meat: A History of Sound in the Arts*, Cambridge, MA: MIT Press

    n.d. *The Arts of Sound Art and Music*, www.douglaskahn.com/writings/douglas_kahn-sound_art.pdf (last accessed 18 August 2012)

Kahn, D. and Whitehead, G. (eds.) 1992 *Wireless Imagination: Sound, Radio, and the Avant-Garde*, Cambridge, MA: MIT Press

Karageorghis, C. and Priest, D. 2008 'Music in sport and exercise: An update on research and application', *The Sport Journal*, 11, www.thesportjournal. org/article/music-sport-and-exercise-update-research-and-application (last accessed 18 August 2012)

Kelty, C. 2008 *Two Bits*, Durham, NC: Duke University Press.

Kidder, R. M. 1982 'Banning the Walkman: What does it mean?', *Christian Science Monitor*, 8 September

Kim-Cohen, S. 2009 *In the Blink of an Ear: Toward a Non-Cochlear Sonic Art*, New York: Continuum

Kindy, H. 1972 *Life and Politics in Mombasa*, Nairobi: East African Publishing House

Kirk, R. 1956 'Learning, a major factor influencing preferences for high-fidelity reproducing systems', *Journal of the Acoustical Society of America*, 28, 1,113–6

Kittay, J. 2008 'The sound surround: Exploring how one might design the everyday soundscape for the truly captive audience', *Nordic Journal of Music Therapy*, 17, 41–54

Kittler, F. 1999 *Gramophone, Film, Typewriter*, G. Winthrop-Young and M. Wutz (trans.), Stanford University Press

Klausen, J. 2005 *The Islamic Challenge: Politics and Religion in Western Europe*, Oxford University Press

Klein, N. 1999 *No Logo: Taking Aim at the Brand Bullies*, New York: Picador

Korczynski M. 2007 'Music and meaning on the factory floor', *Work and Occupations*, 34, 253–89

Korczynski, M. and Jones, K. 2006 'Instrumental music? The social origins of broadcast music in British factories', *Popular Music*, 25, 145–64

Korczynski, M., Robertson, E., Pickering, M. and Jones, K. 2005 '"We sang ourselves through that war": Women, music and factory work in World War Two', *Labour History Review*, 70, 185–214

Krasner, M. A. 1979 *Digital Encoding of Speech and Audio Signals Based on the Perceptual Requirements of the Auditory System*, Ph.D. dissertation, Massachusetts Institute of Technology

Kresse, K. 2007 *Philosophising in Mombasa: Knowledge, Islam and Intellectual Practice on the Swahili Coast*, Edinburgh University Press

  2009 'Muslim politics in postcolonial Kenya: Negotiating knowledge on the double-periphery', *Journal of the Royal Anthropological Institute*, 15, S76–S94

Krims, A. 2007 *Music and Urban Geography*, London: Routledge

Kruth, P. and Stobart, H. 2000 *Sound*, Cambridge University Press

LaBelle, B. 2004 *Site-Specific Sound*, Frankfurt: Errant Bodies Press/Selektion with Ground Fault Recordings

  2006 *Background Noise: Perspectives on Sound Art*, London: Continuum

2010 *Acoustic Territories: Sound Culture and Everyday Life*, London: Continuum

Lacan, J. 1979 *The Four Fundamental Concepts of Psycho-Analysis*, A. Sheridan (trans.), Harmondsworth: Penguin

1993 *The Psychoses: The Seminar of Jacques Lacan, Book III 1955–56*, J.-A. Miller (ed.), R. Grigg (trans.), London: Routledge

Lacasse, S. 2000 'Listen to My Voice': *The Evocative Power of Vocal Staging in Recorded Rock Music and Other Forms of Vocal Expression*, Ph.D. dissertation, University of Liverpool

Lahire, B. 2003 'From the habitus to an individual heritage of dispositions. Towards a sociology at the level of the individual', *Poetics*, 31, 329–55

Laing, D. 1969 *The Sound of Our Time*, London: Sheed and Ward

Lakoff, G. and Johnson, M. 1980 *Metaphors We Live By*, Chicago University Press

Lander, D. and Lexier, M. (eds.) 1990 *Sound by Artists*, Banff: Walter Philips Gallery

Landers, D. 1985 'Psychophysiological assessment and biofeedback: Applications for athletes in closed-skill sports', in J. Sandweiss and S. Wolf (eds.), *Biofeedback and Sports Science*, New York: Plenum Press, pp. 63–106

Landes, J. B. (ed.) 1998 *Feminism, the Public and the Private*, Oxford University Press

Landy, L. 2007 *Understanding the Art of Sound Organization*, Cambridge, MA: MIT Press

Lasch, C. 1978 *The Culture of Narcissism: American Life in an Age of Diminished Expectations*, New York: Norton

Lash, S. 2002 'Foreword: Individualization in a non-linear mode', in U. Beck and E. Beck-Gernsheim (eds.), *Individualization*, London: Sage, pp. vii–xiii

Lastra, J. 2000 *Sound Technology and the American Cinema: Perception, Representation, Modernity*, New York: Columbia University Press

Lathion, S. 2006 'Muslime in der Schweiz: Identität zwischen "Rathaus" und "Moschee"', in U. Altermatt, M. Delgado and G. Vergauwen (eds.), *Der Islam in Europa: Zwischen Weltpolitik und Alltag*, Stuttgart: W. Kohlhammer, pp. 97–105

Latour, B. 1999 *Pandora's Hope: Essays on the Reality of Science Studies*, Cambridge, MA: Harvard University Press

2005 *Reassembling the Social: An Introduction to Actor-Network Theory*, New York: Oxford University Press

Lauer, J. 2008 'Alienation in the information economy: Toward a Marxist critique of consumer surveillance', in N. Carpenter and B. De Cleen (eds.), *Participation and Media Production: Critical Reflections on Content Creation*, Newcastle-upon-Tyne: Cambridge Scholars, pp. 41–53

Law, J. 2010 'The materials of STS', in D. Hicks and M. C. Beaudry (eds.), *The Oxford Handbook of Material Culture Studies*, Oxford University Press, pp. 173–88

Lawton, J. 1998 'Contemporary hospice care: The sequestration of the unbounded body and the "dirty dying"', *Sociology of Health and Illness*, 20, 121–43

Lederman, A. 1988 'Old Indian and Métis fiddling in Manitoba: Origins, structure and question of syncretism', *The Canadian Journal of Native Studies*, 8/2, 205–30

Lee, T. S. 1999 'Technology and the production of Islamic space: The call to prayer in Singapore', *Ethnomusicology*, 43, 86–100

Lefebvre, H. 1991 (1974) *The Production of Space*, D. Nicholson-Smith (trans.), London: Blackwell

  2004 *Rhythmanalysis: Space, Time, and Everyday Life*, London: Continuum

Leitner, B. n.d. 'Investigations 1971–1976', http://bernhardleitner.at/en/73unters1_2.html (last accessed 1 March 2008)

  (ed.) 1978 *Ton, Raum = Sound, Space*, New York University Press

Lenderman, M. 2006 *Experience the Message: How Experiential Marketing Is Changing the Brand World*, New York: Basic Books

Leppert, R. 1998 'Desire, power and the sonoric landscape: Early modernism and the politics of musical privacy', in A. Leyshon, D. Matless and G. Revill (eds.), *The Place of Music*, New York: Guilford, pp. 291–321

Lessing, G. E. 1779 *Nathan, der Weise: Ein dramatisches Gedicht, in fünf Aufzügen*, Berlin: C. F. Voss

Levin, T. Y. 1990 'For the record: Adorno on music in the age of its technological reproducibility', *October*, 55, 23–47

Lévi-Strauss, C. 1966 *The Savage Mind*, University of Chicago Press

Lewis, S. 2003 'The integration of paid work and the rest of life. Is post-industrial work the new leisure?', *Leisure Studies*, 22, 343–55

Leyshon, A., Matless, D. and Revill, G. (eds.) 1998 *The Place of Music*, New York: Guilford

Licht, A. 2007 *Sound Art: Beyond Music, Between Categories*, New York: Rizzolli International Publications

Lippard, L. 1973 *Six Years: The Dematerialization of the Art Object from 1966 to 1972*, New York: Praeger

  1997 *The Lure of the Local: Senses of Place in a Multi-Centered Society*, New York: New Press

Lorimer, H. 2005 'Cultural geography: The busyness of being "more-than-representational"', *Progress in Human Geography*, 29, 83–94

Lott, E. 1993 *Love and Theft: Blackface Minstrelsy and the American Working Class*, New York: Oxford University Press

Lysloff, R. T. A. and Gay, L. C. (eds.) 2003 *Music and Technoculture*, Middletown, CT: Wesleyan University Press

Mac Daily News 2006 'The making of Apple iPod+Nike sport kit and there's more to come', 24 May, http://macdailynews.com/2006/05/24/the_making_of_apple_ipodnike_sport_kit_and_theres_more_to_come/ (last accessed 18 August 2012)

MacAndrew, C. and Edgerton, R. B. 1969 *Drunken Comportment: A Social Explanation*, Chicago, IL: Aldine

MacDonald, D. A. L. 1956 'Mombasa: The "Arabian Nights" port', *The Montreal Gazette*, 13 October

MacKenzie, D. and Wajcman, J. 1999 *The Social Shaping of Technology*, Milton Keynes: Open University Press

MacKenzie, D., Muniesa, F. and Siu, L. (eds.) 2007 *Do Economists Make Markets?: On the Performativity of Economics*, Princeton University Press

Maguire, J. S. 2008 *Fit for Consumption: Sociology and the Business of Fitness*, London: Routledge

Mahmood, S. 2005 *Politics of Piety: The Islamic Revival and the Feminist Subject*, Princeton University Press

Manitoba 1956 *Acts of the Legislature of the Province of Manitoba 1956: Passed in the Session Held in the Fourth and Fifth Years of the Reign of Her Majesty Queen Elizabeth the Second, and being the Third Session of the Twenty-Fourth Legislature Begun and Holden at Winnipeg, on the Thirty-First Day of January, 1956 and closed by Prorogation on the Twenty-Third Day of April*, Winnipeg: Queen's Printer for [the] Province of Manitoba

Mason, N. 2004 *Inside Out: A Personal History of Pink Floyd*, London: Weidenfeld and Nicolson

Massey, D. B. 2005 *For Space*, London: Sage

May, J. and Thrift, N. J. 2001 *Timespace: Geographies of Temporality*, London: Routledge

Mayer, J. 2008 *The Dark Side: The Inside Story About How the War on Terror Turned into a War on American Ideals*, New York: Doubleday

Mazrui, A. M. and Shariff, I. N. 1994 *The Swahili: Idiom and Identity of an African People*, Trenton, NJ: Africa World Press

Mbembe, A. 2001 *On the Postcolony*, Berkeley: University of California Press

McAdams, S. and Bregman, A. S. 1979 'Hearing musical streams', *Computer Music Journal*, 3, 26–60

McCarrey, M. W., Peterson, L., Edwards, S. and Von Kulmiz, P. 1974 'Landscape office attitudes: Reflections of perceived degree of control over transactions with the environment', *Journal of Applied Psychology*, 59, 401–3

McCartney, A. 2004 'Soundscape works, listening and the touch of sound', in J. Drobnick (ed.), *Aural Cultures*, Toronto: YYZ Books, pp. 179–88

McColl, S. 1996 *Music Criticism in Vienna, 1896–1897: Critically Moving Forms*, Oxford University Press

McCormack, D. P. 2008 'Geographies for moving bodies: Thinking, dancing, spaces', *Geography Compass*, 2, 1,822–36

McCormick, L. 2009 'Higher, faster, louder: Representations of the international music competition', *Cultural Sociology*, 3, 5–30

McCoy, A. J. 2006 *A Question of Torture: CIA Interrogation from the Cold War to the War on Terror*, New York: Metropolitan Books

McIntosh, J. 2009 *The Edge of Islam: Power, Personhood, and Ethnoreligious Boundaries on the Kenya Coast*, Durham, NC: Duke University Press

McLuhan, M. 1964 *Understanding Media*, London: Routledge

McNally, M. D. 2000 *Ojibwe Singers: Hymns, Grief, and a Native Culture in Motion*, Oxford University Press

MCP [Mombasa Conservation Project] 1990 *A Conservation Plan for the Old Town of Mombasa, Kenya*, National Museums of Kenya, Municipal Council of Mombasa, United Nations Development Programme and UNESCO, Mombasa

Meintjes, L. 2003 *Sound of Africa!: Making Music Zulu in a South African Studio*, Durham, NC: Duke University Press

Middleton, J. 1992 *The World of the Swahili: An African Mercantile Civilization*, New Haven, CT: Yale University Press

Middleton, R. 2006 *Voicing the Popular: On the Subjects of Popular Music*, New York: Routledge

 2009a 'Introduction', in *Musical Belongings: Selected Essays*, Farnham: Ashgate, pp. ix–xxiii

 2009b '"Last night a DJ saved my life": Avians, cyborgs and gendered bodies in the era of phonographic technology', in *Musical Belongings: Selected Essays*, Farnham: Ashgate, pp. 211–52

 2009c 'O brother, let's go down home: Loss, nostalgia and the blues', in *Musical Belongings: Selected Essays*, Farnham: Ashgate, pp. 253–70

 2009d 'Global, national, local: Or, a hysteric's account of negative dialectics', in *Musical Belongings: Selected Essays*, Farnham: Ashgate, pp. 293–305

 2009e '*Vox populi, vox dei*. Or, imagine, I'm losing my religion (Hallelujah!): Musical politics after God', in *Musical Belongings: Selected Essays*, Farnham: Ashgate, pp. 329–52

Milner, G. 2009 *Perfecting Sound Forever: The Story of Recorded Music*, London: Granta

Minard, R. 1996 *Sound Installation Art*, Graz: Institut für Elektronischen Musik

Mitchell, J. 2003 *Siblings: Sex and Violence*, Cambridge: Polity Press

Mitchell, K. 1997 'Conflicting geographies of democracy and the public sphere in Vancouver BC', *Transactions of the Institute of British Geographers*, 22, 162–79

Mitchell, T. 2002 *Rule of Experts: Egypt, Techno-Politics, Modernity*, Berkeley: University of California Press

 2007 'The properties of markets', in D. MacKenzie, F. Muniesa and L. Siu (eds.), *Do Economists Make Markets?: On the Performativity of Economics*, Princeton University Press, pp. 244–75

Mol, A. 2002 *The Body Multiple: Ontology in Medical Practice*, Durham, NC: Duke University Press

Moore, A. F. 1993 *Rock: The Primary Text*, Milton Keynes: Open University Press

 1998 'In a big country: The portrayal of wide open spaces in the music of Big Country', in R. Monelle (ed.), *Musica Significans: Proceedings of the 3rd International Congress on Musical Signification*, London: Harwood Academic, pp. 1–6

Moore, A. F. and Dockwray, R. 2008 'The establishment of the virtual performance space in rock', *Twentieth-Century Music*, 5, 219–41

Moore, B. C. J. 2003 *An Introduction to the Psychology of Hearing*, 5th edition, San Diego, CA: Academic Press

Moore, W. E. 1963 *Man, Time and Society*, New York: John Wiley

Morrissey, B. n.d. 'Digital campaign of the decade: Nike plus', *Adweek Media*, www.bestofthe2000s.com/digital-campaign-of-the-decade.html (last accessed 18 June 2010)

Muniesa, F. and Callon, M. 2007 'Economic experiments and the construction of markets', in D. MacKenzie, F. Muniesa and L. Siu (eds.), *Do Economists Make Markets?: On the Performativity of Economics*, Princeton University Press, pp. 163–89

Murray, D. R. 1989 'Producer's Note', from CD liner notes to EMI CDC 7495412, 8

Myatt, T. 1998 'Editorial', in T. Myatt (ed.), *Sound in Space, Organised Sound*, 3, 91–2

Nancy, J.-L. 1991 *The Inoperative Community*, P. Connor, L. Garbus, M. Holland and S. Sawhney (trans.), Minneapolis: University of Minnesota Press

  2000 *Being Singular Plural*, R. D. Richardson and A. E. O'Byrne (trans.), Stanford University Press

  2004 *All'ascolto*, E. Lisciani Petrini (trans.), Milan: Raffaello Cortina Editore

  2007 *Listening*, C. Mandell (trans.), New York: Fordham University Press

Nattiez, J.-J. 1990 *Music and Discourse: Toward a Semiology of Music*, Princeton University Press

Ndurya, M. 2009 'Now coast MPs seek complete autonomy', *Daily Nation*, 9 November

Neuhaus, M. 1988 'LISTEN', *Elusive Sources and 'Like' Spaces*, Turin: Galleria Giorgio Persano, www.max-neuhaus.info/soundworks/vectors/walks/LISTEN/ (last accessed 18 August 2012)

Neuhaus, M. and Loock, U. 1990 'A conversation between Max Neuhaus and Ulrich Loock, Milan, March 25 1990', in M. Neuhaus, *Elusive Sources and 'Like' Spaces*, Turin: Galleria Giorgio Persano, www.max-neuhaus.info/bibliography/ConversationwithUlrichLoock.htm (last accessed 18 August 2012)

Nike Corporation 2009a 'Nike's online privacy policy', 23 June, nikerunning.nike.com/nikeos/p/nikeplus/en_US/support#/faqs/article/3395 (last accessed 18 June 2010)

  2009b 'Get ready to run with Nike+', 27 July, inside.nike.com/blogs/nikerunning_humanrace-en_EMEA/2009/07/27/get-ready-to-run-with-nike (last accessed 18 June 2010)

  2010 'The anatomy of a PowerSong', 22 January, inside.nike.com/blogs/nikerunning_sportmusic-en_US/2010/01/22/anatomy-of-a-powersong (last accessed 18 December 2010)

Nike+ Pro 16. 2010 'Human race 2010??', 5 October, http://forums.nike.com/thread.jspa?threadID=28110&tstart=0 (last accessed 16 December 2010 – content no longer accessible as of 22 May 2012)

Norrington, R. 1989 'Performance note', from CD liner notes to EMI CDC 7495412, 5–7

North, A. C., Hargreaves, D. J. and Hargreaves, J. J. 2004 'The uses of music in everyday life', *Music Perception*, 22, 63–99

Notley, M. 1999 'Musical culture in Vienna at the turn of the twentieth century', in B. Simms (ed.), *Schoenberg, Berg, and Webern: A Companion to the Second Viennese School*, Westport, CT: Greenwood Press, pp. 37–71

Nyman, M. 1974 *Experimental Music: Cage and Beyond*, Cambridge University Press

Ochoa Gautier, A. M. 2006 'Sonic transculturation, epistemologies of purification and the aural public sphere in Latin America', *Social Identities*, 12, 803–25

OED Online 2010 'tune, *n.*', Oxford University Press, November, www.oed.com/ (last accessed 18 August 2012)

Osborne, T. and Rose, N. 2004 'Spatial phenomenotechnics: Making space with Charles Booth and Patrick Geddes', *Environment and Planning D: Society and Space*, 22, 209–28

Osterwold, M. 1998 'Terry Fox: Economy of means – density of meanings', in T. Fox (ed.), *Works with Sound/Arbeiten Mit Klang*, Heidelberg: Kehrer, pp. 17–30

Oswalt, P. 1991 *Iannis Xenakis's Polytopes*, www.oswalt.de/en/text/txt/xenakis.html (last accessed 18 August 2012)

Otterman, M. 2007 *American Torture from the Cold War to Abu Ghraib and Beyond*, Victoria: Melbourne University Press

Ouellette, F. 1968 *Edgard Varèse*, New York: Orion Press

Ouzounian, G. 2008 *Sound Art and Spatial Practices: Situating Sound Installation Art Since 1958*, Ph.D. dissertation, University of California, San Diego

  2009 'Impure thinking practices and clinical acts: The sonorous becomings of Heidi Fast', *Organised Sound*, 14, 75–81

Pateman, C. 1983 'Feminist critiques of the public/private dichotomy', in S. I. Benn and G. F. Gau (eds.), *Public and Private in Social Life*, London: Croom Helm/St Martin's Press, pp. 281–303

Patmore, D. and Clarke, E. F. 2007 'Making and hearing virtual worlds: John Culshaw and the art of record production', *Musicae Scientiae*, 11, 269–93

Patrix, 2005 'Don't come Bach', *Nerve Endings Firing Away Blog*, 10 January, www.ipatrix.com/dont-come-bach/ (last accessed 18 August 2012)

Pearlman, J. 2008 'Gonna fly now', *Runner's World*, July, 76–82

Peisner, D. 2006 'Music as torture: War is loud', *Spin*, 30 November, www.spin.com/ articles/music-torture-war-loud (last accessed 18 August 2012)

  2009 'Annotation to "Music as torture: War is loud"', *Spin*, April, www.spin.com/ articles/music-torture-war-loud (last accessed 18 August 2012)

Piekut, B. 2011 *Experimentalism Otherwise: The New York Avant-Garde and Its Limits*, Berkeley: University of California Press

Pinch, T. 1993 '"Testing – one, two, three … testing!": Toward a sociology of testing', *Science, Technology and Human Values*, 18, 25–41

Pinch, T. and Bijsterveld, K. 2004 'Sound studies: New technologies and music', *Social Studies of Science, Special Issue on Sound Studies: New Technologies and Music*, 34, 635–48

Pohlmann, K. C. 2005 *Principles of Digital Audio*, New York: McGraw-Hill

Porcello, T. 1998 '"Tails out": Social phenomenology and the ethnographic representation of technology in music-making', *Ethnomusicology*, 42, 485–510

Porter, M. A. 1995 'Talking at the margins: Kenyan discourses on homosexuality', in W. Leap (ed.), *Beyond the Lavender Lexicon: Authenticity, Imagination, and Appropriation in Lesbian and Gay Languages*, New York: Gordon and Breach, pp. 133–53

Povinelli, E. 1998 'The state of shame: Australian multiculturalism and the crisis of indigenous citizenship', *Critical Inquiry*, 24, 575–610

  2002 *The Cunning of Recognition: Indigenous Alterities and the Making of Australian Multiculturalism*, Durham, NC: Duke University Press

Prestholdt, J. 2010 'Superpower Osama: Symbolic discourse in the Indian Ocean after the cold war', in C. J. Lee (ed.), *Making a World After Empire: The Bandung Moment and Its Political Afterlives*, Athens, OH: Ohio University Press, pp. 315–50

  2011 'Kenya, the United States, and counterterrorism', *Africa Today*, 57, 2–27

Prichard, C., Korczynski, M. and Elmes, M. 2007 'Music at work: An introduction', *Group and Organization Management*, 32, 4–21

Qureshi, R. B. 1996 'Transcending space: Recitation and community among South Asian Muslims in Canada', in B. D. Metcalf (ed.), *Making Muslim Space in North America and Europe*, Berkeley: University of California Press, pp. 46–64

Rajan, K. S. 2006 *Biocapital: The Constitution of Postgenomic Life*, Durham, NC: Duke University Press

Rebelo, P. 2003 'Performing space', *Organised Sound*, 8, 181–6

Renaud, A. and Rebelo, P. 2006 'Network performance: Strategies and applications', NIME 2006 Network Performance Workshop

Revill, G. 2000 'Music and the politics of sound: Nationalism, citizenship, and auditory space', *Environment and Planning D: Society and Space*, 18, 597–614

Rice, T. 2003 'Soundselves: An acoustemology of sound and self in the Edinburgh Royal Infirmary', *Anthropology Today*, 19, 4–9

  2008 'Sound and the boundless body', in V. Hume (ed.), *Transplant*, London: RB&H Arts

  Forthcoming *Hearing the Hospital: Sound, Listening, Knowledge and Experience*, Wantage: Sean Kingston Press

Rickard, J. 2006 'Rebecca Belmore: Performing power', in *Rebecca Belmore: Fountain* exhibit catalogue, Kamloops Art Gallery, www.rebeccabelmore.com/assets/Performing_Power.pdf (last accessed 18 August 2012)

Robbins J. 2000 *A Symphony in the Brain: The Evolution of the New Brain Wave Biofeedback*, New York: Atlantic Monthly

Robertson, E., Pickering, M. and Korczynski, M. 2008 '"And spinning so with voices meet, like nightingales they sung full sweet": Unravelling representations of singing in pre-industrial textile production', *Cultural and Social History*, 5, 11–32

Rodgers, T. 2010 *Pink Noises: Women on Electronic Music and Sound*, Durham, NC: Duke University Press

Rogers, L. 2008 'Classical music in Second Life', *Bread and Roses: Music, Art, Politics and the Intersections Between Them in Real and Virtual Worlds Blog*, 18 February, http://breadandroseslife.blogspot.com/2008/02/classical-music-in-second-life.html (last accessed 18 August 2012)

Rohrhuber, J. 2007 'Network music', in N. Collins and J. d'Escrivan (eds.), *The Cambridge Companion to Electronic Music*, Cambridge University Press, pp. 140–55

Rose, N. 2007 *The Politics of Everyday Life: Biomedicine, Power, and Subjectivity in the Twenty-First Century*, Princeton University Press

Roseman, M. 1984 'The social structuring of sound: The Temiar of peninsular Malaysia', *Ethnomusicology*, 28, 411–45

Ross, D. 1992 'Introduction', in T. Fox, *Terry Fox: Articulations (Labyrinth/Text Works)*, Philadelphia, PA: Moore College of Art

Rothenbuler, E. W. and Peters, J. D. 1997 'Defining phonography: An experiment in theory', *Musical Quarterly*, 81, 242–64

Rowland, M. (ed.) 1969 (1923) *Bert Williams, Son of Laughter*, New York: Negro Universities Press

Russell, R. 2007 'Richard Thalheimer, founder of Sharper Image, talks for the first time about his ouster', *San Francisco Weekly*, 24 October, www.sfweekly.com/2007-10-24/news/ironic-breeze/full/-1/ (last accessed 18 August 2012)

Sahlins, M. D. 1974 *Stone Age Economics*, London: Tavistock

Salim, A. I. 1973 *Swahili-Speaking Peoples of Kenya's Coast, 1895–1965*, Nairobi: East African Publishing House

Salter, C. 2010 *Entangled: Technology and the Transformation of Performance*, Cambridge, MA: MIT Press

Samuels, D. W. 2004 *Putting a Song on Top of It: Expression and Identity on the San Carlos Apache Reservation*, Tucson: University of Arizona Press

Samuels, D. W., Meintjes, L., Ochoa, A. M. and Porcello, T. 2010 'Soundscapes: Toward a sounded anthropology', *Annual Review of Anthropology*, 39, 329–45

Sandstrom, B. 2000 'Women mix engineers and the power of sound', in P. Moisala and B. Diamond (eds.), *Music and Gender*, Urbana: University of Illinois Press, pp. 289–305

Sandweiss, J. and Wolf, S. (eds.) 1985 'Introduction', in *Biofeedback and Sports Science*, New York: Plenum Press, pp. xi–xii

Sassatelli, M. 2009 *Becoming Europeans: Cultural Identity and Cultural Politics*, London: Palgrave Macmillan

Sawday, J. 1995 *The Body Emblazoned: Dissection and the Human Body in Renaissance Culture*, London: Routledge

Scales, C. 2004 *Powwow Music and the Aboriginal Recording Industry on the Northern Plains: Media, Technology, and Native American Music in the Late Twentieth Century*, Ph.D. dissertation, University of Illinois at Urbana-Champaign

Schaeffer, P. 1966 *Traité des Objets Musicaux*, Paris: Le Seuil

Schafer, R. M. 1994 (1977) *The Soundscape: Our Sonic Environment and the Tuning of the World*, Rochester, VT: Destiny Books

Schenker, H. 1979 (1935) *Free Composition (Der freie Satz)*, E. Oster (ed. and trans.), New York: Longman

Schmitt, B. 1999 *Experiential Marketing: How to Get Customers to Sense, Feel, Think, Act, and Relate to Your Company and Brands*, New York: Free Press

Schoenberg, A. 1978 *Theory of Harmony*, R. Carter (trans.), London: Faber & Faber

Schubert, E. D. 1978 'History of research on hearing', in E. C. Carterette and M. P. Friedman (eds.), *Handbook of Perception, Volume IV: Hearing*, New York: The Academic Press, pp. 41–80

Schulz, B. (ed.) 2002a *Resonanzen: Aspekte der Klangkunst/Resonances: Aspects of Sound Art*, Heidelberg: Kehrer

Schulz, B. 2002b 'The whole corporeality of hearing: An interview with Bernhard Leitner', in B. Schulz (ed.), *Resonanzen: Aspekte Der Klangkunst/Resonances: Aspects of Sound Art*, Heidelberg: Kehrer, pp. 81–8

Schutz, A. 1971 (1964) 'Making music together: A study in social relationship', in A. Brodersen (ed.), *Alfred Schutz: Collected Papers II: Studies in Social Theory*, The Hague: Martinus Nijhoff, pp. 159–78

Scruton, R. 1997 *The Aesthetics of Music*, Oxford: Clarendon Press

Seabright, P. 2004 *The Company of Strangers: A Natural History of Economic Life*, Princeton University Press

Seesemann, R. 2007 'Kenyan Muslims, the aftermath of 9/11, and the "War on Terror"', in B. F. Soares and R. Otayek (eds.), *Islam and Muslim Politics in Africa*, New York: Palgrave Macmillan, pp. 157–76

Sennett, R. 2002 (1977) *The Fall of Public Man*, London: Penguin

Serres, M. 1977 *La Naissance de la Physique dans le Texte de Lucrèce: Fleuves et Turbulences*, Paris: Les Editions de Minuit

  1994 *Atlas*, Paris: Juilliard

Sharrock, J. 2008 'Am I a torturer?', *Mother Jones*, 22 February, http://motherjones.com/politics/2008/02/torture-playlist (last accessed 18 August 2012)

Shaw, R. 1999 *Reclaiming America: Nike, Clean Air, and the New National Activism*, Berkeley: University of California Press

Shepard, R. N. 1964 'Circularity in judgments of relative pitch', *Journal of the Acoustical Society of America*, 36, 2346–53

Shields, R. 2006 'Knowing space', *Theory, Culture & Society*, 23, 147–9

Shore, C. 1980 'Kinds of art that vanish as they are being done', *Oakland Tribune*, 13 January, G32

Sime, W. 1985 'Physiological perception: The key to peak performance in athletic competition', in J. Sandweiss and S. Wolf (eds.), *Biofeedback and Sports Science*, New York: Plenum Press, pp. 33–62

2003 'Sports psychology applications of biofeedback and neurofeedback', in M. S. Schwartz and F. Andrasik (eds.), *Biofeedback: A Practitioner's Guide*, 3rd edition, New York: Guilford, pp. 560–90

Sinclair, S. 1997 *Making Doctors: An Institutional Apprenticeship*, Oxford: Berg

Smalley, D. 1986 'Spectro-morphology and structuring processes', in S. Emmerson (ed.), *The Language of Electroacoustic Music*, London: Macmillan, pp. 61–93

2007 'Space-form and the acousmatic image', *Organised Sound*, 12, 35–58

Smith, B. R. 1999 *The Acoustic World of Early Modern England*, University of Chicago Press

2004 'Listening to the wild blue yonder: The challenges of acoustic ecology', in V. Erlmann (ed.), *Hearing Cultures: Essays on Sound, Listening and Modernity*, Oxford: Berg, pp. 21–41

Smith, M. M. 2001 *Listening to Nineteenth-Century America*, Chapel Hill: The University of North Carolina Press

2004 *Hearing History: A Reader*, Athens, GA: University of Georgia Press

Smith, S. J. 1997 'Beyond geography's visible worlds: A cultural politics of music', *Progress in Human Geography*, 21, 502–29

Smith, S. 2005 'Cairo dilemma over prayer calls', *BBC News*, 29 April, http://news.bbc.co.uk/2/hi/middle_east/4485521.stm (last accessed 18 August 2012)

Smythe, D. 1977 'Communications: Blindspot of Western Marxism', *Canadian Journal of Political and Social Theory*, 1, 1–28

Snow, C. P. 1964 *The Corridors of Power*, Kelly Bray: Stratus Books

Solomon, T. 2005a '"Listening to Istanbul": Imagining place in Turkish rap music', *Studia Musicologica Norvegica*, 31, 46–67

2005b '"Living underground is tough": Authenticity and locality in the hip-hop community in Istanbul, Turkey', *Popular Music*, 24, 1–20

Sorkin, D. J. 2008 *The Religious Enlightenment: Protestants, Jews, and Catholics from London to Vienna*, Princeton University Press.

Stanyek, J. and Piekut, B. 2010 'Deadness: Technologies of the intermundane', *TDR/ The Drama Review*, 54, 14–38

Starrett, G. 1995 'The hexis of interpretation: Islam and the body in the Egyptian popular school', *American Ethnologist*, 22, 953–69

Stasiuk, A. 2009 *Czekając na Turka*, Wołowiec: Wedawnictwo czarne

Steiner, G. 2008 *My Unwritten Books*, London: Weidenfeld and Nicolson

Sterken, S. 2001 'Towards a space-time art: Iannis Xenakis's Polytopes', *Perspectives of New Music*, 39, 262–73

Stern, D. N. 2004 *The Present Moment in Psychotherapy and Everyday Life*, New York: Norton

Sterne, J. 1997 'Sounds like the Mall of America: Programmed music and the architectonics of commercial space', *Ethnomusicology*, 41, 22–50

2003 *The Audible Past: Cultural Origins of Sound Reproduction*, Durham, NC: Duke University Press

2006 'The MP3 as cultural artifact', *New Media and Society*, 8, 825–42

2012a *MP3: The Meaning of a Format*, Durham, NC: Duke University Press

2012b *The Sound Studies Reader*, London: Routledge

Still, A. and Costall, A. (eds.) 1991 *Against Cognitivism: Alternative Foundations for Cognitive Psychology*, Hemel Hempstead: Harvester-Wheatsheaf

Stockfelt, O. 1997 'Adequate modes of listening', A. Kassabian and L. G. Svendsen (trans.), in D. Schwartz, A. Kassabian and L. Siegel (eds.), *Keeping Score: Music, Disciplinarity, Culture*, Charlottesville: University of Virginia Press, pp. 129–47

Stokes, M. 1994 *Ethnicity, Identity, and Music: The Musical Construction of Place*, Oxford: Berg

Story, L. 2007 'The new advertising outlet: Your life', *New York Times*, 14 October

Strathern, M. 1988 *The Gender of the Gift: Problems with Women and Problems with Society in Melanesia*, Berkeley: University of California Press

1990 'The concept of society is theoretically obsolete', in T. Ingold (ed.), *Key Debates in Anthropology*, London: Routledge, pp. 60–6

1996 'Cutting the network', *Journal of the Royal Anthropological Institute*, 2, 517–35

Straw, W. 1991 'Systems of articulation, logics of change: Communities and scenes in popular music', *Cultural Studies*, 5, 368–88

Strawn, J. 1978 'The *Intégrales* of Edgard Varèse: Space, mass, element, and form', *Perspectives of New Music*, 17, 138–60

Strehlo, K. n.d. 'A few great references and sources for iPod running song iLists', marathonman.typepad.com/marathoning_matters/a-few-great-references-and-sources-for-ipod-running-song-ilists.html (last accessed 18 June 2010)

Sundstrom, E., Burt, R. E. and Kamp, D. 1980 'Privacy at work: Architectural correlates of job satisfaction and job performance', *Academy of Management Journal*, 23, 101–17

Taylor, F. W. 1911 *The Principles of Scientific Management*, New York: Harper Brothers

Taylor, T. 2007 *Beyond Exoticism: Western Music and the World*, Durham, NC: Duke University Press

Terranova, T. 2000 'Free labor: Producing culture for the digital economy', *Social Text*, 18, 33–58

Thatcher, R. W. 2004 *Fighting Firewater Fictions: Moving Beyond the Disease Model of Alcoholism in First Nations*, University of Toronto Press

Thompson, E. A. 2002 *The Soundscape of Modernity: Architectural Acoustics and the Culture of Listening in America, 1900–1933*, Cambridge, MA: MIT Press

Thompson, E. P. 1967 'Time, work discipline, and industrial capitalism', *Past and Present*, 38, 56–97

Thorsén, S. 1985 'Musik på en fabrik. En intervjuundersökning om music, arbete och fritid', unpublished report, Gothenburgh University

1987 'Från spinnvisor till P3-musik: En historisk diskussion av arbetsmusikens funktioner (From spin-melodies to P3 music: A historical discussion of the functions of music at work)', *Svensk Tidsskrift för musikforskning*, 7–36

Thrift, N. 2006 'Space', *Theory, Culture & Society*, 23, 139–55

2008 *Non-Representational Theory: Space, Politics, Affect*, London: Routledge

2009 'Space: The fundamental stuff of geography', in N. J. Clifford and G. Valentine (eds.), *Key Concepts in Geography*, London: Sage, pp. 95–107

Throop, C. J. and Murphy, K. M. 2002 'Bourdieu and phenomenology: A critical assessment', *Anthropological Theory*, 22, 185–207

Topan, F. 2000 'Swahili and Ismāʿīlī Perceptions of "Salāt"', in D. Parkin and S. C. Headley (eds.), *Islamic Prayer Across the Indian Ocean: Inside and Outside the Mosque*, Richmond: Curzon Press, pp. 99–115

Townsend-Gault, C. 2002 'Have we ever been good?', in *Rebecca Belmore: The Named and the Unnamed* exhibit catalogue, The Morris and Helen Belkin Art Gallery, University of British Columbia, www.ccca.ca/c/writing/t/townsend-gault/tgault013t.html (last accessed 8 February 2011)

Toynbee, J. 2000 *Making Popular Music: Musicians, Creativity and Institutions*, London: Arnold

Trieb, M. 1996 *Space Calculated in Seconds: The Philips Pavilion, LeCorbusier, Edgard Varèse*, Princeton University Press

Trimingham, J. S. 1980 (1964) *Islam in East Africa*, New York: Books for Libraries

Truax, B. 1998 'Composition and diffusion: Space in sound in space', *Organised Sound*, 3, 141–6

UMASC [University of Manitoba Archives and Special Collections] 2002 *Winnipeg Tribune* Newsclipping Collection, 'Indians' files, consulted

Valiquet, P. 2011 'The spatialisation of stereophony: Taking positions in post-War electroacoustic music', in M. Adkins and B. Isaacs (eds.), *Proceedings of the International Computer Music Conference 2011*, Centre for Research on New Music, University of Huddersfield, pp. 41–8

Vanderbilt, T. 1998 *The Sneaker Book: Anatomy of an Industry and an Icon*, New York: New Press

van Meel, J. and Vos, P. 2001 'Funky offices: Reflections on office design in the "new economy"', *Journal of Corporate Real Estate*, 3, 322–34

Varèse, E. 2004 (1936) 'The Liberation of Sound', in C. Cox and D. Warner (eds.), *Audio Culture: Readings in Modern Music*, London: Continuum, pp. 17–21

Verran, H. 1998 'Re-imagining land ownership in Australia', *Postcolonial Studies*, 1, 237–54

Villa, D. 1996 *Arendt and Heidegger: The Fate of the Political*, Princeton University Press

Voegelin, S. 2010 *Listening to Noise and Silence: Toward a Philosophy of Sound Art*, New York: Continuum

Vološinov, V. N. 1986 (1973) *Marxism and the Philosophy of Language*, L. Matejka and I. R. Titunik (trans.), Cambridge, MA: Harvard University Press

Wakefield, G. and Smith, W. 2011 'Cosm: A toolkit for composing immersive audio-visual worlds of agency and autonomy', in M. Adkins and B. Isaacs (eds.), *Proceedings of the International Computer Music Conference 2011*, Centre for Research on New Music, University of Huddersfield, pp. 13–20

Wark, M. 2007 *Gamer Theory*, Cambridge, MA: MIT Press

2009 'Introduction', in Guy Debord, *Correspondence: The Foundation of the Situationist International (June 1957–August 1960)*, Los Angeles, CA: Semiotext(e), pp. 5–27

Warner, M. 2002 *Publics and Counterpublics*, New York: Zone Books

Weheliye, A. 2002 '"Feenin": Posthuman voices in contemporary black popular music', *Social Text*, 20, 21–47

2005 *Phonographies: Grooves in Sonic Afro-Modernity*, Durham, NC: Duke University Press.

Weiner, I. 2010 'Listening in: Reflections on studying sound and noise across religious boundaries', Paper read at the International Association for the History of Religions XXth Quinquennial World Congress, Toronto

Weintraub, J. 1997 'The theory and politics of the public/private distinction', in J. Weiner and K. Kumar (eds.), *Public and Private in Thought and Practice: Perspectives on a Grand Dichotomy*, University of Chicago Press, pp. 1–42

Wessel, D. L. 1978 *Low Dimensional Control of Musical Timbre*, vol. XII, *Rapports IRCAM*, Paris: Centre Georges Pompidou

1979 'Timbre space as a musical control structure', *Computer Music Journal*, 3, 45–52

Whitely, S. (ed.) 1997 *Sexing the Groove: Popular Music and Gender*, New York: Routledge

Whiteley, S., Bennett, A. and Hawkins S. 2005 *Music, Space and Place: Popular Music and Cultural Identity*, Burlington: Ashgate

Whittall, A. 2007 'Messiaen and twentieth-century music', in R. Sholl (ed.), *Messiaen Studies*, Cambridge University Press, pp. 232–53

Wikinvest n.d. 'Nike', www.wikinvest.com/wiki/Nike (last accessed 18 June 2010)

Willis, J. 1993 *Mombasa, the Swahili, and the Making of the Mijikenda*, Oxford: Clarendon Press

Windsor, W. L. 1995 *A Perceptual Approach to the Description and Analysis of Acousmatic Music*, Ph.D. dissertation, City University, London

2000 'Through and around the acousmatic: The interpretation of electroacoustic sounds', in S. Emmerson (ed.), *Music, Electronic Media and Culture*, Aldershot: Ashgate, pp. 7–35

Wishart, T. 1986 'Sound symbols and landscapes', in S. Emmerson (ed.), *The Language of Electroacoustic Music*, London: Macmillan, pp. 41–60

1996 (1985) *On Sonic Art*, Amsterdam: Harwood Academic Publishers

Wolf, R. K. 2009 *Theorizing the Local: Music, Practice, and Experience in South Asia and Beyond*, Oxford University Press

Wood, N., Duffy, M. and Smith, S. J. 2007 'The art of doing (geographies of) music', *Environment and Planning D: Society and Space*, 25, 867–89

Woolf, M. 2006 'Cliff vs the ASBO kids', *The Independent*, 11 June, www.independent.co.uk/news/uk/crime/cliff-vs-the-asbo-kids-481920.html (last accessed 18 August 2012)

Worthington, A. 2007 *The Guantanamo Files: The Stories of the 774 Detainees in America's Illegal Prison*, New York: Pluto Press

    2009 'Tortured in the "dark prison"', *Counterpunch*, 15 December, www.counterpunch.org/2009/12/15/tortured-in-the-quot-dark-prison-quot/ (last accessed 18 August 2012)

Yahya, S. S. 2010 'Who owns the Kenya coast? The climaxing of land conflicts on the Indian Ocean seaboard', Conflict Vulnerability Analysis: Issues, Tools, and Responses (USAID and CERTI), unpublished paper

Young, L. M. 1969 'Notes on continuous periodic composite sound waveform environment realizations', *Aspen*, 8

Young, L. M. and Zazeela, M. 2000 (1968) From 1968 programme notes, reprinted in 'Notes on the Theatre of Eternal Music and *The Tortoise, His Dreams and Journeys*', www.melafoundation.org/theatre.pdf (last accessed 18 August 2012)

    2010 'Dream house: Seven+eight years of sound and light', New York, NY, www.melafoundation.org (last accessed 8 February 2011)

Zak III, A. 2001 *The Poetics of Rock: Cutting Tracks, Making Records*, Berkeley: University of California Press

Zarda, B. 2008 'Nike's human race', *Popular Science*, 7 May, www.popsci.com/score/article/2008–05/nikes-human-race (last accessed 18 August 2012)

Žižek, S. 1989 *The Sublime Object of Ideology*, London: Verso

    1996 '"I hear you with my eyes": Or, the invisible master', in R. Salecl and S. Žižek (eds.), *Gaze and Voice as Love Objects*, Durham, NC: Duke University Press, pp. 90–126

    2000 *The Fragile Absolute: Or, Why Is the Christian Legacy Worth Fighting For?* London: Verso

    2002 *For They Know Not What They Do: Enjoyment as a Political Factor*, 2nd edition, London: Verso

Zuckerkandl, V. 1956 *Sound and Symbol: Music and the External World*, Princeton University Press

# Discography

Amacher, M. 1999 *Sound Characters (Making the Third Ear)*, Tzadik TZ7043

Berlioz, H. 1974 *Symphonie Fantastique*, The Amsterdam Concertgebouw Orchestra, cond. Colin Davis, Philips 416659–1

    1988 *Symphonie Fantastique*, The London Classical Players, cond. Roger Norrington, EMI CDC7495412

Björk 2001 *Vespertine*, Polydor 589000–2

Garland, J. 2001 (1961) *Judy at Carnegie Hall*, Capitol Records 724352787623

Goldfrapp 2000 *Felt Mountain*, Mute Records CDSTUMM188

Leitner, B. 2003 *Kopfraüme/Headscapes*, Edition ZKM 978–3–7757–1298–9

Pink Floyd 1971 *Meddle*, Harvest SHVL795

Richard, C. and the Big Stone Band n.d. (*c.* 2004) *Family Tree*, Apple Blossom Studios compact disc

Schaeffer, P. and Henri, P. 2000 (1950) *Symphonie pour un homme seul*, Philips 464533–2

Varèse, E. 1960 (1958) *Poème électronique*, Philips A01494L

Wainwright, R. 2007 *Rufus Does Judy at Carnegie Hall*, Geffen Records 1755358

Wells, K. 1994 'It Wasn't God Who Made Honky Tonk Angels' from Various Artists, *Country Classics: 18 Country Greats*, AAC audio album from iTunes Store, K-tel

Williams, B. 2004 (1906) *Bert Williams: The Early Years, 1901–1909*, Archeophone ARCH5004

Williams Jr, H. 1993 *Hank Williams Jr's Greatest Hits*, Curb Records D2–77638

# Index

Printed in Great Britain
by Amazon.co.uk, Ltd.,
Marston Gate.